Hazzard
AND
Harrower

BRIGITTA OLUBAS is a professor of English at the University of New South Wales. She is the acknowledged expert on the writing of Shirley Hazzard and Hazzard's authorised biographer. She co-edited the first collection of essays on the writing of Elizabeth Harrower and is the author of *Shirley Hazzard: A writing life* and *Shirley Hazzard: Literary expatriate and cosmopolitan humanist*.

SUSAN WYNDHAM is a journalist and writer. As New York correspondent for *The Australian* newspaper and literary editor of *The Sydney Morning Herald* she interviewed Shirley Hazzard and Elizabeth Harrower. She is the author of *Life in His Hands: The true story of a neurosurgeon and a pianist* and editor of *My Mother, My Father: On losing a parent.*

'This collection is vital, compelling, terrifying, revelatory – and a literary pleasure in its own right. *Hazzard and Harrower* sheds light on one of the tragedies of Australian literary history: why Elizabeth Harrower stopped writing. We watch her let herself be dragged into situations where other people's needs – including Hazzard's – trump her own, bringing her possibly closer to life, but certainly further from art. Harrower's own words about what a novel comprises best describe the content of her letters, and Hazzard's: "All of these beautiful, severe, true things, lying about waiting to be understood."'

ANNA FUNDER

'Beautiful, wise and unflinching. Will we ever have a chance like this again to eavesdrop on two great writers as they talk books, people and the world for forty years?'

DAVID MARR

'I read these letters with mounting excitement. There is a righteous delight in seeing female talent reclaimed: two great Australian writers finally treated with the care and rigour they deserve. But even for those who haven't read Hazzard or Harrower's work, there's also the voyeuristic thrill of gaining intimate access to a complicated friendship.'

DIANA REID

'*Hazzard and Harrower* is an engrossing portrayal of forty years of complicated friendship between two writers, only one of whom has the steel – or is it the ruthlessness? – to put her art before everything else. These letters are both public and personal, forming an important record of an especially vibrant time in Australian culture, while poignantly reminding us of how profound is the gift of a vivid, cultivated inner life. A wonderful book.'

CHARLOTTE WOOD

Hazzard

AND

Harrower

THE LETTERS

Edited by
Brigitta Olubas
and
Susan Wyndham

NEWSOUTH

UNSW Press acknowledges the Bedegal people, the Traditional Owners of the unceded territory on which the Randwick and Kensington campuses of UNSW are situated, and recognises their continuing connection to Country and culture. We pay our respects to Bedegal Elders past and present.

A NewSouth book

Published by
NewSouth Publishing
University of New South Wales Press Ltd
University of New South Wales
Sydney NSW 2052
AUSTRALIA
https://unsw.press/

A catalogue record for this book is available from the National Library of Australia

ISBN   9781742238180 (paperback)
        9781742238913 (ebook)
        9781742239873 (ePDF)

Internal design Josephine Pajor-Markus
Cover design Debra Billson
Cover images Shirley Hazzard in New York in 1984, photographed by
    Lorrie Graham. © Lorrie Graham. Elizabeth Harrower in the 1980s,
    photographed by Jacqueline Mitelman. © Jacqueline Mitelman
Printer Griffin Press

This book is printed on paper using fibre supplied from plantation or sustainably managed forests.

Contents

Introduction

Shirley Hazzard and Elizabeth Harrower met in person for the first time in London in 1972, six years after they began a correspondence that would span four decades. They exchanged letters, cards and telegrams and made occasional phone calls, their mail travelling (often with maddening delays) between Harrower's home in Sydney and Hazzard's in New York and Italy. They wrote about their lives, friendships, their writing, and reading, about politics and world affairs. And they wrote about Hazzard's mother.

Kit Hazzard, charming, lonely, and mentally fragile, had brought the two writers together. In 1966 she was a familiar figure in the streets around her home in 'The Chimes' apartment building in Macleay Street, Potts Point, in Sydney's inner east. Harrower recalled that the owner of the Macleay Bookshop, Norma Chapman, had introduced her to 'Shirley Hazzard's mother', after becoming concerned about Kit's welfare, perhaps with the thought of a therapeutic literary connection. Harrower admired Hazzard's stories, which had been appearing in the *New Yorker* magazine since 1961 and, as Chapman pointed out, both writers were published by Macmillan. Kit took immediately to the much younger Harrower, and Harrower was charmed enough to stay in touch when Kit took off shortly after on one of her regular, doomed, trips around the world.

That August, while visiting her daughter in New York, Kit wrote to Harrower, and Hazzard added an appreciative note, to which Harrower replied a few months later. At first, their letters were short and courteous, but when they turned, as they quickly did, to the saga of Kit, they became longer and more intimate. Quite early on, Harrower became worried about Kit's mental health and took her to seek advice at Sydney's Callan Park Hospital (Hazzard later spoke of her mother having been diagnosed as 'manic depressive', a condition now known as bipolar disorder). Thereafter she took on greater responsibility for ensuring Kit saw her doctors and psychiatric nurses regularly, for making sure she had somewhere to live, and then, through the years that followed, for providing ever more mundane necessities. While Hazzard was clearly uncomfortable with the extent to which Harrower shouldered the burden of her mother, she allowed it to continue for over a decade. This strange arrangement raises many questions that simmer at the heart of this great and important friendship. On the one hand, there is certainly exploitation on Hazzard's part; exploitation of a friend for whom she bears great affection, and whose work she admires and encourages. How could she do this? Harrower's actions and her motivations are just as much a mystery even to herself: why would someone take on such a burden for someone else's mother, and why keep doing it for so long?

Hazzard and Harrower – three years apart in age – shared memories of the hilly streets of Mosman on the northern shore of Sydney Harbour, where both lived at different times in family-tainted houses above the golden crescent of Balmoral Beach. Hazzard's home at 30 Stanton Road and Harrower's at 5 Stanley Avenue were separated by just a few blocks and both had wide views of the bay and headlands, with passing yachts and ocean-bound liners. Hazzard and her parents had left the suburb, and the country, in 1947, long before Harrower briefly moved into her mother and stepfather's house in 1960 on her return from London, and then returned there in 1976, this time for two decades. The idyllic Sydney vista gave the two women a connection, a sense of a shared past even though their lives there had never overlapped. Hazzard wrote in a letter: 'It seems odd that 1972 was the year of our meeting – to me, it is as if we had met back in those summers of childhood, a pair of banded panamas above school ties...'

What they shared, rather than these imagined summer days, was unhappy childhood, with its intractable darkness shadowing both their lives ever after.

Shirley Hazzard was born on January 30, 1931, at the Bungalow Private Hospital in Chatswood on Sydney's north shore. Her parents had met while working for Dorman Long, the company that built the Sydney Harbour Bridge; both came with grim backgrounds of poverty and illegitimacy that they obscured through their lives as their social circumstances improved. Shirley and her older sister Valerie continued the deception, as they weathered the deep incompatibility of Reg and Kit Hazzard that issued forth in rages and emotional violence, often prompted by Reg's long-time marital infidelity. In the wake of the Second World War, and Reg's postings as Australian Trade Commissioner, the family travelled to Hong Kong, then New Zealand, then New York, where they all went their separate ways; Shirley to a stenographer's job at the United Nations. Shirley had always been a particular focus of her mother's fraught attentions, and told the story that Kit had asked her, aged six or seven, to join her in a suicide pact. She took on a horrified responsibility for her mother at the latter's inevitable divorce in 1953 but was never able to manage the burden with any sanguinity, nor to gain real perspective on her mother's condition, believing that, one day, Kit would settle somewhere and stop being miserable. It didn't help that Valerie was unwilling to take on much responsibility for Kit, despite living, mostly, in the same city as her mother.

Hazzard's own life took on a happier cast after a posting to Naples in late 1956, which began her great romance with the city, where she continued to live for part of each year for much of the rest of her life. In 1963 she married the esteemed and much older Francis Steegmuller, a biographer and translator of mostly French literary subjects. He had inherited an income, and a substantial collection of art, from his first wife Beatrice Stein Steegmuller, who had died in 1961. These funds allowed the Steegmullers to devote their time to writing. They rented an apartment in Manhattan and others in Capri and Naples, where they wrote and read and met with wide circles of literary and artistic friends. Their shared life – Kit referred to it, enviously or disparagingly, as their 'lovely life' – was as far from Shirley's uncultured and emotionally fraught childhood as it could be, but the past was always there in the figure of Kit, who kept up a shuttle of ocean voyages between London, New York, and Sydney; leaving and coming back, lugging trunks of old clothing and other objects from her married years, that she never unpacked and refused to throw out. Shirley and her sister Valerie never agreed on how best to manage Kit – or, violently, on anything else – and Kit continued to threaten her own death, or disappearance, or another sea voyage back to the last place she had run from.

The unending concern for her mother might have slowed Hazzard's writing but didn't stop it. Her work first appeared in *The New Yorker* in 1961. She published two books of short stories, mostly from *The New Yorker*, four novels and three books of non-fiction. Her first two novels are really novellas; both set in Italy, both telling of the mystery and ephemerality of love. *The Evening of the Holiday* (1966) plays pastoral against elegy; it was described as 'one of the most beautiful short novels ever written'. One reviewer praised its 'almost miraculous ability' to give 'living balance and proportion' to 'the great moral design of human fate' and noted Hazzard's own place as a literary outsider, describing the book's protagonist as 'half English, half Italian, and wholly antipodean'. *The Bay of Noon* (1970) is a meditation on time and the complications and aberrations of love. It too was much praised by reviewers, particularly in the US where it was shortlisted for the National Book Award (then dropped from the list when it was learned that Hazzard was not a US citizen). Ten years later she published *The Transit of Venus*, which won the US National Book Critics Circle Award. Recently (2021) reissued in the US, and acclaimed all over again as a masterpiece, *Transit* is one of the great novels of the century. Its densely wrought plot traces the lives of two Australian sisters across the post-war globe, through marriages and love affairs, to deaths prefigured but not told. *The New York Times'* John Leonard wrote that he had finished the book 'angry and in tears'. Its business, he said, was 'to break the heart'. The poet John Malcolm Brinnin wrote to Hazzard that he was reading it 'in a sort of enchanted jeopardy: I swear you write just for me'. It was another twenty-three years before the appearance of *The Great Fire*, which won the National Book Award and the Miles Franklin Award and was shortlisted for the UK Orange Prize. In this final novel, Hazzard returned to scenes from her youth in post-war Hong Kong and Hiroshima, and to a re-worked account of her first love affair. Interspersed through these years were two books about the United Nations, groundbreaking and trenchant if somewhat dense, and a more writerly memoir of her long and often prickly friendship with the writer Graham Greene.

The increasingly long breaks between her novels mark a shift in her attentions, with the need, from the early 1980s, to care for Steegmuller, who was living with dementia for the last decade of his life and relied on her help to produce his final books. She was also drawn away from fiction to produce what she called her 'public writing'. The breaks led to her being forgotten by readers and then rapturously rediscovered, and rediscovered again. In her fiction she drew unquestionably from her life, above all for her novel worlds – she is one of the great novelists of place – and for the experiences of often excoriating love affairs, and of persistent melancholy. At the same time, she presented to the public a version of her own life that was sharply edited and rearranged to obscure some of its obscure beginnings. With Steegmuller she mixed in elevated circles of an older literary Manhattan, privileged and discreet and full of erudition and engaged thought; a world she embraced as an antidote or counterweight to her past. They were, both, hardworking writers, committed to a tradition of belles-lettres commentary, producing, in addition to their books, dozens of essays and articles for the many magazines that paid well in the post-war decades. Today Hazzard's reputation remains secure, but it is perhaps as a writer associated with the cities of New York and Naples, or with a world that is wholly literary, imagined, rather than as an Australian, that she is and will continue to be remembered.

Betty Harrower was born on February 8, 1928, at Nurse Johnston's Private Hospital in Newcastle, the industrial port city 120 kilometres north of Sydney. She dropped 'Betty' for Elizabeth as an adult, and often said she was born in Sydney 'because I don't like Newcastle'. She too would forever edit her personal history in conversation and interviews, leaving out unwanted details and the worst experiences. But she returned to them in her fiction, in characters, relationships and places, always veiled but nonetheless recognisable. In a letter to her older, Scottish-born cousin, Margaret Dick, from London in 1972, she wrote that she had no desire to go back over her unhappy childhood, as others seemed to want to do: 'I must have cast off mine (and it really leaves me unmoved and has for years) partly because of writing, and partly because I told you and you listened and thought it hadn't been right or fair.'

Both sides of her family came from Scotland, a country to which she felt a strong attachment all her life, though her relatives tended towards a stern, practical and unpoetic nature. In Australia most of the men worked in coalmines, or in steelworks and ironworks. Her mother, Margaret Hughes, migrated with her family from Kelty, a coalmining town in Fifeshire, and was just nineteen when Betty was born. Newcastle-born Frank Harrower was an itinerant worker for the Railway Commissioners, who lived apart from the family after Betty was aged about seven. The date of their marriage, May 14, 1927, suggests Margaret might already have been pregnant, and the relationship ended long before the couple divorced in 1941. Through these years Betty lived with relatives in Newcastle, mostly without her mother, who worked as a nurse in Sydney. Her maternal grandmother, Helen Hughes, also a nurse, ran a private hospital and a boarding house, where her steelworker husband, Robert, was often drunk and abusive. That marriage ended in divorce in 1943.

Harrower recalled that as a child, she 'never saw any happy marriages'. She brushed aside inquiries about her father and her stepfather – 'that man' – and described herself as a 'divorced child' who was bullied by other children. Neglected and lonely, she recalled late in life that around the age of eight she lay down in the middle of the road outside her home, hoping that a car would come. The first story she wrote, 'The Fun of the Fair', is told from the perspective of Janet, described by one critic as 'an unloved, unwanted orphan, who is shunted between various triangulated relationships in which she is the third wheel'. She left this first unsettled household aged twelve and moved to Sydney with her mother, who made a second bad marriage to Richard Kempley, an accountant and hotelier who would bring material comfort but also emotional misery. He was, Harrower wrote to Hazzard, alcoholic and perhaps mentally ill. Kempley made at least some of his money in dubious enterprises.

After leaving school, Harrower began work in city offices as post-war Sydney came back to life. Outside work hours, her pleasure came from books that she borrowed from the City Library, housed in the Queen Victoria Building. She claimed to have read her way through the shelves of non-fiction and literature, but had not read an Australian book before she was in her thirties. Hazzard, too, was consumed by great literature as a salve and alternative to the uncongenial world of her dependent years, and like Harrower, only came to Australian writing later in life.

In 1951 Kempley took his wife and stepdaughter by ship to Europe and drove them across the Continent in a Jaguar. When the Kempleys left for Sydney in 1952, Harrower stayed in Britain, first with relatives in Scotland, and then in rented rooms in London. She began to study Ancient Greek in order to enrol in a psychology degree at London University, but didn't continue. Already she had plenty of material for the fiction that would pour from her in the following decade. Her novels and short stories would all be intense psychological studies of oppressive relationships, orphaned and abandoned children, damaged and manipulative adults. In a 1980 interview, asked how her fiction reflected her life, she said, 'The emotional truth is there in the books but none of the facts.' The books certainly track the phases of her life with artfully compressed and heightened intensity. *Down in the City* (1957) portrays a young woman's relationship with a heavy-drinking petty criminal against the seedy glamour of inner Sydney after the war.

The Long Prospect (1958) goes back to her disillusioned childhood. It tells of a child living with her domineering grandmother (Fiona McGregor calls her a 'little despot of a little world,') in an industrial city called Ballowra – she still couldn't bear to name Newcastle. The child, neglected, overlooked, but observant, forms an attachment to one of her grandmother's boarders, who gives her conversation, thought, 'more than anything, a manner of thinking', the possibility of a world beyond Ballowra and her terrible family. *The Catherine Wheel* (1960), set in a London bedsit like the ones she was writing in, further raises the level of emotional claustrophobia in the relationships between a law student from Australia, an alcoholic failed actor and his older mistress. By the time the third novel appeared, Harrower had travelled home, ostensibly to visit her mother before returning to London, but also to escape the hardships of her life there.

Harrower was accompanied on the ship back to Sydney in 1959 by Margaret Dick. Harrower had met Dick, her mother's first cousin, in Scotland and the two young women shared a flat for a time in London. Dick also published some stories and two novels. The visit to Sydney became permanent for both, and they would be sisterly confidantes and mutual supports until Dick's death in 2014. Dick published one more book, a critical analysis of the novels of Kylie Tennant, with Rigby in 1966, the same year Macmillan published Harrower's fourth novel, *The Watch Tower*.

This masterpiece of psychological abuse was autobiographical, Harrower told friends in the last year of her life. Laura and Clare Vaizey are abandoned by their widowed mother, who returns to England, and go to work in a factory owned by Felix Shaw. He offers marriage as a businesslike contract to provide security to Laura and her schoolgirl sister. In reality they become slaves to his business, his household and his volcanic moods. Like Harrower, Clare finds a way out. The story readily offers itself as a fictionalised version of the second marriage of Harrower's gentle mother to the domineering Kempley, the sisters stand-ins for mother and daughter, a relation that marks both Harrower's youthful dependence and her sense of her own moral maturity. While, like Hazzard, Harrower always resisted the label 'feminist', *The Watch Tower* dramatises the subjugation of women in the harsh domestic world of post-war Sydney.

The Watch Tower remains Harrower's greatest achievement and one of the greatest Australian novels. Reviewers noted a likeness to the work of

Patrick White in its 'insight into evil and the blight that afflicts Australian suburbia'. White himself admired the novel, and withdrew *The Solid Mandala* from contention for that year's Miles Franklin Award, believing Harrower deserved to win, but the prize went to Peter Mathers' *Trap*. (Hazzard's first novel *The Evening of the Holiday*, also published in 1966, would not have been eligible for consideration due to the award's then tight constraints around representation of Australian life.) The two novels were reviewed together in September that year by John Colmer, who praised Harrower's control of the novel's imagery, describing it as 'simultaneously illuminating the darkness in the human soul and the corresponding sterility in society' and her striking portrayal of Felix Shaw: 'The accounts of the proposal and marriage brilliantly suggest how Felix reduces all human relations to a matter of property ownership.' Colmer heaped praise on Hazzard, likening her to Flaubert, Turgenev, Chekhov and James, while also overtly cutting her down to size with a reference to Françoise Sagan. He pronounced *The Watch Tower* 'a great advance in Miss Harrower's career as a novelist' and praised the 'consummate artistry' of Hazzard's 'remarkable first novel'. Harrower and Hazzard don't seem to have discussed the review with each other. Its importance lies in the fact that its publication marked a crucial point in the careers of the two writers, a crossing of trajectories. In 1966, both appeared to be in the ascendency; however, over the next decade, while Hazzard's output and reputation grew, Harrower's faltered and then stopped altogether in the 1970s. The reasons were complex and not entirely clear even to Harrower herself, but some threads are significant.

Harrower was awarded a Commonwealth Literary Fund Fellowship in 1967 to write her fifth novel. *In Certain Circles* opens in a 'square stone house on the north side of Sydney Harbour' and is a composite of Harrower's familiar concerns and fresh observations. The complicated plot, about two brother–sister pairs, is driven by social and gender inequalities, psyches damaged by war and grief, and a suicide note. By this time, Harrower and Hazzard shared a publisher, Alan Maclean, at Macmillan in London. Harrower submitted the manuscript in 1970 and her own doubts were confirmed by a critical reader's report written three weeks before her mother's death. She pushed through the haze of grief to tighten the writing. But in March 1971 Macmillan's independent reader, C.H. Derrick, gave a second report, which saw the novel failing due to 'a feeling of unreality, of diagram, of theory'. He concluded: 'The subtlety and even brilliance of the author's mind is obvious: I find this book at once empty and stifling.' Maclean maintained his offer to publish but Harrower's English agent urged her to put the novel aside and start another. Harrower conceded that the obligation of a grant had produced a lifeless story without the organic urgency of her earlier books. In an interesting coincidence, C.H. Derrick had been the reader who, in 1963, had recommended Macmillan against publishing Hazzard – as 'an accurate (though morose and mildly obsessed) observer and a needle-sharp commentator, she is not by temperament a creator of large positive things' – advice disregarded by Maclean. When *In Certain Circles* was finally published in 2014, Harrower reflected: 'I suppose I have been very good at closing doors and ending things. But the other mystery is why I was so angry, annoyed or self-destructive as to make up my mind that I would spare the world any more of my great thoughts.' She felt, she said, looking back, that she had overreacted and 'decided to destroy my life'.

In these early years of their friendship, the late 1960s and early 1970s, Hazzard and Harrower exchanged only half a dozen letters, and Kit was mostly in London (the burden of other of Hazzard's friends there). However, there seems to be no doubt that Kit's needs had become one important factor in Harrower's new inability to write. Patrick White certainly believed so. In a postcard sent to Harrower in 1971, he and his partner Manoly Lascaris sounded an early warning (that was already too late): 'Were alarmed to hear Mrs Hazzard had broken a leg & was returning to Australia. Keep well away, or you'll be landed with her for ever.' In March 1971, on the eve of yet another of Kit's voyages, Harrower wrote to Hazzard offering ongoing help, and musing that she wasn't sure how she 'gradually became involved', speculating that it was because she had finished her novel and her own mother had just died. It is astonishing that this is one of only two mentions by Harrower of her mother's sudden death aged sixty-one. We know from other accounts that she was immobilised by shock and grief, in her own words 'absolutely frozen'. Perhaps Kit's troubles, less close to home, filled different kinds of gaps in her life at that stage. A few years later, with Harrower enmeshed in Kit's troubles and those of several of her close friends, Patrick White told a mutual friend: 'She is living a novel instead of writing one.' He even wrote pointedly to Hazzard in 1980: 'Elizabeth keeps her principles. Whether she is also <u>writing</u>, I have given up asking in case I get the wrong answer. Too many vampires make too many demands on her...'

Harrower was attracted in life, as in fiction, to complex, damaged people, some of them dangerous. She was closely involved with the problems of the writer Kylie Tennant – a dear friend – and her family. Tennant's husband Lewis Rodd (Roddy) suffered from depression and in 1961 threw himself under a train, losing an arm and a foot. Their son Bim suffered from a fatal combination of drug addiction and schizophrenia, and was killed in 1978 in a horrifying incident. Tennant herself spent years being treated for cancer, and was both needy and evasive about her troubles. The two writers had met when Tennant was literary adviser to Macmillan in the 1960s and she helped Harrower secure a job as manager of the British publisher's Sydney office, overseeing book orders and deliveries. They were neighbours in Hunters Hill in the 1970s and bought a rustic house together at Blackheath in the Blue Mountains, where they intended to write but, as Harrower's letters show, were increasingly derailed by chaos.

Another difficult friendship was with Cynthia Nolan, a writer of travel memoirs and wife of the artist Sidney Nolan. At first, relations were warm. Harrower stayed at the Nolans' Putney house in south London for six months in 1972, after her mother's death and her loss of confidence following the Macmillan rejection led to an emotional crisis requiring a change of scene. Even now there was little respite – Kit Hazzard wrote to her sixteen times during the visit. She also needed a break from the Tennants, as she wrote to Margaret Dick: 'I wouldn't mind the stress if it let me write, but it doesn't.' The following year, she was persuaded, against her inclinations, to accompany Tennant, her daughter and her father on a cruise to Japan. Cynthia Nolan had seen Harrower's distress in London at ongoing dramas in Tennant's family, and warned her against the cruise. When Harrower went ahead anyway, Cynthia refused to speak to her, and the friendship never recovered. With her heightened flight reflex, Harrower jumped ship after travelling only as far as Brisbane and returned to Sydney, holing up at Katoomba to avoid seeing anyone she knew, especially Cynthia.

Hazzard and Harrower were always in fierce agreement about Kit – her charm, humour, and her darkness – and Harrower never voiced any complaint, at least not to Hazzard. Hazzard seems to have taken her friend's courteous reticence as licence to go on asking her to do things. Alongside this skewed balance sheet of efforts and favours, there came other pressures, small but cumulative differences which reached a peak in the years between 1980 and 1985. These are barely marked in their correspondence, or, rather, any references to them are couched with great discretion. Hazzard's sustained and repeated criticism of the nationalism of the Australian arts scene, her sharp retorts to Patrick White's rudeness (to her in particular but other friends, too, including on one memorable occasion, Harrower herself), all left their mark. Harrower's responses were restrained, but there are occasional tense moments. In 1984, Hazzard and Steegmuller finally persuaded her to accept their long-proffered gift of a trip to Europe and New York. Harrower was always a reluctant traveller, anxious about money and time, and it seems likely she was starting to feel affronted by her friends' single-minded pursuing of the matter (Steegmuller was delegated to write most of these letters). None of this was recorded in their letters, but according to Hazzard's diaries, Harrower was prickly from the moment she arrived in Rome (she commented repeatedly that the room Hazzard had booked for her at the Hassler Hotel had no view) and had refused to engage with any activities Hazzard organised ('There you go again; I don't accept orders'). At lunch on Capri one day, Harrower spontaneously proposed a toast: 'To Francis, the kindest person at the table'. She left early, travelling to Paris, England and Scotland, then returning directly to Sydney, dropping the New York part of the trip. Hazzard wrote, but not to Harrower, of her hurt at these developments, speculating about their cause: in her diary she recorded that perhaps Harrower had hoped, unconsciously, to 'provoke' an angry response from her 'thus facilitating her precipitate, longed-for return'. To another friend, who had met and liked Harrower, she wrote of her sadness about the visit, observing that it seemed the matter was, for Harrower, 'far more complicated than she is prepared to admit to herself'. They spoke on the phone, and their letters remained amiable but with moments of crisp refutation ('No, I didn't say...') without apologies or explanations. Interestingly, from this coolness, this shifting of tone and focus, a new warmth develops, at least within the scope of the letters, which provide a less fraught account of their days and lives. Through this and beyond, there was something of a contradiction in Harrower's bearing. She often spoke to her friends mockingly of what she saw as Shirley's pretensions and claimed not to like her writing. And yet the correspondence shows affection and admiration – with, particularly in the last years of their writing, a desire for contact – that belies, or complicates, this disdain.

In the last years of her life, when Harrower was interviewed by a number of writers who were researching Hazzard's life, she spoke coolly about her old friend. She said that over the years Hazzard's 'tone' had become 'very grand' and expressed some contempt for what Kit called Hazzard's 'lovely life'. Perhaps she resented also the material and emotional security that allowed Hazzard to write, even though Harrower was herself rather more secure in financial terms than she admitted, through ownership of several properties, while Hazzard lived mainly on the sale of Steegmuller's art collection and, in her late years, on the generosity of friends.

However mixed her feelings for Hazzard became, Harrower adored the towering, kindly, intellectual Steegmuller. She wrote to Margaret Dick from London in 1972, after their first meeting: 'Why aren't there lots of Francises about? Not fair.' They sometimes exchanged their own letters or he added a note to Hazzard's; he showed her novels to his agent, Cyrilly Abels (who said they would not sell in the US due to their Australian settings – Steegmuller was mortified). Harrower admired his books, possibly more than she admired Hazzard's (although her responses in letters to each new novel published by Hazzard are full of praise that does not feel forced). Harrower did not marry or have children, and friends of later years were unaware of any romantic relationships. But she was very fond of several married men, including the Russian-born communist writer Judah Waten, and a South African-born architect, Ferdi Nolte, who encouraged her to join the Australian Labor Party. Among her close friends were many gay men, notably White and Lascaris. White urged her to write, invited her with Margaret Dick to lunches and dinners at his Centennial Park home, and for years they spoke by phone every Sunday morning. In 1996, after his death, Harrower won the Patrick White Award, set up by her friend with his Nobel Prize money.

On the evidence of their correspondence, there was genuine regard and much in common between Harrower and Hazzard. The letters are suffused with discussion of books and the arts, a shared passion for politics, and a nostalgia for declining values of decency, nobility and learning. Harrower carried her working-class roots into lifelong support for the Australian Labor Party. She became politicised in London, where the scars of war were visible in the 1950s. Her excitement at the election of the Whitlam Government in 1972 became another distraction from writing as she joined campaigns, formed and ended friendships on political grounds, then slumped after the dismissal of the Government by the Governor-General in 1975. Gough Whitlam himself was a hero and became a friend, invited to the party she arranged for Hazzard's visit in 1976. For her part, Hazzard was transfixed by Harrower's accounts of a new Australia, under Whitlam. She wrote animatedly and often, in letters and for publication, of this achievement, comparing arts policies in Australia favourably to New York (Steegmuller likened Whitlam's Australia to the New Deal United States, which he had lived through). Much of her knowledge about contemporary Australia, and many of her contacts, came through Harrower's generous and astute commentary, and she is fulsome in expressing her appreciation of this to Harrower. Hazzard was, too, a committed follower of world affairs, of US and Italian – especially Neapolitan – politics. She was less partisan than Harrower, but also a furious opponent of successive Republican presidents (she wrote to another friend that each of these 'makes the next one possible – as Johnson made Nixon possible. Nixon is satanic. Something that came in with Reagan is a new dimension of blatancy in evil – whereas Nixon's speciality was diabolical hypocrisy'), of the rise of Berlusconi in Italy and the persistent taint of the Camorra in the local politics of Naples.

Although Harrower produced only a few short stories in the 1970s and little after that, she was always busy with the background business of being a writer. There were requests for rights to republish and translate her novels, to include her stories in anthologies and interview her for scholarly publications; she was writer in residence at a technical college, reviewed books, judged literary awards, wrote an introduction to Cynthia Nolan's posthumous collected travel writing. Several reissues of her books were frustratingly short-lived. Many friends she made in later life did not know she was a writer. She almost disappeared from public attention until her books were reissued by Text Publishing in the years 2012 to 2015, along with the first publication of *In Certain Circles*, which had sat among her papers in the National Library of Australia, and a collection of her short stories, *A Few Days in the Country*. In her late eighties by then, Harrower said she had always been sure her work would be rediscovered after her death. But how much better that the renaissance came in the last years of her life. Harrower flourished in the attention and made her first appearances at writers' festivals in the protective company of Michael Heyward, her publisher and literary saviour. Harrower's penetrating insight and chiselled sentences impressed critics again, even more deeply with the burnish of fifty years. Her first four novels are 'beautiful little nightmares', and Harrower 'one of the sharpest authors of psychological fiction in Australian literature', wrote one critic in a review of *Down in the City*. In 2014, Jessica Au declared that '*In Certain Circles* is subtle yet wounding, and very much alive', and in *The New Yorker*, James Wood found her body of work 'witty, desolate, truth-seeking, and complexly polished'.

Hazzard was unaware of her friend's late-blooming success. Over the last decade of their friendship, their correspondence slowed and the last surviving letter was written in 2008. Even before the death of Steegmuller in 1994, there is an increasingly elegiac tone to their exchanges as one after another friend leaves the world, a melancholy sequence broken for a time by Hazzard's excitement at the huge success of her own last novel, *The Great Fire*, in 2003, critically acclaimed and a bestseller. They spoke occasionally by phone until about 2010 when Hazzard began to decline into dementia and frailty, dying at home in New York on December 12, 2016 at the age of eighty-five. Harrower was socially active until the last year of her life when, also suffering from dementia, she left her Cremorne apartment for a nursing home, and died on July 7, 2020 aged ninety-two. Unlike Hazzard, the constant traveller, she had not left Australia for thirty-six years. The enduring legacy of these two extraordinary women is, of course, the books – too few – they wrote. And also, now, their remarkable correspondence.

Editors' note

The distinctive literary styles of the two correspondents are displayed in their letters and a pleasure to read in dialogue: Hazzard erudite, poetic and emotional, tending to prolixity; Harrower elegant and outwardly calm, as opinionated and forthright as Hazzard about politics and world affairs and literature, but on personal matters reserved to the point of secrecy. With sincere curiosity as a shield, she deflects attention to others. Each is an observant storyteller, and an appreciative reader of the other's offerings. The correspondence is truly an extended conversation in which both voices are clear, the shifts in relationship and mood subtle but cumulative.

They wrote on manual typewriters or by hand, with the well-formed sentences and precise punctuation of the professional writer. They included newspaper clippings, often the prompt for discussion. In the early years, some letters, caught up with the grim detail of Kit's travails and what to do in response, run on for pages and pages. They joke that the correspondence could be more substantial still, as they were often prevented from writing by other responsibilities; in these instances they speak of sending 'a telex' – an unwritten, unsent, but intricately thought-through missive. With passing time and deepening friendship, the tone becomes more conversational, words are abbreviated, the grammar is looser. Were they writing for posterity? Certainly they kept most of the correspondence and deposited it with their papers. Sometimes they express themselves as if for future public consumption – with careful exposition and infuriating discretion (requiring detective work by the editors of this book to explain their half-references) – but mostly they are friends sharing candid thoughts as if sitting together over a cup of coffee. Their dry, dark humour is often a conspiratorial antidote to the drama of Kit, who soon became 'MM' and 'YM' (My Mother, Your Mother). Shirley occasionally took up the schoolgirl slang of her earlier correspondence with the writer Muriel Spark ('splenders', 'agoggers').

As editors, we had to drop whole letters and cut many others in order to turn almost 400000 words of correspondence into a more acceptable book length, a painful process when the writing is so fine and their news the stuff of biography and world history. We reduced the circular repetitions of Kit's bipolar excesses and the details of Harrower's care to an essential account and removed many mentions of medical tests and (in hindsight) minor illness among the correspondents. We had to trim fascinating – sometimes obsessive – outpourings on politics in Australia, the United States and Italy but valued their knowledgeable eyewitness accounts of important events. Wherever possible we retained insights into their writing lives. Even before our culling, there were missing letters – undelivered, lost, perhaps discarded – and lengthening silences as the friends age, fall out, and lose Kit's centripetal force with her death in 1985. There were also pauses in letter-writing when the friends met in Sydney and Europe or when they exchanged urgent news or affection by cable or phone, with greater frequency as telecommunications improved and intimacy grew.

For ease of reading, we have made invisible cuts of a few words or an insignificant sentence or two, while marking longer cuts – sometimes several paragraphs – with ellipses within square brackets. Idiosyncrasies of spelling and usage remain as the authors wrote them; we have also left unchanged some expressions, common at the time but no longer in use. Inadvertent errors have been corrected to avoid confusion, but readers can be assured that there were few of these from such meticulous writers.

PART ONE
1966–1975

When Hazzard and Harrower's first letters were travelling between New York and Sydney, Australia had followed the United States into the Vietnam War and remained there until both countries withdrew their last troops in 1973. These were years of deep, shared personal and political engagement for the writers. Harrower celebrated the election in 1972 of a Labor government under Prime Minister Gough Whitlam, then mourned Labor's historic dismissal in 1975. Hazzard was aghast at the Watergate scandal that led to the fall of President Richard Nixon in 1974, and continued to criticise the failings of the United Nations. The 1973 Arab–Israeli War provoked an international oil crisis, inflation and unemployment. Their correspondence from here on records an unrelenting disappointment, and often despair, at the state of the world, all the while rejoicing at daily beauty around them and the deep pleasures of reading and friendship.

200 East 66th St New York NY 10021 | Aug 30 1966

Dear Elizabeth (if I may call you that??)

My mother has let me read your so nice letter, with its lovely and generous words about me. I'm happy that you liked 'Nothing in Excess', because it's part of a book I am working on just now and alternately despairing of and pressing on with. I'd like to read your writings one of these days and look forward to that. Also perhaps to meeting you eventually, in London or here?

With very best regards –

Most sincerely Shirley H-S.

6 Want Street, Mosman, N.S.W. | 16th November, 1966

Dear Shirley,

I was so pleased to have your note along with your mother's letter.

Since the time I found your first story for myself I have taken an exclusive sort of interest in your work and watched for it in The New Yorker. I like it very much, find it extremely congenial and, as I seem to remember saying before, in some mysterious way that I probably could – but won't – pin down, a great relief. When circumstances organised me into Macmillan's I was delighted to see that they were publishing Cliffs of Fall. Then recently I so enjoyed meeting your mother. We were well disposed towards each other, of course, because of our common enthusiasm, but it turned out that we would have been well disposed anyway. I was sorry we met so late in the day, so close to your mother's return to New York.

Someone was arguing the other night to the effect that Australian writers had to live abroad if they were to write anything of any consequence. Your name was then brought in to support this idea. You would not have been writing about the United Nations if you lived in Australia. Since nothing of international importance ever happens here, this journalist went on, writers were at a great disadvantage. – If people write about public events, I suppose this is true, but if they write about people, the only handicap here or anywhere else is a lack that no change of continent would be likely to alter. Since your work seems to me at all times extremely private, I was taken aback to hear this and could only feel that you had been misunderstood by my acquaintance. However, this sort of thing has been gone over too often already, though not by me.

It would be pleasant to meet sometime. After eight years in London I came back to Sydney for a visit, stayed, and now seem very disinclined to wander. Still, it is nice to see new places.

I am sending you a copy of <u>The Watch Tower</u>, my new book, under separate cover.

I wish you well with your new novel, and look forward to seeing more of it in The New Yorker before long.

All good wishes,
Elizabeth

New York | 20 December 1966

Dear Elizabeth –

Please forgive this delay in replying to your so nice letter of last month. I have been finishing a book and have not lifted my nose out of my pages for weeks. Tomorrow I go to Paris to join my husband for Christmas – he has been there since the end of November, beginning a book of his own, a biography of Jean Cocteau. So I'm here among the suitcases and the tissue-paper. We come back to New York at the end of Jan. I'm sorry to leave my mother alone for Christmas but she will spend it with friends in the country outside New York and will be looked after well in our absence. She has told me so much of your kindness to her and how she enjoyed seeing you in Sydney.

All congratulations on your own book. I'm looking forward so much to receiving The Watch Tower; many many thanks for this kind thought of sending it. Blessings on it and its career. And thank you too for such kind words about my own work (at present, having finished, I feel I will never never begin again – you know how that is?). No, of course I don't feel that writers have to leave Australia to write anything of consequence – why should that be so? It is true that when I was growing up in Sydney there <u>was</u> a sort of inferiority feeling about domestic products – that a writer from Europe or America must somehow have a larger and truer idea of the world and human experience (I am talking, of course, about a general public attitude, not about particular people or artists themselves). But I feel, from what I hear, that this must be changing, or already much changed. Then too the world has become so much smaller that it is a more normal thing to travel and invite experience in that way. But naturally a gifted person need never whizz about; just observe. My organization book, the one I have just finished, is a satire set in a large international organization (!), and of course it would not have been written if I had never left Australia. But I might have written something else that used the same things in myself... Well, I'm sure we agree on all this.

My mother has posted you one or two of Francis' books – I only wish he had been here to inscribe them to you. So you must truly come to New York one day – I feel you will. Meanwhile, I send you all good wishes, and again thanks for such a nice letter. A very happy Christmas and 1967 – I wonder if you are at work on another book?

Most sincerely, Shirley.

Want Street | 17th May, 1967

Dear Shirley,

I was so happy to have your letter just before you went to Paris, and I did write to your mother to thank you both for your kindness in sending me two of your husband's books, and to say how much I had enjoyed them.

Like Herzog (and half the population) I write numerous letters that never see paper or the post, so I feel as if I have already passed on to you news of the Australian literary scene, and other matters that may have been of interest.

Your new book is listed in the Publishing Programme now, and I look forward with particular pleasure to reading and re-reading it. That it will be greatly appreciated – and widely – is something I don't doubt. I wish it every success.

Are you working on something else, I wonder? Or knee-deep in proofs? When I heard from you, you were just beginning to enjoy the wonderful feeling of not writing. Unfortunately that good feeling of something accomplished, something done, etc., lasts such a short time!

Your mother wrote the other day from Southampton. I hope the summer is fine for her, and that circumstances arrange themselves in a kind and friendly way. Later on I'll send her reviews of your book and, meantime, news of Sydney and Blackheath.

A pity the Herzog letters were never written. This might as well be a telegram for all that's in it. Still – it was only meant to send greetings, and good wishes to your new book.

Sincerely yours,

Elizabeth

New York | 24 June 1967

Dear Elizabeth,

Please excuse me for such a delay in writing to you, and especially in telling you how much I have enjoyed The Watch Tower. I felt I got to know you in the reading of it, and was absorbed in the story, told in your very special, clear, poetic voice. It is a powerful theme – I admire you for tackling it and succeeding so well. I liked too the atmosphere of the city, still very fresh in my memory even after (perhaps because of) so long an absence. I'll be looking for more of your work – I didn't know until reading the flap that you were already the author of other books, though I knew the stories.

I have been under a mound of galleys, and now page-proofs, for my book (to be published this October here and in England), trying to get these done before we leave for Europe early in July. We come back in September. Yes, I've been enjoying the freedom of not writing – but how right you are, it doesn't last: one starts to feel at odds with oneself for not having something on the desk or on the typewriter. I am beginning, very tentatively, a new novel, but at its present rate it will be light-years before it is done. What about you?? Here we have been in the front trench of the useless battles carried on among the world's leaders – if we weren't all so inured to it, the pettiness of the absurd arguments that lead us into wars would be horrifying... As it is, most people seem to be fatalistic, even bored, feeling they can do nothing to influence the course of events...

My mother is in London and of course we are going to see her there, and will perhaps take her for a while to France or Italy to give her a change. I am worried about her – I hated to have to leave her here, as she insisted we must, and feel that she is very lonely and at loose ends in England. The logical thing would have been for her to stay in New York with us, and I hoped that she would let us arrange that for her. She refused, saying that it would make her too materially dependent on us – as if the worry of having her alone in London is not an infinitely greater burden. Shifting countries is an undertaking at any time, and I think very demoralising at her age. She loved meeting you and seeing you in Sydney and often spoke about you when she was here.

[...]

Please let me know about your work, and about you. And thank you again for your book and for your nice letter –

Most sincerely

Shirley

Want Street | 2 August 1967

Dear Shirley and Francis,

[A friend has] asked me to keep his television set (he's left & gone to Europe) & to my horror two evenings have been absorbed by it. Irritated with even the thought of it, the flickering screen, the advertisements & the cacophony I can only report two very enjoyable sessions – an interview with Kruchev and tonight an absolutely delightful adaptation from Luigi Barzini – his voice is intelligent & with a suitability for his ironic commentary & the screenplay of his characters, the whole gains much more impact on me than just the reading of his book. I hope you've seen it. [...]

Quite accidentally I have partly designated this summer & smog to the pleasure of discovering Francis – seeking a Christina Stead in the public library I found instead a delightful small boy at a 'Christening Party'. Returning a week later, still for Stead, I found Apollinaire – fascinating possibility of the King of Rome's paternity! [...]

Your last story made a very suitable closing theme – a sort of 'Good night sweetheart' without the playing – just a hint, a trace. But then your stories always touch so lightly. – Love to you both

Elizabeth

Want Street | 13 December, 1967

Dear Shirley,

I was so pleased to have your letter. You were knee-deep in proofs at that time. Now your book is out and I hear of excellent reviews everywhere. Many congratulations! I read it in The New Yorker, then in page proofs, then finally read the printed book. So good, so pleasing in so many ways. I'll watch for local reviews here and send them to you.

When you wrote to me – at that time – Israel and Egypt were fighting. Since then so many other ghastly things have happened that it becomes harder and harder to respond to world events in any rational way. In Australia it is peculiarly easy for people not to notice what is going on, because the newspapers give so little space to overseas news. Vietnam, of course, does get space because there are Australians there...

How is your mother? She writes to me every few weeks. You said you were worried about her, and I can understand that well. London does not sound the most cheerful place in the world just now, and it is possibly the place where she has fewest connections. (I have a gentle, intractable mother who worries me, too, and am apt to run on, giving her good advice which she listens to with interest and takes no notice of.) [...] In Sydney as you know your mother and I met towards the end of her stay, and did not see so much of each other, but did see each other in a real way. She was clearly not very happy, but she took the trouble to be entertaining, and to make me laugh, which I thought was very generous and gallant. (She and my cousin, Margaret, agreed that being born in Scotland was enough to blight anyone's life. They felt for each other. Australia's not perfect, heaven knows, but it is better as a birth place, I'm sure.) Anyway, having an excessive talent myself for happiness and unhappiness, when there are reasons, and there usually are, I sympathized with your mother. So now I'm conscious of her being there in London and think of her and wish her well.

Earlier this year – about September – Sidney and Cynthia Nolan were in Sydney for a couple of months for the opening of his Retrospective Exhibition and the publication by Macmillan of a book about his work, and one by Cynthia – Open Negative – An American Memoir. The Nolans are immensely likeable and added much to the Sydney landscape for those few weeks. The exhibition was quite overwhelming. It reminded me that there were probably better ways of passing the time than in my very comfortable and pleasant office, and I applied, after resisting the idea for years, for a Commonwealth Literary Fund Fellowship. The application went in three weeks after the closing date. My friends were ready to murder me because of the indecision and alarm all round. So the application stayed in, and I did get a Fellowship for 1968. They give me $6000, and I am supposed to write a book. (There's no time limit, of course.) So this is pleasing and alarming. As I must resign from Macmillan's and do not feel that I have any capacity for supporting myself by writing, the future seems dark and precarious, and the application quite reckless and silly. On the other hand, if you want to write...

The latest drama on the literary front blew up last Monday. The General Council of the Encyclopaedia Britannica Awards Committee rejected the advice of the Literary Committee, and said there would be no award for literature this year. ($10,000 each for various branches of the arts and sciences.) The next day, Patrick White wrote to the Herald disclosing (and deploring strongly) the fact that it was Christina Stead who was turned away from the door, because she has not lived in Australia for many years. Sidney Nolan was passed over for the Art award for the same reason. Patrick's letter stirred things up and today there is a leader in the Herald about it. But the Committee is not likely to budge. Really, really.

Thank you again for your letter and for liking The Watch Tower. Let me hear from you sometime when there's time. – Happy Christmas.

Sincerely,
Elizabeth

New York | 7 December 1970

Dear Miss Harrower –

Hearing about you often from my mother who loves you dearly and enjoys her times with you, we want to be in touch – and, as she has told us the exciting news that you had a new manuscript, we both wanted to say how very much we hope it will be in print this year. 'The Watch Tower' has been an unforgettable book for both of us; and while it is selfish to urge another writer for one's own pure pleasure, we are feeling that it is high time for another Harrower. We also hope that we can meet one day and I can thank you then, too, for all your friendship to my mother in Sydney. Meantime, with my warmest greetings –

Shirley H-S

Dear Miss Harrower –

I find The Watch Tower <u>very</u> strong and impressive & I am its and your great admirer. Please accept my warm congratulations for such an accomplishment – F. S.

Want Street | January 10th, 1971

Dear Shirley and Francis Steegmuller,

Do please call me Elizabeth. I hear of you often from your mother (and Kit) and feel, too, as you say, that we are in touch.

[...]

After meeting or speaking to your mother, and certainly after reading <u>Bay of Noon</u>, I have often intended to write to you. Reading your novel gave me more than pleasure; it really made me happy. Your writing is felicitous, and I have thought so since I read your first stories in The New Yorker. Apart from making everyone not living in Italy dissatisfied with his existence, it's a beautiful book. My cousin, who reviewed it for The Herald and was sorry not to have more space for her enthusiasm, was inclined to say afterwards, about any novel set in another place, 'It isn't <u>Naples</u>...'

As a preparation for <u>Cocteau</u>, I've recently re-read some of his work, and now look forward to the biography.

Your mother tells me she is having her sailing date moved from February to April. I ask her if this journey back to England is any sort of answer, but she seems to feel it necessary. Because it's warmer here (not that heat is so marvellous) and less overpowering than London when one is in the wrong sort of mood, I am sorry that Sydney hasn't worked out better. Kings Cross is probably the least neighbourly and sociable area in the country. – I haven't been able to do very much. Some time ago I tried to persuade her to see a diagnostician, in the hope that he would consider the whole person and perhaps find some way of relieving stress and tension, as well as attending to any physical problems. But beyond a certain point, it's more harassing than useful to press people, so I let the idea drop.

– Frequently, after I've worked out and propounded a particularly intricate argument in favour of some constructive attitude or other, your mother has replied, 'But that's exactly what Shirley says!' At first, I was quite surprised (evidently believing my thought processes to be unique!). – In general, over coffee in town, we talk about books and places and people we've liked, and exchange the more cheerful and enlivening pieces of news.

You mention my new manuscript. Alan [Maclean] accepted it for Macmillan's in London, but we both know (though he is too compassionate to say so) that it is disappointing. Whether it will be more inhibiting in the long run to publish and face justified harshness from critics, or to write off two years' work and the CLF's $6,000 is the choice. There was an interesting book to be written, but I blocked it for all sorts of reasons and my concentration disappeared. People. Since January 1st, I've been cutting and re-typing. Alan will be here shortly, and I'll probably give it to him. Then the way may be clear for something better.

When Kit worries that you are both working too hard, I assure her that the only pitiable state for a writer is the opposite one. It wouldn't be human to tell any non-writer how enviable it is – in its peculiar way – to be engulfed in work, or what it adds to leisure and enjoyment.

On this strenuous note – warmest good wishes to you both for 1971.

Yours,

Elizabeth

New York | 24 January 1971

Dear Elizabeth –

We came back from a European trip two days ago and found your delightful letter. Thank you so much for it – we both enjoyed all your kind words, and I must say at once that Alan showed not the least sign of 'disappointment' about your new work when we saw him in London. In fact he told us that you had seized it back for some changes, and that he was cheered because now he felt that you would be sure to publish and with an easier mind. We told him how much we were looking forward to the book's appearance and, I need hardly tell you, he shares our admiration for your work completely.

We came home to find several letters from my mother. [...] I so appreciated your wise and understanding and sensitive words about her – she has so much intuition and indeed artistry in her make-up, and I wish it might have found a channel of expression and interests. Her difficulties go back so far, and have done her so much harm, and I wish more than anything that there would be serenity for her in these late years. I smiled over your description of our thought processes having led to the same deviously-arrived-at suggestions – I do hope she will take notice of yours, as she never will of mine! I love her dearly, and agonise over her, and worry much about the future. I so agree that professional help – a diagnostician, as you say – would relieve her of much strain if properly offered; yet I have never succeeded in any attempt to persuade her to this. I cannot tell you the comfort it has been to me to think that you were in touch with her at Sydney – she writes of you so warmly and affectionately, and your presence in her life has provided the dimension of imagination and understanding that she so appreciates and is so deprived of. [...]

Do you ever come in this direction? We hope so very much. (We were going to come to Sydney about this time, had my mother not decided to leave. As it is, we might still come, but not for another couple of years. It is expensive, and one needs time – it would be a big thing for me to be in Australia again, and I'd like to spend a couple of months there if possible.) How right, about being glad to work hard if one is a writer. But why do people never see this? – or I suppose do see it and resent it. I am at the beginning of a book – have thought about it a lot, and hope it can now be written fairly consecutively. But of course it is all horrors and groans and staring into space, and one can only hope it will be better than one feels as it goes on to paper. I have to work on it full-tilt for the next few months and be ruthless about distractions and housework and the rest of it, as it has been so interrupted during the last years. I loved yr cousin's nice words about my 'Bay of Noon'. I think it took a long time to shake off the influence of that book and begin this one...

Francis feels somewhat that way about Cocteau – though at last that devilish personage (whom we both came to hold most dear!) is receding from our lives. I have been so pleased about the good reception of his book, it was a tremendous labour (with a lot of fun in it too) and deserved to be heaped with laurels.

Yours – Shirley.

Dear Shirley and Francis,

Warmest congratulations on winning the National Book Award for <u>Cocteau</u>. It's a glittering piece of work. An inspiriting, life-enhancing book. What labour, but what a pleasure, it must have been to trace the movement of that most ambivalent of natures! And to sustain that glittering (sorry I can't think of another word) analysis to the end! My sincere admiration. When we heard the news, my cousin, who reviewed Cocteau for the Herald, rang to tell the literary editor. Her notice will appear tomorrow. – Knowing that it was a very big book, I asked Margaret when she came in for coffee one day, 'How are you getting on with <u>Cocteau</u>?' She was silent, looked at me with a sort of vague desperation, then burst out most uncharacteristically, 'It's so <u>exciting</u>.' She said afterwards that she hoped she had done it justice; she wanted chiefly to make people want to read it. – Congratulations, too, on the <u>Bay of Noon</u> nomination. Both of you! That was so nice.

Shirley, I was delighted to have your letter. Thank you for it. Don't feel you are about to be deluged with correspondence from Sydney – not so. But I wanted to write about <u>Cocteau</u>, and also to say that when your letter arrived, your mother had finally gone to a doctor. That meeting (and subsequent ones) worked out so well that I was tempted to write to you at once, but in the end waited until Kit had mentioned it herself. (I did write, but tore the letter up.) Ordinarily, I'm in favour of non-interference in someone else's life, but this time, the situation with Valerie had intensified your mother's depression to such an extent that I was alarmed. We spoke one evening then, as I was going into town next morning, arranged to meet for coffee. That day we saw one doctor at a hospital. She talked to your mother for about an hour, gave her anti-depressants and a letter to be taken to another doctor at a city clinic two weeks later. At the end of two weeks, your mother was sleeping better than she had for a very long time, but was still telling me that she wishes they had given her methedrine. However, by the greatest good luck, she and the second doctor – a Dr. Andrew Robertson, a youngish Scotsman – liked each other well. He confirmed what Dr. Burkitt had said about this particular drug – that it has a gradual, cumulative effect, and that at the end of a month she would feel vastly different; if not, he would increase the dosage. Meantime, if she wanted to talk or visit Dr. Robertson at his clinic, she could do so at any time. (All these consultations and drugs are free, to my amazement!)

Now, after just a few weeks, she is like another person and looks about ten years younger. Just as the doctors predicted, her spirits and general health picked up slowly and then all at once everyone began to tell her how well she looked, not knowing that she was having any sort of treatment. Even she (and even I) began to believe that this rather miraculous thing was happening. I was so pleased and relieved.

[...]

Dear Alan has flown in and out. It was lovely to see him again. There was a Macmillan party and then lunch. We managed to exchange lots of news. He said he would be at his London desk on March 14th, so word of some sort about my manuscript should filter back soon. (I did my best to turn him against it: his decision will be the right one, whichever way it goes.) Meantime, now that I am less involved with solicitors and legal affairs following my mother's death, and having finished the weeks of typing and cutting, I must think of new work. There are piles of notes already.

[...]

Soon I'll be writing (work, I mean) and then I never, never, write letters. You'll be relieved to hear this. I've quite out-done the original long-winded lady!

Very best greetings to you both,

Yours,

Elizabeth

New York | 23 March 1971

Dear Elizabeth –

Your more-than-kind letter came this morning, giving us both great pleasure, and I send this off at once to thank you for it and for all the thoughtfulness and understanding it brings. Yes, it was marvellous that the NBA judges did the right – indeed obvious! – thing, and Francis will want to add some words of his own to thank you for your good wishes. What is also good news is that you have 'piles of notes already' towards a new book – that is the nicest thing an author can say or hear. We are hoping that Alan is going to publish the new manuscript;

and I think too your own feeling about it is more affirmative now as you grow away from the process of its creation, isn't it? Feeling badly about one's work is inescapable if one truly cares about it, and I do believe that suffering of this sort works to the benefit of the product... It is the most unshareable anxiety, though, and unexplainable. [...]

How right to never-never-write-letters when doing your own work; though we'll regret this, we respect and honour it! This won't mean we won't be thinking of you and wishing well to both you and your work. With more thanks than I can say, and with warmest wishes from Shirley.

Want Street | March 24th, 1971

Dear Shirley,

Our letters crossed. You will realize that I had very much wanted to write even earlier about your mother, but hesitated for the rather conventional reasons you can imagine. If I had had more sense and fewer scruples, it might have been a good thing.

[...]

On Monday night, and then again this morning on the phone (I have not yet mentioned receiving your letter yesterday), your mother spoke of your letters and cables urging her to leave some of her luggage etc., as mystifying. She wondered why you minded so much this time that she should leave Australia. What were your motives? I said there was nothing mysterious about your motives at all; that sooner or later we must all decide to live <u>somewhere</u> and that if I did not like the picture of her trailing off into the blue, how much more distressed you must feel. [...] There had been a reply from a boarding-house in Southampton offering accommodation at $1.50 a night. What should she do with it? 'Tear it up!' She said, 'And then if I make a booking and Shirley and Francis come...' So she is prepared for the likelihood of your arriving to meet her, but will protest violently till the very last. And the protest will be completely genuine, and yet not, at the same time.

[...]

On Monday night I was dismayed to hear her say casually that after paying her whole fare and making all her arrangements, she had been thinking a little of the tours she might have taken if she had stayed. I was slightly stunned to see that even this decision to go to England – unwise though it seems – was not firm. (Yet, of course, she did not mean to change her mind.) The remark simply illustrated the alarming vagueness of the entire project. I do wish I could be more cheerful about it. Dr. Robertson's drugs have helped, but performed no miracles. This morning she said she had found some sixteen-year-old methedrine tablets. (I had hoped never to hear of methedrine again.) I told her not to take them, and certainly not to mix them with the other drug. She has to see Dr. Robertson again, and I'll press her to ask him if the dosage of his prescription can be increased.

From your mother and from your letters, I know how more than willing you and Francis are to help her. But she will say there is nothing she can do for you; your life is perfect but for her. [...]

Apart from a trip to Scotland, I have heard only of trips along the south coast to look for villages full of decorative cottages and welcoming neighbours. She will find a 'mousehole' where she can hide away, where she can do nothing to offend, and she herself cannot be offended or hurt.

[...]

If your mother comes back to Sydney and it's at all helpful, please do keep in touch with me. I don't know how I gradually became involved. (Partly, my novel was finished, and my mother died, and I had some time between tasks when things began to fall to pieces a bit for your mother. At other times, in the middle of a book, I know I've let other people sink or swim.) But although we are very different, I'm fond of your mother and understand the way she thinks, disastrous and one-sided though it frequently is.

While everything I've said here is true, please don't weigh it too heavily. When you meet everything will be different.

Very kindest regards and best wishes to you both –
Elizabeth

New York | 26 March 1971

Dear Elizabeth –

I shan't bore you with more and more thanks, but they are more and more in order, and nothing can really express my feeling for your generosity, of mind, heart and time, and all the help you have given.

I feel a great relief for your work that my mother is leaving, as preoccupation with others' troubles – or even having to resist it – is a desperate imposition on one's book. And I was touched by your reference to my own struggles in this regard – I need not tell you that all these convulsions my mother goes through are a series of depth-charges and torpedoes into my efforts to write, or even to achieve a writing state of mind. Many people have much more to cope with; but one's case is unique. (You'll agree that if ever there was anything unique it is My Mum!)

[...]

Of all the contradictions, fantasies, self-dramatisations, etc, I say naught – since I see you understand it all, and also know the odd mixture that lies behind it. How can she be 'mystified' by our anxiety over her leaving Sydney, when she herself has done everything to exacerbate it by writing about disappearing into a 'boarding house in Southampton' etc. etc. etc. is something which defies analysis. I do feel the announcement of a $1.50 a day room in an unknown provincial town was almost consciously intended as a shocker; but in fact such things always get a Pavlovian desperate response from me, and not entirely irrationally as I have been the one everlastingly appointed to dig her out of such situations and to be ripped apart by it all having happened. [...]

One day we shall meet and burst into mad laughter. With most heartfelt blessings and embraces – Shirley

Want Street | April 21st, 1971

Dear Shirley,

A final word before thinking of work. – You will know by now that the Northern Star was successfully launched on April 10th. Already there has been time for a cheerful letter from your mother. [...]

There was a good deal of last-minute social life as well as business, and this included lunch at Margaret's flat on the Sunday before sailing. Then there was a valedictory visit to Mr. Robertson, at the clinic. [...] He gave your mother 'a family sized' bottle of anti-depressants, and a letter to be shown to other doctors. He said she had been 'a classic patient'. I think he's fond of her.

On Easter Saturday, Margaret and I went to the ship at four. Your mother and Valerie and the children had arrived earlier with the luggage. All bars were closed, and all public rooms full of a very Australian crowd drinking quantities of beer brought on in cartons (if not kegs!). We were hoarse trying to talk above the roar. The ship was due to sail at six, and we waited on the wharf amongst the streamers for about forty minutes, but gave up the vigil when we heard there was a delay of half an hour. The departure went off in an atmosphere of relatively total calm. Margaret and I reeled away as though we had been present at a moon-rocket launching. It is a relief to feel, from the tone of Kit's letter, that she is set to enjoy herself.

[...]

After a reader's report and a letter from Alan (in which he generously did not withdraw his offer to publish), I decided finally to shelve my novel. Alan wrote so kindly, such considerate, morale-building letters, that it almost seems nothing bad has happened. But it does make you hesitate to dash in to the next thing.

[...]

Warmest and best wishes to you both –

Elizabeth

New York | 27 April 1971

Dear Elizabeth –

Thank you once more for such a kind letter, as always telling just what is helpful and what one wants to know. You've played a great part in keeping my mother on an even keel as she has managed at Sydney, and it is all more appreciated than I can say. The doctor is a marvellous development that I can only pray he will not dissolve, get promoted, move, or otherwise let us down before my mother's return. Return I think she will – her letters are already shaped to that end; and such a semblance of 'plan' gives of course a far more pleasurable and less rending aspect to the trip. I too have already had cheerful letters from her (she was seasick in the Tasman Sea, lost (and found!) a suitcase, is 'terrified' of the Purser, and generally having wonderful time...). We will be over to meet her at Southampton on the 20th, and spend the following month with her. [...]

Shall keep mum on the subject of yr manuscript – as naturally we wish you <u>would</u> publish, and naturally we should say nothing, you being the onlie arbiter and true sovereign of the situation. One thing certain is that nothing there can possibly be lost – not simply because you probably will use all or part of it, but it is all a sort of literary life-experience that makes for knowledge and self-knowledge. Well, you know all this. You wrote once that you had a pile of notes towards the next book – so one hopes that means, before very long, a new ms. and a new publication.

Francis flew to Venice (yes!) for a few days, to attend the ceremonies for interment of Stravinsky. He has written about this for the New Yorker, for the issue of 1 May we hope. Was v. moved, and felt it was the last great 'event' in a way. Everything a Carpaccio procession, the real evocation of past being possible probably only in Venice where there are no cars and few big-city noises... I was v. envious, but could not have interrupted work, even apart from expense of it all, as am trying to get to some (undefined) encouraging point before breaking off to go to England. Yes, the interruption is always painful and haunts one – for me, most of all the disruption of a working state of mind, belief in characters and time-sequence.

Next voice you hear will be a cheery 'Here we are!' from one of those mythical destinations – Anne Hathaway's hollyhocks, or the Radcliffe Camera... Again with all thanks for the pleasure your letters give, and with very best and warmest greetings from us both – Shirley

London | 26 June 1971

Dear Elizabeth,

Thank you again and again for your letters and all your thoughtfulness. In fact, I don't know how to thank you for such practical and reassuring kindness, all of which I feel is a distraction from your work and days. [...]

Two nights ago we went to Putney to the Nolans, which was heaven, really, the best of our evenings here. We (F & I) spent an evening with the Nolans and Macleans, then drove out to the house. One sees (hears, rather) that Eliz. Harrower is loved; Cynthia thought you & I had met. Well, I feel we have, but would like it to be even truer in fact as well as thought. [...]

May I send warm affection, which is only a fraction of what I feel? – Shirley.

Want Street | August 16th, 1971

Dear Shirley,

I did enjoy and appreciate your last letter from London, all the news.
[...]

I think your mother is in a much stronger state than when she left, though not by any means reconciled to Sydney. Obviously, in spite of the disasters involved, seeing you both and living that 'lovely way of life' for a time was enormously important to her. And no doubt (again, in spite of everything), it was to you, too. Of course, she has powers of exasperating that are way above the ordinary. There is this verbal, lifemanship, game you find yourself involved in – and <u>losing</u>, half the time – when you're with her. And yet, and yet... That doesn't seem to be what matters most. I must try to think of people I know who don't work during the day. Practically everyone does. Will do some brain-racking and bringing together.
[...]

Your evening with the Nolans sounds delicious. If you felt that I was loved, this is certainly reciprocated. They usually come back once a year towards the end of our winter, the beginning of spring, and their friends look forward so much to the general flurry of spring flowers and Nolans. Cynthia and I write erratically between times.
[...]

Must stop raving on. My typewriter has been fighting back today. We have frequent tussles and I am certain it's because, after the deepest brooding, and with justified misgivings, I overcame scruples, prejudices and dark feelings, and bought a <u>German</u> typewriter. (The Olivetti that season were either very frail, or bright red, or turquoise.) Everyone was heartily sick of my moral dilemma by the time I bought the Olympia, and couldn't see that it mattered all that much. When I heard weeks or months after this that you had <u>resisted</u> a German machine, I thought how wise!

Oh dear. A call from Valerie – at your mother's request. The flat fell through and no-one is in good spirits now. Back at Park Regis in a slightly bigger apartment next door to the old one – same price. So please forget all I've said (I daresay that would be wisest in any case. I mean – not to quote me. – And while you're not quoting me, forgive my graceful way of expressing myself.) Things and people went agley, temporarily.

Best regards and greetings.

Affectionately – Elizabeth

New York | 29 Aug 1971

Dear Elizabeth –

You are so good to us – not only to send us news and give us a real idea of what is happening, but to make us laugh and cry and give us shocks of total recognition. Your rendering of the 'verbal, lifemanship game you find yourself involved in and losing half the time' – well, it is all certainly very fresh in memory...

[...]

I am writing this v. late at night after a day of slavery at the (US-manufactured) Smith-Corona typewriter. Am writing a long long article on bureaucracy which I have had in mind for many years – something has happened to make me want to bring it all out, if I can, fairly soon, so am trying to get at least all the references down on paper and prepare a sort of draft before we leave for Rome. [...]

What we hope is that you are working, and to your satisfaction; and well and prospering and pleased. I wish we could meet. [...]

With such good wishes from us both – Shirley.

New York | 20 Oct 1971

Dear Elizabeth,

[...]

Our trip just now was just about as different as could be – I worked harder, I think, than I have ever done except perhaps when I've been at the very end of a book; my essay on bureaucracy has now turned into book length – and I think that is the only way it will be published, as it is too long for magazine publication and in any case – even in these times – too controversial. I'll send it to you, if I may, when it sees the light of print. I was working on this book in the most beautiful places imaginable – and managed to do five or six hours every day except when actually on the road. Francis wrote his Rome article; and we went to Geneva to see Stravinsky's son, Theodore, who lives there. [...]

In London, where we were only for a week or two, we saw Alan of course, and Robin; which was lovely. They are very dear friends – I admire Alan more and more for he only gets wiser and kinder as the world gets worse. [...] We always hope to hear from him – or from you – that you have a new ms. for Macmillans. If not tactless to enquire, can one ask if your new book is, in fact, going on?

Speaking of good books, working on this odd subject made me feel cut off from imagination – partly because the only thing I've been reading was my own ms. However, have read two books I liked since surfacing – Graham Greene's 'autobiography', 'A Sort of Life'; and a novel by Nicholas Mosley 'Natalie Natalia'... It is nice when a newly published work gives pleasure – most pleasure I get from reading these days is not from new books. All the more reason there should be a new Harrower on the presses as soon as poss. With many good thoughts and greetings, and with the warmest good wishes of Shirley.

Want Street | December 13th, 1971

Dear Shirley,

[...]

We are in the middle – or perhaps at the beginning – of a bus strike. After exchanging notes and sending telegrams, your mother and I both hiked into town on Saturday morning and had some coffee. I hesitate to say anything good because the situation always reverses itself if I do, but she still seems to me so much better than last year... [...]

No telephone. It really is hard to keep in touch without one. I tried to persuade her not to cancel the application, but as there was some idea of moving into another place in the same building in December (which hasn't come off yet) your mother said it wouldn't be worth while paying for the installation for only six or seven weeks. I disagreed strongly, but to no effect. Valerie agreed with her to my disgruntlement. To someone living alone, a telephone seems as important as water and electricity, I'd have thought. Expense or no expense. However. [...]

For possibly two or three months, although it feels more like six months, I have been undecided about whether to go to London for a while. Having to store things and vacate flats, and what to do with papers, and how to go away from people I don't want to go away from... When I remember how easily your mother takes herself away, I am quite mortified. The trouble is, I don't really want to go, but can't <u>see</u> this place, or anything, after being back in Sydney and moving seldom for ten years...

[...]

Did you see that Margaret chose <u>Cocteau</u> as her first 'book of the year' in the Herald Christmas list? If allowed, I think she might have chosen it three times over. Last year her selection wasn't printed because one was also 'too controversial' and didn't fit the Herald policy. <u>Bay of Noon</u> was one of her three choices. – We've both admired the Doris Lessing novel <u>Briefing for a Descent into Hell</u>. – You ask about my pile of notes. I've written two poems and seen people and wasted my time badly which is why I had better be exiled.

[...]

Warmest greetings and good wishes to you both –

Elizabeth

Want Street | December 20th, 1971

Dear Shirley,

[...]

I decided on Saturday, two or three days ago, to go to London for four or five months. I sail rather than fly to avoid six weeks of saying goodbye, <u>and</u> of all the weird coincidences I sail on January 3rd on the Fairstar, the ship your mother came home on! Needless to say, as I am giving up the flat I've lived in for eight or nine years, and Christmas and public holidays are almost on us, it is all a little complex and busy. I'll be at the Nolans' place in London, and that should be nice. I'll hope to do some work, but that – is what I hope and intend. Home about May. It's a fearful wrench to go.

One thing you might like to hear which I don't remember mentioning before: Margaret reviewed E.M. Forster's <u>Maurice</u> in the S.M.H. It isn't in the same world as his other books; nevertheless there were things that needed to be said (especially in Australia). Then just the other day M. had a letter from a man visiting Sydney in whose house Forster lived the last several years of his life and where he died. He and his wife are here briefly. He seemed touched and pleased. I mention this because your mother said you used to like Forster so much.

Heaven knows how a person passes a month on a ship. I wish, I wish, I could switch my mind to work again. Forgive all this egotism.

Warmest and best greetings to you both –

Elizabeth

New York | 20 December 1971

Dear Elizabeth –

What we hope for you in 1972 is that miraculous, as it does seem, coming together of all your creative activity and expression of the last two years and more, and of the intervals when the mind's eye seems to bend itself on vacancy but is often at its most perceptive, and most nourishing to one's unconscious. If you take a trip to England, we hope we can manage to be there. [...]

I am in some subterranean world of the deadline which [...] keeps me just about from all contact with the world of Christmas, or indeed anything else. Doing this present book has been a weird and gruelling experience, and v interesting to me, and I hope never never to have to deal with 'facts' again. [...] It is a lonely book to write, and once in a while one wonders whether all the abuse one is going to get is really worth going through to tell the truth. (It is, however.)

[...]

Many many blessings for Christmas and 1972. We wonder what your decision will be about a journey in the coming year – the world is in such extremis that one sometimes has sensations of sitting tight just in order not to rock one's mental boat. Our journeys are refreshment to us – but we wish more and more to go to what we know and love and to feel continuity rather than change; as change is now the whole of life and continuity is nowhere. With great greetings, and warmest affectionate wishes – Shirley.

Dear Elizabeth

Of course you must by now realize that you have become part of our folklore – a kind of literary & household goddess; & as such I pay you all

kinds of tribute, including thanks & affectionate greetings. We must meet –
it seems almost weird that we <u>actually</u> haven't met! Happy 1972 to you –
Francis

New York | Christmas Day 1971

Dear Elizabeth –

Just a rushed note hoping to reach you before the Fairstar (of many
good associations!) brings you in what we love to think of as this direction.
We are certainly going to try to get to London while you are there – there is
a good chance of it anyway, and now we have an added incentive. It is, I'm
sure, a right and good thing to be doing – and what we both hope is that
these months away will be filled with pleasure, and eventual productivity,
for you. I'll write you c/o the Nolans, if I may. (By the way I should mention
that strangely – to us – we have never had a reply from them to a letter
written after we had run into them with the Macleans in London last June
and spent what was for us a lovely evening at their house. We sent them,
shortly afterwards, from here, a letter rejoicing in our new friendship and
asking if we might possibly buy a painting of Sidney's we had particularly
admired, and how we should go about it etc.) Anyway, let me say that your
rhetorical wondering as to 'how a person passes a month on a ship' is, we
hope, going to resolve itself into notes, or lines, or impressions... I'll be
interested to learn whether one can write on a ship (some ships are short on
privacy, others seem to have particular lounges where no one ever goes).
        [...]
The very best of bons voyages from us both, and warmest wishes for joy
in this venture – Shirley

FAIRSTAR | 4 February, 1972

Dear Shirley and Francis,

This is more in the nature of a telegram than a letter. We're on the way
to Lisbon and the end of the voyage is – at last – rushing towards us. I did
want to send a letter before London, but dishes have been smashing all day,
and people fell out of bed last night, and the Fairstar is having a rough time.
The mail closes shortly...

Your letter came just before Christmas and, as always, made me smile with interest and pleasure. I know what's involved in turning from work to letters and more words, so I appreciate and thank you twice over for all you say.

[...]

We picked up some London newspapers in Tenerife yesterday. They've given horrid shocks to many innocent Australians on board. Suddenly there's no sun in the morning, not even a chink of light, and then these black newspapers. After living inside <u>M. Hulot's Holiday</u> for four and a half weeks, the change is daunting. The distance between Australia and Europe is a matter of so much more than miles.

There were letters yesterday from, among others, your mother and Margaret. I was delighted to hear that the new flat has been achieved (<u>now</u> perhaps we'll go on to greater things like the telephone and television set), and also that Mr. Robertson is prescribing something even better than the yellow pills and visiting your mother. He's so nice. Obviously the January 14th appointment was kept as promised. Really, this is all very cheering. And the kitten is gorgeous. [...] Oh, Margaret told me earlier that she had forwarded on some letters to Fremantle, including one from you, and the big envelope containing them never arrived. I feel like a miser defrauded, and have brooded over those lost letters on and off since hearing of them.

[...]

As you can see, the Olivetti is hostile; and in the cabin everything's sliding about. Too distracting. And your letter isn't answered... Hope to send something more coherent from London.

With most affectionate greetings and wishes –

Elizabeth

New York | 23 April 1972

Dear Elizabeth –

We're just back a few days, from what was a beautiful and therapeutic and interesting trip. As Italy is in a desperate situation (desperate situations these days being the norm) and facing very frightening elections (in fact the electorate is so frightened of the obvious real force of the two extremes, the fascist party and the communists, that there will probably be a last-minute reinforcement of the middle of the roaders – i.e., the Christian Democrats who with their corruption, supinity, and bureaucracy have sold the moderate and well-meaning majority up the river these past years), it is remarkable that we did even achieve a sense of being away and fugitives from the horrors of the world. Anyone who can achieve moments of serenity these days is a true man of action, I say, even if – or most of all if – fugitive serenity is all we can hope for. One of the great things of our trip was of course meeting you.

[...]

What we'd like now is news of your present, your plans, your state which we warmly hope continues happy and, as we divined, glad of having made this great change. With great affection – Shirley

PS: While away, we both read The Watcher on the Cast-Iron Balcony, and were tremendously moved by it. Shall write Hal P. Why is such a book not world-famous anyway?

79 Deodar Road, London SW15 | April 26th, 1972

Dear Shirley –

[...]

I'm glad you both admired <u>The Watcher on the Cast-Iron Balcony</u> so much. Why is it not world-famous? I should think for no other reason than Hal is Australian and that it is written about Australia. Do you know him? We met twice years ago – once at a party in Adelaide, and then he was in Sydney and took me to dinner. He seemed to me that night completely truthful and completely unaffected, and I liked him. No-one agrees with my description, and I quite believe he can be the very opposite, but that was how he was then. There's a fair amount of jealousy on the literary scene in Australia (as elsewhere), and people are belittled, their achievements are belittled, because they have human failings like everyone else. The book did receive a lot of acclaim at home; everybody talked about it. (This reminds me of something that happened at Boulestin's, when there was some talk, I think, about Muriel Spark; and I remember your saying quickly to Alan, and glancing at me, something like, 'Yes, but she did write those other books.' And I was pleased and interested to see that you felt, too, that the value of someone's work was not negated by the passing of time or the most recent book.) The Watcher is Hal's best book, and on the strength of it, if he had never done anything else, (and he has) I feel he should be declared a National Treasure. Some of his short stories are very good. There's one called, I think, Francis Silver. If you haven't read it, I'll try to get it for you when I go home. Years ago, I read a poem of his in the Herald, The Moon is Round, the Snow is White, and meant to write to him about it, but never did. It was published in a different form later; he must have tinkered with it... Much more could be said about the literary scene. Hal and Patrick don't care for each other.

[...]

It goes without saying that I so much enjoyed seeing you both. Well. It really does go without saying. It's a permanent pleasure to know you're about. – You realized, no doubt, that I don't live perpetually on that plane of euphoria and enthusiasm (that would be rather wearing all round), but after some less than good years I was relieved to find so much buoyancy left. London has continued to provide enormous interest, treats, entertaining and/or surprising company – above all, variety. The Nolans are due back on May 4th.

[...]

With much affection to you both –
Elizabeth

London | June 15th, 1972

Dear Shirley,

[...]

The other day I remembered Francis asking if I had an agent. I said yes, but that was hardly true. There is a man here I've exchanged a few letters with, but we've never met and there's no point. He hasn't done anything, or liked anything of mine. All Alan said, years ago, about him was: 'He won't do you any harm.' In Sydney I've written stories and put them in a cupboard, simply not knowing what to do with them. I suppose unworldliness, or idiocy, can be carried too far. At one time Patrick offered me his agent, but I did nothing about it and she's on the point of retiring. At the moment, I haven't anything wonderful to offer; on the other hand, it's inhibiting not to have someone who is on your side when you do produce something. I've had some people, but never an agent on my side. Anyway. Perhaps it doesn't matter. Maybe a good thing would beat its way even out of a cupboard.

[…]

It doesn't seem very likely now that I'll fly home in time to see you in New York. That would have been so enjoyable for me; though I trust I'll still see you both again in Australia. It is so pleasant, so stimulating, here, that I feel I must be mad to think of going home. The Nolans could not be easier or nicer or more considerate; they both want me to stay longer and have plans – enticing plans – including me lined up into the future to tempt me to stay. (They like it here, and I think it's good for me to be away from Australia.) However, I miss Sydney and my life and people there and must wrench myself away from London soon. (The matter of the letter and the painting remains deeply mysterious to me. I feel too baffled to ask.)

The garden is a marvel; C <u>works</u> in it. Scotland was ravishing… Probably I'll go home in the second half of July. When there's a new address in Sydney, I'll send it to you. Meantime, many good wishes and affectionate greetings to you and Francis.

Elizabeth

New York | 20 June 1972

Our dear Elizabeth –

It was with so much pleasure that we read your letter this morning – also your v. welcome one of last month. We now have a date for arrival in England (about 21 July) for one week, en route to Italy. Please do still be there! – your letter says you'll be departing 'the second half of July' and we can only pray that we'll arrive beforehand.

<u>Distinct</u> impression that your time in England has been exceedingly good, and good for you (two things not usually found together); how glad you must be that you didn't whizz home in May. I know what you mean about the polarising attraction of home, even when one knows that one is having a better time (as the absurd saying goes) elsewhere: I don't think I could have so much pleasure from our travels if I didn't have 'home' looming at the back of it all – even if home is this extraordinary, inhuman, alarming, scruffy, and just about desperate New York. Also, I don't find it

possible to enter into a writing state of mind away from home, at least in any protracted sense. Do you? (intrusive question) – we have idyllic mental glimpses of you, pen and pencil on your knee, composing in the Nolans' garden: I suppose it is possible to compose in such circs, but only <u>very</u> stark material... That garden, seen by us in moonlight, remains a strange enchantment, the house too.

About My Mum! So many sagas have roiled around since last we exchanged news... But let me thank you so much for writing realistic and positive news of her, as you always do. [...] The best news I have from my mother is (aside from THE ALL-HALLOWED KITTEN!) the constant mention of people dropping in – Margaret (about whose recent visit I had the most delightful and cheering letter); Daphne, Dan, and even Joan Lemon who, although often afflicted with domestic woes, seems to be often on the phone or the threshold.

[...]

I've been so sunk in these interminable galleys and annotations that I hardly know what else has been going on – ghastly things in the world at large, of course. [...] I have just read the Holroyd life of Strachey (engrossing and amusing and, somewhat, amazing) and the companion vol. When I have finished this weirdo book of mine I am madly looking forward to lots of real reading, and hope never, never again to set eye on books with titles like 'Dag Hammarskjöld: Custodian of the Brushfire Peace' or 'The Limits of Power' or 'The Legislative Struggle' or... We are all so protected, we little realize how very few books, of the inundation published, are written by <u>writers</u>. [...]

With all great greetings, until we meet, dear Elizabeth; and most affectionately from – Shirley

8/20 Joubert Street, Hunters Hill, NSW 2110 | September 20th, 1972

My dear Shirley and Francis,

Many happenings since my London postcard, some of which I'll set down rapidly now, in a jumble.

London to Sydney was easy, comfortable and as untiring as could be. (Thank you for the advice about the seating on jumbos. Followed it.) Beautiful and enriching as London was, I was ready to go home; so as soon as the plane took off and headed for the southern hemisphere, it could do no wrong. We had no turbulence, no delays anywhere. I did hear 'Greensleeves' about five hundred times on the 'classical' music programme, but even that was all right. In no time, a marvellous sunrise, Sydney airport, and the impression that someone had switched on – out there – much more radiance than falls on any other place on earth. It isn't so, but it often feels like that, and I just happened to arrive at the beginning of a run of spectacular days.

At the moment I'm in Blackheath (also radiant, smelling of clover, violets, cut grass, and buzzing, alas!, not only with bees but blowflies), recovering from the uncharacteristic nest-building involved in moving to the flat at Hunter's Hill.

[...]

September 24th

Interruptions. I must have gone out to look at the pear tree, or just to admire the rural scene. There are six hens, six ducks and numerous parrots dropping in to eat the remains of the hen and duck food. On a dismal day it all looks sordid and slummy, but there haven't been any dismal days and it looks idyllic. Ripples, the cat, is a hunter, so we try to save the parrots.

Anyway, back in Sydney. Yesterday Kit came over for lunch, catching a ferry and a bus. My flat costs $6.00 a week more than hers, but you will imagine it's something magnificent when she tells you about it. She was funny. She brought me some home-made pie, but she didn't tell me about it till we were driving her down to the ferry in the evening; when she did mention it, it was only to say she was taking it home with her. [...]

Keep well and keep writing. It's so nice to know you're both about somewhere. Greetings and love, Elizabeth

New York | 3 October 1972

Our dear Elizabeth –

What pleasure to get, first, your card; and then to come home to your letter. London definitely lacked some quality we had so quickly come to expect of it, without you; we both felt it natural to have you there, and in fact to have strong-armed our way into your life with every intention of remaining there until (god forbid) forcibly evicted. We've both thought and spoken of you and congratulated ourselves on our connection with you over and over. [...]

We welcomed, as a pure crystal fountain in the desert, <u>favourable</u> impressions of Australia (which have been, as you'll imagine, sadly lacking in our correspondence since your departure at the beginning of the year...). I liked the word radiance, which was my childhood impression of the city of Sydney when we drove sometimes into town in the early morning and its (then) towers (now no doubt diminutive or demolished) came into sight as one crossed the bridge. There was in fact a golden sun – sheer radiance! – on top of the building that housed the Sydney Sun. The whole thing, always, enchanted place to me when it suddenly appeared. (Then, few minutes later, descent into the narrow dark of George, Pitt, and Castlereagh, toast-rack trams, smell of sooty-city, lights on sometimes on winter mornings... Surfacing again in the shimmering aquarium of David Jones...). How right you have been in realizing, and doing, what was perfect for you – departing in the first place, much pleasure and friendship and interest in the contrast, then choosing the appropriate moment for resumption; it has, as one knew and as one sees from your letter, all achieved a harmony. We think of the difficulties you were facing on return – sometimes one is much stronger at these things when enjoying your present perspective and equilibrium, and we hope it may be so.

We were abroad two and a half months this trip, always in hotels; we loved it all, but there is the ineffable moment of turning the key in one's own particular oilèd wards – and the even more ineffable moment of finding that the New York terrorists have not yet torn one's place apart in one's absence. We both slaved most of the summer – I had a terrific job to do on my galleys (and the reference apparatus makes the checking a fearful undertaking), and am now facing another siege with the page-proofs that arrive in two days; publication is set for the beginning of March. Macmillans are really taking quite a bit of trouble to publicize the book and one hopes that it will have some favourable effect. [...] Francis' 'Flaubert in Egypt' is triumphantly launched in England [...] F. is now working away on the checking of the French translation of his Cocteau, then will return in earnest to his treatment of the correspondence of

Isadora Duncan and Gordon Craig. [...] Craig was a monster; and obviously a beautiful and electrifying one.

Oh my Mum, My Mum... Thank you for wise and, as always, understanding words on this theme... I had just had a letter from Joan, pouring on insoluble woes (and taking, I may say between us, a somewhat bossy tone with what can only be called insanely impracticable proposals...), but thank heaven not reverting to her previous idea that my mother should go into the real estate business in Portugal (I swear that this is true). [...]

Nice to be home – days of an almost-Sydney radiance, and New Yorkers confounding one's knowledge of the situation by being maddeningly kind and helpful and acting pleased to see one again... Perhaps this state of continual beleaguerment is going to bring out the best in us... As to the elections, we just pull the covers over our heads and cry. Fond love to you, dear Elizabeth, from Shirley

New York | 7 Oct 1972

My dear Elizabeth –

A post-telephonic word to say – well... to say thank you, first and last; and also to say that it would be so much more appropriate to telephone you for the purpose of exchanging joy and laughter, instead of with such an imposition as today's. What I dread is that too-much-Mum should becloud our friendship; or that one should trespass on your own goodness and your presence there, which one will try rigorously not to do. (It is not enough to urge you to hang up on us in such a situation – obviously one should not put you in position of doing so; the exchanges of letters and cables with my mother in the past few days had driven us so bonkers that we fear having exceeded delicacy.) It is of course maddening to have a sister there who is not only not helping but who is exacerbating the situation and who is, in fact, the last person one could turn to. As you are so much the first person one would turn to, one would not wish to overdo.

What was marvellous was to hear your voice, within thirty seconds of giving your number (little did I think that number would so soon be dialled from here...). It was about 7 a.m. here – we'd tried you in the evening (i.e. morning) before, with no luck, and hoped to calculate the time so as not to disturb you late at night (?). I had written out 'Things' – but all disappeared in my transoceanic yelps. [...]

Much love to you, dear Elizabeth – Shirley.

Hunters Hill | October 8th, 1972

My dear Shirley and Francis,

[...]

Your letter was such a pleasure to me, as your letters always are. [...]

Did you like hearing about beautiful Australia? I'm glad. Last week, from Tuesday to Saturday, I was driving out in the west of NSW with Margaret. We didn't go so far, just over the Blue Mountains, and on to Bathurst the first night; then we stayed at Parkes (saw the radio-telescope); then at Cowra, then at Katoomba (of all places). But arriving was nothing much and travelling was everything. The light is really ravishing. It transforms everything. Bathurst, Orange, Forbes, Parkes have trees everywhere now, wide clean empty streets and footpaths (more or less). We saw rolling hills and wheat and galahs and cockatoos and had to stop while sheep and lambs surrounded the car. Some parts reminded me very much of some of Sidney's Dimboola paintings with little mop trees scattered sparsely over the landscape, each with its shadow, and little dams seeming to run uphill. There is a drought, needless to say, and they were feeding the sheep by hand outside Parkes. The ground was cracked open and the creeks were dry. And yet it was, to me, enchanting and magnetic and I couldn't bear to turn back to the city. Finishing on another airletter. Love to you both, Elizabeth

Hunters Hill | October 10th, 1972

My dear Shirley and Francis,

Letter 2. I hope they arrive together. It's hard to have any faith in Post Offices.

We were still in the country in the other letter, and I am almost as reluctant to stop thinking about it, as I was to leave it. While we were away, I was cast down to hear the Government announce that Bathurst and Orange had been chosen (lucky them!) as 'growth centres' and that the long-discussed decentralization was about to start. They have about 20,000 people each and almost no industry. Anyway, such is Australia and its light, silence and air. When I was in London, people would write would-be pathetically to me to the effect that I'd find it provincial when I came back. (They seemed to forget that I'd been away before, for a much longer time.) To my surprise, I did find it provincial. Even now I can't look at a newspaper and can't care much about what's going on. The General Election will be held on Dec. 2nd, it was announced today, and perhaps, perhaps, Labour might win after about 25 years. That's all I know of current events here. But the planet can have sometimes so much beauty that I am terribly glad that people in the rest of the world don't know about it. They would run here, maybe, and it would be like everywhere else. Whatever I mean by that! God knows in many respects there's so much room for improvement. Still, enough of all that. Oh, David Jones' threatened to close down in four years' time because of Land Tax and water rates. It is the only place, just about, that was here when I was 17 and if any more of the background changes it will be too much.

[...]

More another day. I'm glad you're glad to be home. Much love to you both,

Elizabeth

Hunters Hill | October 16th, 1972

My dear Shirley,

[...]

On Saturday we went to see the new wing of the Art Gallery of NSW, which was long, long in the building, and then back to see Kit on the way home. Everything – by which I suppose I mean general health and emotional balance – seemed pretty fine, and Margaret, who was with me, thought so, too. Your mother did start out to list a catalogue of negatives describing herself, and Margaret and I listened in that sort of dumbfounded, hypnotised way one sometimes does, but instead of contradicting I asked for a cup of tea and the subject got itself changed...

[...]

I spoke to her today and everything had slumped again. The cat seems to be destroying everything at high speed, and your mother said that she was an expense, and would keep on being an expense, and seemed to have some idea of parting with her permanently. I said money could put things right, but was told that even I, even I, wouldn't want to keep something that was a perpetual worry and drain on the resources. We then got involved in some tacky philosophy in the course of which I invoked the sun, moon and stars, the tides, the good and bad in all things, etc. Even I (to quote your mother) should have been ashamed to be so shameless, but the fact is I believed what I was saying. Well, that was all rather gloomy and enough to make me want to take to the woods. (You know I have some dearly loved and alarming neurotics all of my very own, and they aren't in a good way, either. Luckily I have a few staunch and stalwart friends about, too, who are very reliable.) [...]

I like to hear of all the work going on. Difficult for me, in view of what's above, to blame other people for my lack of work. I look forward greatly to your book, Shirley. [...] And I can see Francis going over that enormous ms. with a tuning fork – I think one of the most absorbing and enviable occupations in existence.

Much love to you both,
Elizabeth

New York | 17 Oct 1972

Our dear Elizabeth – Your two letters arrived today: they are inestimable, and so are you.

[...]

Our telephone call was a chaotic greeting on your return from your trip – oh what a description, though. Of course I was seeing a series of 'Nolans' as I read your words aloud to F – the mop trees, the split ground, and the light that SN paints as Monet painted his (different) light, like painting the air; well, the Steegs will see it one day (and that day not too distant, by the look of things!). [...]

Yesterday... a most extraordinarily useful day. My page proofs being ready in Boston, I got up at 6am, took the plane to Boston, and spent the day going over them with the splendid chief proof-reader of the Atlantic-

Little-Brown empire – a dear woman and a totally professional being in the right sense. What was marvellous was that all my little excesses and overflows were not only accommodated but accompanied by heartfelt remarks. Of the right kind.

[...]

18 Oct: This morning, a brief letter (somewhat cheerier) from My Mum, enclosing the splendid Margaret Dick review of F's Stories & True Stories – we read it with delight, and are proud to claim connection with so penetrating a reviewer! [...]

Oh Elizabeth, at the end of my mother's letter yesterday was the coup de grace – and it really did pierce to the heart: to the effect that I'd be finished with my book now and surrounded by all the fun and congratulations of friends... I hope Mum will never know what pain and anxiety and depression have gone into this book; but this is too much! It made me feel like withdrawing into the real estate business in Portugal.

[...]

Much love – Francis and Shirley

Hunters Hill | November 3rd, 1972

My dear Shirley and Francis,

[...]

Margaret was so pleased that you both liked her review. After all, all I had said was, 'You used "especially" twice.' Wasn't that helpful? It was in <u>print</u>. [...]

A week of Blackheath in heavy, heavy rain, with four, five and sometimes six of us confined to what is scarcely more than a fibre tent with very few amenities. What was once meant to be a place to work has become a sort of halfway house for hippies. Long-haired boys who take drugs and think (and worse, keep telling you) that they're The Universe drift tiredly from bed to table. Twas somewhat chaotic and unexpected because visits are usually planned not to coincide. By some miracle or other – with all that mud, rain and close confinement – the situation didn't deteriorate; but I tottered away from a week of Ritual Magic, I Ching, Tarot cards, Om, Rolling Stones, assorted mystics and Great Teachers, with my mind slightly mazed. They talk in blocks of words, slogans and curses, and show no sign of pausing to think at all. My mind, such as it is, seems to sit about thinking profound thoughts like: Oh, the pity of it!

[...]

Francis, thank you for talking to your agent about The W.T. I know about the difficulties of an Australian background, because I didn't read an Australian novel myself till I was thirty-one, and even now read South African (and similar) writers with reluctance. Not in a strong position to blame anyone else. Because this is the way it's happened, I've learnt not to expect anything of writing but the satisfaction of having done something that seemed impossibly difficult while it was going on, and friends. Since the satisfaction and the friends are important to me... And it's always a relief, very welcome, if someone not here says in effect: you can do something. Artur Lundkvist took The WT home to Sweden with him in the hope of getting it published there for me. Resistible there, too. – I think backgrounds are confusing, as you say; the only time they're not is when you're writing a novel. And then, if the people are right, they master it and loom larger – according to my lights. [...]

I see jacarandas from my window looking like smoke almost amongst the eucalypts.

The ABC reminds me (not necessary) that you'll be voting tomorrow. Mournful day! – But now I must rush out into the sun for shopping and exercise. Thanks over and over for all you say.

Much love, Elizabeth

Hunters Hill | November 18th, 1972

My dear Shirley,

[...]

Oh, the party, the party. Last Saturday we all rolled up at The Chimes. [...] There was no general talk of New York, but the party did go very well. It went on from two till six with lashings of goodies to eat and drink, and as much animated conversation as the room could hold. It was fun. Your mother said it was the best birthday she'd had for years. I think Valerie must have talked to Joan (a good-looking but somewhat startling lady) and Jean.

[...]

Election Day. We listened and listened to commentators. Everyone thought it was no contest, and so it turned out to be. No-one liked Nixon (these were the reports we heard) but he was in office; he had been to Russia and China; the Democrats were stuck with a radical label; New York was wilder than ever, and Nixon was for law and order – and so on. Yes, the Vietnam ceasefire (so we thought!) on the very eve. Oh, cynicism! Really, there is no word for it... You say horrific things portend and while I can believe it, I wonder what you mean specifically. We have our Election Day on December 2nd. It won't make any difference to the world, and I'm not even optimistic especially about the difference it could make here. But the Liberals should just go...

[...]

Much love to you both –

Elizabeth

New York | 26 Nov 1972

Our dear Elizabeth –

Since I wrote, Nixon has triumphed, to no one's surprise; and we have again had wondering thoughts about our future, and some hankerings for having a toehold elsewhere – though it is true that the only 'elsewheres' are places that will doubtless become Nixonised in due course. There have been, since the installation of the Nixon Supreme Court, such changes in the judicial system and such infringements on citizen's right under law as can only bode very ill indeed for people like us (as this week, a ruling from the Supreme Court that the government may decide what evidence should be admissible in political cases). How long our few little scraps of protection took to build up, and how quickly they are cast away before the eyes of an inattentive and indifferent public.

[...]

What are you doing, Elizabeth – what reading, any writing? (excuse that last impertinence, however). It is nearly a year since you flew the coop: a good year, don't you think? Also for us. It's only the world that drives one bonkers. Yes, one's mob does notice the difference, isn't it strange, interesting and true? Of course, there is also the precedent of you having flown said coop, you could do so again, and that may be subliminally recognized.

[...]

Great affection and friendship to you, chère amie, and as ever from us both – love – Shirley

Hunters Hill | December 5th, 1972

My dear Shirley and Francis,

I must tell you that I, and my Mob, and half the population are THRILLED about the change of government. At last. And they are speaking so rationally, simply, unaggressively, unoratorically – it's heaven. It can't last perhaps, but it has started very, very well. From not being able to read an Australian newspaper, I am reading four a day. You become so used to living in a condition of public shame, vicarious shame, that you forget what – no, have never known what – it might be like to agree with those who speak for us. I found myself in a little local bus – all strangers, all Labor voters and hopers (before the results were known) – you can see I'm quite incoherent, overcome and in no state (as the New Yorker says) to just 'give you the news'. Anyway, on the bus, all so varied, we were bosom friends by the end of the journey. I took champagne, balloons and heaven knows what to the house of other hopeful friends. It had to happen, but it seemed too miraculous. And that's how it continues. Enough of this raving.

[...]

Under separate cover I am sending you some cuttings about the elections, some editorials from local newspapers. Do be interested. It's the most exciting thing that's happened in this country since I've been born. And that's quite a time ago now. – There has also been a lot of Nolan publicity because of Snake and the film and the opening of his exhibition at the Marlborough all in one week. Both C and S invited me to stay on for this week, and perhaps I might have... But then – think what I'd have missed here! Much love to you both, Elizabeth

Hunters Hill | December 10th, 1972

A PS to that last note – just to say that I spoke to Kit yesterday and we had a talk about television sets. She said if she is to stay here, she must have one; after six in the evening the nights are long and drag. When she comes home, she and I are going to inspect sets together and choose one; and if I haven't spent my all on other household items, I may get one at the same time. (My present Whitlamania can't bear to be deprived of television news.) So it seems that with your talk and my talk over this last shortish time, Kit has been persuaded that this is an essential possession. Hurrah!

[...] We are all dazed by the thrill of having things happen (constitutionally, within the law) that should have happened years ago. The mood among liberals with a small 'l' and Labor supporters is like nothing I've experienced before. We are all in love with each other. I remember in <u>The Heat of the Day</u>, Elizabeth Bowen said that all the people left in London during the war were in love, and that's just what it's like here. I can't help feeling thrilled and joyful, and I have so much company [...] Perhaps it's unwise to hope for so much and to react (as so many of us are) like emancipated slaves, etc, etc., <u>but</u>...

[...]

Dear friends, happy days. I hope so much that all is harmonious and pleasing as could be imagined. Your plans sound super (to use my Deodar friend, Mrs. Fox's word), sumptuous. – Many affectionate greetings and love to you both –

Elizabeth

P.S. Come west.

Hunters Hill | December 23rd, 1972

My dear Shirley and Francis,

A pre-Christmas word from sticky Sydney – a hundred and four degrees and a hot, hot wind; all week it's been like the summers of my childhood. What happened to September's radiance?

[...]

Here, we are coping with our prolonged heat-wave and Christmas frenzy, and suffering slightly from schizophrenia in that we are still truly thrilled and amazed by our good fortune in acquiring such a government. They were actually <u>working</u> in Opposition. Even on Saturdays and Sundays we wake up to good news. People are always coming through a door announcing new good tidings. None of us has experienced anything like it before. Whitlam knows <u>Greek</u> (a peculiar touchstone of mine).

But the other side, of course, is that we are terrified by the ghastly events in North Vietnam. While everyone's been asking for years if Presidents might not be literally mad, the question presents itself again today with a piercing reality... Listening to the news in bed this morning – London and New York views of the bombing – I felt frightened. What <u>can</u> Nixon intend to do next? [...]

Meantime. While they're still in existence and we are, we've reached agreement with China and East Germany, and today the Australian dollar was re-valued upwards (as they put it). [...] This morning I was momentarily startled to hear that Mr. Whitlam is broadcasting to the world tomorrow. That statement brought a tentative alarm, but such is the general confidence that a broadcast on shortwave radio about our foreign policy (considering what that has been for so long) seems – not injudicious. We continue to hope.

[...]

For the first time ever people are coming to me for Christmas, instead of the other way round. So like Shirl I'm thinking of turkeys and plum puddings – but only the pud will be hot. After the 25th there may never ever be more eating or shopping done at 8/20. But it should be fun on the day.

Dear friends, a happy and peaceful and hard-working New Year. Love from E

Hunters Hill | January 5th, 1973

My dear Shirley and Francis,

Thank you, thank you, for that so-nice postcard (from all three) and for the New Year cable – a lovely surprise. I've had a happy, joyful letter from your mother. Don't you think things have altered rather wonderfully? I've only had time to write once to her, but I so look forward to hearing all the details of this holiday when she comes home.

Oh, whenever I think of those first post-election air letters I sent you, I really laugh. Very high marks for incoherence. But if I'm incoherent, think how the Liberal and DLP voters sound!

And Vietnam. I very nearly rang to see what <u>you</u> both thought was happening.

Started the new year by sitting and typing from old diaries and notebooks – not with the feeling that this was especially useful in itself, but with the intention of re-establishing work-habits, and also with the hope that my mind might begin to stir, wake up and take an interest. So there has been what feels like constructive activity all week. And as the rule is that I must finish anything that's started, this particular chore will keep on for two or three weeks; after that, sitting and typewriter-brooding should come naturally. No more chat just now. I'll take this up to the little Post Office.

[...]

Many greetings and much love to you both

Elizabeth

New York | 5 January 1973

Our dear Elizabeth –

A very very happy 1973 is what we wish for you – at least as many good things and good surprises as in 1972; and – we can't help selfishly wishing the year will include a reunion among us all. It seems odd that 1972 was the year of our meeting – to me, it is as if we had met back in those summers of childhood, a pair of banded panamas above school ties... Let me thank you at once most warmly for two marvellous letters, which delighted us, and for the envelope of clippings which maddened us with envy. The newspapers here have also been carrying a lot of Australian news and it pierces one to the heart to see that it can be done and that even in this decade of reaction it is possible for an electorate and a government to do new, rational, and right things and to be brave. Through the nightmare of the December bombings there ran, here, the super-nightmarish undercurrent of realization that this country had just re-elected the 'maddened despot' (as the NY Times described him) by a huge plurality and for another four years. Our despot has not even been inaugurated yet, for his second term.

The visit is THE GREATEST SUCCESS – my mother is really loving it, and we are getting pleasure out of seeing her enjoy herself so much. We've been living our lovely life at a rate that boggles imagination and beggars description, and I could not begin to recite all our excursions and incursions even if you had patience to hear them. So far the climax has been our splendid New Year's Eve – when we were the guests at the opera in the box of the manager who is a chum of ours. [...] Sutherland, in glorious voice, proceeded to sing a high-camp and highly entertaining Daughter of the Regiment, to thunderous applause.

[...]

Something pleasant about stopping dealing with world affairs has been reading real books again, instead of ghastly (and often deceitful) tomes on international events. The natural antidote has been poetry, which stands in shelves adjacent to the world-horrors books in my study, as dock leaves to nettles...

[...]

More soon, dearest Elizabeth, and tremendous good wishes from us all. And utter determination on the Steegs' part to arrange a reunion in '73. Our love to you – Shirley

New York | 13 January 1973

Our dear Elizabeth –

Thank you again for, as always, a delighting Elizabethan document.

[...]

You'll scarcely believe the horrific letter Valerie sent my mother a few days ago – of a forced tone that made the toes curl, no mention of us, and enclosing a clipping (no, not of old Shirl) of a suicide at The Chimes – which greatly upset my poor old mother, as she had known the girl and often spoken with her. [...]

Wot else? – well, tomorrow is departure day. And so far all is on schedule and my mother should reach Sydney in the morning of Tuesday 16th. [...]

The book actually exists in US edition, and a mysterious box of rush copies (intended for supposedly potential reviewers) reached me a couple of days ago – so I have been able to give one to my mother. As soon as there are more, you shall have one pronto. The horrors of the war – with, now, the injection of a nuclear weapons note – and the dictatorship we are living under here have made me feel more than ever that anyone who was at the scene of the crime must come forward with their evidence... You cannot imagine (or rather you can, but most people can't) the invasions of rights and privacy we are living under here, and the attrition of the free press and freedom of speech. In New York the news still comes through loud and clear and furious, but NY is now like a separate country, or the last fragment of what America was in these respects. There has been much praise of the courageous Australian actions, and this week the New Yorker carries passionate editorial and article on the war invoking the Australian and Scandinavian reactions. (You realize, of course, that this does no good whatever in Washington; we are all talking to ourselves; and Nixon has recently been re-elected by a landslide...)

No more of these nightmares. We grinned with pleasure to picture you typing from old notebooks and diaries – it is like a painter setting up canvas, putting brushes in turpentine, etc. It is good news, more news of the kind, please. Blessings on you, dear Elizabeth, and much love from Shirley.

Hunters Hill | January 19th, 1973

My dear Shirley and Francis,

[...]

It looks as if the war might really end – <u>again</u>, it looks as if the war might really end, and though meanwhile we see vapour trails from bombers on the news... Here we seem to be all set to send diplomats, missions, assistance, to Hanoi. Is this really Australia, or Through the Looking Glass? Amazing days. [...]

Oh, Kylie says she would be v. interested to review 'Defeat' if it comes her way, which it easily might. She cares a great deal about what is happening everywhere, and is predisposed to be on your side. Not that there will be any shortage of supporters here or elsewhere, I'm sure. Wonder who would be best?

[...]

My typing goes forward by jerks; there have been crises since before Christmas, but everyone is now attending doctors and hospitals and I trust all is calm and bright again. Patrick spoke to me sternly about my life this morning. He thinks that I should be writing more books, which knowledge encourages me.

Must go out and <u>buy some clothes</u>. I do wish they would just arrive without being sought. – I have your address in Italy (Florence) if anything of interest happens.

Much love to you both

Elizabeth

New York | 26 January 1973

My dear Elizabeth –

[...]

This in haste, as am flinging my rags into bags for departure, and galloping to the post office to send you, by air, a copy of my book. It could, of course, be ten times as long; I have such a mass of material and so much more to say; but the pressing need to me seemed to be to get some suppressed essentials and a mass of documents into print while they could do good and before they made me a human wreck by obliging me to devote my life to them ever after. I would be thrilled if Kylie Tennant is interested to review it; and of course I greatly hope that it does come to the attention of serious people who 'care a great deal about what is happening everywhere'. In any case, I'd be proud and so pleased to think she had read it, and shall get Macmillan's to send a first copy to her in Australia.

[...]

Good for Patrick, as I boldly call him, urging you to the typewriter. One never knows quite whether one can do this without annoying – the typewriter is so much where one wants to be and sometimes the injunctions touch one on the raw. But that is where we are greatly and deeply hoping that you are and will be spending much of your time... One feels from your letters that you <u>are</u> tending in that direction???

Love to you, dear Elizabeth, from us both – your Shirley.

London | 23 February 1973

Elizabeth dear –

How to thank you for your wonderful cable, which greeted us here and warmed my heart and blood stream. You are, in effect, the person the book hopes to reach – so it has already done its stuff if you think well of it. Thank you.

[...]

Shall write properly from N.Y., where we return tomorrow – all here is a hive of publishing, babbling, interviewing etc. It's nice to be in London, but so rushed... My dear mum – from whom the most delightful letters here – told me you were looking for a Tarot pack, & we found this one opposite the British Museum, along with a booklet also enclosed... (You may have 100 of them by now, but if so, then – as the Japanese say – laugh at it and throw it away...)

Alan and Robin in fine form – we dined at sacred Boulestin's last night, and sent waves of affection in your direction. We also spent two days at Cambridge, where F did useful work in the library – on way back to London, drove to Ely: the light and huge sky over the Fens was (I suppose, literally) heaven. Such clouds and space and changing. Back to the well-scraped sky of NY... Love, thanks, and blessings from us both – Shirley.

New York | 4 March 73

My dear Elizabeth –

If the writer's craft ever appears over-stern to me, I'll take out your inspired and blessed letter of the 22nd and glory in my lot. You are a dear friend, and a great writer and reader, and one feels (however unworthy) as one read your words, that one is rising to an occasion. Dear Elizabeth, thank you for thinking and saying these things – so true to my intention, and just what an author longs to hear (and almost never does, praise not necessarily coming from those who have understood best, and so seldom from one who understands completely). I felt acutely what you said about the false indulgence – the tolerating of the intolerable out of the superficial wish to be 'charitable'. [...] The treatment of this theme is one of the qualities I prize in the early – or rather, the earlier – books of Muriel Spark – she is on to this in a flash, can spot it at fifty yards. Not for her, the

embracing of evil just in order to show the length of one's own arms...
As I say in my opening chapter, what this attitude in effect amounts
to is the position that 'We're only inhuman'. [...]

Tomorrow is publication day, and some good things have already
happened – although the abuse-mongers have of course yet to be heard
from. The NY Times gave it a splendid, and rather amusing, review last
week – a great relief, as there is a strike of NY newspapers and many
books in any case are not reviewed for weeks after issue. Also, some
other good reviews known to be coming up. The BBC called from
London on Saturday to do a telephone interview – I gave them an earful
(dignified, I hope; but to the point: they asked me what I thought of
UN administration and I said, 'It makes Parkinson's Law look like
jurisprudence'). It comes out in the UK in mid-April, and of course I am
wishing there were copies in the shops so that BBC listeners could get out
and acquire them... But these are the wild ravings of an unrealistic author.
[...]

An adorable cable and good & comforting letters from my mother –
who (WHAT NEXT???) reports a plague of fleas in her flat. I have written
the obvious – for heavens' sake, get the exterminator, take the puss to be
de-flea-ed, etc. How awful, I hope this crisis at least has passed by now...

Elizabeth, my father is dying. The ghastly death from cancer – at any
moment the end may come, and indeed one can only pray that life won't
be extended in such suffering. I've written to break this news to my mother
[...]. There will be many thoughts and feelings for everyone concerned;
one's own mortality will loom, as will all the past. [...] We are entreating
my mother to accept an invitation to visit Hobart in April. Meantime,
we wonder if you are to go to Japan – incredible sentence! – on the 21st??
I can't tell whether the Nolans arrive before? Please give them warmest
greetings.

Our best love to you – Shirley.

Hunters Hill | March 5th, 1973

Dearest Shirley and Francis,

Just to say – it will be over (in one sense) by the time you receive
this – but, just to say you are both being THOUGHT OF on book day.

On Friday evening at Kit's, Margaret and I were thrilled to see the cable about the NY Times review. It's one of those tide-turning books, I think, because it will give other people the energy and courage to search around for their best selves... Kylie is reading it now, so I haven't had a chance yet for a second reading. That a book so concerned in so detailed a manner with the workings of anything, any organization, should also be a work of philosophy, and poetic, everything taken into account, everything in focus, yet not confined but made free, quite dazzles me with pleasure. It's the truth that has that effect of course... In London years ago I saw some of the McCarthy trials on BBC television. Quite unforgettable. Quite unbelievable, even while you were watching them, too. I remember the maniacal questioning of a tall gentle man from some university about a society he'd belonged to in his youth. The questioners sometimes ignored him, giggled and smirked at each other, whispered and giggled together constantly. You know it all so well; I wasn't <u>telling</u> you, only remembering.

Thank you for the lovely surprising packet from London, and for your letter. – Oh, and the Tarot cards and booklet. You might well wonder why your rational-seeming friend feels the need to go in for fortune-telling. I have what amount to visitations from one and sometimes two boys who have addled their poor brains with drugs. After I came back from London I spent, on and off, odd hours and days over a period of months, trying to persuade one in particular to see some professional person. After dreadful dramas and traumas help was found, and no sooner found than the same kind of dramas and traumas were traversed, like going through a mincing-machine twice, in order to abandon that help. (I've told your mother nothing about this because it's too sad and too full of grief for too many people.) Anyway, such boys wonder what Fate intends, and see signs everywhere. So if real help is rejected and if, as seems likely, I continue to receive visits, they have to be met (as far as possible) at the level they exist on. So at their place I play these games, or to the alarm of my ears listen to records or tapes. Now at my place there will be Tarot cards – as well as Nescafe and sandwiches – to divert them and, more important from my point of view, help to protect me. – Of course, if I become very very expert I could always SET UP and receive paying customers. That would be something!

[...]

Cynthia and Sidney arrive next Friday evening. No-one knows much about their plans. S usually flits about quite a lot – his family is in Melb. They slip in and out very quietly as a rule (unless there's an exhibition or something). Perhaps I should practise making spinach soufflés, and other light and approved dishes. Fun to see them again. It's rather bad timing that I'm perhaps disappearing to Japan nine or ten days after they arrive, disappearing into debt (!) and onto a ship. Long Bay would be preferable because at least stationary. And Patrick had made arrangements to go off for a holiday about this time, too, which is a pity. (P said there was an interesting piece about your book in The Observer; he'll pass it on to me.)

The typing of ancient stuff continues and doesn't feel purposeless though not immediately useful either. It's just right to be sitting down typing and considering most of the day. Happy days.

[...] Greetings, thoughts, love to you both –

Elizabeth

New York | 13 March 73

Elizabeth, my dear –

[...]

Are you really sailing? – my first journey from Aust was a five-weeks Syd to Japan trip on a ship taking wives to the Occupation forces in 1947... excitement, enchantment, indescribable. Would one (ever) feel like that in our day, at our age? – Should be more excitement, as one would now perceive more. So I say, yes: do it, you'll be glad. Yet who am I to say who will be glad of anything? – So I then tell myself: Shut Up, Shirl. If you are going, then an address please. And terrific wavings from this far-off pier. Surely it will be nice, and strange.

Please, also, our hearty greetings to the Nolans. It must be fun to be with them again, and to see them, chez vous. If they think of going home via NY, then we will start boiling the billy at once.

[...]

My mum wrote so sweetly about yr evening together – you and Margaret are so good; I wish I'd been there. [...] Bless you, dear Elizabeth; and bon voyage if you are voyaging – Shirley.

Hunters Hill | March 18th, 1973

My dear Shirley,

[...] I was so pleased that you were pleased with my feeling about your book. I wrote about it so swiftly without even looking for typing errors because I felt strongly about it and didn't have to hunt about for my reactions. [...]

Guess what? Cynthia and Sidney came here on March 13th. Patrick and their other close friend, Bill Cantwell, kept ringing and we were all going on about their arrival. Then I heard Cynthia was ill, which she was and still is. But she won't see me! We've had many long talks on the phone, but she is so opposed to my going on this cruise that she can't bear to see me. It would upset her too much. I can't believe she meant it. Then I remembered she felt and talked this way about Jinx, her daughter, when she felt Jinx was wrecking her own life; and later Margaret said C had said this to her, that she felt about this as she did about Jinx. So today we spoke again, and she's lying about in her motel, and Bill is visiting her often, and she's had dinner with Patrick, and I said what about relenting for half an hour and we'd talk of non-controversial things, but she said it would upset her too much and there we are. I'm sad about it, but she _is_ fragile, and I've seen her ill, and down physically and psychically – all ways. She thinks I am used, apparently, and credits me with a rather frailer and simpler character than I possess. If I want to be compassionate, C says, I should be a nurse or a doctor. In other words, our conversations have been irrational. Of course, we haven't parted bad friends, but it is a pity. The others are not unnaturally surprised that she feels so extremely and passionately about it. They think I've unwisely let myself in for this cruise (!) and that it's my own fault, and I'd better make the best of it and wring some advantage from this self-inflicted adversity. Separately, I'll send a list of ports, and if you could just send one buoyant postcard it would be a charitable and friendly act – helping to keep me and the ship afloat.

[...]

Yes, I did give Cynthia and Sidney your greetings and talked about your book, too. They are going on to Japan, perhaps to China, though C isn't really well enough. [...]

Best love to you both.

E

PS I was sad to read in the Observer the other day that Elizabeth Bowen had died.

Hunters Hill | March 20th, 1973

My dear Shirley and Francis,

Your letter was here – and no doubt with Andrew – this morning. I've just tottered back from town and was delighted as always to see signs of New York in with the snails and dead leaves.

Tomorrow I'm really, really going on that ship. As I told you in my last letter, Cynthia is so incensed about it that she has refused to see me. It's quite staggering to me. We've spoken a number of times, and I've said, 'You can't be serious,' and things like this, but no, it would upset her the way Jinx upsets her. Then their friend Bill Cantwell, who has been up at the Town House every day, said to C, 'I just don't know how you can do this to Elizabeth,' and C replied, 'That's what Siddy says. But I can.' Then, I was in town yesterday, in Elizabeth Street, going towards Market, outside DJs' and I saw Sidney getting in or out of a cab just ten yards away. So I of course went up and said hullo and so on. Cynthia was sitting in the front seat next to the driver; she (after thought) wound the window down and we looked at each other (as well we might in all the circumstances!) rather ruefully. Sidney was embarrassed and kept saying that as soon as C was better they would ring me and meet. This was – felt – so strange and sad and silly when we all looked so familiar to each other. And it appears that Patrick has had something of an earful about me and this voyage... [...] Nothing C does really surprises me, though I couldn't believe at first that she intended to keep up this embargo as a kind of punishment. – There are other fairly interesting (I think) ramifications to all this, but I'll spare you.

[...]

Do send a postcard and some thoughts to me in the midst of all that water. You'll be certain to receive some impressions from somewhere –

Thoughts and best love to you both
Elizabeth

PS. Don't feel that all is over between Eliz. and the Nolans; all is just a bit dramatic.

New York | 31 March 73

My dear Elizabeth –

I was about to send a great many of my defective thoughts, and much
of my affection, to you at one of those ports – when my mother's letter has
come telling me that you abandoned ship. My first and continuing response
is relief – only because you were always somewhat in two minds about
the venture and it had in the event caused you so much suffering; and also
due to a fondness of mine for just putting a stop to something when it has
become trouble and indecision and is not doing anything for anybody, least
of all oneself. But I know it will all have been a distressing series of events
for you, and I hope that the recompense of coming into your own flat and
feeling released from equivocations was a comfort. [...]

This tirade may arrive when all is harmonious – which, of course,
I hope for (though I also hope it is not simply because you gave up the
trip...). As when one is close to people, one can only hope to sustain
understanding through it all. But I cannot help saying how it moved me
for you – the account of that taxi meeting was like a surrealist film, or
like a monologue (that we found unforgettable) in Albee's play 'All Over'.
A lot of what Cynthia has dished out to you seems Lesson 1 for Freud,
and it hardly needed the news that Cynthia was recalling her relations
with her daughter.

Well, dear Elizabeth, please forgive so much talking out of turn.
But we have both been boiling like the radiator of our 1930s Austin when
it reached the uppermost slope of Bulli Pass. And we wonder whether you
yourself are getting over the drama and feeling a bit detached from these
horrid events? [...]

Bless you, dear Elizabeth, and our many (and, to some extent,
indignant) thoughts to you and our best love – Shirley.

Hunters Hill | April 10th, 1973

My dear Shirley,

You are kind. I appreciated your letter more than I can say. It arrived
on Friday (this is Tuesday) almost two weeks after my flight from the ship,
when I was still suffering from self-inflicted shock. I felt understood. [...]
Truly, there have been pressures on my soul. They started the day I

returned from London – tragic, heart-rending. It's been like being in a war, receiving startling dispatches at all hours, and often contradictory ones. You do what practical things seem possible and that's all right. But if people you care about suffer, you suffer with them and for them – probably excessively, sometimes possibly more than they suffer for themselves – and this is what's so wearing and tattering.

The prospect of the cruise was almost forgotten, not taken seriously, with so many events bombarding us, till the last moment. In between bombardments, I liked my flat, saw friends, and was beginning to feel furnished and settled. I didn't at all want to go, disliking the sea and ships as I do, and dreading that stultifying feeling of drifting in a circle to no purpose. However, my company was wanted and I felt bound by loyalty to go, and even hoped that I and everybody else would have a happy time. I don't know… On the ship, which was a nice one, I looked about and took in the indications. It seemed to me that no-one would collapse if I removed myself. They were tired and needed a rest… I often order my self about and it usually responds to some inevitable situation and behaves well. This time it seemed very sullen as though dragged along in chains, like a prisoner. All this would have been unnecessary if I'd had the brains simply to say 'No' in the beginning, and everyone would have accepted it. I think I hoped someone would rescue me, see how desperate I was, and say firmly, 'She cannot go, and it isn't her fault.' However, this desire to be faultless and blameless turned out to be my undoing. Friends <u>told</u> me not to go, but that didn't constitute a rescue. The ship lingered in dreary Brisbane for two and a half days. On the very last morning I thought (with terrible self-pity), 'No-one rescued me.' Then I was (really) gripped by the original idea: 'Then I'd better rescue myself.'

I had got into a double-bind where my idea of myself was bound to be damaged anyway, whatever happened. Although I felt horrible, rushing away, I'd have permanently despised myself if I'd stayed. (And there were other reasons apart from boredom and sea: I couldn't take any more stress.) But you see the confusion! Of course, when you are usually reliable and not excitable, it's all the more staggering to other people when you do something so apparently out of character.

Needless to say, I didn't rush back to see Cynthia. She was far from my mind. Above all, I wanted not to have people talking at me, so I went to Katoomba for a few days – hideous place, ravishing skies. Currawongs warbled, and I walked a lot. It was very strange up there – I mean the people I encountered were strange. There is much in this that I could and should write about. I feel something like your 'Harold' who said, I think: 'They keep coming all the time.' He meant his poems, with me it's experience – or so it seems... I could have stayed in the mountains for ages, but it wasn't practicable or sensible. Only three people knew I was back and I'd only seen Margaret once. Deliberately, I didn't ring anyone who knew Cynthia till I was sure they had flown off.

[...]

Heartfelt thanks for your understanding words, and my best love to you both –

Elizabeth

New York | 22 April 73

My dear Elizabeth –

It is wonderful to have a friend to whom each of my letters begins with prayers of thanks – what I hope is that it is not an imposition and a burden on the blessed friend. Your phone call was such a help and comfort in every way – and most of all for the thought that prompted it and for hearing your voice. And of course I would have been wondering what on earth would happen to my mother over the long Easter weekend. How kind you are, to sacrifice privacy and silence and work in such a way – one can but say, it changes not just the days when the comfort is being given but life as well, because of the sense that there is compassion and concern. After we'd spoken, it occurred to me that you would be taking on Pussy as well – oh lord, poor Elizabeth! [...]

My poor father – as he must be described, after the dreadful end of his life – died after months in hospital and such terrible operations (the last one, to relieve agony, left him completely paralysed). I hope my mother can somehow, after this, bring herself to feel that life itself is precious and that no further time should be wasted (as so much has been) on going over grievances. [...]

The BBC called me on Thursday morning to do a telephone interview and to talk to me about coming over – which we are doing, as Alan immediately called too, to tell me that my book is off to a fine start and had front page of the TLS (shared with an immense, and dishonest, book on Hammarskjöld by a UN official whom I know) with lots of compliments. [...]

So, Elizabeth Harrower, you rescued yourself. I would gladly have said 'Don't go' – and in fact, one of the unresolved questions of life is when can one do this without falling into the very ways we are deploring. I had a dream of being you and wanting to leave the ship and not being able to pack my bags... Oh, I know that self one has, that is sometimes dragged along in chains – it looks like Caliban. What you fled from – rather, what must have been the aura of your feelings in the place – sounds like (if one can still invoke Forster) telegrams and anger. If one says one hates disorder, that sounds prim – however, there is a disorder of the soul, combined with actualities, that is like having physical wounds: you know you will have to get cured, healed, convalesce, etc. Oh I do hope that the process is going on. I know how you felt, not wanting people buzzing at you. [...]

Dear Elizabeth, grateful embraces and apologies and great solidarity, and much love from Francis and Shirley

Hunters Hill | May 6th, 1973

My dear Shirley and Francis,

[...]

Now you're either in beautiful London or beautiful Capri, where I was once for about a fortnight in 1951. I thought it was heaven, and seem to remember having some Great Thoughts in Anacapri. There was only one hotel up there in those days, and it was out of season in September, so the place itself was wonderfully available...

[...]

A certain welcome calm seems to be about at the moment. The typewriter now lives on the kitchen table. No point in sending such an epistle to blue Capri; it can go to New York. Have happy times. Grateful thanks and much love to you both –

Elizabeth

Hunters Hill | May 16th, 1973

My dear Shirley and Francis,

A ravishing, beautiful day. [...] Yesterday the Herald asked Kylie if she would review 'Defeat' and they would hold it till publication day. Macmillan hadn't sent her a copy yet (or the Herald), but she borrowed mine, and having heard about the US and UK notices, wondered if I had any. Naturally, she has her own highly individual thoughts about everything, but it's always interesting to see what other people have said. So this was a good reason for me to (virtually) cartwheel my way into town for coffee with Kit, to catch up with her news and collect some notices for Kylie.

Kit had had her hair cut and permanently waved recently, and it was highly successful. She had on a very becoming hat with the brim turned back – red velour – and looked extremely well. [...] Today, Pussy was very popular. Valerie's past misdeeds were thought of only for seconds. Folkstone – I was told – is a very pretty place. Francis had looked at a flat in London costing scarcely more than the one at The Chimes. [...]

Of course, Mr. Whitlam alarms me by threatening to call for a double dissolution of parliament: the other parties have control of the senate and can and do block Labor's legislation. A controversial industrial relations bill is about to be axed in the senate. I feel like sending him urgent telegrams: 'Don't do it!' He thinks the sense and wisdom of his actions will be clear to all and that he (Labor) would for this reason win both houses. When did wisdom ever have such a very great appeal? A private member last week introduced an abortion law reform bill to the House of Representatives. There was a free vote. The campaign launched by the Right to Life association was like nothing that ever was on land or sea. The bill was thrown out by 98 to 23, and the scenes outside the house sounded (on radio) like something from the nuttier shores of Ireland. – It is so nice after a lifetime to be represented by Us instead of by Them.

A pity to take any more attention from Capri and hols. Many thoughts and best love to you both – Elizabeth

Villa Oreste, 53 Capri (Napoli) | 1 June 73

My dear Elizabeth –

After unrecountable horrors of the Ital. mails, we hit the jackpot with a concentration of your letters, and had a delicious and literary time reading them in, yes, Blue Capri. I sit typing this looking into our horizon of blue Rothko, against which psychedelic notes are struck by pots of lobelia and geranium. We are in paradise here; it is so natural to be in paradise that we are having second thoughts about the doctrine of original sin... No cars (in this part of the island) in itself would be such a holiday; added to that such beauty and calm and incredible weather. We get up early, have breakfast in the sun, inspect sea, mountains etc. with critical eye, work, sit in café and read papers, take long walk, read, eat, go to bed. It is as if there never was anything other. The tourists are beginning to come in droves (literally, for they are mostly in accompanied groups that stay for a day or two), but one need not be near them as they all stay in exactly the same three or four places. This week there were two holidays, Thursday and Saturday, so an ingenious workforce added two days of national strike to close the country down for the week; who knows whether it will ever reopen...

Speaking of which, we tank up on Watergate via the foreign press. The most frightful part is that there is scarcely a surprise in it for those of us who assumed all along that this was the pattern of White House activity: obviously, much more will come out as they turn on one another, good and proper, and when the trials open, and it may well be that Nixon will fall. Historic devel., if so. It would be traumatic, yet it seems to me much better than going on with the lies and hypocrisy we had before: all parliamentary systems have had such crises and have had to surmount them – in the case of England, with constitutional reforms such as now obviously urgently required in the USA. (Provision for vote of No Confidence, etc). The Presidency had become a virtual dictatorship, through which an undeclared war, disapproved by Congress, could be prosecuted for years. Well, it is all fascinating. The most depressing aspect, perhaps, is the lack of fundamental public concern and understanding – there seems to be no comprehension of the significance of Nixon's claim that he was up to all these tricks on behalf of 'national security'; in other words, the pretext of all totalitarians. (Of course, many people in the press and in govt have been outraged by Nixon saying this, but the nation itself is generally uncomprehending and indifferent.) How nice, on the other hand, that you can write of being governed by 'us' rather than by 'them': I cannot ever recall living under a system of which I felt this. (Though of course with degrees of disaffection). Whitlam is much reported in the British press – wondering whether Nixon will see him as he has dared to criticise, etc. So we are all to keep quiet as if we were behind the Iron Curtain???

[...]

In our first few days here we had nice times with GG, with whom we've had nice times at other Capri convergences. He has a charming house, (in a sort of little white casbah, all of its own) in Anacapri; has had it for twenty years, comes here v. little – couple of weeks in spring, couple of weeks in autumn, sometimes a week at New Year. He is extremely nice and real and like his books. Just finished yet another novel, 'The Honorary Consul', which appears in September. Elizabeth, how does a novelist do this? – a novel every year, almost, for decades.

[...]

May this arrive without too much difficulty in the post. My love to you, dear Elizabeth, and more thanks than one can say for all the pleasure, stimulus, laughter, and comfort your letters give. An embrace from Shirley.

Hunters Hill | June 17th, 1973

My dear Shirley and Francis,

[...]

God, Watergate, Nixon. On it goes. It seems impossible that he'll fall, whatever is revealed. After all, how much must be revealed before a rational majority appears? Is the alternative Agnew? And if so, how is that bearable? Yes, indeed, when you hear those famous words 'national security' emerging from innocent transistors, you wonder where to move on to from stupefaction. We hear Watergate every day, of course.

[...]

The Anguses were here, and Kit saw them a number of times and enjoyed their company. But money seems to be what stands between her and Hobart, Craigieburn week-ends, mountains week-ends, trips to Singapore like Valerie's, a bigger flat, and even catching buses instead of walking. The exchange-rate isn't good. – Yes, the paper is being delivered still, or was quite recently, because I saw a Herald with 58 pencilled on it when I was there. The cupboards have quite good stocks of food in them, but I don't know if it's kept for visitors. Sometimes she looks frail, and sometimes very well, and this is not unnatural, I suppose. The other day she was annoyed that she never went to parties at night! That quite floored me, and I felt rather helpless to combat it, but I know from experience that these moods pass. – We met another day last week in town and that was very lively and diverting. I never think of Kit as being any particular age. She understands so much. We stare unblinking at each other across the little table exchanging great thoughts. She is never dull company.

[...]

Meantime, great thanks for all the pleasure your letters bring, and my love to you both –

Elizabeth

New York | 6 July 73

My dear Elizabeth – your letter of the second just came, with pension application enclosed, and – bless you another thousand times – there seems quite a chance that this venture may be made to prosper, as ventures do in which you've had a hand. [...] My mother sent a sweet cable for H of Commons day – I in turn regaled her with every last detail (I quailed to think these boastful renderings will reach yr ears – but my Mum likes to hear them, so I tell All). It did go, I think, very well. I was quite prepared for an audience of three cats in a basement room – but no, an excellent and attentive audience in a solemn chamber with long windows on the Thames (the room itself was in the House of Lords, and there were members of Commons and Lords present, as well as all the rest). I may publish the talk here in a magazine; in any case, Parliamentary group will send the official report to me, and I'll send it on to ye Chimes.

Bless Kylie Tennant – I vastly enjoyed seeing the very compass-points that should be indicated brought out in her cockle-warming review. [...] I saw a couple of horror reviews from Australia sent on to me by Macmillans there – I suppose you saw them, nice Elizabeth, but suppressed them: good for you! Sounded very much an inside job. Am used to that, but on the whole reviews have been serious and favourable, they only really interest me – and this is not bravado – when they understand the book and one feels a bond and a mutual wave-length with the reviewer, as in Kylie T's review. Do you think my social duty is now done, Elizabeth? – all I want is to go on with my novel, though I suppose this world govt thing will nag at me until someone else takes it over as a life's work. I get masses of mail from (good and intelligent) people who care about all this, and one must respond. But wot of art? It matters most.

[...] More soon – Our best love meantime – your Shirley.

New York | 15 July 73

My dear Elizabeth –

I'm always promising (you and myself), no more impositions. But am writing on rebound from a real old-timer of a letter from my mother, reminiscent of the awful pre-yellow-pills era – you don't think she has stopped taking them again? She may have climbed out of her depths of woe and her mood of alone-against-the-gods by now; I certainly pray so, for her sake and the sake of her friends. She has written totally irrationally about money again – really as though she had nothing. In fact and truth, both the capital and her income are gaining well and she will have the best financial year of her life, even allowing for devaluation, cost of living, etc. However, by some wild deduction, my mother imagines herself getting more out of her money in England, and the 'rooming house in Devon' is back on the nightmare map. Elizabeth, I know, I know: nothing so insanely self-destructive, and destructive of us, will eventuate. But the horrid fantasy of it depresses me beyond belief. Also the cruelty of parroting that business of 'not being ill or dying near anyone': she knows this is monstrous, to imply that her dying alone would be a relief to me.

[...]

England is no longer financially possible for us, let alone for her; quite aside from total unfamiliarity in a country she deeply hated when living there. I don't suppose the adverse position of the dollar will continue, but as long as it does our travels have to be financed from pre-paid undertakings – travel articles on Italian or French subjects, things we never previously would want to do. It's not only the exchange of course but the world-wide rise of costs.

It is enough imposition that you should have had to hear the foregoing, but I have another thing to ask. Which I <u>beg</u>, you will sign off from if it looms as a bore and a trouble beyond even what I imagine. Elizabeth, you have done so much and one blushes to ask further. Could you possibly hand in the application and ask whether questions might be relayed or answered by you? I would send the application to you; it would need my mother's answer on a few dates, but I can fill it out for her otherwise; and she should sign it.

[...]

As ever, I'm struck by the weirdness of even asking you such things when I have a sister in Sydney. Even if V did not give my mother any affection or companionship, she could perhaps have done a few practical things for her. But never.

[...]

There were funny things to tell you; but all I can remember now is that Nixon is in hospital with a cold... We get bulletins... One wonders, why don't they put him out of our misery???? The hearings are a drug – we don't have a telly, but I turn on the radio and despite myself can hardly get it turned off: Mitchell on the stand was as Francis said, like a hardened criminal – lie, lie, lie, and sticking to the lie even when six witnesses testified to the contrary. However, he confessed to obstruction of justice (former head of the Justice Dept...), so the first count is already in. I suppose the reason that not one of these people arouses the pity usually felt for someone who has been caught is the terrible harm they did; but there's even more than that, they scarcely seem human in any sense recognisable to people like us. They really don't care about respecting themselves: self respect is just a banality to them and a weakness.

Great heat – followed last night by explosive storm and cool day. Plagued by brown-outs, power-cuts, petrol rationing, etc. etc., New Yorkers stagger about to work and shops and muggings and generally demonstrate the excessive adaptability of the human animal. We read some new novels (wish they were yours or mine...) – did I tell you we liked Graham Greene's new 'Honorary Consul' v. much? An amusing Kingsley Amis, 'The Riverside Villas Murder'. What relief after those UN docs. An outing to the Bolshoi Ballet – v. exciting variety, from treacley romanticism to exquisite austerity to almost athletic feats, with one act that was almost circus-like in physical dexterity.

[...]

I close with love – Shirley.

Hunters Hill | July 22nd, 1973

My dear Shirley and Francis,

[...]

I had a call from Daphne last Monday morning to say that Kit was 'very low'.– I rang Kit, rang Andrew, and went over to The Chimes at two. He arrived (with yellow pills) at three, and we stayed (in spite of being invited to go!) till about seven-thirty. By which time we'd all had three cups of tea, three brandies and three cups of coffee and snacks, and by which time the scene had improved considerably.

When I first got there I thought Kit must have taken ten tranquillisers all at once, she was so sunk and inert. After great talkings and silences and arguing (and she doesn't always feel friendly towards Eliz. and Andrew, so it might be best if you never said a kind word about us: by alleviating her position even slightly we remove some of her ammunition to be directed at you...) we learned the reason for this bad slump. She had run out of and deliberately stopped taking the yellow pills. Then, at Valerie's two or three weeks ago, she saw the children and V. regarded her as a mad old woman to be laughed at and despised. (This was the very worst thing, and I don't doubt it's true.) Then, her cheque for $1000 turned into $700 Australian dollars.

[...]

She was bullied and cajoled into taking the pills again. They need about two weeks to have their full effect, but meantime they give her proper sleep at night. If she hadn't agreed to take them again, Andrew said he would put her into hospital that night. She knew he meant it, and was finally persuaded...

[...]

Before we met at the flat, while we were arranging to meet there, Andrew said she'd told him she knew more people in England, and spoke of some woman on the south coast. I said the only woman I'd heard of there, in the Folkstone area, was one who'd committed suicide years ago. He revised his ideas, and when England was mentioned he said she wasn't fit to travel and he'd sign papers to say so. (He has the gift of saying disagreeable things without being disagreeable.) When we suggested local holidays, she said she couldn't afford them. (No wonder the doctor has given me a bottle of tranquillisers this week. I despise myself rather for needing them. But My Weird Mob, dear friends that they are, always have sad, bad times at the same time.) Oh yes, I think it was when she said to Andrew that she had been unlucky and never found anyone, any friend, to listen to her troubles – it must have been about then that we all had a third brandy to console ourselves.

[...]

If you can give your mother something to look forward to, some idea that she'll see you again, this will be what will settle her and calm her, I think. She did apparently say to Andrew that nothing on earth would make her go to New York again for Christmas. He said had you asked her, and she said no, but she wouldn't go anyway. – Today she was going to Valerie's (!) for lunch, with Mavis Lonsdale. Not being a mother, I can't help feeling I'd get very jaded about anyone who treated me as V. does your mother, and cast her off. – Margaret feels indignant about all this on your account, or just 'feels' might be more accurate. – I remember one of your characters saying that she could only hope to see <u>less</u> clearly, and I thought at the time: how true! So, I suppose we all see the sadness of Kit's situation, and care about her, and feel she's a demon, all at the same time. Well, I'll leave this subject. Forgive the jumble. As Margaret and I used to say, nervously, handing over manuscripts: 'It's a first draft. It's a first draft.'

Yes, yes, I do think you have done your social duty. Do, please, go back to your novel. Leave the letters from good and intelligent people concerned about the world cruelly unanswered. Art does matter more. Patrick was here the other night, and he was thinking of you and your book and duty v. art. (He has got involved in local issues in recent years, and knows the time it takes to go to meetings and make speeches and so on.) It was marvellous that you did this book, and you did it marvellously well, but no-one who cares about fiction can say other than – please, write your novel. – I did see some anti-book reviews, but people who think 'idealist' is a dirty word don't stir me much, and I certainly didn't feel they would disturb you. I wasn't protecting you: I knew they wouldn't affect you. But I've been leaving it to your mother to send reviews. [...]

Thank you for letting me know that Cynthia had even the faintest doubts about my wanting to talk to her again. I am fond of her, but I'll eternally wish she had spared me that extra stress earlier this year. All that tumult really wrecked my health. One way or another I feel that this will sort itself out. If there is ever time when we're in the same place, I'll tell you some of the ramifications. It was strange.

[...]

So, that's about all for tonight. We were worrying about Kit last Monday, but now she's stable, or more stable, and making pastry, and taking pills, and wrested out of that gloom I do hope. I'll see her this week. Just try to think of something she can look forward to and all will be calmer, I believe. (These aren't instructions! Sorry if they sound like that. I'm, by this time, sort of mumbling to myself, and listing advice that's meant for myself as much as anyone.)

Andrew's a sonsie boy with a kind heart... It's on his conscience that he hasn't written to thank you for your book.

Something much cheerier next time, dear friends. You're both wonderfully kind and good to Kit. (Margaret says to her: 'You should see the scraps I write to my mother – in Scotland – at irregular weekly intervals.') My love to you both –

Elizabeth

Hunters Hill | July 25th, 1973

My dear Shirley and Francis–

God! We should have a Telex installed. No sooner had I wandered up to post my airletter and come back, than the phone rang. Kit. She had had your letter – 'pages and pages and two pages from Francis. They're dear people...' She sounds miles better. She thanked me about the pension thing and didn't seem to mind (which I was afraid she might be) that I'd been making enquiries. Her whole tone was different. I was so relieved. ... She said it's hard when your mind feels young and your body is old, but she was pleased to be herself tonight and that was so good to hear. ... I've told her to buy some eggs tomorrow and to eat one a day. She's promised.

Before I forget. Nadine Gordimer is coming here next year in about March for the Adelaide Festival. My South African friend, John Brink, rang to see if I could rally the forces to bring her from Adelaide to Sydney. I'm not active in any organizations but know who is, and of course we'd want her to come over. Do you know her? I admire her work. And John said she's a good speaker too. He no doubt hopes that she will spread the word about conditions in S. Africa.

Saw 'Last Tango' yesterday. I suspect – I know – if it hadn't been Marlon Brando I'd probably have thought it trivial. Well, I don't know... What I usually feel when I see him is what a tragedy it is that marvellous actors, actresses, are so often in parts that are unworthy of them. And they get older, and then it's over. There were good Aussie ladies eating Minties behind us, tutting and talking all the way through. At one point Brando was lying alone on the floor, fully clothed, and he simply leapt to his feet. Those ladies said: 'Isn't he agile?' There seemed to be something sad and real and some quite bad, halting fiction mixed up together.

Also went to a meeting of the Australia Party which confirmed me in my allegiance to Labor. I'm not sure I have a moral leg to stand on if I don't join. But I hate joining.

[...]

Tonight Hunter's Hill is turning out to see a local group perform a play of Kylie's, never before performed, though published and prize-winning, produced by a friend who has never before produced a play. Kylie said there was no need for me to go and wince, too, but on the other hand there was pressure on all (from said producer) to put in an appearance.

I look forward to the new Graham Greene. Patrick has a new novel out in, I think, September or October – The Eye of the Storm. Margaret has at last started writing again, but there's no doubt it's hard to fit it in at week-ends. She says at night she's too tired to write, because she works quite hard in her office. However, she seems to be in quite good spirits. The main point is that she is rooted again, as one is when working... She tells me I must either start a book or go out and get a job. How awful! This is what I know, myself. Patrick has said to someone who couldn't resist telling me: 'She is living a novel instead of writing one.' He, too, wants me to 'do something' by which he means only to write.

The days have been beauteous – brilliant mornings, skies, rainbows... There are 400 buildings going up and coming down in the square that goes from the Quay to Central Railway, and up to the Cross and down to the docks. Cranes everywhere. There is a new feeling of aliveness about; I wish it had been like this years and years ago, but I'm glad it's happened at all. [...]

Best love,
Elizabeth.

New York | 1 Aug 1973

My dear Elizabeth – your marvellous Telex letter just came now, as I was sitting down to this. I read it aloud, and we both heaved up a great sigh of relief from fathom five, and – as ever with your Teleces (?) – with gratitude, laughter, and self-congratulation on having such a friend. What guilt when we got to the part where the 'kind friend' relayed the comment that you were living in a novel instead of writing one, at least some macabre passages of that novel you are living must be designated 'KIT'. I have myself always felt the mighty unfairness of not getting – directly at any rate – stimulus or, if one can use the ghastly word, material out of the torments of it all which has just seemed to wring me, exhaust me, use me up, and leave me quietly moaning inside as if I were lying in the road after an accident... (This seems to have got on to me rather quickly, so I hope the tendencies are not hereditary.)

[...]

Yes, I do admire N. Gordimer's books and her life very much, her last book, a long & v. serious approach through art to public affairs, quite unlike any other. She has stories in The New Yorker, and I think comes here once in a while; but I've never met her. Would like to. What can it be like to be a good writer and live in S. Africa? [...]

All this question of pub. affairs and/or one's 'own' work, which much exercises me, does not I suppose arise for a novelist whose public concern, so to speak, is inextricable from what she most deeply wants to write. Graham Greene says he is this way, yet I think the truest and best of his work is detached from social conscience, at least from any obvious message-ness. As a writer of fiction, I do enjoy writing about bureaucracy because it is life (in a manner of speaking!) and I've observed it and experienced it. But if I had a message to give it would have to be done in the way of my last book, as reporting and with docs, because 'message' is not sufficiently interwoven with my own message.

[...]

I saw an exceptionally well-expressed statement in the TLS for Patrick W's new book. We are both agoggers for this, it is the best kind of looking forward, when there is a new book by a writer who gives great new pleasures always, and is increasingly exciting to read as one increasingly enters the wavelength and the whole unfolds itself. As for you, EH, one feels you will root yourself in your work in spite of all our exhortations to you to do this. If one is a writer, one will write if one can; one sometimes has to wait. Graham Greene endeared himself more than ever to me in Capri in May by talking about a gifted novelist he had published years ago who then gave up after early books. He said, 'Fiction is time as well as the rest of what it is: novelists sometimes can't believe this or they know it but give up.' He meant of course novelists of quality. It was all balm (barm?) to me, as time slipping away without pages mounting sometimes sends me up wall. Everyone is different; but a job is the last thing for me – I did begin to write while I had a job, but could not have gone on that way: job used me up. Others tell me it stimulates them – I admire Margaret immensely for doing homework in the evening: I used to do this, it was so hard to come home and begin when one was wanting to stop. Also she does work all day that uses up her word box, and that is another thing that has to be recharged. How good that she is writing, for herself I mean and eventually for us.

[...]

Whitlam was here yesterday and today. There has been a lot of interest, and of course all our Mob are highly disposed in his favour. He is the leader acting like a person one might allow in one's living room. In the press, much criticism of Nixon for almost snubbing him; so patently because of Whitlam's not acting like a sycophant. Oh E, it is utterly engrossing, the unveiling of Nixon's paranoia, his feuhrer (sp?) complex.

Watergate. How everything comes round to language. The incapacity – which one could describe as physical – of these people to say anything authentic or direct. It is fascinating. Last night we were talking with some friends here about the study that might be done of Watergate from the linguistic standpoint. One can scarcely believe the lingo that comes out of these mouths; and the mouths themselves are no minor item I can tell you. Has the following reached Australia: 'at this point in time' invariably instead of 'at this time'; similarly, 'in this timeframe'; 'there was a level of concern', rather than 'We were worried'; 'on a basis of consistency' instead of 'consistently' (not to speak of the howlers of different sort: 'hurling epitaphs at one another' etc). The evil that comes out, with dogged unresponsiveness to reason or humane considerations or common sense or absurdity, leaves me either howling or speechless. The exposure, day after day, is terribly important; it couldn't have been done in the courts, and the cumulative effect certainly has frightened even some of the goon element. The horrors revealed are already enough to send the pack to gaol indefinitely – but will the country ever grow up?? It is interesting that the old guard (southern racist senator such as Ervin, 76 years old) has been the element that ultimately came down on Nixon. If it had been a younger group, against the way, in favour of civil rights, etc., they would immediately have been tagged 'radical' or irresponsible in some way. But here are these (really rather dreadful) old senators coming on talking as if they were Thomas Jefferson & constituting a now unstoppable juggernaut. Oh it is riveting. The power these people have had, and the Nazism they expound (an over-used word, but it is the only one here), gives the whole such dimensions.

[...]

Mitchell, Ehrlichman, Haldeman, are men from Mars: there is no conceivable human response in them on our terms. I do feel that it will lead to Nixon's removal in some way – it is scarcely possible to go on with Nixon for three years after this. [...] What I wonder is whether there is going to be any real correction, or whether this is the last throe of real democracy in this country? [...]

I know what you mean about political parties – I could never join one. I hate joining – even good groups have group leaders and group followers and one is constrained to swallow what one doesn't like because of 'good cause' or common cause, or cause of some kind. I feel I might become a U.S. citizen if Nixon is impeached. Even sometimes now I think one should show solidarity with a country that is actually doing this and trying to get back from the abyss. But the act of it, the making of the gesture, falls on the non-joining blank in my nature. We'll see. I can have both nationalities, so there is nothing to renounce. Besides, I don't know if they'd have me once they looked at my dossier…

Do tell us what Kylie's play was like when produced at Hunter's Hill. I have always envied playwrights – dialogue is what I like to write, I sort of wait for it to come along on the page. Then, one thinks – what thrills to stand at the side watching people play out one's ideas and hearing audiences laugh at one's words (where meant to laugh, I would hope…); on the other hand, how much one is at the mercy of all the intermediaries, producers, actors, facilities, etc. I'll be interested in how Kylie's intentions were treated. (I call her Kylie, please excuse…). We haven't seen Last Tango, though we've meant to go every morning, night and noon. […] We'll get to it when Watergate closes…

[…]

Your description of the new building at Sydney brings me to 'our trip to Australia'. We have talked and talked about this – it is involved with so many things. Utterly between us, I think we <u>may</u> come out about March of next year. We have to try to get some kind of assignment – magazine articles, lecture, something of the kind (I don't suppose the Adelaide Festival would want me at short notice…) – because the expense for two of us is quite a sinker, and work would otherwise be suspended on our mss. for weeks at least if not months.

[…]

Francis is nearly through with a first draft of Isadora – it is marvellous, and marvellously moving. Craig is a monster, a monster, but oh, they are all electric, Ellen Terry, Isadora, Craig; it was easier to be electric in those times, before mass-ness descended on us like the night. I don't mean that existence was pleasant or social conditions were other than hell: I mean that personality and temperament were in great and spontaneous variety, breaking out all over and even in barren places, and with no relation whatever to the 'celebrity' cults of today.

[…]

With the best love of – Shirley

Hunters Hill | August 13, 1973

My dear Shirley and Francis,

This is no attempt to answer the marvellous all (thank you many times over!) – only to give the latest news for the moment. Monday. I spoke to Kit last night and went over with my typewriter plus cautiously selected documents. After sounding moody and difficult on the phone, making me wonder more than ever what should be revealed and what concealed and how all should be approached, Kit made me quite ashamed of myself and my intended deviousness by being so helpful (though not interested), unquestioning, meek, gentle. I thought she might mind producing bankbooks and things and offered to show her my bankbook and cheque book to keep everything fair. Quite unnecessary – we filled in the gaps: divorce – Sydney January 1954; the ship – Jervis Bay; Bank of New South Wales [account details] and the balance was $1056; approximately $6.00 on hand; rent $30.00 a week; Catherine signed with a C. Then, feeling virtuous, we had some sherry, coffee and sandwiches, and discussed our characters. (Yes!)

[...]

When I went up to the P.O. to post the form, I had a parcel to collect for myself – an airmail copy of Patrick's new book from Jonathan Cape in London. He's just gone off with Manoly for 12 days to Queensland and the Barrier Reef.

[...] I have half-joined the Aust. Labor Party. It made me feel quite poorly, because it goes so against the grain to give yourself up. On the other hand, what moral legs did I have to stand on, so approving, a freed slave and all that, if I didn't join? So I filled in a form, and it goes before the credentials committee and at the next meeting they either take me or reject me. (I don't belong to a trade union so perhaps they'll reject me.) If you are accepted, and attend four meetings in a year, you are entitled to vote at pre-selection ballots and might – would – help choose the State and Federal candidates. Even so, it's enough to make a person think!

Would you like me to ask Geoffrey Dutton (who lives in Adelaide and knows everyone connected with everything) about the Adelaide Festival? Whether you might be invited? I know you could be invited any time you liked, but this time it's a question of how far their programme is made up. What do you think? ... – Dr. Fisher, seen after a fortnight on his little tablets, says I have an enlarged heart and high blood pressure (always low before). Now everyone is cross with me because they think I'm mortal and it's my fault! I feel just the same but had better avoid stress/ships/getting on and off. That was a bad time. It's that world of telegrams and anger that wears me out. Kit is nice to me and <u>doesn't</u> constitute stress. This is true.

Much love, dear S and F – Elizabeth

New York | 1 Sept 73

My dear Elizabeth – yesterday your letter of last week arrived – the 'good news report': indeed any letter from you is a good news report by definition, no matter what its contents – we read it, and Francis put it down; then he looked into space for some moments, then he said, 'this woman is incomparable'. That is the only suggestion I can offer of our feelings. Had it not been for your telephone call, we would not have had time to get the goods from the Soc. Sec people. Had it not been for your letters we would have been bonkers. Had it not been for... you name it. And all with such feeling and understanding, it is incredible. To business – the enclosed <u>live</u> cheque is just on account, towards the next tension-pension.

[...]

Whitlam question. Could you also – again no hurry – ponder whether a letter written by me, about a scandalous UN system of importing indentured Australian girls as typists, could ever be addressed in such a manner as to get to Whitlam's own attention? Of course, I would like to interest him in the larger matter of the UN; but this is a particular monstrosity that has gone on for years with the connivance of the US authorities and the Australian delegation to the UN here, to allow the UN Secretariat administration to get cheap labour from Australia and the Philippines. There have been occasional press pieces about it here & in Australia, but nothing real or influential. The Australian girls (whom I've never met) write me constantly in distress, and I have tried to interest Australian interviewers in the matter. Of course I have documents, etc. but, since the Delegation and External Affairs have turned a blind eye for years, & will not help the girls in the least, one would have to begin at the top to get attention and change. Scores of girls, or even hundreds perhaps, are involved, and – because of the canniness of the original snare – can get no redress as long as the authorities are all in collusion. Perhaps this is a pest – but if you <u>do</u> have an idea... Dear Elizabeth, so much more to say. It's good – no, <u>you're</u> good – to have written Cynthia; it must be best, otherwise ill-feeling spreads like stain. Our love too – Shirley.

Hunters Hill | 2nd September, 1973

Instructions: Drink something nice before, or while, reading.

My dear Shirley and Francis, – I hope, hope, that I didn't frighten you out of your wits or add to alarm and depression. Of course, I <u>must</u> have. Do forgive me. One should never ever take any single day's events (involving Kit, especially) as final, irrevocable. When will I learn? Just a few days earlier I'd sent the 'good-news' report and promised, like Herzog, 'not a single word' more; then I take to the telephone! (In London I discovered how easy it was to ring Sydney, and one thing leads to another...) It was nice to hear your voices – pensions/tensions: same thing, as S truly remarked.

[...]

As there is, unusually, carbon paper in the kitchen where I'm typing, because the day has been spent on passionate letters written all over the place in defence of the Minister for Social Security, I'm doing a copy of this letter for N.Y. as well as Capri. (Still no faith in the Italian postal service.) In passing, the Minister for Social Security, Hayden, is trying to introduce a national health scheme: the private health funds and the general practitioners are hounding him. I saw them baying at him on television the other night. What faces! What expressions!

[...]

Your so-nice letter. My famous enlarged heart. I'm sleeping and sleeping a lot, and have to see the doctor again this week. Dear Judah Waten in Melbourne (Communist-Jewish-novelist-friend) instantly consulted a medical Prof., and asked for explanations in simple words of E's complaint. Pictures must be taken of the heart, etc. This will happen or everyone will go on remorselessly. There are only two or three members of my Mob who are dangerous to me. As you say, simply telling one's pals that one should avoid stress only brings them on thicker than ever. Ah well. I do thank you for your 'heartfelt telex'. I have written to Geoffrey Dutton about the Adelaide Festival and told Patrick this today. [...] I told Patrick Francis likes/collects paintings; Patrick also likes/collects... September 6th is his publication day. Margaret finished The Eye of the Storm this morning. She says it's a marvellous book. Terrible, but marvellous. He says it's black. I'm wondering how Kylie has reviewed it. She and M., both admiring, obviously, would do it so differently... Well, before your letter came I wondered, too, what you would do. I had begun to think, disinterestedly, that it would be good and do good (to you, too, in roundabout ways) if you came.

[...]

Next morning.

[...] That was terrific to send tickets for the Opera House. Almost certainly it would be tactful and placating to take Valerie, but that was so nice of you to think of me. And your mother will be thrilled. She loves occasions so, and the Opera House is extraordinary. While it was going up, I spent years converting the drivers of Red Taxi Cabs to the idea that it was a Good Thing... M and I loved to think of Francis reading Dumas and even getting some fun out of it. And, as I said before, we come very high on the list of those delighted by the Cocteau/Paris launching. Beautiful September has arrived. So bright and clear. Freesias and boronias making their presence known... A whole year since I returned from London, and only notebooks typed up and diaries typed (a decade of them) but no real writing. I said to Patrick: 'I feel like Oscar Wilde when he left Reading Gaol. That I wrote before I knew about life. Now that I know...' He said, 'That sounds very mysterious.' It is mysterious even to me. Because I certainly thought I knew about life from a very early age. Someone seems to have broken some illusion (though 'illusion' can't be right) or my confidence... I'm not sure what the answer is, because I don't want to do anything else. Perhaps a permanent absence from some of My Mob. A little rose-covered village in England??? – Meantime, Oscar-Wilde-complex notwithstanding, I don't feel a bit dreary, or that I'm just 'sitting waiting for Fate'. Far from it. Just puzzled. Maybe it's only laziness and having lost the proper routine, which used to be so inflexible but satisfying.

[...]

Blessings, great good wishes, greetings from M as always, and best love – Elizabeth

Capri | 11 Sept 73

My dear Elizabeth –

You'll get bored with every letter beginning with our marvelling at your qualities, but this is your own fault for having them. [...]

Before departure, tried to get Patrick W's book – but not yet in NY. However, shall grab it at first opportunity. All reading here so far is Thomas Pynchon and Compton MacKenzie ('Vestal Fire' is really v. amusing, especially read here) and a million Neapolitan newspaper articles on the cholera epidemic. When we arrived, there was suddenly a possibility of our doing a New Yorker piece on cholera at Naples, and we started to bone up on this melancholy (but quite dramatic) event, cables flew etc. However, the epidemic seems to have subsided and the magazine has doubts about getting space in time, so – somewhat relieved – we are amateurs again, and only know what everyone knows... Capri is almost devoid of tourists, at a time when the centre is usually bedlam. I disgraced myself by saying (to a Caprese merchant friend) that I much prefer it this way, and now no doubt infamous throughout the island as having spoken favourably of cholera itself... The weather – hot, magnificent.

Thursday – meantime, box arrived with typewriter. The cholera subsides in Naples at the mo. Poor place, it is a cholera microbe's dream – whole regions without proper sanitation, whole buildings where 'running water' is a tap in the courtyard. The sewers open into the bay just a few yards out from the waterfront. For a few weeks we will have a farce of 'hygiene' at Naples, then relapse into total negligence once more. Capri of course is incredibly clean, the sea is transparent; there is a vaccination crew upstairs at the post office and everyone has been 'done' and talks about their reaction... [...]

Must gallop to post office – I pray this will not be masticated by the mails. Our intense feelings (it runs in the family!) to you, dear Elizabeth, our best greetings to Margaret, and love from Francis and Shirley

Hunters Hill | September 25th, 1973

My dear Shirley –

So much to say... The Italian P.O. is improving like anything. Your letter crossed the cholera-barrier and fought its way to Australia in only ten days. Now there's a strike at Redfern Mail Exchange, but that's another matter. Thank you for writing. I love your letters. They always make me laugh and feel enlivened. But, O, I felt sad and indignant, too... We'll think about that later.

[...]

Patrick's book came out on September 6th and has just reached the shops (container demarcation strike). It has a bad review in The Observer (Paul Bailey), but good ones in the New Statesman, The Guardian and numerous other places. He said Graham Greene's new novel also had a bad notice in The Observer. Some papers or reviewers feel an obligation to knock writers down. We were talking this morning. I am to see the film Cries and Whispers, which P says is exceptional. Unfortunately there were gigglers in his audience.

[...]

Patrick asked about my heart, which organ I feel should be referred to in inverted commas, since it's only noisy and has already survived much since the doctor's announcement. In an effort to save me from myself, or for some reason I'm not sure of, I'm being given a grant to get on with a novel. (This was not my idea.) When this happens, at the beginning of November, there are going to be changes in the Harrower regime. I'll only be sociable at night; and, as the phone can't be switched off, I'll have to warn everyone to lay off. So this grant is one of the crimes I've had to answer for. The others recently are a) not inviting someone to dinner when Patrick was coming, and b) not being a Christian. About the grant, I said to P, 'If I'd just written a wonderful book, I'd feel it was justified.' He said, 'You might write a wonderful book...' While I can afford to stay home and not go to an office, I have to be very careful with money, so this will mean a certain loosening up, which will be nice; but much more than that, it will provide a spur, and an obligation of the kind that most people can recognize. It could be – quite non-financially – a lifesaver. Margaret could do with it more. She has to go out to work. I don't like to be the one on whom all the goodies shower, but it wasn't a matter of either/or, so such feelings aren't very useful.

[...]

Why did I feel sad and indignant when I read your letter? Because YM doesn't ever think that anyone else has a tether to come to the end of. Her daughter, for instance. She can be exceptionally winning, and she can be merciless. They say that every difficult soul affects the lives of fourteen others. As one whose life has been affected by an alcoholic grandfather, step-father (possibly also mentally ill), and lover; by a few genuinely depressive bosom friends; by acquaintances who were raving mad; by several youthful drug addicts; and, almost worse, having had to witness others having their lives affected, others who were lovable, gentle, intelligent, considerate, talented, with capacities for life and laughter, I can only say that my wholehearted sympathies lie with the fourteen damaged, rather than with the person causing the destruction. (And I have really cared for some of them.)

[...]

I told M about your friend Patricia Clarke and her mother, snatched back to life and bored to death in the country. Margaret laughed and shook her head. She has strong feelings about mothers, having had one herself.

Saw a play called Jugglers Three on Saturday. David Williamson (about 30) wrote The Removalists, which I've only read, and thought violent and crude. Before that (while I was in London, so I missed the stir he was beginning to cause) he wrote Stork. Then Margaret and I saw Don's Party – funny, but the characters were types, and there were so many four-letter words you couldn't hear the dialogue. Now Jugglers Three (all the plays written very swiftly and very close together) seems a great leap forward. It was very witty, and decidedly cheering to see something good and Australian in the theatre. Recently, The Removalists had a short season at the Royal Court in London, but wasn't well received. With any luck, he'll keep on and extend his range. At the moment he has to have a brutal or stupid or corrupt policeman in every play.

A letter from Christina Stead from London. She has the same agent in NY as Francis and speaks always very nicely about her. She (CS) is an interesting and brave woman. Strange, but kind. She's ill now, with heart-trouble. But she's had a triumphant, if hard, life.

[...]

Greetings and best love to you and Francis –
Elizabeth

Hunters Hill | October 2nd, 1973

My dear Shirley and Francis –

Yes, we <u>did</u> go to the Ball, and sumptuous and beautiful and exciting it was. That was so thoughtful and kind of you to think that I might go, too. Thank you, thank you. The seats were perfect. We drank champagne and investigated Sydney's Elsinore. The building had only been open for two days, so it was particularly elating to see it and be in it this very first week-end of its life. We've watched from ferries and from the Quay daily, or weekly, for so many years. Truly, it's an interesting building. Utzon should have been given his head. The opera theatre itself is much reduced in size from what he'd intended. The ABC and the Department of Works wrested the main hall away from him and from opera for their concerts. It's said that <u>War and Peace</u> was chosen as the first production so that they could show off the ingenious stage machinery and make use of the whole ensemble. It was – opera, and building, and first production – thrilling. The theatre itself has little to distract the eye. You concentrate on the stage. At last we have a <u>building</u>. To whom should we give thanks that our first building is not dedicated to sport?

[...]

Blackheath – Thursday

Came up yesterday for a week. Heavy rain, mud, ducks, pear blossom, boronia, wisteria. A box of new chickens <u>in the spare room</u>. Rather too much nature around here, but the sun's coming out this afternoon, and it's just today that the boronia opened its flowers. (The chickens have vacated the spare room and are with their brother and sisters in the chicken-house, or else making friends with the ducklings. This is a ridiculous place.)

[...]

At The Chimes, waiting to go to the Opera House, I read your London talk. Heavens. It was so good, such a relief to see something that matters so much expressed with beautiful logic and clarity. Would you mind if I had a copy made to share around? Or at least to read again myself? It's difficult to concentrate, reading in company, or to give anything as much time as you'd wish.

[...]

In the letter to Mr. Whitlam's right-hand woman I told her – no, I asked her if she could see that a letter from you reached Whitlam himself.

There was no suggestion that it was anything serious. While I do know a few people who call Whitlam Gough, the general feeling (you'd think I'd conducted a nation-wide poll!) was that this was the best thing to try first. There is industrial chaos in NSW just now. The Liberal Askin Government will take no action, and every one of the disputes involves State laws. Askin knows that the Federal Government will receive all the blame. The newspapers are all owned by Liberal supporters, naturally enough. We are having widespread and prolonged blackouts daily and nightly; this is affecting industry and jobs. There are 16 million unsorted letters and parcels at the Mail Exchange. Sydney Airport has closed down because of radio technicians striking. I forget the other troubles looming or present. On Tuesday night I attended an ALP meeting at Hunter's Hill to meet the candidate for our electorate in the State elections, which will possibly be held very soon, in November. He – the Labor candidate – could do nothing but attack Federal Labor and Whitlam for not consulting him, and us, the rank and file, before combing his hair or changing a shirt. Really, I was cast down by the general stupidity. Our brilliant candidate blamed Whitlam for inflation. He seemed to feel that he would know the solution to the world's financial problems. Most of them (members and speakers) seemed to me quite dotty and out of touch with reality.

[...]

Great greetings, thanks and best love to you both –
Elizabeth

Capri | 15 Oct 1973

My dear Elizabeth –

Many many – MANY – thanks for your letter of 25 Sept which was here when we returned from Paris, and which gladdened our hearts and minds. Most of all we enjoyed the news, so off-handedly handed out, that Elizabeth has a grant and is to get on with a novel: Oh Elizabeth, this is rejoice-worthy and rightful, and we are so pleased for you. Our opinion of the Australian art scene is sky-rocketing, if the right things are landing in the right places. Yes, changes in the Harrower regime perforce – and this must include less of My Mum and her troubles (her terribles, as a Turk at the UN used to misrender the word), and less of Shirl on the telex.

Not only will we understand like mad, but it is the thing we understand best. Will they really let you alone until nightfall? – and will they all pump you so full of terribles after dark that they use up the daylight hours too? If you have a turn-off-able phone, it helps; or if people can be urged to write to you instead of phoning or turning up – this last is the best, as most people don't manage to get around to writing, it is too much trouble, too revealing, and on a different-time-wave; besides being not nearly so much fun as dialling and pouring forth the jolly old terribles in person... Good On Patrick, of course you may write a wonderful book; and if that isn't the point, what is?

How well expressed – Labour can't afford to be less than perfect. Indeed, it is so. Any person or group that is brave enough to assume real (not hot air) moral leadership and is seen to be genuinely making an effort is scrutinised for the least defect or defection. Thank you v. much for looking into the UN discrimination matter – I'll hope to hear from someone at the horse's mouth. What I want to by-pass is the so-called proper machinery – which would be an inquiry to the Aust. delegation at UN, via Dept of Ext. Affairs, who would report that all is well, or that there was a little difficulty in the past but now straightened out, or that any such report is vastly exaggerated, etc. If I can tell the tale to someone who will be willing to read the docs, interest themselves in the girls themselves, get the truth (without subjecting the girls to UN reprisals), that is the only hope. It is a ghastly scandal.

I am a tremendous admirer of Christina Stead. I suppose she gets fatigued with readers' enthusiasm for The Man Who Loved etc., but what an extraordinary work it is. Yes, she has Cyrilly Abels as NY agent – Cyrilly is splendid, and very nice. I will go to her when my agent retires. I have – between you and me – a hopeless agent, but she is elderly and ill & I can't get up my courage to leave her as she is v. sweet etc. etc. I long to fling myself into Cyrilly's bosom and will do so as soon as humane-ly possible.

[...]

Yes, we saw Observer reviews of P. White's and G. Greene's novels – we liked all the others we saw much more. Both those reviews brought blood to our eye, the patronising viciousness of these little people whose incomprehension leaps from every line. That review of Graham was just about intolerable – P. W. at least was commended for the body of his work.

I care much less about these things for myself – it makes me furious for a day, then I forget – than when I see the books of others subjected to it.

[...] Much to say about cholera, about being here, about silence and awayness. Even about autumn! Next letter. The great pleasure, unalloyed, pure, shining, in coming to Australia would be to see Elizabeth; and to meet Margaret. I embrace you, thank you as ever and always from the heart, and send my love – Shirley.

Hunters Hill | 20 October 73

My dear Shirley–

Enclosing note from Elizabeth Reid. I think she would bring the UN girls' plight to Whitlam's notice.

Great great joy here because of Patrick's Nobel Prize and the opening today of the Opera House. The timing was somehow marvellous. Everyone is terribly happy for Patrick. He just wants to get on with his work.

Best love to you both –

Elizabeth

Capri | [Undated, October 1973]

Dear Elizabeth –

With what pleasure your letters, of 2nd and 12th, were read here this morning. And we know you will be feeling much pleasure too in the splendid news about Patrick White – how joyful and rightful, and how nice that it comes on the heels of his new book (we loved Kylie's review, and cackled over the opening para about the pack who hoped he would somehow come a cropper...!) We sent him a congratters cable c/o you, and hope this eluded the Italian Telegraph system (which acts as if Marconi had never been born) & that you didn't mind this imposition – but we did not know how else to address him. This and your own grant are cheering devels; and we cheer.

Also – oh, cheers for the pension. ALL DUE TO YOU. How can you be so many things to all of us, and how can one express what this means? And how can you be so good humanly and do work at the same time? – you can't, obviously. [...]

Oh Elizabeth, MM saying 'Why not relax & enjoy yourself'…!!!!!
Oh the chaos in USA, and one has to remember that it is chaos-with-power, and that the world is now divided into mighty blocs none of which
has political morality. The nations where reason still limps along and a
measure of justice prevails are nations without power. Here at Naples –
a city, a region, forced to its knees. Naples is an ominous, unemployed
silence, broken only occasionally by riots. Nothing is so far done – what
will happen? Did I tell you that Muriel (Spark) once said to us, 'Don't
you sometimes feel that one of these days we'll all be down at the railway
station fighting for a couple of potatoes?'

[…]

My love to you dear Elizabeth. Please renew our great greetings and
rejoicings to P. White when you see him. If the collecting of the prize and
its contingent lolly is likely to bring him through NY, would he possibly
let us know and let us roll out the red carpet we've been conserving for
your own visit? – it's time that carpet had a trial run at least – Shirley.
PS: When I was sending the cable to Patrick White in our little post office
here the cable boys (far from the imposing stern professional ethics of
indifference to message) were thrilled, having just read the news in the
papers. 'Dev'esser bravissimo! Auguri!' Auguri indeed.

Love to you – S.

Hunters Hill | October 24th, 1973

My dear Shirley and Francis–

[…]

Quite euphoric days, nights, events followed [my last letter]… Agnew
evaporates; everyone asks if Nixon is resigning tomorrow or announcing
his own descent into insanity; Middle East cease-fire; tickets arrive today
(this is something of a paella) for a performance of Hamlet to be given
in the presence of the Honourable E.G. Whitlam; and fireworks, terrific
fireworks, are let off for the opening of the Opera House (O, happy day!);
and Patrick wins the Nobel Prize! All very mixed and marvellous.

[…]

Next day

Patrick, Manoly, Margaret, and Judah's daughter, Alice, were here for
dinner, the night before the awarding of the Prize. We didn't mention it,
though The Australian had that day reprinted from a Swedish paper a very
favourable review of The Eye of the Storm by Artur Lundkvist, a member
of the NP selection committee. (He came to Sydney a year or two ago and
was nice, I thought.) Apart from the main course, which was disastrous
because I was interested in the conversation and didn't stay stirring in the
kitchen long enough, we had a very happy night. Alice is a marvellous girl
who spent six years in Moscow studying the violin. They all liked each
other greatly, and Manoly even praised my cooking. (They know they're
going to live dangerously when they come here.)

The next day, Thursday, M and I found out from the Swedish
Consulate that the decision would be announced at ten that night.
I listened to the news and rushed to the phone. I was much more excited
than Patrick, who had heard only half an hour earlier when reporters
started banging round his house. He was very calm. I stayed awake
all night. He didn't see the reporters that night. Next day there was a
tremendous delight loose everywhere. Everyone seemed so generously
delighted that it was an extra sort of happiness to feel the responsiveness
of strangers as well as acquaintances and friends.

Then on Sunday (after Saturday's official opening of the Opera House
by the Queen, with doves, balloons, bands, millions, F111s flying past,
big and little boats with flags and decorations, and the fireworks at night)
Margaret and I met Patrick and Manoly – as arranged the week before – to
look over the Opera House and to hear the Moscow Chamber Orchestra.
I thought P might have a rest instead, but I was glad he came. The place
was swarming with people and probably for the first time in the history of
Australia, a writer was recognized in public. Everybody was smiling. And
the Orchestra made very beautiful sounds. I told you there was euphoria
to follow the sad bits.

[...]

You're both so kind to be so pleased about my old Fellowship. It hasn't
started yet, but soon I'll feel its existence. Somehow, somehow, I have
before then to wrench my mind and heart away from those who do not

really want me but won't let me go. Heavens, this is becoming something of an ancient story and I should spare you. It's just so weird and sad, and destructive (as is your mother's situation of you) of peace of mind, concentration, pleasure in other people. And so many people are terrific, kind, affectionate.

Best love –
Elizabeth

New York | 3 Nov 1973

My dear Elizabeth –

[...] As ever, so much to say – your letters bring so much of life ('lovely life'). A kind letter from Mr Colin Horne of the Adelaide Fest. Writers' Week Committee. Of course all is suspended with us, in mind, while F is having this upset and these tests.

Elizabeth, how wonderful that P. White is giving away his prize to other writers. What a great man he must be. Can I ask if you received a cable from US to him c/o you, sent on the day of the announcement? I'd be very sorry to think this didn't make its way through the Italian Telegraph barrier since, while we can send it again, it had an element of instantaneous rejoicing. However, we can also rejoice at leisure, and do.

Yes, the Whitlam lady had a letter here awaiting, and I am going to tackle the mass of stuff on my desk today. Thank you!! As MM says, 'Elizabeth gets things done'. [...]

Our best & most fond love – Shirley.

Hunters Hill | November 25, 1973

My dear Shirley and Francis–

A quick note to say that, having dreamed of you both last night (we all met somewhere, somehow, and were wafting about smiling and talking; I think you had come here, but don't be nervous – I've only had two prophetic dreams in my life, both concerned with Patrick, and all the rest, most of the rest, have been just interestingly symbolic).

[...]

My God! The energy crisis! What is happening in New York, and I wonder what you think will happen next? Kissinger's threat of reprisals seemed from here not v. likely to succeed. And the stock-market? Britain's State of Emergency. No Sunday motoring anywhere. The Shock is more Present than Future, I'm afraid. Here, we have at the moment more jobs than people. They can't find anyone to pick fruit in the Riverina, and David Jones' can't find women to sell dresses. NSW returned the Liberal government, in spite of Ferdi being at the polling-place from 8 till 10 and Eliz. there from 10 till 12. We were so hypnotized we kept floating back there all day. We were at a little stone church just near here, with trees everywhere, cicadas, summery scents from old H. Hill gardens. In Japan, they say, people are sweeping the shelves bare as they did in war-time. What are you going to stockpile? I'd thought of a bicycle, but there must be easier ways to die. Even motorbikes have to fight their way through cars, without any rights of their own. In Putney, and in Piccadilly, it quite staggered me to see old ladies on bikes. – Thinking of Putney reminds me (perhaps I've already told you, or you knew) that Sidney is going to Stockholm to collect the Prize for Patrick. He (P) is pretty well now and doesn't want to risk the northern winter. There are interviews, many events. You could see how this could change a life that was not highly disciplined. Luckily, the discipline that produces the work isn't easily affected. He can take pressure, but I hope it begins to ease off after Christmas anyway.

[...]

My fellowship hasn't started yet but is very close. I have been locking myself up in the hope of either boring myself to death or bringing about a confrontation with the typewriter. [...]

Great good wishes, best love, Elizabeth

New York | 1 Dec 1973

My dear Elizabeth – such a pleasure to have two letters of yours, one received just now as I was about to reply. [...]

Before getting engulfed in MM, I mention less consequential items – the fuel crisis, the Middle East, UK state of emergency, Liberals in NSW... Also, the Adelaide Festival to which I am almost certain now not to be able to go, as so long a journey – and then more exigent travel at the end of it – will probably not be possible for F so soon. [...] Can I ask you for some reading advice about Australian Lit? The US scene is shamefully devoid of almost any consciousness of Australian writers, and I keep up to some extent through the TLS, who do that occasional issue on Australian authors; I then either get a few works from our London bookseller, or look for paperbacks etc. when we're in England. This is scarcely called keeping up. The last Australian published here to any critical notice at all was Thea Astley. A. D. Hope is The Australian Poet (there being room in the USA for only one, it appears) and of course P. White has a following of devoted and serious readers and will now have many more. I don't think Hal Porter has even been published here. But of the new people, whom I get from the TLS, whom do you like? I see that Judah Waten has a new novel out – set in Melbourne – do you like? Shall I get? Who else? – I mean, of real quality, not necessarily widely known even in Aust. Please tell.

(Among poets, I should have said perhaps that Judith Wright is known here but only just.)

VERY GOOD NEWS that you are thinking of working, and also working. When I am thinking of working, that is when most gets done. When I make the hideous effort to get to the typewriter, quite a lot seems to have gone through the hoops in my head. You have two well-wishers here for your thoughts and their outcome.

[...]

Fuel crisis keeps us in sweaters and on our toes. Stock market is down – but it is so volatile, and the country so immensely prosperous still, that it could go up at the drop of a tarboosh. Surely it would be better to tighten belts and declare the USA not dependent on Arab oil, which is feasible, rather than show ourselves ready to compromise and capitulate – which can only have infinite repercussions. As to Nixon, if we had a less than geriatric Congress he would have been out weeks ago. Yes, I believe he will go – the Republican Party is facing elections next year, & have to get this albatross off their necks. Apparently the country is waiting for Nixon himself to provide 'conclusive evidence' – which by now amounts to murdering someone in public, as the evidence is in slag heaps all around us. He is so bonkers that he in fact does continue to destroy himself, producing bombshells every week. The trials of the big fish (Mitchell, Stans, Haldeman, Ehrlichman etc.) are soon to begin, and we shall see some action from that end too. Time is wearing those villains down – Mitchell is said to be drinking himself to death before a telly in an NY hotel, he lives under assumed name, for example – and Nixon is in the hands of all of them...

[...]

As to rose-covered England, I pray to heaven that MM has some faint idea of what is going on there at present. Alan telephoned us on his return to London, and said that they arrived home to a blackout, no heating, no light, queues at London airport for transport into town, queues everywhere, petrol coupons, the lot. He said it is hellishly uncomfortable and no one knows what is coming, as the coal miners are on a go-slow with threat of strike. [...]

A page from a Dutch newspaper reviews Patrick White's book and my own – plus a few hangers on...! Wish I could read Dutch but I can tell it's favourable as P. White is 'het epische en psychologische karakter van zijn vertelkunst' And, as for me, I can guess what 'een soort prehistorisch monster' means when I see it... After this, Waltzing Matilda on a Chinese tape will be nothing to me.

[...] Do let me know about Australians to read, do let us have a prospect of a Harrower to read. With best love to you from us both – Shirley.

Hunters Hill | January 13, 1974

My dear Shirley – Such a long time since I wrote, or perhaps the eventfulness makes it seem long. The other day I was determined to send that postcard, at least; when I came back from the P.O. and shops with the Herald, there was that piece about Patrick having been discovered by New York, and an extract from your review in – due to be published the following Sunday in the N.Y. Times. And how exceedingly well you do always say what you want to say, dear Shirl! It is always a sort of joyful relief to read anything of yours. As I have been known to say before. And always with heartfelt truthfulness. Patrick was talking to me yesterday and said he had received a copy of the review (probably from Viking). I'm sure he was pleased. [...] It wasn't my 'lovely life' or Christmas cheer that kept me from cabling or writing, it was visiting at Gladesville Mental Hospital and coping with the subsequent horrors (exactly like last Christmas). That has quietened down and cheered up and so on but, as always, these events are wearing to the supporting cast...

[...]

– Forgive me for not responding sooner to your request for info about Aust. Lit. In fact, there is not a great deal of it. Some promising young men are writing plays. I myself haven't read a new Australian novel for a long time. (Apart from <u>The Eye of the Storm</u>. I do so want to know what you thought, and what you said.) None of us (US, whoever we are) much like Thea Astley's work or, indeed, Thea Astley. There was, a few years ago, a huge fuss about Thomas Keneally, but that is over. The literary entrepreneurs look for someone to boost and often in their excitement do everyone a disservice. When I first came home from London in 1959 the quarterlies were putting Randolph Stow through the mill. It happened to Patrick, too, but he was older and better able to withstand the pressure of so much analysis and attention. For some years there was (and in some of those already mentioned) considerable Patrick-copying. They seemed to feel that the significance of his work lay in its syntax. Then there was a lull, and now we have a very few youngish men writing in another peculiarly Australian and peculiarly awful style. Perhaps it's supposed to be hilarious and shocking. Hal Porter of course is – Hal Porter, and stands where the real ones stand. Which of his books have you read? Would you like me to send some others? Have you read Randolph Stow? He's older now, but I still think of him as a poetic boy... Recently Geoff Dutton discovered (for Macmillan?) someone that Patrick liked, and Kylie reviewed this novel and liked it. She showed it to me and I wasn't drawn to it at a glance because it seemed to be in the tradition now current, of facetiousness, which I find so boring. Using capital letters all the time and funny names and funny punctuation. (Funny?) Still it isn't likely that P (who wasn't drawn at first, either) and K could admire or like something not good. It's only published here in Australia, I think. Perhaps I could get it, read it, and pass it on. Judah Waten has kept writing steadily. Everyone admired his short story collection <u>Alien Son,</u>

which was his first book. He's a good, kind-hearted man. Perhaps being political, Communist, has got in his way – in his mind – a bit. I thought <u>Distant Land</u> was done well. There's Barry Oakley (facetious), David Martin (much better), Frank Moorhouse (trendy sex), David Williamson (playwright), Alex Buzo (playwright)... There aren't many stayers among the novelists. Perhaps this will change now that so much money has been given out, although money can't (alone) buy novels. As for poets apart from A.D. Hope. I think Margaret said Patrick likes Les Murray. Then there are R.D. Fitzgerald, Kenneth Slessor, Geoffrey Lehmann, Judith Wright, Francis Webb, Bruce Beaver. Really, I must try to send you something instead of throwing names around like this. I'm not very good about judging newish poetry somehow. – When I told Margaret you would like some info about literary things here she was instantly fired with a desire to communicate all, and M's judgement in my view is highly reliable. However, when it comes to letters those instant fires are inclined to fade as instantly. The novel P and K liked was by David Foster and was called (something like) <u>North South West</u> or <u>North North West</u>. There is a sort of wistful looking out for new people (the same anywhere, I know, but there are fewer of us here and the climate is so against literary effort – physical and mental climate) and so when something that <u>isn't bad</u> arrives everyone thinks: perhaps this one will keep on and develop. Oh yes, there was William Marshall (also Macmillan). In all this, leaving the poets aside for reasons stated, there is – Patrick, Hal Porter, and Randolph Stow aside – no-one I feel you should rush out to read. Martin Boyd? Must give this more thought later, or encourage M to think.

Yes, it is so that Patrick would not have his books entered for the Miles Franklin Award or others. At first he did win the Miles Franklin and then was offered another, bigger prize a year or so later, but refused it. Weeks ago, you said if he ever passed through NY you would like to entertain him, and I told him. He said this was very kind. I imagine he'll stay put all this year, working, but when you do meet you'll like each other well. Hope I'm around.

[...]

Best love to you both as always–
Elizabeth

P.S. You might not have meant only new Australian writers. I remember reading <u>Landtakers</u> by Brian Penton, and <u>The Young Desire It</u> by Seaforth Mackenzie and admiring them. Both wrote in the thirties and forties and are dead now. Was aged myself before reading <u>Maurice Guest</u> H.H. Richardson or <u>anything</u> written in Aust, feeling allergic to homeland and contents. Changed days.

New York | 3 March 1974

My dear Elizabeth –

A telex to send you our love and blessings, which we send you every day in every case, and to let you know that MM splashed down here this very morning exactly on time and is in wonderful form. Came off the plane pretty squashed-looking as – despite fantastic efforts on our part with the airline beforehand – no one helped her with hand baggage, etc, and her first words were 'I'm simmering with rage!'!! However, in no time she was beaming and admiring everything in sight as we drove into town, even gasometres and junk yards.

[...]

No word to me from Elizabeth Reid, although she is mentioned in the press as attending UN meetings, so is here. I wrote her c/o the Aust Delegation, proposing a meeting, and at least a telephone talk, and shall feel that there is not much hope for the Aust girls if she does leave town without being in touch. [...]

As to Watergate, Elizabeth one can hardly believe it is happening, as these supreme pests who persecuted us for years are one by one led forward to their Nuremberg. Mitchell is already on trial, Ehrlichman and Haldeman are to be tried in late spring, etc. Yes, it is awful of course, but at the same time it is immense relief and health and justice. Even for worst criminals on trial I usually feel the awfulness of it, and just see human wreckage; and am rather enjoying the new experience of hearty pleasure as these gauleiters are brought down, who did so much damage to every one of our liberties and to so many persons. I don't know if I told you that last summer we had dinner at a friend's house with Alger Hiss, who remarked that if Mitchell (former head of justice dept) went to gaol (as he almost certainly will), then he (Hiss) did feel sorry for him, as the gaols are mainly occupied by persons Mitchell put there, who cannot wait for his arrival in order to make hell for him. Mitchell is ghastly – the sort of man you cannot possibly imagine as a child.

[...]

I had a very amusing telephone call the other day from Sumner Locke Elliott who is at the Adelaide Festival now – I've never met him, but he was cheerful and would have been fun at the Jamboree had we gone together. He was full of praise. It is so far, and such a rearrangement of life, one simply has to know something ahead of time. I was sad not to go, in the end, despite all the crocodiles waiting at Edgecliff – it would have been a terrific evocation of just about everything... It shall be done, one of these days.

Yes, of course I do feel for the miners in UK – besides, don't you think Heath is dumping the blame on miners when the inflation and chaos of the last two years is at the root of much trouble and the complexities are far greater than a single go-slow or strike? What interests me is that no one in authority seems to realise that the time is quickly coming when no one will go down a mine, or do any of the other appalling things everyone is counting on for their daily well being. It will be no use taking sides for or against miners, when there no longer are any. It baffles me that this cannot be realised, and people go on talking about what they can be prevailed upon to do. Britain is in such a fearful state, one sometimes imagines it will just submerge like Venice – do you think there could ever be civil violence, though? I don't picture any appreciable amount of that, it is not their temperament; just as in Italy, where there is every cause for revolution and the govt leaves one speechless with indignation, there is no heart for uprising either. One just keeps gawping and wondering what on earth will be the outcome.

Please give greetings to P. White and thanks for his hopes that we were coming out – meeting him would have been one of the great pleasures; seeing you would be another, the greatest. [...] With love – Shirley.
PS: How good they are filming Voss – if they do it right at all.
PPS: Yes, Ford is appalling; but would have little power as a successor to a disgraced Nixon, & almost certainly not re-elected. Besides, essential to exorcise Nixon...

Hunters Hill | March 15, 1974

My dear Shirley –

I had just finished an airletter to YM when your telex appeared in the letter-box. Twas a tonic to me.

[...]

On Sunday night I went to Patrick's. I knew Cynthia and Sidney were to be there (flown in from Adelaide), and felt somehow listless about that. In the event, affection lived and breathed (in me, anyway), and that was a relief and very nice. They were tired. I expect to see them again when they come back from Adelaide on Saturday. The occasion, which Patrick has mentioned to M and me before, was the handing over of the Nobel Prize medal and Diploma by the Swedish ambassador. He had come up from Canberra with his wife (a beautiful woman, not young, Italian-Swedish). P hadn't wanted to go there for a formal dinner. So there were just eight of us, and the ambassador performed his part with such – amiability, such a likeable lack of calculation or affectation. I thought it was v. agreeable of Patrick to ask us, because he really has a great many good friends.

[...]

Those miners. Well, yes. A bright friend of mine from London sent me a seven-page letter explaining in ludicrous detail that a miner earns as much as a parson. And she told me, quoting Juvenal, I think, that things were as bad in Rome. Some time ago. 'They should build a Temple to Cash.' This presumably directed at the miners! Oxford, classics, and she should know better. No, civil violence in England is impossible to imagine. It was more surprising and interesting to me that you feel the same about Italy. As you say, one just keeps gawping.

Yes, I'll gladly give greetings to Patrick. He likes to hear news of you.

[...]

Greetings and warm love to you both –

Elizabeth

Hunters Hill | March 25, 1974

My dear Shirley and Francis –

[...]

Margaret went to something at the Opera House the other night for the writers from Adelaide Festival, and met Sumner Locke Elliott. She liked him very much. We'd both read one of his most recent novels (title unfortunately escapes me), set in the Blue Mountains and Sydney, and been gripped. I saw his play 'Rusty Bugles' at the Independent just after the war, or perhaps while it was still going on. Someone in it said 'bloody' or something similarly depraved, and there were court cases and prayers to the Almighty. It seemed to me a very good and funny play. And his novel 'Careful, He Might Hear You' won the Miles Franklin Prize here some years ago. Also good.

The Nolans. They leave tomorrow night (Tuesday) for some part of the US (not NY) and no, I have not seen them again. Probably if P hadn't asked us all to that so-nice, celebratory dinner we'd never have met at all. So affection was obviously only living and breathing in me. Afterwards, I rang C once, and then she rang me once and had a longish talk, sounding much as ever but, clearly, with little intention of meeting. [...] They've seen a fair bit of Patrick. He has known them long and is their good friend. So, Elizabeth, who did not obey, has been cast out. I suppose it ceases – all ceases – to be the sort of thing you can take seriously. Which in a way is everybody's loss. The evaporation, deterioration, of good feeling between two persons has always seemed at the very least regrettable... So there we are. Since it obviously had nothing to do with the London period (although I don't doubt that that, too, has deteriorated in memory), only with my failure to, so to speak, choose C and do her bidding, it is so silly.

[...]

I am trying to work and there certainly seems to be a lot in my head. If only I can sort it out and use it properly. If not, everyone will cast me off. And that would be a pity. I did a piece, a sort of story, unpublishable but fun to do. And I remembered that marvellous feeling of being interested and absorbed and feeling it mattered... Margaret has started to do some reviewing again, which is good. But doesn't lessen my obligations, of course. That was a smokescreen. My love to you both, dear S and F –

Elizabeth

Hunters Hill | May 15, 1974

My dear Shirley –

Your letter of May 8 arrived just now...

[...]

Oh, Shirley. Did you get any of my letters about the election? It happens on May 18 and if Labor does not get back there'll be (I hope) a revolution. We've been having a staggering time; we're all nearly demented with the suspense. I've been to Whitlam's opening campaign rally at Blacktown, to a huge Lane Cove meeting – Whitlam and one of his Ministers, and just this Monday to a MARVELLOUS meeting at the Opera House. Patrick agreed to come out and speak for Labor and there were two, more, advertisements to 'come and meet the Prime Minister at Lunch-time'. They hired the concert hall at the Opera House; it was a heavenly day. Thousands and thousands crowded there. Ferdi and I were in the front row. Glee! [...] Three thousand in the hall and about 15,000 listening outside. While I was standing clapping, and Patrick (on stage) was standing clapping, he saw me and laughed. Others spoke for Labor (all well) then Patrick was called and he, too, received a standing ovation. He made a fine speech, and so did Professor Manning Clark, other professors, a dear young surfer who had won an award – best surfer – and turned his money over to Labor. This is – we have seen a stunning display of democracy in action. The Liberals have millions, the support of huge mining interests and god knows what. Labor's coffers really were empty. I have door-knocked, put leaflets in letter-boxes, handed out leaflets at an Eliz. Reid meeting (for our local candidate), sent off more money than I could afford, and clapped my hands off. Oh, yes and written indignant letters to the papers – one of which got in. And so have all my friends. [...]

I'm about to be collected to see Him (as Helene says) on television tonight after dinner. On polling day, Ferdi is going to be at the polls for 12 hours and I'll be there for 6. Margaret (even) is going to do duty at Mosman, and has letter-boxed. [...] My letter in The Australian was headed 'Effrontery' and referred to the Leader of the Opposition. Oh, Judith Wright spoke at the Opera House, too, and – in her case as in all others – I was deeply relieved to hear true statements about the situation. Only in

office for 16 months! I can't bear it. But what a wonderful crowd that was in the Opera House. I don't think I've ever felt so surrounded by people of goodwill – all ages, all stations. It was heartwarming.
Later

Home again after dinner and hours of politics on television. If Australia rejects Labor and Whitlam I'll want to change my nationality. All at the Opera House said they'd been proud – at least able to stand upright – to be Australian at last these 17 months.

[...]

It's almost midnight. As I type, I'm confusingly listening to an opinion poll on the election and falling into despair at the sound of Liberal opinion. They keep saying Whitlam is a friend of the communists, that they believe in freedom, that he wants to get rid of God Save the Queen and use (there was a public poll) Advance Australia Fair as a national anthem. At Snedden's rallies they all stand and sing God Save the Queen. Pray for us, S and F.

Must to bed. I am keeping watch over YM as far as possible. Although she is sad and worn she seems less threatening, threatened than sometimes. I'm hoping for a good resolution. They have occurred before after such trials. Keep well. Warm greetings and love to you both –

Elizabeth

Capri | 21 May 1974

Oh my dear Elizabeth –

Your heroic & intensely appreciated letter of 11 April came yesterday (yes), our having received a much later one in the meantime about which I wrote you distraughtly from Naples. We were moved to write you at once but waited until this morning's papers gave what was to be the final result of the Australian elections. Well, it still isn't final, at least from reports here, but it seems like Whitlam. We've been holding our breath and thinking of you and feeling for you – as well as for all Antipodeans. We read a splendid article about Patrick's speaking to an audience of angel-siders on Whitlam's behalf, and were sure you would be there. He is (Whitlam), as far as I can see, the only leader who is real and inspired, and therefore inspiring. [...]

The news from the USA is – mind-boggling. Thank god it is all happening: imagine what these outlaws would have achieved by now if they had had no opposition, no exposure. (What is being done by Nixon's Supreme Court, however, is heart-sinking: that reckoning is being stored up for some Orwellian future…)

Had we not in the meantime received your later letter, I think I could not have borne the revelations in the one that arrived yesterday. I opened my mouth to gasp helplessly – How could, How can, Oh, this is monstrous… But you know it all. It is useless to make logical responses about all you have done and are doing – logic, and indeed rationality, not operating in this situation. That you should be informed by Valerie that you have not spent enough time… No, here again one simply moans inwardly, & outwardly. […]

Do you not think that an element of [MM's] show of resentment at you is some form of transposition of me and my inadequacies as felt by her? They used to be only me, and now there has been you – someone doing things, caring, understanding, not (as in other cases) giving up and giving in. A writer, and without obvious claims of offspring, etc. Don't you think you have been getting some of what would rightly (though that's not the word!) be coming to me? Above all, also because you have done and been, and therefore would be the elected? Thinking of it, I put my head in my hands, literally as well as figuratively. […]

Something favourable here has been the result of the iniquitous referendum on divorce – a referendum that was sought only by bigots and fascists, with everyone else begging them not to put the country through such an exercise. Well – they got their proper punishment in the result, which will be a turning point for all sorts of reforms (if they can ever stagger through the administrative turmoil of this extraordinary nation). A tremendous blow to all wowsers, as the supposedly 'reactionary' south did not even vote solidly for the cancelling of the divorce law – many places surprised by voting to retain divorce, even in the strongholds of wowserism. And of course, the remainder of the country came out solidly for reason. An elderly Neapolitan friend of ours said to us, 'Since I attained the age of reason, this is the first time my country has done a public action of which I can be proud.'

[...] Bless you, dear Elizabeth, and know that we honour you. With love – Shirley.

Hunters Hill | 26 May, 1974

My dear Shirley –

This may never struggle through the world's post offices to Capri and S and F, but here is the news, and here's hoping.

[...]

Now, since I have appointed myself yr political correspondent, I feel you should know that these have been extraordinary times... Money, foreign interests, electoral boundaries, have kept Labor out of office for decades. Then, as you know, they were in for 16 months, transforming the country and its citizens, and battling against a hatred so naive-seeming that we tended not to take it seriously. Major bills were rejected twice by the Senate and finally our conservative friends took the unprecedented step of blocking a Government supply bill, so that there would have been no money for the day-to-day running of departments, for paying salaries. Then there was the double dissolution and the Opposition crowing that they'd been planning this from the moment Whitlam got in. After that, indescribable things kept happening and the population has been reeling from shocks, hopes and too much suspense. Eight days after May 18, election day, we are still not certain of the result. [...] Last Saturday, 18, was election day. After beautiful weather it was cold, black and rain pelted down all day. With our three papers to fill in – 73 Senate numbers, 4 referendum questions, 4 House of Representatives numbers – the Electoral Office expected chaos and it was right. People queued at 7.45 am to get into the local church hall to vote. Our 'secret ballot' in these circs meant that we stood – as in a crowded train or bus – and wrote on our papers wherever we could find space. We were sodden, and the officials hadn't even enough ballot boxes to hold the papers, and now casual labour taken in off the street is counting the confusing result. Ferdi and I were at the polling-booth nearby for six hours officially and more unofficially. Friends donated sun-umbrellas to keep us and our how-to-vote cards moderately dry, but you had to keep going out to give cards and we all caught colds. Volunteers kept arriving to relieve those at the booths, but we didn't want to leave. There was an extraordinary feeling of – oneness. [...]

It has been so strange. No-one could guess which way the country would vote. And there was a feeling of forces having been let loose, powerful feelings let loose, and there have been floods everywhere, in unheard of areas, so it has been a little like the end of the world.

I do realize that Watergate reaches new heights and depths daily, and that Ireland is about to explode, and that the Middle East may not – just yet. But when numbers here were planning to take to the streets if Labor was forced out without having served one term, it was – for lotus-land – very traumatic. Headlines suggested the CIA had a hand in things and that perhaps Australia was to be another Chile, because of mineral reserves, useful sites for bases and so on. Anyway, so it goes.

In a fit of enthusiasm I sent you many cuttings, some of which may reach you in Capri.

[...] It's good to know you are 'working and working'. Greetings and best love to you both –

Elizabeth

PS. That day, mentioned by Muriel Spark, when we'll all be fighting for a potato seems closer, but probably it's (the seeming) only the result of listening to too much news.

More greetings and love

Elizabeth

Capri (en route, on wing, for Tuscany and NY) | 6 July 74

My dear Elizabeth –

With what pleasure we received a hugely delayed and hugely welcome letter from you – our only news from Australia in weeks. In the same mail, an envelope solely of clippings from MM – I do not know if this is a massive remonstrance or merely that one thing that has got through the hideous mail-traps at your end and at this. (Oh Italy – what utter irremediable chaos. Half the country is preparing for its summer holiday at the seaside, and the other half for civil war...) We leave here in two days' time, after much serenity, much joy, much work, much anxiety over MM, some health setback for F, now in pink. [...] The lack of news from MM has been as desperate-making as the news when it has come. Bless you for being, in all this distress and confusion, a source not only of fundamental information, but as ever, of strength and sense and kindness.

[...]

Elizabeth, we are truly excited and thrilled to read of the great Whitlam meeting of true spirits, of which you sent clippings and of which we'd already read something in the English papers. It is a once-in-a-lifetime thing – once-in-this-world, I fear – not because what it represents can't go on, but because that wave of belief and truth can only come spontaneously. We wished ourselves there – we there in the sense that all persons of goodwill and conscience made part of the presence. One felt, reading, that – well, that the drongos had not yet won. It is important that Whitlam is happening somewhere in this world – he is the only one, so far as I know; yet one might be enough (though I think of the Cities of the Plain and a little moan escapes...). The library fees for authors, the generous thinking, (thinking!) that is going into his policies surely could not be totally reversed by the Sneddens if they ever got back. (Snedden's remark about the 'real Australians' is very Nixon-like – Remember Nixon's 'silent majority'?) Oh lord, what a long suspense for you and Whitlam over the result – we were groaning over our newspapers, 'poor Whitlam, poor Elizabeth' – but one has so little faith in the electorate that one can only rejoice that something disheartening didn't happen, landslide for Snedders, etc. It is exciting, in the way that good government ought to be – It is also the answer to Nixon's position on official crimes: 'Everyone does it'; not only that Whitlam doesn't do 'it', but that one sees how ready people of goodwill are to interest themselves in authority when it is candid and imaginative.

[...]

When we get out of this mail-less Italy, I'll be a more consecutive and coherent correspondent, I hope. This letter should be about real and important things – the bougainvillea massed below our balustrade, F's birthday dinner last week (just the two of us at the rickety table of a trattoria in the full moonlight, looking over a cliff at sea and out all the way to the mountains above Salerno – which, I should explain, you could see before the moon took over), and a heavenly trip for a couple of days to Paestum, indescribable beauty. A deposition of terracotta figures, more than lifesize, in the Church of Monteoliveto in Naples – the Mazzoni Lamentation, it's marvellous. One has not been idle. Even – even – work has been done.

Bless you, dear Elizabeth, and bless your work also. We will be in touch again very soon, from a real post office. We think of you and send constant teleces of one kind or another. May we meet soon. With love, as ever – Shirley.

Hunters Hill | 14 July, 1974

Dearest Shirley and Francis–

As I so often write when events are not joyful, I thought it would be a happy change (and only fair!) to send news of improvements and smooth seas. [...]

We're still recovering from the election. It gave everyone a jolt. Afterwards, since then, the unions have gone raving mad, and inflation has taken another great leap forward, but Parliament has started again (July 9) and now we begin to feel we'll all survive that election setback. (Whitlam was shaken, temporarily, we felt. Saddened, dismayed.) ... Patrick has just given twenty-four more of his paintings to the Art Gallery, including a big Nolan. He's being got at rather in reviews of his new short story collection. [...] – Meeting a number of poets all at once – Bruce Beaver, Geoffrey Lehmann, Rodney Hall; listening to Joan Sutherland on radio, here for a short opera season; Patrick, Judah, visiting. All I really care about and all that worries me just now is work. And I wonder if I'll ever sort out and find ways of transmuting... I'd better.

Dear friends, I hope you both feel well and marvellous, and that you've worked like anything and had happy times. – More and better news next time. Till then, greetings and love –

Elizabeth

Hunters Hill | 26 August, 1974

My dear Shirley –

I have just written to Francis about Isadora. Isn't it a beautiful book? It was <u>so touching</u>. What could be sadder than to see so much love go to waste? [...]

Events, events. And you've lost Nixon! All events leading up to it breathlessly followed here (as all round the world!), and I thought often of you and what you were making of it. What now? Do you think he should be prosecuted and gaoled? Will that happen?

A while ago I sent you some clippings about the state of this nation. While not of the Nixon order, they've been dismaying. On August 6, the first joint sitting of Parliament ever held was called to pass the six bills rejected by the Senate before the May 18 election. Till the very afternoon before, the session was in doubt, because the Opposition Senators had challenged its validity in the High Court. Whitlam not only has an Opposition, he has his own Caucus and the Trade Unions to handle. Just three days ago he had to deny that he was about to resign. The press is fiendish. [...] Then we've had Jack Mundey (President of the Communist Party of Australia) telling us that he wants to call a general strike, 'like the spring and autumn offensives they have in Italy and Japan' later in the year. He is going to put up barricades all over the city at Christmas-time, if the Council doesn't ban all private cars. He became well-known, a celebrity, when his union – The Builders' Labourers' Federation – was called on by some ladies (I mean ladies: known to me) in Hunter's Hill to put a 'green ban' on a piece of land called Kelly's Bush. After that, they – the BLF – scattered bans all over Sydney saving buildings and open spaces. But if you go outside the law for your own purposes, you have to be conscious of some of the possible consequences.

[...]

I hope all's very well with you both. Greetings and best love –
Elizabeth

New York | 29 Aug 1974

My dear Elizabeth –

With what enormous pleasure your letters have been received, & at perfect Harrower-timed moments, the dear letter received on our return (& answered, uselessly, in mind many times over). [...]

So much to say – Thank you, thank you for all news and clippings. I love Whitlam's phrase, 'the white ants of democracy', it sets these twirps in perspective. We were sad about Mr Mundey, who has done good, but as you say, become irresponsible.

[...]

Elizabeth, might I ask you – if you think it appropriate – if you could sometime show the piece about suppression of Solzhenitsyn's works to Patrick White? Perhaps you think this unsuitable, in which case disregard, please. But I felt that perhaps some confraternity of Nobel Laureates should have an inkling this sort of thing is going on. The UN press release (which I have, if needed) is appalling. It almost surprises even me. Jerzy Kosinski has sent an excellent letter to Waldheim on behalf of PEN. But most people prefer not to reflect on issues of this kind – ie, Solz. is alright as a clear-cut hero; but not when he makes it necessary to criticise supposedly 'good' institutions.

[...]

NIXON!! Wot did I tell you!!! Smiling damned villain. That last speech was the ultimate in defiance and total absence of human grace. Much as Ford & Rockefeller would love to close the books on the case, I don't think it is that easy. The 'little' Watergaters are serving sentences already, the bigger ones are about to go on trial, and much more evidence has yet to be released. It may not be possible to let Nixon off before the whole world, when all his underlings are (rightly) getting it in the neck. What days, what months. We two sat and drank champers and listened to the wretch on the radio. A feeling of enormous relief. Ford & Rockefeller are awful – completely representative of corporation interests – but we are rid of one salaud and are back at least to a normal level of grumbling, instead of in the grip of a psychopath.

Elizabeth, thank you so much for putting Mr Geering in touch – he wrote me such a kind note & sent copy of the cockle-warming brochure in which Harrower and Hazzard figure gracefully. I have written him, and hope one day we'll meet. Meantime, I received a set of galleys of The Cockatoos from Viking – have put this in the port for the trip & immensely looking forward to it. Have had a re-reading this summer of all P. White, except the earliest books, which I have never been able to get, and poems. The grandeur of this body of work – in which so much wit and humanity are mingled, and an almost Shakespearean range of private insights – moves me more than ever. He redeems literature – modern literature – practically single handed (I don't mean there aren't other modern writers I greatly respect and enjoy; but there is a different dimension here). I called Viking and said I only wished I could review again, but not possible so soon! But would be proud to quote, if any use. So we'll see.

[...]

Dear Elizabeth, what about your own work? Do you find, as I do, that all this being anxious or furious about The World takes away from time and silence and thought for real work? Yet one cannot refrain from taking some part – it is no longer possible for writers to do that, alas. The Watergate thing here has been a strange dichotomy of horror and hearteningness – but does it not seem strange to you that these American people, who have ultimately shown an interest in liberty in their own country, seem almost unanimously indifferent to the sorts of nightmares their country is encouraging in Saigon, Seoul, Chile, Cyprus, etc? I suppose this is a case for that overworked word, Imperialism?

[...]

My love to you, dear Elizabeth. Thank you for such letters, and such friendship – your Shirl.

Hunters Hill | 18 November, 1974

My dear Shirley –

[...]

Loved hearing from you the other day. Thank you so much for the news, and copies and all. I've posted off the Solzhenitsyn letters to Patrick. If you'd like my opinion of the letters, it is that those characters are insane to argue with you. – Still, deliberate public lies, private lies, are very weird manifestations. You talk about the herd instinct of intellectuals and the way they attach themselves so carefully to the 'right' causes. It's – naturally – the same here. All those shrewd eyes and unexamined motives. [...] I have two good friends and one sterling acquaintance (two of them <u>writers</u>) who would not hear a word in favour of Solz. during all those ghastly days. They have such long-lasting uncritical feelings about the Soviet Union that they could hate him in that situation of extreme horror, and consider him a traitor, a publicity-seeker! For himself. I marvel at the power of fixed ideas. What happened after your last letter? Any further developments?

[...]

Nadine Gordimer's new novel sounds terrific in the Observer review. The Conservationist. Must get it. – You'll see from clippings somewhere in this envelope that Patrick's first Nobel P. prize was won by Christina Stead. I was so pleased. She's a splendid person.

I'm always promising a better letter another day. Still. There'll be a better letter; this is just a telex of sorts. But it was SO NICE to hear you last night, and to hear <u>about</u> Francis. With fond love to you both –

Elizabeth

New York | 24 Nov 1974

My dear Elizabeth –

How nice you are – it is a joy every time to see your envelope, as we know that generosity and wit and wisdom are about to visit our rooms. [...]

I was so happy to find Christina Stead had won the PW prize. She is a splendid writer – I think I told you that she became known in this country only in the last few years, in spite of having lived here and having a high reputation in England. That is what I mean about the hopelessly ingrown & parochial nature of 'criticism' here. It is true there is cachet in knowing certain developments abroad – mostly French, or Japanese! – but a real fear, I think, of finding out that a tremendous figure like Patrick (as I call him) has been out of their orbit all this time. In recognising him, they have to admit, even if tacitly, that they have been in error. I hate all that 'police-station of the arts' element of criticism – indeed, I rarely read criticism and have little interest in it as a genre, only for the occasional statement or essay

that rings true and <u>wants</u> books to be good, rather than showing relief
& satisfaction when they're not.

[...]

A terribly nice letter from John Colmer. He's also, of course, pleased
by the money Whitlam is giving for the arts and to young writers; and
speaks so warmly of you. He recommends Naipaul to read, particularly
<u>A House for Mr Biswas</u> – have never read N., and shall. Must also get hold
of the Nadine Gordimer, you speak of, of which I've seen nothing here.

Now for MUM. [...] She is angry at us because we cabled to ask
whether a cheque for A$1000 posted in August registered, returned by her
unregistered via the Italian mails ('Leave it just now, honey'), returned by
us registered six weeks ago, and unacknowledged had ever been received.
(Yes, received and deposited.) But we should not press any such matter, is
the mater's message.

[...]

It is so depressing that she not only will not do minimal things to help
herself out there, but seizes on any suggestion or request of mine about
such things as an object of resistance and a source of antagonism. Thus a
telephone call to the Anguses, her friends in Hobart, to find out – simply –
how they are, when coming to Sydney etc. and to find out, more essentially,
whether she would find them there if she made a trip to Hobart for a week
or two in January (my long-ignored idea to give something to look forward
to over the Xmas nightmare) – becomes An Issue. I beg, she ignores, & so
on, month in, month out to no conceivable purpose. Francis writes, she
then answers: 'I called them a year ago but they were out.' Even she must
wonder what satisfaction this gives her, and why.

[...]

Have just seen Gordimer novel got good prize in England. I am
wondering about Harrower works, and wondering about Hazzard works.
When I see pages strewn about all over desk, typed and scribbled on,
I wonder how anything coherent or properly incoherent, can ever emerge.
Let us pray.

Captions under 'social' photographs in copy of Aust Women's
Weekly sent to me (with UN article in it) seem all to have been composed
by Patrick White: 'Mrs P. Groom, of Indooroopilly, arrived at Ballymore

Rugby Union Club in a long denim skirt, matching jacket and yellow accessories'. (Actually, Mrs G. one of better-looking customers therein.)

Next week Sumner Locke Elliot is coming for a drink – have never met him. We spoke on phone and he said his real failure in Australia last March was not seeing you – you had tried to be in touch and he (I think) was just leaving for a PEN Bring Your Own Bottle party at Parramatta. I am only reporting what he said! I should add that he was overwhelmed by the beauty of the setting of the city: 'I'd creep away from gatherings in the evening just to take a round trip on the Cremorne ferry – the blue lights of the bridge and the lighted opera house were so beautiful. No one noticed that I'd gone and come back.' (Imagine coming <u>back</u>.) I shall let you know – he is funny & cheerful on phone.

[...]

With a great embrace, dear Elizabeth, and again, thank you for a letter with such pleasure in it. I send as always and ever, my love – Shirley.

Hunters Hill | 29 December, 1974

My dear Shirley and Francis –

Isn't it lovely that Christmas is over? Oh, the beautiful relief of coming home after two radiant days in the mountains (Christmas, Boxing) with good company, food, wine, wonderful trees, blackbirds, butterflies and a black cat!

But poor Darwin! Late on Christmas Day I went out on to the verandah and someone said in a wondering tone, 'Darwin's been wiped out.' Just nine weeks ago the Government set up a Natural Disasters organization and it has, with the help of all the voluntary welfare organizations in the country, and the services, done marvels. Mr. Whitlam flew back from London. (I worry about his health. He is good.) Everyone wants to help – plumbers, bus-drivers, pilots, doctors, technicians.

[...]

I was given the Nadine Gordimer novel and feel so disappointed not to like it more. My novel-loving mind had to be driven to it. Maybe Christmas aftermath. Maybe, in something so complex it was cruel to the reader and unnecessary to abandon inverted commas. Some wonderful writing, but… The London critics think it's colossal, all that a novel should be. I've admired most of her other work very much.

[…]

Solzhenitsyn. No, it isn't magnanimity that makes me refrain from berating his detractors. Years ago I stopped arguing with anyone dead drunk, insane or drugged. Elizabeth Bowen said: 'to so much as argue was to injure honour,' and there are times when you feel this so strongly that nothing could make you speak. Totalitarianism is ghastly insanity. The subject arises briefly, and hatred appears in the eyes, and your heart goes cold, and you feel deep surprise and disappointment, and realize that this person you've liked isn't ever to be counted on again. (This isn't to say I don't argue constantly!)

Yes, I know about that cheque flitting to and fro, with YM waiting for the Australian Government to devalue the dollar. 'They like me to bank the cheque straight away.' 'It's very inconvenient if people don't.' 'That's what they say.'

Wonder how you got on with Sumner Locke Elliott. Margaret encountered him at some parties and liked him, I think. Much laughing. His novels are complicated and good. (I've only read two, both set in Australia.)

[…]

I'm glad to think of you both working. Francis says he's all thumbs. That's hard to believe! But it often feels like that, with words like cement blocks. The Gordimer was so dense and wrought. Everything has to be deliberate, but when it looks deliberate, it's – very troubling to this reader. I like some artful artlessness, a little appearance of spontaneity, breath, transparency. And to be there. Want too much?

Meantime, trying to work (like you, I feel two years of monthly cheques – and from Mr. Whitlam! – impose an obligation), ever thinking thoughts, and wrestling with Great Moral Problems, and finding everything very interesting.

All happiness, health and hard work for 1975, dear friends. I appreciate you – and who wouldn't! My love as ever to you both –

Elizabeth

New York | 5 Jan 1975

My dear Elizabeth –

We snatched up your letter with the usual surgings of pleasure [...]
We were at the opera v. late last night – a new Boris Godunov, with a
monolithic Finn called Talvela; much praised by all, but a disappointment
to us; a faint air of MGM, much thin-ness of conviction, good singing, but
none of the majesty and soul of Christoff's rendering which we have seen
various times and loved. Your letter is the best thing since the cessation of
Christmas. [...]

The Darwin calamity is hard to take in. I kept thinking of the storm
in The Eye of The Storm – the experience of force, annihilation. Am
sending to MM a wad of clippings about it from here, thinking it might
interest her to see how widely it was reported in America; and am asking
her to hand them on to you just in case you'd like to see. [...] What will
become of the evacuees? – is there to be compensation for those who
simply lost their entire assets? It is corny to say one feels spared and
grateful, a tiny minority of the globe who are not being crunched (as yet)
in the awful maw of fate. But I do feel so. Existence has become so intense,
precarious – always was so, no doubt, but not previously charged with
universal awareness of that fact.

[...]

On New Year's Eve we were quietly sitting, having just posted a
New Year's note to Patrick White, when a messenger struggled to the door
with a huge box containing Viking's new editions of all his works as far
back as The Aunt's Story. I had been promised this a year ago, as a prezzie
from publisher; it just made it in the door in time for 1975. We spread all
the books out, it looked as if PW was coming to dinner. (Wish he were.)
I'm disappointed about the Gordimer – from what you say, I fear that
MESSAGE has taken over. That would also account for popularity with
critics, who love Message these days and are recalcitrant when not given
large helpings of it. A pity though, as she is a fine writer. The new Elizabeth
Bowen book (a posthumous collection of fragments mostly) is much
more interesting than I'd expected – fearing that it was some publisher's
dodge to pad out a volume that Elizabeth would have shuddered at. No,
there are truly illuminating and highly intelligent things, and it all makes
you wonder about who is valued and why, in the literary world. I loved

Elizabeth's remark about its being dishonour to so much as argue – that is how one feels in such circs, dishonoured. [...] Did I ever tell you how Elizabeth described to us being in a supermarket in the King's Road & finding herself stared at as she stood in checkout queue; and realising that she had been looking about her & saying out loud, 'O the squalor, the squalor'. How often one feels like that, & towards the whole world at times.

Otherwise have not been reading much (a puzzling, informative but I think defective good book on Thomas Hardy by a fine biographer, Robt Gittings – Hardy being one of my heroes, perhaps I feel that nobody would do him justice), but trying to work. [...] World is awful, also a constant infringement on the sort of thought-space one has to have to write in. A nice surprise was a cheque for $35 from the Aust. Govt. as first instalment of their royalties from libraries system. Good for them. So few governments are doing anything good and most of them don't even want to. Among the clippings I'm now sending to MM are screeds about the CIA. We all knew this was going on, but were helpless – only the changed climate of post-Watergate is making it possible to bring the stuff out. Of course the FBI (domestic spying) has been after us all for years, and has on its own admission spied on millions of civilians – in cases like ours and most, just for protesting the war, speaking against Johnson or Nixon in public, sending unkind letters to the White House etc. But the CIA is even so another dimension – it is 'foreign' intelligence – in other words, the persons spied upon were being treated as 'foreign agents' and liable to charges of treason. This sounds incredible, but is the case. Had Nixon not blundered into Watergate, I am certain that by now we would have been joining MM in that rose-covered cottage on the boat deck of the Port Line.

The Watergate verdicts an enormous relief. The pardon is an insurmountable wrong. Much justice will never be done. But to see that posse of Hitleristes in the dock was beyond wildest hopes. I do appreciate and admire Whitlam. But some things continue to bother me. I suppose I never expect thoroughly to 'like' a political leader; and in truth I don't see how even the very best leader, which I think Whitlam is in the world today, can govern ideally under present conditions. He is so much ahead of most; & we enjoyed what Gore Vidal, (awful & talented man, intelligent, exhibitionist, amusing, & vicious) said about the unrealized bliss of Australians living in their innocent ideas of a political scandal – compared to what this unhappy USA has undergone.[...]

With all the fond affection possible of your Shirl.

Hunters Hill | 23rd February, 1975

My dear Shirley and Francis –

After I had your last letter I wanted to send cables, or ring up. Then I thought that a little peace, total wordlessness on the M front might be best.

[...]

We went to Aida. There were many stages on the way to Aida – not going at all, giving the tickets away, not hurting F's feelings. I pressed YM to take a companion who owns a car, so that she could be collected and delivered. No, I was chosen and no other would do. Sydney produced (before Aida) a most glamorous, beautiful evening.

The clocks are shifted an hour for Summer Time so it's still light at 7.30, and there was so much summer evening glamour – sea-scents, light breezes, purely decorative clouds, trees, flowers, and the Opera House and champagne – that we were quite transported. YM had been to Dan's for lunch and met Daphne and two other women. Talk was of Europe. However, the evening and then Aida (as you know the first opera performed in the Concert Hall, which was in Utzon's original plan to be the Opera Theatre) overpowered even thoughts of superior places. It was wonderful. They did marvels. We were all thrilled. We wrote that card from our splendid seats in the stalls. Afterwards, as I'd anticipated, there were no cabs, and I fell from favour because we (like many others) had to wait for a bus; then at the Cross we picked up a taxi to the Chimes, and I went on from there. The Cross was choked with taxis. Still, it was a marvellous evening and I was only sorry everyone wasn't there, enjoying it.

[...]

Patrick posted me a couple of books he'd been reading – Edmund Wilson To the Finland Station and Elizabeth Hardwick Seduction and Betrayal. I've put aside the first temporarily, finding it too exciting for bedtime reading: I was having dreams like MGM spectaculars, revelations everywhere. It's bad enough when I'm awake, reading the papers, hearing the news.

[...]

You say Gore Vidal spoke of the 'unrealized bliss' of Australians and he was right. (He is buying some land here, a vineyard, I think somewhere in NSW.) I saw him on television when I was in Blackheath, an hour-long interview. He was so amusing, so startling (to the studio audience); he made so many useful statements, like a series of electric shocks. The audience looked bemused. Sacred cows are still sacred here.

The Opposition keeps threatening to force a new election. The Queensland Premier is blackmailing Japan: if they won't take beef, he'll cancel huge coal contracts. The NSW Premier is breaking the convention that any casual Senate vacancies must be filled by a Senator from the same party as the resigning or deceased Senator. The Attorney-General, Murphy, has gone to the High Court and the next NSW Labor Senate nominee should be selected. No. Lewis is just going to pick someone of his own choice. Poor Dr. Cairns is distraught because of the alluring Junie Morosi. He may resign, after spending the best part of his life to get Labor in and reach a position of influence. Mrs. Cairns is distraught. I said to YM on the phone that I was sorry for him, or for her. YM said sharply, 'I'm sorry for me.' [...]

Dear Shirl and Francis – goodwill, affection, love and great wishes about work and happiness from

Elizabeth

New York | 23 Feb 75

My dear Elizabeth –

Barely surfacing after a bout with a UN article for a political magazine here (The New Republic), which has nearly killed me. What emerges is, one hopes, useful; but I could have written a chapter of me novel in the same time if the same frightful consumption of energies had been applied. One has to amass so many (hideously boring) facts in order to extract the meaning and make it into something illustrative & forceful. Anyway, it's done.

[...]

As to Adelaide: I have not heard anything from the Festival people, and wonder if it is too early to inquire from them? We had a delightful and very kind letter this week from Patrick W. asking if we were coming in '76, and magnificently saying he would stay in residence if so. [...] Patrick writes that the Opera House has altered Sydney, 'We can't imagine how we got along without it'; its moment had obviously struck.

[...]

Elizabeth, a thousand thanks for sending the forms for library royalties. I had already received a few first fiddlies for one book, and now applied for all the others. This is an immensely civilised development. Thomas Keneally and I were asked to be on a radio programme to discuss Australian literary devels, which we did. He's a Harrower enthusiast, a White enthusiast, etc, & generally spoke well abt the indigenous nature of new writing in Australia. (He's immensely enthusiastic about Les Murray, only one or two of whose pomes I've read, so I've asked MM to send me a paperback of same.) [...] He seemed pleasant, intelligent, & I'd certainly have picked him right away for a lapsed Catholic priest living family life at Avalon. Anyway, Keneally coming for tea tomorrow, so I'll get to know him better. He wants to talk about the UN. [...]

Reviews of PW's Cockatoos, apart from a quite understanding – but not brilliant – one by Eudora Welty, made blood boil. Anatole Broyard not only savaged Patrick (who, weirdly, had been recipient of his praises for EYE OF STORM), but gave such a hideous review to Sumner Locke Elliott's new book that only a timely and plushy sale to the movies can have saved Sumner from seppuku. (Not that one should even notice evil reviews – but this one struck us as being practically insane with vituperation; and that of the Cockatoos, only less so.) In this and many, many other connections, we beg you to give us the source of the beautiful Eliz. Bowen quotation you sent us? 'It would be dishonour to so much as argue.' This has not only saved our sanity on many recent occasions, but even seems to have done something for us retroactively.

[...]

With love from both of us – Shirley.

My dear Shirley,

A report from the battlefront: the war is over. It seemed an age, didn't it? [...]

When your cable suggesting NY now was rejected the upheavals were awful, awful. I rang Andrew for help and he received his share of upheaval and was ordered out of No. 58. Like you, we felt 'The hopelessness of building up any feeling of having helped at all gets one down.' Those days of crisis and the letting loose at Andrew and then your last letter all combined to end the stress. Yesterday I saw YM. She was worn but sweet. I was just worn. I said, 'Don't you realize how many people are concerned about you?' 'No,' she says, giving my arm a hug.

[...]

Nolans. A long call from Cynthia, who isn't well. She only weighs 6 stone 7 lbs. They're in Canberra, Adelaide, Melbourne, then briefly back to Sydney. I don't know if we'll meet. Like you, I feel there's mortality and I knew Cynthia well. Nadine Gordimer. No, I didn't think this was a 'message' book, but too wrought, too tight, with no space for the reader. Margaret is reviewing it. She admires NG's work and admires aspects of this, but knows what I mean. Judah Waten. A very good friend, a good writer, a kind-hearted man. Here in Australia the Communist Party has split into pro-Moscow, pro-Peking and maybe pro-Trotsky groups. Judah has belonged since he was 16 to the pro-Russian side and he is now 63. At least one Left group (but not his) wants to destroy Labor.

[...]

Elizabeth Bowen. <u>The Heat of the Day</u>. That novel said so many true things. 'To as much as dispute with him was to injure honour.' Chapter 7. Then there is this: 'At the worst there came out of it a warning to the bottom of her heart, that no return can ever make restitution for the going away. You may imitate but cannot renew safety.' Then, '"It may still be the first of many more evenings, but what will they be worth? This is the truth," she said... "He cannot bear it; let's hope he will forget it – let's hope that; it is the least we can do; we're all three human. At any time it may be your hour or mine – you or I may be learning some terrible human lesson which is to undo everything we thought we had. It's that, not death, that we ought to live prepared for."' No, there are so many pieces to quote and perhaps those last two weren't the first to mean something to me – the first always did.

Best love and greetings to you both as always –
Elizabeth

New York | 26 March 75

My dear Elizabeth –

[...]

After you had told us that MM seemed a little more accessible to the idea of a 'home', and that Andrew felt it was best hope, we noted a mention of such (even if faint) interest in a MM letter. She did mention the totally fantastic place in Florida, which I decided not to respond to in any form. As to 'saving her money for S & F' – you can imagine how this piece of grotesquerie makes my head sink into my hands. She also wrote me she was 'saving' for a trip to NY, or 'any trip'.

[...]

During these days of MM war, have kept on even keel (says she in an ocean-floor voice) by reading a marvellous new translation of The Iliad by Robert Fitzgerald (who previously translated the Odyssey). It is superb. The slaughter makes one speechless – it is so like everything that has ever been. And trying to get my paws on The Conservationist – it is just out here – before leaving for Italy. A couple of days ago we again saw Nadine Gordimer – just for a little while, & with other people; but she is a person one feels a kind of love for as soon as one sets eyes on her. We agreed to meet in peace and quiet within a year – she is coming back here, & might be in Italy sometime – and I do believe it. These last days in NY before departure are moving with a sort of disjointed velocity, like an express train that stops at every station. Too many people and activities and items – some of them nice, some merely necessary.

[...]

I listened for a while on the radio to the UN panel discussion that launched their ludicrous 'Women's Year'. Shall restrain myself on this disheartening rhetorical exercise, held in a building where women are massively discriminated against – a fact which no one at the conference seemed to give a damn about, or even, mostly, know about. UN's Women's Year activities, mainly financed (ie, all congresses, no acts) by Iran, a country with, as Amnesty International puts it, 'possibly the world's worst record on human rights in recent years' (and think what a distinction that has to be!); the Shah's twin sister is the nominal directress of the whole shindig... etc. The entire Conference syndrome, as exercising self-esteem and ego-building – and waste – had seemed to me a male manifestation; and I suppose the current jamborees are to show that women can recycle hot air as well as anyone else. The condition of UN women was raised for a moment or two in the day-long meeting, and quickly sunk. [...]

Well, shortly after this I was invited, for the first time in 25 years' association with the UN, to meet a representative of my own country. Invitation to reception for Reid was telephoned to me here the day before. We were going somewhere else – as they had hoped – but decided to look in for a while so as not to give another opportunity for saying she had tried to be in touch without success. UN Australian mission housed in totally inappropriate super-rich building where Rockefellers live (all UN missions like this – why allowed?), but with saving grace of having several particularly splendid Sidney Nolans – one very pewter-coloured, sombre, large, unforgettable. Head of mission on leave, chargé d'affaires greeted me, looking at me like rabbit at a cobra; introduced Miss Reid saying 'I believe you've corresponded'. I said, 'I've done most of it.' Reid genial, v. impressed with her assignment, travels, etc, obviously no intention of asking single question about UN women, Aust. women, or any other kind of women. The mistake is ever to think there would be interest in actual cases, rather than 'prestigious statements'. However, then nice thing happened, as – moving on to room of Nolans, SH surrounded by Australian UN secretariat women, Pour It On, Let Me Shake Your Hand, Good On You. This cheering and cheerful. The awful place (UN) is so exposed in this context that something will happen to benefit UN women generally – & then no doubt we'll hear, thirty years too late, that it was thanks to the heroic efforts of conferees...

I need hardly say that there was not one question, either, from any official of the Aust. mission. Far from it. Two corpse-like manifestations of External Affairs, men, vaguely inquired whether anything was wrong with women's lot at UN, never having heard anything about it. On hearing there was, they disappeared in the direction of the bar. One said, 'I try to know as little about the secretariat as possible', which was supposed to be witty. Doubtless only reason to invite me was apprehension of another article in print; which they might well indeed apprehend. Gorge rises.

Gorge is not adequate word for what rises over news of the world. Dear Elizabeth, this nightmare of carnage in South East Asia is like blood over all our souls. The terrible helplessness to put a halt to it, the imagination boggling in daily horror – and this government of remorseless inhumans having no idea but to put in more and more US armaments and destroy the last thing that lives. What terrible retribution will come out of this?

[...]

Press here covers such things as Darwin, disaster, v. widely; but so little written about quality of the country, or Australian developments. For instance, excellent piece could now be done by NY Times contrasting Aust. Govt's policy on the arts with calamity situation here, where every cultural enterprise is at the brink of financial collapse & govt spends virtually nothing on arts, & in fact discourages a wide interest in – well, thought. When we have been at Adelaide, Sydney, etc, shall try perhaps to get something into print about this here.

[...]

Elizabeth! MANY THANKS for the Eliz. Bowen trouvailles. (Your own first version was really the noblest of all, but I like having the Bowen one too, & knowing where it comes from.) [...] Jacques Barzun said the other evening – talking about Auden – 'it is very difficult for an artist to be intelligent'. This especially true of poets. For novelists (Patrick, e.g.) easier, though still hard; Elizabeth Bowen managed this wonderfully, at her best. [...]

Best and rarest love to you, dear Elizabeth – from Shirley.

Capri | 23 April 75

My dear Elizabeth –

Just to greet you and send friendship and affection from this island, which is the perfect antidote to the horrors of the world (as I type that, fascists are planting bombs under trains a few miles away, and unemployed are marching in thousands...). This chunk of limestone in the sea is burgeoning with wisteria, Judas trees, iris, lilac, a million varieties of wild flowers, and the invincible <u>ginestra</u> yellow on every slope. I think of what you told us about hillsides in Scotland – 'I felt it almost required some action from me' or words to that effect... There could not be a better place to be, in this awful global moment, than where a multitude of children are happy, healthy, adored and intact. It reminds one that massacres are not universal, as they had begun to seem.

If only we could talk (and not about MM!), if only we could stop at Putney one fine summer morning and take you aboard, then down to the Oast. If only you were here, where we sit by the forno (a huge old fireplace where the bread was made in Capri in the Middle Ages) at a little trattoria in the sooks. I should add here that it's only the evenings that require <u>forno</u> treatment; the days have been glorious, summer. Well, we will do it somehow, somewhere. [...]

With love to you from yr devoted Steegs, dear Elizabeth; and our best greetings always to Margaret – Shirley.

Hunters Hill | 2 May, 1975

My dear Shirley and Francis –

Indeed, if only we could talk! I'm sorry to have been so apparently silent lately [...] But some dear friends nearby have had tragic things happening to two or three people in one house. My part hasn't involved much more than appearing fairly frequently, eating, drinking, talking, being another presence from the outside world. But it takes time.

Yesterday the end of the war in Vietnam. Last night (visiting) I saw television films of the war. I remember the faces, eyes, of individual civilians as the camera closed in. Then a two-hour radio programme came on, going back to the distant beginning. I only listened to part of it. Some of the time I try not to remember we live in a world where so much is – and ever was – truly insane. Or I try not to dwell on it. It startles your mind so much.

Oh, to beautiful things. The exhibition. It's marvellous, of course, and it's a very cheering sign here that more people have gone in in three weeks than in three years. I read that in 1939 there was a fine exhibition, the only one comparable with this, and even the gallery director ridiculed it. Now the crowds are not only going, but appreciating. We have gone in and staggered out, calling for oil paints to be brought at once. We've sat about, musing away, and pored over the catalogue like old children looking at our picture books, pointing out our likes and dislikes. And art books in general have been brought out and swapped about. Telephone calls to and fro about the paintings. Inspiring, it is.

[...]

Patrick is working away as always. He said recently he'd heard from you. We met up at Lawson in the Blue Mountains at Nancy and Pete Phelan's for lunch not long ago. (Nancy writes travel books and is published by Macmillan.) A beautiful day.

[...]

Greetings and best love, dear friends,
Elizabeth

Capri | 16 July 1975

My dear Elizabeth –

In a few days, we leave Capri, having been LUCKY, LUCKY to stay so long; next week at this time will be back in NY, flying home from the chaotic hellhole of Rome airport. Some work done, both; some sanity regained, after punishings of winter in the thick of things. I remember how one's heart was lead with helplessness during fall of Viet Nam, those hideous scenes which were only a tiny suggestion of the reality; and take a huge breath before being plunged back into that state of indignation once more. Here there is so much to remind one how agreeable the earth might be, even with human beings on it. Salutary reminders. We're going back to a bankrupt, decaying NY, where every cultural institution is facing collapse, and the CIA or some other murk-sifter is prying over one's shoulder. Yet the old place has some attraction, obviously, or why would we return? (Do not ask that I analyse that magnetic pull, however...)

[...]

A really rather intimidating situation has been developing in Italy since the regional elections last month, when the Communist Party made very big gains. The Christian Democrats – inert, corrupt, shameless – have made a present on a platter of this poor country, delivered up to extremes. There is also the lack of responsible citizenry, absence of any tradition of civic conscience & collective pressures – Italians have been told what to do for so long, (paying attention only in varying degrees) that it does not occur to them to reverse the process in any democratic form. [...]

The Cairns debacle depresses us, as also the environmental, or anti-environmental, developments in the handling of them – ie, tone and language. If we should not be depressed, you'll tell us. But, for me, important to be <u>as</u> depressed by acts of those we want to prosper, as by same acts by those we want kept out. That said, I myself don't feel partisan for Labour, or any other party anywhere in the world: only partisan for good policies and actions. Given the goon-awful Opposition in Australia, Whitlam has a moral duty to stay in office, I shld think. I don't suppose The Times of London particularly wants to support him, therefore their reporting wld tend to harp on troubles rather than achievements. On the other hand, never seen a word there for Liberals, except for bewhiskered dreadful platitudes once in a while about Menzies. In fact, until Whitlam, Australia virtually unreported in world's press. The wealth tax in Britain seems designed to put a stop to the arts (taxing owners of paintings on their value, increasing tax as value of picture increases etc), while we hear that the taxes on big business in fact have subtle loopholes to allow 'wealth' to burgeon in that sector. Australia – and perhaps Canada – only countries I know of where official policy favours arts. US Govt abominates them, it is from 'arts centres' such as NY that all the exposure and criticism of recent years has come, protest against the war, NYC voted for McGovern etc. Thus the refusal of Washington to bail out NYC in its present bankruptcy, letting tens of thousands join the ranks of unemployed overnight. If we want work, we should join the Philistines.

[...]

Love to you – Saluti! – S.

Hunters Hill | 11 August, 1975

My dear Shirley and Francis –

[...]

Over here we've had our political troubles. [...] When things were so ghastly and suspenseful I began to see how a whole population might develop ulcers or have a nervous breakdown. The left wing of Labor has always supported Cairns, and even now, after his incredible behaviour, they are using his dismissal against Whitlam. There are many real enemies of Labor inside the party machine; they don't want a democratic-socialist government, they want a revolution. [...] I haven't been swayed by a charismatic leader; Whitlam just simply stands against the fanatics of the left and right; he is stable, consistent, brilliant, good-hearted and has commonsense. Brave and witty. Even in these dark days he makes us laugh. If someone tackles so much, accomplishes so much, acts and decides, not everything will be right, or work out as expected, but I don't distrust his motives. There are some very good men in the Cabinet – Hayden, the Treasurer, McClelland, many others. Inflation is so bad, and no-one here in the press is willing to notice that it is world-wide: it's generally agreed that Labor will go out when there's an election in the greatest landslide ever seen. The few papers and television networks are owned by the same two or three men; the tone adopted towards the Government is almost invariably hostile, sometimes vitriolic. So in answer to your question, please do go on being depressed about the Labor Government's chances. The country has wakened up, however, changed. I don't think, couldn't bear to think, it will slide back to the old position...

Margaret is leaving on 13 September for a month in the UK, Edinburgh and London. She'll certainly see vast changes. She left in 1959 and has never been back.

[...]

Is it possible that S and F might be here in 76? Crossing all fingers to help it happen. Would be so nice to see you both again. Many greetings, much love –

Elizabeth

New York | 1 Sept 75

My dear Elizabeth –

You should hear the note of relief and joy with which F says, 'It's from ELIZABETH' when he hands me yr letter(s). A particular contrast in a period where we had been learning to wince at the sight of an Australian stamp, MM being in such a trough, slough, hough. [...] The photographer Stieglitz once said 'Everything is relative except your relatives: they are absolute.'

[...]

Leave this vale of troughs. Must mention right away that as we may pass through London in October, returning here, can we please have Margaret's UK address if there is any chance she might be in Lon. and as late as third week of Oct? BON VOYAGE MARGARET, good works and great pleasures. It is fine to think that, if we can't meet over a chop in SW-1 in Oct, then we can really think of getting together at last in early 1976. It seems ages since we sat in the potted-palm-court of the Ritz and met Elizabeth in a chic suede jacket. I find myself looking back on that as the world of stability – it was actually mayhem – which just shows how much more rife everything can get than one believes is possible. Does the news get out to Aust. that New York City is bankrupt, for instance? Well, we read it each morning in our NYT, then put away the butter and go to our desks, only vaguely wondering when the bailiff will show.

[...]

This week – in pursuance of Lovely Life – we are expecting to dine with Isaiah and Aline Berlin, and I think they are in a few weeks going to Australia. Do you by any chance know them? I thought I might, if you would not mind, give them your name and address – I think he is going out to lecture, shall find out more when I see them. Do you think I might in this case give Patrick's address in a tentative and guarded way (ie saying that he likes to keep to himself)?? Needless to say, not something I would usually do, but I think both you and he would find Isaiah good company and very sympathetic. Perhaps you or P knows him already. He is erudite, amazing memory for his knowledge, most entertaining talker of high velocity but not a mere assertive monologist – he is kind, has charm. Perhaps his contribution (as the saying goes, as if life were a collection taken up in church) has been in teaching – he is at Oxford – rather than his few writings; and also in conversation, really. A tremendous appetite for social life no doubt uses up his powers – yet in the end and perhaps that was what he preferred and could do best, talk, life; hard to say. His wife is charming, from a French banking family, has children from former marriage. If they turn up, I am sure you will like.

[...]

Enclosing a couple of clips. The Jean Rhys needs no comment from any daughter of MM! [...] By the way, do you like Jean Rhys? – I do, immensely, especially WIDE SARGASSO SEA and VOYAGE IN THE DARK. A v. unusual talent, and I don't readily think of another modern writer other than a poet who can transform self-pity into art. Have been reading many things, especially old Greeks who take one's breath away: after them, all literature comes in gasps. (No, not true, there are great inhalations* like Shakespeare; but few.) For my essay (on Style & Criticism, oh heavens) had to expose myself to some modern criticism, against which I've written a tirade. What hatred, what envy, what gross opportunism, what vanity, what obtuseness. Keep thinking of that 'review' of Hurtle Duffield's show of paintings, in The Vivisector. What a marvel Patrick is.

[...] The magazine FORTUNE are doing a big piece on UN, coming to see me this wk; I propose to give them an earful, but it probably won't get into print at length, and what is needed is a massive investigative job – things will have to change a lot before that gets done. Having got itself into this self-destructive 'economy' – of depletion of earth's resources, pollution, overpopulation, a 'prosperity' of more cars, more armaments, etc. – it is almost impossible to see how the world can get itself out and onto some other calmer, saner set of rails without some godawful convulsion. We go on – as Churchill once said in a different context – 'drinking salt water to slake thirst'.

F has just finished Bellow's new novel, 'Humboldt's Gift' & likes it very much. I also like immensely what I've read of it. Funny, wise. I remember you too are an admirer, at least, of Henderson Rain King?

[...] Again our warmest wishes to Margaret, and our eagerness for the results of this adventure. With love to you, dear Elizabeth – from Shirley.
* I think I mean exhalations?

Hunters Hill | 12 September 1975

My dear Shirley,

Many thanks for yesterday's splendid, lovely letter – heart-warming (because true!) things about Whitlam; the Jean Rhys clipping: she even looked like YM in that photograph; best of all, naturally, all the news, conversation. This isn't a proper answer at all, only to say that Margaret leaves here tomorrow. [...] It does seem that you'll just miss each other. Pity! I'd love you to have met there.

[...]

Yes, I do very much like Jean Rhys. No word wasted and great emotional force. A bleak and devastated view, but so good. When I read Quartet again recently I nodded, wishing I knew much less well what that was all about.

That would be splendid if Isaiah Berlin did get in touch with P or me. Quite recently, only a couple of weeks ago, we finished hearing a series of his lectures. Terrific! I envied his young students because they'd have heard more.

I wonder which of the old Greeks you're reading. I used to be deeply addicted...

Recently keep meeting more and more poets – and as far as I can judge, good ones. Bruce Beaver and Geoffrey Lehmann... Must find and send you some. Books!

There is a most most beautiful big sky outside my window, with lit-up pearly clouds...

Elizabeth

Hunters Hill | 21 September 1975

My dear Shirley and Francis –

[...]

I loved hearing from you, dear Francis. Thank you for writing. I thought of you the other day (I often think of you both) when I took Kylie Tennant and Christina Stead to lunch. Somehow or other they had never met. Christina said she had just that day had a letter from her NY agent, who is also your agent, I think, to say she was giving up her work. C is extremely fond of her, and was very sad about it. K and C and I all exceedingly different from each other; they were united anyway in hating <u>Herzog</u>. Ah well... It made me quite nervous to have brought these so-different consciousnesses face to face. [...]

Spoke to YM last night and she is on a better track, deeply pacified by S's 'eight-page letter, and every line of it interesting'. She had the pleasure of chiding me for having refused some desirable invitation to dinner. It is not so often that she can feel other people are doing wrong, and put them right. Or not quite in this way! Wit's Endville... A whole crowd of us – at least S and F, and Andrew and E – may wake up there one morning as in some novel by Marguerite Duras, all brooding about YM.

Yes, some writing is happening. Not very euphonious, quite cement-blockish, but going on anyway.

[...] Meantime, affectionate greetings and love, dear friends from Elizabeth

Hunters Hill | 23 October, 1975

My dear Shirley and Francis –

[...]

Patrick has an early copy of <u>Humboldt's Gift</u> and let me have it as soon as he'd finished. A wonderful wise and funny book. In a way I grudged picking it up and reading it because I didn't want it to be over. (Like a long-awaited letter.) Stayed under cover with it for days and nights. Francis, I agree it's long – though I hadn't expected to think so. It deserves more time and less greed. So much to think about!

Australia. Yes, we're in mid-crisis again. The Opposition (never reconciled to a period out of office) hired consultants to take a public opinion poll: would anyone care if they blocked the Budget? Only about three per cent of the population, they were told. The ALP has a majority in the House of Representatives and is the Government. They (the two parties) had equal numbers in the Senate and there were two Independents – both leaning to the Liberal Party. Since the last election – forced by the Opposition after Labor had been in power for eighteen months – two Labor Senators have gone – one to the High Court and one to his death. Breaking a never-before-broken convention – the NSW and Queensland Liberal Premiers appointed arbitrarily one of their own choice rather than men nominated by the Labor Party. Casual vacancies in the Senate are automatically filled by someone of the same party. With this sort of assistance, they blocked the Budget. Everyone was amazed. Even Liberal supporters were alarmed to see how far the conservatives were prepared to go to take over again. The two Liberal-leaning Independents in the Senate voted <u>with</u> the Government, saying that they had a majority in the House of Reps, had battled nobly, passed many splendid bills, had made mistakes, had a philosophy different from theirs, but were entitled to serve their three-year term. There has been a tremendous public reaction against the Opposition. <u>They</u> are amazed. The Government is united, galvanized. Even the papers, having egged Fraser on, are now afraid of general strikes, and fighting in the streets, and are thinking of exits. Whitlam will never have an election just because the Opposition wants to get rid of him and his Government. Fraser can't back down without terrible loss of face. Meantime, the Government is running out of money for everything – Public Service salaries, pay for the armed forces, pensions, schemes to combat unemployment, students' allowances, building... This is a crisis of the Opposition's making. Everyone, even the hostile press, agreed that Hayden's budget was good, sensible, deserved time to prove itself. It's agreed that Whitlam now has the best men about him that he's ever had. [...] This week-end there will be big rallies. The Labor one comes first and unfortunately it's wild wet weather; everything is sodden... Parliament resumes next Tuesday. Will the Governor-General act? And what can he do? And what is he like?

[...] Love, dear S and F. More letters soon. Love, again
Elizabeth

New York | 30 Oct 75

My dear Elizabeth –
Your splendid letter just arrived. I feel as if coming back from Space, though I hope with more interesting things to report than those related by the astronauts. The big step is the idea that by putting this in the postbox I may actually manage to be in touch with you. [...]
First let me say that, thanks entirely to your intercession, a letter arrived here, just at the moment of our return last weekend. From Geoffrey

Dutton, saying that we are invited for Writers Week and very kindly sending literature etc. This is sobering and awesome, and we think also immensely generous as they must be worried about future at this time of crisis. So, Elizabeth, there we are. She's on, as they say. I feel various tremors and apprehensions, but also excitement and great curiosity. The wonderful part will be seeing dear faces: yours; meeting Margaret; meeting Patrick (to whom I'll send a note, as he had some time ago written, to ask if we were likely to attend). Doing – oh... oh... oh... doing whatever we can for MM. Surely giving her some diversions & something to look forward to? Oh I hope so.

[...]

Elizabeth, the chaos that fell on us, tooth and claw, when we put our foot off that beloved island does give us paws. To sketch in a few essentials – we left Capri in violent storm, after weeks of such Sept-Oct beauty as you never saw! We swam in mid-Oct just before storm broke, marvellous. Arrived in Naples to spend the night before taking train to Rome. Shoot-out at side of hotel, just around the corner in Via Santa Lucia. Battle between contraband-bands of drug & cigarette smugglers. Street of 1890s buildings, each palazzo closing its big portone doors as fast as possible while desperate pedestrians sought to be admitted, in flight from hail of bullets. (No danger to us, just saw and heard.) Hotel informed us that train might not leave on morrow as all trains suspended between Naples and Rome because of bomb threat on line. Did leave, however. Uncheerful feeling of being first to try out minefield. Arriving Rome, no message at hotel from Muriel S, to whom I'd written and telegraphed asking her to dine that evening. Tried to telephone. Operator asked, What number are you trying? Oh yes. Don't you read the papers? The Rome telephone exchange was blown up and set fire to two weeks ago, and that whole area of Rome without telephone. [...]

Arrived Rome airport (a hellhole at best of times) to find Air France on strike from that moment. Waited five hours, managed to get ourselves on Alitalia flight. Arrived Paris, Shirl's luggage missing. All Shirl had was, what she stood up in. The proverbial toothbrush was absent. Took taxi to Grand Palais straight from airport – cab driver said, 'Mais les musées sont en grève.' At this point Francis said, I feel your mother is along on this trip.

No. Musée en grève day before, now re-opened. Found Villon would be open until 8:00 pm, so went to hotel where there was, for me at least, no necessity to unpack. Returned to Villon show for evening. Spent next day at

Villon show and in other such nice places. [...] Paris desperate but of course many beauties still. Two years since we were there, and flabbergasted to see the buildings are already well on the way to getting grey again. Happy to have seen them pale gold (not to speak of buttercup yellow against a great snowfall one winter).

Two nights in Paris. Luggage found morning of departure. [...] Within sight of Orly, perhaps three-quarters of mile, all traffic ground to halt. Cab-driver tells us, Air France strikers blocking road to airport. Hundreds of taxis and cars completely stuck. Thereupon, desperate scene of car doors being flung open and frantic passengers getting out and trying to drag their heavy luggage along the grass at side of road, the rest of the way. Dreadful. Fellini. One man's face I'll never forget. God knows what was to befall him if he did not catch his dreadful plane.

[...]

London distressing. Beautiful days, trees, porticoes. Dear London friends. But tattiness overtaking the place, cheapening of everything, loss of style. Also, everyone is worried of course, and beyond the worry there is the strain of the unspeakable violence that can afflict anyone anywhere. Moments of sadness.

[...]

Returned of course to nightmare crisis of NY. Unspeakable. [...] Yesterday Ford spoke to the nation abt the Cities of the Plain – the iniquities of NYC, & how we should be punished for them. No help, let them kiss the rod, good for them. Now of course the city has been pawn of mass corruption and graft from all sides – banks, corporations, unions, the Mafia. And it is odd to find oneself on its side. But the idea of letting ten million people in America sink, and the only really interesting place in America (don't quote me!) go down the drain out of low political malice makes the collective gorge rise. I dare say some kind of last-minute support will be provided, in a back-handed way that won't lead to any real reforms and will come down hard on ordinary citizens & leave the grafters untouched. But the hatred of the wowsers for the place where the ideas (and the exposure) come from is quite a spectacle.

I don't want to be in town the day that a million welfare cheques don't arrive in the monthly mails... Bearing in mind that most of the unemployed are Negroes, and pretty fed up anyway before all this began.

Must thank you for your terrific clippings, all of which will be read with care. Some quite good reporting in the UK papers abt horrific dealings of Opposition in Aust. I don't see why anyone should ever vote Liberal again after this – though I can't say I saw before, either. Please tell us what will happen. What a frightful situation – I suppose it is better than NYC because the blockage of money is technical, whereas NY has in fact piled up staggering debts in the billions which can never be paid. NYC has more unemployed than all Australia, & as many as all England. [...]

Among good things, of which – yes – there are still many – have been re-reading George Eliot, that is to say Daniel Deronda and Felix Holt, which I had not read for years. I remembered, who doesn't, that Dan. D. 'goes down' in second half of book, and began it with some trepidation as not wishing any disappointment from author of magnif. Middlemarch & A. Bede. At page 508 I said to Francis, 'Well I know it goes down after this, but as I'm at p. 508 and every word so far being marvellous, I don't see how I can lose.' TERRIFIC. The psychological mastery of the scenes between the two (as I think of them) main and real characters of the book, Grandcourt and Gwendolen, made one say things out loud, This is wonderful, and so on. There is something so natural in her brilliance, an authority that is never heavy when she is really managing what she wants to do. A wholeness; so that even the keenest perception comes with stature rather than with a narrowing of the eyes.

[...]

Dear Elizabeth, you will be fatigued by turning these pages. Bless you, thank you. Tremendous appreciation for interceding with G Dutton (shall write to him today). Love to you from your devoted F and Shirley.

Hunters Hill | 17 November 1975

My dear Shirley and Francis –

I loved hearing your voices this morning. That call cheered me greatly, in spite of its being impossible to say much. [...] There is always so much to say: this time with Festival and Kerr's coup, there is so much more.

On the Sunday before YM's birthday, I rang Christina Stead in Canberra and said I could go down for a few days. She had asked me several times. Trained off for Canberra early Monday morn. Chris lives with relatives (kind but not congenial) in Sydney, and has for the moment escaped to the house of a friend absent in Melbourne. Canberra a change from Sydney for me, too – sweet-smelling and spread out in a great shallow saucer surrounded by hills, and the circle of hills under a circle of purely decorative flat-bottomed clouds. Lovely. I had a passion to go to Parliament House, thinking – as everyone did – that this week the Opposition would crumble and pass the Budget. A few Liberal senators were beginning to feel bad about it and only needed an excuse to cross the floor and vote with the government. And the public opinion polls were turning in Whitlam's favour and against Fraser.

On Tuesday (November 11) two women, wives of profs, came to take us for a picnic on the Murrumbidgee. One knew someone close to Whitlam and was going to ring to see that I could get in without trouble to the Visitors' Gallery. Picnic very gay and lively. Lots of optimistic political talk. Home again with arrangements for Parliament the next day. Telephone rings. I hear Christina saying many times, 'But that's terrible. That's terrible.' Finally she came in. 'What's happened?' 'Malcolm Fraser is Prime Minister. Kerr has got rid of Whitlam.' Horror. Horror and stupefaction. People very nearly fell down in the street with amazement and dismay. Manning Clark (our most splendid historian) said he was literally sick. Switched on radio which was dooming away in stunned voice. Chris offered gin, brandy, sherry, while I paced about holding head and listening to reports. Finally knocked off some Nescafe and took taxi to Parliament House. People surged there from everywhere. It was so AWFUL. Everyone was outraged. Our votes meant nothing. Moderate reform is not allowed to take place here. The new leaders came out on the balcony and laughed like Nazis. Then our deposed mates came outside to the front steps where we all were, to talk to the crowd, and were hugely cheered. Whitlam came out and it was a relief to see him still alive and valiant in the face of all this. To say that Kerr and Fraser have welded the Labor Party together is an understatement.

Telephone calls to and from Sydney where my mates were running temperatures, marching in the city, collecting money for the campaign, signing protests, sending telegrams, talking of Chile and Greece and the death of democracy.

On Wednesday I went again to Parliament House. A great rally in the space opposite the House, the police out in force. They don't understand.

It's good feeling that brings these people together. People only clapped and cheered and called 'Shame!' from time to time. Police moved the crowd from around the steps and doors of PH and directed us across two roads running in front of the building. Whitlam and most of the Cabinet spoke from the back of a truck. The sun blazed down. People handed up ten and twenty dollar notes to Whitlam, who put them in his shirt pocket. I met Manning Clark. We all got sunburned. Labor staff went round handing out little squares of paper, hastily roneoed, to pin on fronts, saying LABOR WILL WIN.

No transport. Had to walk miles. Got blisters on soles of feet. Left for Sydney Thursday night. From station to Craig McGregor's (he's a young writer, very pleasant) to sign protest for full-page advt in The Australian. (It will show, as well as signatures, Labor's majority figures in both House of Representatives and the Senate on a ballot slip torn in two.) Home at 2 a.m. To Head Office next day with Chris's cheque.

Heard on Sunday from one of our Canberra-picnic friends. She was in Sydney briefly. Had heard of very black dealings in the planning of this coup. She had had the Berlins, or one of them to dinner on the night of Nov. 11 and some Treasury officials. (Incidentally, the Berlins, according to Clare, have just gone back to Britain. I was sorry we didn't hear from them. They were no doubt highly organized, as you will be. I enjoyed hearing a number of IB's lectures on radio, and tried to write down some of his many wise words, and witty. Patrick has a long-standing theory that people never use letters of introduction.)

Ah well. Labor made some mistakes, and they admit it. They reached office after 23 years, at the beginning of the world recession. They tried to make up for years of conservatism, dead hands, dead thoughts, inequality and no spending on welfare, cities, transport, women, arts, aborigines. They tried to redistribute wealth. Pensioners used to be hungry, had to struggle to get 50 cents extra once in six years. (Andrew says his organization doesn't now have to spend on supplementary food and vitamin injections since Labor came in.) Education was for the rich. Health for the rich. Australians had to tug the forelock and continue in their old colonial role, saying Yes, sir! to the British and then the Americans, with no independent thoughts about foreign policy. The Vietnam War was something the Liberals had to toady their way into...

The other night when the ABC (radio) finished transmission for the night and played as they do now, Advance, Australia, Fair, instead of God Save the Queen, it symbolised all the great good changes of these three years. I am personally, because of fixed income, quite a lot poorer, and I wasn't – heaven knows! – rich before. But we've had a government full of friends, real human beings.

The extreme Left will take advantage of all this, of course. There are red flags at rallies, and placards calling unhelpfully for a General Strike. They would like violence. So far the sensible crowds have heeded the exhortations from Whitlam, Cabinet and Hawke to stay angry (till Dec. 13) but to stay calm.

What a harangue! I hope you took some refreshment half-way though. Tomorrow night Patrick and Manoly are coming for dinner. I must shop for food.

YM has a sore hand, from having fallen on Melbourne Cup Day, returning to the TAB agency (where bets are placed) to collect winnings. It is getting better slowly, but poor hand did look abused. She has to plunge it from hot to cold water several times a day. I felt sorry for it. She did see the doctor, so it is under someone's eye. There has been quite a lot of social life, and spirits are definitely better. Prospect of S and F visiting no doubt helps a lot, too. She is being best self again. And no self can be more endearing.

Thank you for your letters, thoughts, pictures left in my mind permanently (Paris in snow, Fellini men desperate for plane), and above all for not only being there, but being.

Best love, Elizabeth

Hunters Hill | 30 November, 1975

My dear Shirley and Francis –

I hope you aren't wading knee-deep in the paper clippings I've sent over. But, O!, we're in a fever. What days, what days.

[...]

On Friday Helene and I went to a lunch-time rally – Arts for Labor – at the old Capitol Theatre down in Campbell Street near Central Station. Patrick was to speak there. Everything is arranged in haste and there is so much happening and advertising costs so much that getting the news from here to there has often depended largely on word-of-mouth. Only four people there when I arrived. Horror and dismay. Would it be a fiasco? Oh, Whitlam was speaking too. Did enough people know? Conversations on the footpath with a communist, a midnight cowboy, and an ex-RAAF man. Radical newspapers arrive. We don't buy them. I'm looking for a new newspaper put together to show Labor's view, written by chief journalists from the SMH and the Australian etc. People gather gradually. Helene arrives, and another girl. Patrick arrives and we claim him. No-one else seemed to be there to take him off anywhere. He has been having teeth out but was going to speak anyway. An organizer comes to give us a pep-talk. We tell him we're on his side. But anyway we all surge down to the front row when the doors opened, leaving Patrick to be claimed by the theatre-man who was organizing the day. The theatre was only a third full. We suffer. Then suddenly it's full. Patrick, Lloyd Rees (dear, aged painter), Jackie Weaver (pretty young actress), John Bell (serious actor who, like JW, turned down Royal Shakespeare contracts to stay here and work) all came down from back of theatre and up steps in middle of stage. Cheers and applause. Patrick is asked to speak. Cheers and standing ovation. He says many true things (clipping on way to Steegs). Uproar at the back. Whitlam has flown in from Melbourne and arriving at theatre. More standing ovations, and hand-shakings on stage. Ken Horler (organizer of rally from Nimrod Theatre) says: 'Two super-stars...' Patrick finishes speech, all of which highly approved by audience. Whitlam then speaks. I wish you had been there. It was a noble speech and noble because he means what he says and appeals to the very best in people. At 1pm, after great cheers, he left for an ABC programme at 1.15. Everyone else then spoke – and no-one from self-interest, in spite of the great assistance given by Labor to the arts, rescuing arts from a portfolio including aborigines and the environment, Whitlam taking the arts portfolio himself, and enacting more legislation in that area in three years than in the previous 72. After the suffering and worrying about the size of the crowd, we floated out so stimulated and happy. Oh, Mrs Whitlam spoke, too, and said she was glad Patrick White had mentioned (I don't know exactly) the role of women in all this. Met Frank Hardy (do you know his name?) in the foyer afterwards with a new thing for us to sign. Patrick went off home. (He left another rally earlier in the week, wearing a button that said: RIGHT THE

WRONG – REINSTATE GOUGH. He said you'd have thought he'd brought revolution into the bus, the way people stared.) Helene and I went downtown to have coffee and a sandwich. Also wearing buttons. (Yes. A once inconceivable happening.) [...] Helene had a LABOR CARES FOR PEOPLE button and mine was a SHAME, FRASER, SHAME one.

(The cicadas are incredibly noisy this year as if they know something is UP.)

So we come home to spread the news to our anxious friends that the day had been a huge success. On Wednesday night there was a meeting locally addressed by an ex-Minister, and on Monday 24 we were getting sunburned at the opening campaign rally in the Domain. The crowd covered eight acres and was totally good-natured. At night the campaign was opened in Melbourne, too, in Festival Hall. Whitlam and his wife, and the small team now allowed him, flew 15,000 miles last week.

On Sunday night (I'll stop any minute, I promise), Ferdi and Margaret and I went to a People for Whitlam dinner at the beauteous house of Harry Seidler (architect who built here the Australia Square complex and who is responsible for our vast new embassy buildings in Paris – still in process of going up). The subscriptions all went to ALP funds, all champagne and food donated.

Liberals were picketing this bushy street in Killara and calling out nasty words. There were about 150 or 200 people there, and a thoroughly enchanted evening we spent. The house is in a sort of gulf of trees, and there was – on the gulf side of the house – much glass, open terraces, and that was a pleasure in itself, but as dear Ferdi said: 'Just to think! We've got something in common with everyone in this house!' (Apart from arms and legs etc.) Really, at times like this, to feel yourself in the company of people who care about what's happening as much as do yourself is a great solace and source of happiness. The Whitlams came and stayed for a long time, enjoying it, too, after such a pace. We have worried about the fantastic strain of so much work, so much travelling, such pressure from all sides, but we stopped worrying that night.

Next week, from tomorrow, meetings of one sort or another every day or night. We have been sunburned, blistered, very nearly made bankrupt, for Labor, have caught chills and lost voice standing in the rain.

People say (the other side says), 'How can it not be democratic to have an election?' One answer is that if a Government can be overthrown, dismissed, when it goes through a period of unpopularity in the course of a three-year term, no Government is safe or stable and no Government will dare to enact sometimes necessary but unpopular legislation.

[...]

Liberals instantly wanted to appoint someone to watch and monitor all ABC political broadcasting. A censor. That was quashed for the moment. They are making jeering remarks about the Government having bought Blue Poles, and are promising to destroy Labor legislation concerning the National Gallery in Canberra. Their budget, as Whitlam said on Friday, is directed at businessmen and businessmen only. Fraser was a super-hawk in Vietnam days and got rid of Prime Minister Gorton who was not so warlike. They now cry 'Communist!' all the time, and you feel you are back decades in the fifties. Awful. But Margaret has a dear landlady, a kind woman, who is terrified of Labor and believes the worst they can tell her.

You will be the best-informed politically of all the Adelaide visitors.

[...]

Love, dear friends, from your overwrought

Elizabeth

14 Dec 75 | TELEGRAM

COURAGE DEAR ELIZABETH AGHAST ELECTION AND MOTHER IMMENSE GRATITUDE TELEPHONING CHIMES LOVE STEEGMULLER.

New York | 17 Dec 75

Dearest Elizabeth –

Your health, first, foremost & above all. [...] PLEASE PLEASE LOOK AFTER YOURSELF, even if it means letting us all go to hell. [...] Please, please; we are much concerned.

[...]

To election – ie life itself. How can you want to hear more, as it will all be what you know and all right-thinking bods have said and felt? Well, it is a theme for another letter. We were immeasurably shocked by landslide, beyond everything else. It vividly recalled Nixon's 1972 landslide (which was in fact worse – only one state out of the 50 in the USA voted for McGovern: Massachusetts; and only one city: NYC); by which I mean, a deliberate, self-destructive selection by a population of the group that will bring out the worst in them. A conscious rejection of civilising influence and humane considerations. Something that has been v hard for me to realise, brought home to me by Viet Nam, is the colossal <u>indifference</u> of people generally to evil. I do not want to suggest that other eras were better in this way, but I do think there is something in the mass society, over-population, aggressive materialism, masturbatory advertising, saturation of people's responses with irrelevant urgings and information, that has used up the general capacity for ordinary human instincts and good intuitions. I used to think, if you could bring the truth home to people, they would mostly care. I'm afraid I don't think that any longer. The truth of Viet Nam was brought home day after day, year after year, to Americans, and they <u>did not care</u>. They don't care now, either, and have simply expunged it from their minds. Some of this seems to be in the Fraser–Whitlam result.

[...]

Elizabeth, so much more to say, as ever. [...] No one more deserves a great and good 1976 than does EH, and no one wishes it more for her than her loving Shirley & Francis.

PART TWO
1976–1984

Spirits dipped as politics took a conservative turn with the election of Malcolm Fraser in Australia, Margaret Thatcher in the UK and Ronald Reagan in the US. Harrower was relieved by the return of Labor in 1983 under Prime Minister Bob Hawke. An intense two decades of concern about Kit Hazzard reached a climax, and the relationship between the correspondents shifted again in 1984 after Hazzard delivered the Boyer lectures in Sydney and Harrower made an ill-fated visit to Italy. Friends such as Christina Stead and Lilian Hellman were dying, and their own illnesses and accidents gave glimpses of mortality.

Sydney | 9 January, 1976

Dearest Shirley and Francis –

Your call on New Year's Day gave 76 such a happy start. I was thrilled. It was (practically) uncanny, because there I was with some paper and a pen, wondering at the very moment the phone rang about what sort of dinner or gathering I might conjure up to welcome S and F. Fun! Of course, there is such delay with mail deliveries over holidays, that I was responding to news of horrible letters from YM at a time when much better ones had been received. I was happy to hear.

Your so-kind letter came just two days ago, Francis. Thank you both for all your concern about my health. That frightfully sore throat and wheeze in chest descended on November 16 in one minute. A few days later – no voice. Then I started on the first of five courses of antibiotics. In a very unintelligent way, I put the fever and sickness down to rushing about in the rain and heatwaves. I think now that I was lucky not to have pneumonia. [...] I had begun to grieve about the books I haven't written. It's certainly true that the election was bad for the health of the 43 per cent. (Parliament opens again on February 17 for two months.)

[...]

To move on to more celebratory things... I suggested dinner here at my place to Patrick to meet you. Yes, to that. So perhaps that might be an early (in your arrival) date? I think Patrick would ask you to dinner at his place, after that, to meet a few people who wouldn't be going to Adelaide. (Patrick's dinners are almost always for no more than eight.) He is a marvellous cook and gives his dinners a lot of concentration. That's why (apart from all the other reasons) meeting here first gives people a chance to talk without thinking about the responsibility of it all. Also, if it can be managed, I'd like it very much if you could come one night, a small party, and I could ask: Andrew, Yolanda, (Prof.) Ron Geering and his wife (he wrote Recent Fiction, you'll remember), Nancy Phelan (writes, knows Alan, charming traveller), Kylie, poets Geoffrey Lehmann, David Malouf, Rodney Hall, Bruce Beaver, Nancy (Keesing) Hertzberg and Mark Hertzberg – Nancy is a poet and chair of the Literature Board of the Australia Council – of course Margaret and YM. Perhaps twenty, twenty-five. I wonder if there's anyone in particular that I know that you'd like to meet? Anyway, I think it could be very enjoyable. Patrick might want to ask you both alone by day just to have a proper look at the paintings. It's not easy to disappear in mid-dinner-party to go through the house and look properly. Also, obviously, the light is better by day.

Don't say I haven't given you something to think about!... Judah Waten lives in Melbourne, but he's almost certain to go to the Festival. Alice Waten will be playing in the Australian Chamber Orchestra at the Festival. Judah's a very good friend. The only person that neither Patrick nor I would urge you to meet is Professor Leonie Kramer, Aust. Lit., Sydney University. She has all the bone-deep dislike of art of the dedicated right-winger, is positively damaging to (living) Australian writers. [...] Now that Fraser is in, there is talk that she may be appointed Chairman of the ABC. Horror! Patrick and Christina Stead call her Goneril. Ah well. It's easy enough for us all never to meet.

Oh, Patrick would just ask you, but I would ask YM, too, don't you think? What do you think? I don't quite know... Greetings and much love –

Elizabeth

PS. Seeing Kit in town tomorrow morning.

New York | Jan 17 76

My dear Elizabeth –

Elizabeth, what a splendid story, intensely enjoyed by your admiring Shirl. Did you then understand everything from childhood, as you give the impression of having done? – one always felt you did, but here is the evidence, as these things could not have been remembered with such perfection of placing-and-timing had they not been deeply comprehended then and there, surely. Could not help feeling, lucky grandmothers, to have a gd-daughter like this. Many of the notes perfectly touched also struck chords... It is strange how these 'elders' seem to their intimates-and-victims something other than human, I suppose they know they have special power over us and are not in the range of ordinary human relations. You will imagine what was felt here at some passages – 'I don't count as old' ... BRAVA! More please.

[...]

We will LOVE to come to dinner, and, if it is not awful for you to bother with party, wld love that too. Immensely look forward to meeting Patrick and Margaret our pen-pal. Elizabeth, you are a saint to suggest having MM that night of your dinner. Of course we all know that it would be simpler to meet Patrick without MM; yet, if our meetings with him are to take place in MM-lessness, as they should, it seems it would just be inviting disaster to leave her alone right after our arrival for such a glorious first occasion. At least he will recognise his material, if she comes and sits looking excluded. [...]

Had a v. nice letter from Patrick – how good it will be to earn the right to call him Patrick by becoming friends, as we hope. He told us his teeth had been pulled in conjunction with the depression of the election result, poor man. Great news however is that he has finished his book and – my God – is beginning another. Shall write him.

Much more to say, but how nice that it can soon actually <u>be said</u>. [...] – Shirley
PS: 21 Jan

Various things since closing above. Now confirmed that Shirl is to do a 'Letter from Australia' for The New Yorker. This means I'll v. probably need a few more days at the end of the stay, and definitely scrapping our round-the-world tour, as we'll come back here to see it through galleys etc. Now, Elizabeth, you know how I'll hope to bring through all our feelings abt past and present – particularly as the piece will be in large measure dealing with 'the arts'. There'll of course be some stuff abt govt in it. <u>Can</u> I ask that you put aside, for our arrival, anything you see in the press that particularly suggests the overall outlook of the Fraser govt? (esp. direct quotes of revelatory kind). Not a great many, as my brain will become befuddled, but just yr usual masterly selection. Also, do you think I would be able to see Whitlam for an hour? Does he live in Sydney at all, or always in Canberra? (Shall have to try to see Fraser – these bods usually do spare time for press, espec. foreign press. All this aspect somewhat burdensome to SH but necessary.) Shall be writing Festival people to tell them this, and to ask if I can have some minutes at least alone with Dunstan...

[...]

Love to you – Shirley

Hunters Hill | 2 February 1976

My dear Shirley and Francis,

Any minute it will be too late to write to you! Think of that!
It was good to have some dates, and such interesting news of all kinds...
Thank you.

[...]

I'm glad you liked the grandmothers. Thank you for saying so. Francis,
you made me laugh at the picture of your being lectured about your good
fortune in having a mother. The things people do to children!

[...]

Shirley, very pleased to hear about the Letter from Australia. [...] I
have for you a quite stunning speech about the arts – Whitlam's PLR
[Public Lending Rights] speech in September to the Society of Authors
in Melbourne. We all reacted in the same way – first, wonder and delight
that such speeches should be made at all, this then taken to further heights
when fully realized speech by Prime Minister, terrible sadness then when
the loss remembered. It's full of facts, figures, feeling. Might be very useful.
Nancy wrote to me about it: SIC TRANSIT GLORIA MUNDI. And
she usedn't to like him! It's a tragedy to us. Told Patrick about your wish to
meet for New Yorker. He'll make inquiries.

[...]

Much love –
Elizabeth

New York | 18 Feb 76

Dearest Elizabeth –

Just received your ever good and helpful prose, and am rushing
this into the post thinking it just might precede us. We fly this Saturday
morning. So good to hear your voice on the blower and <u>so good</u> to be
thinking of seeing you. If it were not for you I don't think we'd have the
courage to come. The MM letters, and huge emanations of seethings and
resentments – massing for the onslaught – are frightful. I know these
patterns have been evident always, but in this particular context, where she
seems positively enraged against us by the fact of our coming, I wonder if
it portends some new phase of decline. I have developed weird sensations

in my side – perhaps sympathetic gallstones thinking of how F developed same at previous Adelaide Festival season – have seen doctor but am to see on return if still persisting. F thinks it is all MM, as well it might be. [...] She has really downed me this time.

[...]

So many thanks, dear Elizabeth, for news abt Whitlam appointment possibility. I'm glad he comes to Sydney, so much better to see him out of govt atmosphere. Already have appt with Dunstan in Adelaide. To my relief, Andrew Porter, music critic for The New Yorker, is covering the music at the Festival itself – I was dreading having to pretend competence for that.

[...]

Love to you, au revoir – Shirley.

Hunters Hill | 25 March, 1976

Dearest Shirley and Francis –

Thank you for ringing from the airport. I'm so glad you did. In town all day from nine till six (most unusually with M, who had taken three days hol suddenly and wanted me to shop etc. with her), I did some silent grieving about the departure of S and F and thought of ringing you at the Town House but didn't want to rouse you if you were trying to sleep. However, we did speak and that was so nice.

Last night with all these regrets about your imminent flight, I didn't even remember to thank you for our Tuesday at La Causerie, but thank you now. It was a happy time. It seems to me that all the times were – delighting, and often euphoric. All the more so perhaps because, as you said at Patrick's, 'we've been through so much together'.

[...]

Today the property agent told me that Mr Pope has accepted his notice and will be gone from 5 Stanley Avenue, Mosman, by the end of April at the latest. So the die is cast, alas and alas, and I'll have to take a thousand uncongenial decisions. Property, money, auctions, painters... Having had my own place for years with people coming or going for days or nights but not staying indefinitely, I don't know how it will work out. It's temporary, however, and M and I say we'll just camp there and enjoy it till the business part is organized. We'll ask people over. I intend to work, write, whatever else.

You'll be able to tell Sumner L-E that you arrived in Sydney for the Big Wet – and now that you've gone The Wet has returned. It looks like Scotland outside my window. Judah says maligned Melbourne has had weeks and weeks of sun. He said he looked out for you in Adelaide but was told Francis was ill. He didn't stay the full time.

Thank you again for everything. All sorts of wishes and remembrances from M and many others. Best love,

Elizabeth

New York | 2 April 76

Dearest Mate from Old Sydney Town –

I was so happy to get your letter on coming in just now. Happy, and chagrined because have been wanting each day to write a few necessarily inadequate words abt the joy and friendship you generated for us out there. [...] As F & I have gone over 'high points', they keep coming round to an Eliz-connection. Have had no happier evening than that of the shrimps at yr hallowed board; and the unforgettable rort of two nights later... and so on, and on: high points. (As to low points – well... yet even they are absorbed into the adventure, at least in retro.) Adventure it certainly was. I am looking forward to reading my own article, (scarcely begun!), to see what the main features and content are, memory is such a world of action and event. Here, we feel v smug, as we <u>know</u> and they <u>do not</u>.

We miss you. We miss Margaret, and Patrick and Manoly. [...] Greatly warmed to <u>Prince</u> Andrew.

Felt I would have known, though not dared accost, Margaret had we nearly passed one another at DJ's. Her wisdom emanates. Among the high points, Margaret's novels.

Say the word when we should address our teleces to Stanley Av. Climbing Awaba St in car, I pointed out Stanley to F. What a pleasant place to have a house. Balmoral turned out, for me, the most poignant and pleasant of all places of return. Earliest memories of swimming there, also growing up there, school there. (Place always good, even if not all memories good). This time glimpsed house (textured brick – what a PW expression – three storeys, pretty garden) where lived till age nine or so, corner of Stanton Rd & Glencarron Ave: comfy inside, beautiful view of heads. F and I got out of car and walked around under Moreton Bays at cove beyond Balmoral Baths, where my dad kept first (beautiful, baleful) yacht. Lovely Cove, Beach has kept its humanity.

[...]

Many thanks for SMH article – I must have wildly exaggerated idea of appearance, as all photos look hideously unfair to me. Have yr excellent info here safe, & shall return in due course – how can I ever thank you for the clippings you amassed, and infinite insight? V. sorry not to have met Judah W at Adelaide. Very glad to have met all nice people we did meet – Malouf, Lehmanns, all. And Christina, unforgettable. I will be sending her a poem of Melville we mentioned, so perhaps can address her c/o you?

With fond love, from the heart, Shirley

5 Stanley Avenue Mosman, NSW 2088 | 10 June, 1976

Dearest Shirley,

A brief note from the area known to real estate agents as 'Balmoral Slopes'. The famous move was strenuous but the memory of it recedes as the place is brought into order, with useful men in white overalls rushing around doing good. Autumn has been very beautiful and every day the brilliance of the sea and sky surprises me. I wake up and see the sun rise without having to get up. It is intimidatingly a sunrise.

Today is the day Valerie leaves Australia. We have seen her a few times – or twice? Can't remember. It's impossible not to feel sorry for Kit just now. I don't know how it will all go. [...] Andrew said she was on a self-destructive course and probably no-one could remove her from it, though she could take people with her on it. I know all this. I suppose, seeing her, I only think sometimes you could be AWFUL but lucky. I know some FRIGHTFUL depressives who have had personal slaves, virtually, dancing around them for life. It's never made them happy. And it has greatly bent the life of the slave, and the other anxious characters hypnotised into hovering round All Hail-ing. [...]

Margaret heard a recording of your talk at the Adelaide Festival and reported that it was so good. M agreed with everything you said, and knew

I would have too. The others were (evidently) rather grim listening. Did you hear Morris West? Were you all there together, speaking and listening?

[...]

M and I are rattling round in this biggish house. It looks so different from the way it was when my mother lived here. Neglected, poor thing. I feel I should have it painted inside and out before offering it for sale. It should be at least very clean. Others tell me people would buy it for the position and if unpainted would think they were getting a bargain. However I have no wish to sell it off as a bargain, real or imagined. Painters have walked through and given quotes. It would be about $2200 to have the painting done. As things go, this doesn't seem extraordinary. I miss my Hunter's Hill flat, where I could find every last teaspoon in the dark, supposing I'd wanted to. Here, I wake up at night and go crashing through the undergrowth to find the telephone ringing in another room. (Having walked into walls and doors in the dark, now remember to move the telephone at night to bedside.) [...]

The Fraser Government continues to dismantle every piece of Labor legislation. You can count on nothing but grim times ahead. The whole of life has changed again. [...]

I took Christina to lunch at La Causerie the other week and told her of our lunch there. She has gone to Newcastle as Writer in Residence. Not all that congenial to her, I think, but it provides congenial company possibly. – Must go now and say encouraging words to Alan, who is fixing eaves, windows, doors etc. Trust all is very well, especially Shirley and Francis. Much love –

Elizabeth

Capri | 26 June 76

Dearest Elizabeth –

[...]

Finished 'Australia' – perhaps I already told you this? – but have not yet heard abt it from The New Yorker; hope they will not want any cuts (it got long, and they have space difficulties). You will see how much is owed to Elizabeth, Eliz-docs, Eliz-chums, & the atmosphere of Eliz's Australia. In which regard, let me say that Graham Greene is here for his usual brief spring stay (he has a pretty little house in Anacapri) with his friend Yvonne – in v. good form, we have had nice times. He asked if we had seen Patrick while in Aust., and we poured out our recital of joys with PW. Graham (who also has, especially when younger, avoided celebrity antics, interviews, etc. like the plague, and who lives – though indubitably a man of great wealth – a 'normal', simple life, takes buses, etc.) then asked, 'Where does PW live?' Answer: 'In Sydney overlooking nice park, etc.' 'Yes, but how does he live?' 'Quite modestly, nice house, not large, books, pictures, nice friend.' 'I suppose – service, and all that?' 'No, does his own housework' 'What, really?' 'Yes, the vacuuming, washing, cooking, the lot. No help.' Graham vaguely disappointed, outdone in the race to the simple life. I thought, rather nice this sense of rivalry in who could be less carried away by fame.

Election here has taken up most of the week, with post-mortems, etc. Nothing good could possibly have come out of those elections, nor did it. The only improvement was the loss of ground by the Fascist parties – and heaven knows there are enough fascists in the Demo Christian party to represent them anyway... The impasse is sickening – any resolution of it by a mandate for the Communists would have been pretty sickening too. We are back where we were, except that one never is: everything is intensified, and the real danger – in the face of almost total negligence from govt – is that lawlessness and outbreaks of violence from extreme factions of all kinds will become daily life. Shades of Beirut! The poverty and hopelessness of cities like Naples has to be seen to be believed, and cannot surely be kept in abeyance forever.

Meanwhile – bella Italia! How beautiful it is still, and how humanly delightful in many many ways. Great heat this past few days, Mediterranean glory. We are brown, and happy to be alive & here. A Mozartian sensation. Yes, wasn't the Magic Flute lovely? – we urged MM to see it, but no response. Thank Margaret for kind words about Adelaide panel – it was one I filled in on at last mo, with raging fever. Rodney Hall and Wole Soyinka were excellent – Morris West was... well, Margaret heard it. Now Australia is in the works, shall send a poem (not mine!) to Christina. I think of her with much wishing we could meet again. Wish most of all we could drop in at 5 Stan Ave.

Love, dear E, from Shirley.

Mosman | 12 July 1976

Dearest Shirley and Francis,

Twas so nice to have your letters and cards. Yes, as so often, our post was crossing in mid-air for a while. Australia is having her first national strike today. Margaret (for one) is on strike. Even Fraser's car-driver is on strike. Good!

[...]

Francis, yes, the house is vast if you are the one who has to wash its face. All the space is nice in a way, but the position is marvellous without qualification – all that blue, the birds, clouds, moon-on-water, sunrises, tiny curved deserted beach with little sailing boats at anchor all week. It's a constant surprise. Seeing it when I'm alone, I envy myself and want everyone else to see it too.

[...]

Judah Waten was here the other day. He's a splendid friend as well as a good writer. Evidently at Adelaide Morris West asked why he bothered to stay in Australia and use backgrounds that interested no-one (out in the great world) and made him no money.

Stacks of friends and acquaintances are lying about suffering from a v. bad flu. A virus. It has killed numerous quite young people. So let's all remember if it comes round to take it seriously.

[...]

Take care... Much love, Elizabeth

Capri | 5 Aug 76

Dearest Elizabeth –

Your so welcome telex, just received, was nearly three weeks en route – Australia is the worst served by these appalling Ital. mails, desperate-making. [...]

The thing about Morris West is, he is so outright, blatant, flagrant, undeflected from course. He is abt the only Australian novelist known in the USA – better known than Patrick, needless to say. Had hoped to correct this with my immortal, or mortal, Aust. essay by introducing a few other names... I wrote to the editor of The New Yorker last week, begging him to send me proofs so at least I could correct meantime. I had a story in the mag. recently, of which they sent me a copy – but no news of Aust.

[...] Love to you, love to Margaret. Love to Balmoral, and to the Moreton Bay fig tree at the shore of the little yacht basin near the baths – tree remembered from my earliest toddling days. Your Shirl.

Capri | 10 Aug 76

Dearest Elizabeth –

After sending off a few days ago a dreary-bones letter full of our staple MM vicissitudes etc, etc, have just learnt from MM herself (in a letter showing real concern about your wellbeing) what you have been going through. Elizabeth, what an awful experience, what misery. I've never yet had shingles but have agonised for dear friends who have – it seems to strike at dear friends, ie, sensitive and precious souls who have not developed the usual anti-shingle rhino hide imperviousness to grisly world. [...]

Have just finished Patrick's Fringe of Leaves, which a nice person at the bookshop Heywood Hill got me an advance copy of, bound galleys. Have seldom been so moved and engrossed by anything as the sweep of his great story and his marvellous human revelations, as if by X-ray. Could not budge from the book until after the wreck of the Bristol Maid – the story of the wreck itself a tour de force. The very end again tremendous – it reminded me (but these analogies so often give irritation) of Wm Gosse Hay's 'Escape of the Notorious Sir William Heans', that end part of Patrick's book where the trio of 'authority', 'malefaction', and the female instrument of intercession are balanced as in an opera. Excellent! Bravissimo, Patrizio.

Yesterday we walked up to the palace of Tiberius – beautiful walk, almost no one except us there. Bless you dear Elizabeth. Forget our pestiferous side – we love you, so be careful – love also to dear Margaret – Shirley.

Mosman | 5 September, 1976

Dearest Shirley and Francis –

Until today I have found it <u>impossible</u> to write letters or even postcards. So this has been another way in which I have felt unlike myself. Your friend has had a severe fright, shock, to the system. Even today, though I HOPE and HALF-THINK (touching wood) that I'm much better, there are still enough signs and symptoms to make me nervous. There have been some funny moments, and I've learned things, but it's been a drag. [...]

On September 18 Margaret has some time off, so we're hoping to drive away into the country. [...] Things have deteriorated on every front controlled by Fraser. Every enlightened piece of legislation has been undone and a new Cold War stepped up. 'Life was never meant to be easy,' says Fraser, millionaire, to aborigines, migrants, women, artists, conservationists, community self-help groups, homeless vagrants. The conservatives dismiss all demonstrators as hooligans. If (as hoped) huge crowds of non-feared persons of all ages arrive at the Town Hall and people like Manning Clark speak, it will be harder to ignore. [...]

We haven't read Patrick's new book yet, so it's exciting to hear how much you've both enjoyed it. He's terrific, isn't he? At the moment he and Manoly are still in Greece, finding Athens much polluted, and beginning to look forward to coming home.

[...]

Francis, you've had shingles, too! And Cynthia wrote to me. She, too. The most recent theory seems to be that it's caused by a chicken pox virus that lies dormant from childhood and then for mysterious reasons attacks. My (young and insecure) doctor kept saying, 'There's nothing we can do.' But I later heard of an acquaintance who had been given a cortisone-type injection and tablets and recovered quite quickly.

[...]

Margaret sends love. We think of you often. Much love
Elizabeth

Capri | 13 Sept 76

Dearest Elizabeth –

It was a joy to get a letter in your own unwavering typewriting and feel that you were slowly emerging from the hell into which the President of the Immortals had cast you. The wretched helplessness we felt while you were enduring your ordeal would have intensified if we'd known you had a doctor who wrung his hands and 'couldn't do anything'. It is very good news that you and Margaret are getting away for a bit. I'm sure you'd like a change of scene from what must have seemed Job's own parlour for a while. Also good that things are moving on the house and that there is a prospective (and shingle-veteran!) client. You deserve some splendid surprises now, and plain sailing.

[...]

As to My Mum. As you know, appalling. As you also probably know, MM wrote to 'Henry', our NY trustee and hers, accusing F and S of embezzling not only her assets but her American Social Security... I gather she has broadcast this unhappy development at Sydney too. Of course we are aware that it is now a matter of ANYTHING in order to be able to slam us, and thus reach us, and compel attention etc. etc; but this particular form is among the most unappealing of her slams. [...]

As to Fraser, you'll see what I think of him if my article is ever published. I am still, incredibly, awaiting the galleys. [...]

Best and greatest love to you and Margaret – Shirley.

Postcard, Murrurundi NSW | 29.9.76

A word from the bush, dear friends. A heavenly day & an incredibly pretty valley, remote, sunny, sweet cool air. M & I on way back to Sydney in two or three days after two weeks of driving through country. Was v glad to get away from Sydney Harbour. The Monday 20 Sept meeting at Town Hall for Constitutional reform was packed & overflowing. All ages, & all relieved & happy to see each other still caring. As much as ever. Those who fall away because they only want to be on the winning side are well lost. [...] Patrick will be home when we get back. Hurrah! Christina says to me 'Patrick & Manoly are your brothers' – and I do count on them as if they were. Though I have never felt that relatives mattered more than friends.

Spoke frequently to YM. She had had cable from Francis. Will see her on return. Much love, E.

New York | 6 Dec 76

Dearest Elizabeth –

I have been expecting day after day to be telephoning you to say that my ineffable article is in the works, and to have pow-wow. Never such an experience – how lucky we are to be fiction writers and not go through this ordeal of work that dates while magazines don't publish...

[...]

Millions of thanks for marvellous clippings, all of which put to use. Hope to be worthy of such helpfulness. You probably know that Murdoch has bought the NY Post. That was all that NY newspapers needed to complete their disgrace. A number of newspapers (most of them pretty bad; one goodish one) have been forced out in the last 15 years by stupendous demands from the unions combined with union action against the (inevitable) automation. Newspaper workers (typesetters, etc.) are tremendously highly paid. After collapse of various papers, all that remains is NY Times – a baffling, huge mixture of unfair biases (all kinds), serious reporting on the city itself, some good feature articles, excellent science etc., gauleiter culture approach, detestable weekly book section... Then a right-wing gutterish paper called the Daily News, huge circulation, lots of sports and comics, crime, scandal. And the Post, a liberal paper as far as politics go but pretty cheap stuff. Murdoch, interviewed in the Village Voice (a weekly), now says the Post is too stuffy and he is going to jazz it up...

SO GOOD to talk to you. When we talk, or get yr letters, I have utter feeling of having just seen you, more than with anyone else from whom so separated. Our reunion in the lobby conversation-pit of the Sebel seemed more like continuation than resumption. Got to get reunited again soon, also with Margaret who has been a precious addition to our (perforce minuscule) directory of great souls.

[...]

Oh – Carter. Having a vote for the first time in my life, I intended to abstain. But Ford's threatening to win was too much for me. Carter is a dreadful little twerp, I think (his only truly good factual record is on environment, which I suppose – grudgingly – might suggest better qualities than have as yet been aired). Why he should have been virtually the only person served up for reasonable people to vote for is a mystery yet to be unravelled – I am certain he did not just sit up in Plains, Georgia, and decide to be president. No doubt there is power, and economic power, behind it somewhere. [...]

On the anti-Kerr demos, you'll think Shirl a wowser but I dislike above all things the shouting down of speakers – whether they are speakers I abhor or not. I see all that as a chain-reaction of violence and blockheadism, and a point at which everybody begins to be on the same (wrong) side. It is hard to concede rights to those who violate them, and heaven knows we get plenty of provocation to become emotions instead of minds; but otherwise it seems to me protest will become useless as the other side will have won by making 'us' like 'them'... Also, I wld think it quite likely that some of these anti-Kerr demos are incited by Fraserites. That was certainly the case here during the Johnson and Nixon presidencies, when anti-war protesters were discovered time after time to have been inflamed into rowdiness and violence by planted agents. If this comes out in Australia, only those who were 'against' the rowdies would be in a position to criticise, surely.

[...]

Patrick wickedly said on phone (when I called him last month to be sure I cld quote something abt Kerr) that he had not known where we were in Europe and thus could not be in touch abt meeting. Well do I recall writing it all out, including the number of steps up to our front door... In fact, had we known he was in Rome (and had we been, as MM would put it, wanted) we'd have gone up from Naples to see him and Manoly, in default of their promised trip to Capri.

Last week we took a trip up to the East Bronx to visit a former maid of mine (lovely and saintly woman, a negro from Virginia) who, poor one, has had her leg amputated for diabetic gangrene. I wish I could describe to you in any adequate terms the horror of this region of NY, which, over the past dozen years has been gradually abandoned because of crime. Mile after mile of gutted and vandalized tenement buildings, looking like Beirut; heaps of garbage in vacant lots, stray dogs wandering starved, endless vistas of uninhabited desolation. The area is that of a small city. We had gone up in a cab (took about half an hour); came back by walking a few blocks to a bus (a dangerous thing to do, especially for white people – the area is almost exclusively black) in a more inhabited region where hospital is; then half an hour through Beirut in bus; then tube for fifteen mins. A grisly and fascinating journey, with the city turning into something recognizable to us only in the last couple of tube stops when complexions, dress, expressions etc. were transformed. Until then we'd been about the only white people on the train; after that, few blacks. What will be the outcome of people raised in those conditions, with little hope of employment and no prospects of decent life one does not imagine. The unemployment rate in the city here is 10%, the majority of them blacks.[...]

On returning from above excursion, we congratulated ourselves on surviving & sank down, chastened, in our chairs. To learn, on turning on radio news, that an appalling double murder (old couple in their eighties) had been committed in a suave building across the street from us, and police were swarming among television cameras in our street... Appointment in Samara.

Shall be in touch soon, possibly by Singing Out. Best and fondest love always, and yours timidly – Shirl.

Mosman | 31 December, 1976

Dearest Shirley and Francis –

As ever, when we spoke those two weeks ago it seemed in all respects as though you were close by. [...]

Margaret rang this morning from her office. The Financial Review has quoted from your piece in this week's New Yorker. Whacko! It's in print! M has copied the F.R. comments in the office machine. You must be so immensely relieved to have that out at last. It must have begun to feel like your life's work. You can imagine how we are <u>longing</u> to read it. You'll also realize that the word has been spread.

[...]

No, no, of course I don't think you're a wowser for not liking above all things the shouting down of speakers and so on. I am glad that opposition to what happened is still visible, but find egg-throwing, car-kicking and chanting depressing. People who see the letter I wrote to the Governor-General divide into those who know why I used all the proper forms of address and those who are automatically derisive because it wasn't frothing with rage. No, in private and public life I am sure the object (one object) of the spirit, attitude, view of life that must always be opposed is exactly that – to make 'us' like 'them'. (I said this better in a book. It's in print. So it must be true.)

Christmas. We called in to see YM on Christmas Day and took her a bottle of Scotch. She went out to Joan's at night – from five till twelve. 'It lasted too long,' she said. And, 'It just goes to show that nothing's as bad as you think it's going to be.' Our visit went off very well. Judah is up from Melbourne. Nancy is back from Morocco and India. Ferdi is in Capetown, Jerusalem and Athens. Christina stayed with Ron and Dorothy Geering for Christmas. Manoly is getting slowly better and Patrick is working hard. Lots of people have been over including, yesterday, a dear little baby called Sophie. Eight months old. You could not doubt that her character is all there already and arrived with her.

Just about to have hair fixed so must rush off now not to lose appointment with Ulrik. A proper letter soon to answer yours. 'Twas marvellous to hear – A happy, hard-working, super-healthy New Year, dear friends. Take care of yourselves. Fondest love,

Elizabeth

Mosman | 16 January, 1977

Dearest Shirley and Francis –

A telex to describe events here and to answer yours, dear friends.

[...]

M and I had dinner at Patrick's last Wednesday. There were two conservative friends present. It became very lively. You must share some of the (entirely good) responsibility, dear Shirl, because some of the first words exchanged were about your letter. 'Lucid', 'explains it just as it was', 'had to be said' all with speaking looks.

[...]

We were very pleased that the ABC went into action with the a.m. interview. Everyone listens to that programme. The advance announcements that yours was the longest article written about Australia in the outside world for 25 years would have caught attention, too. It would be too painful to describe in detail the warnings <u>days</u> before this event to YM to organize transistor, batteries, alarum clock, God knows what else. On the morning itself, four or five calls. Then she missed it.

Perhaps you know from someone else by now that Cynthia committed suicide. She tortured herself so. Or (as she would have seen it) others tortured her. She was intense and complex and (as Patrick said) this was no blessing to her. Manoly spoke so lovingly of her the other night. Sidney and Jinx are coming out in April.

[...]

Christina (Stead) rang the other day. If I intended to stay put, she wondered about coming to live here in part of the house and being my tenant. She's a splendid, interesting woman, and I wish she lived somewhere that she liked, but this wasn't possible. As you say, houses have insides and outsides and someone forever must be doing something about them. If you're the one who owns the house you're always having to make rather tedious decisions. I felt I couldn't complicate things by introducing another person into a scene I hope to change.

[...]

Saw a BBC production of <u>Candide</u> on television. It was <u>delicious</u>. Had never seen it produced before anywhere.

Take care of yourselves in all that snow. Fondest love,
Elizabeth

Mosman | 4 Feb 1977

Dear Shirley and Francis –

[...]

In general, here, we are tottering about with not much energy and faintly addled by the heat. YM said she was 'disintegrating'... In all sorts of ways she seems better. [...]

M and I read Sumner Locke Elliott's <u>The Man Who Got Away</u> last week and enjoyed it terrifically, were gripped. Like a thriller, a mystery, but what he's tracking is character.

[...]

What of work, dear S and F? Does it have any chance in New York? Patrick said recently that he had too many friends (don't quote me!), and you must sometimes feel like that. I feel like that, and think of removing myself from Sydney for a while. The telephone rings... In between times we seem to do lots of laughing. It's easy, too, to fall into dreams watching clouds, sea and birds over Balmoral. Yesterday huge express clouds from bushfires raced overhead and out to sea, looking ominous. Then a few evenings ago Helene and Ferdi were here and suddenly the most wondrous rainbow appeared, complete, brilliant and quite close. Everything inside its arch looked painted, ideal, and everything outside was in another dimension. We couldn't leave it. It was (literally) enchanting. Ferdi said he had been waiting for a sign for 1977 and this was it. He has a lovely good nature, Ferdi... But nothing pleases you if work is too much interrupted. One survives, but it takes the edge off.

We think of you both often. Greetings and fond love,
Elizabeth

New York | 5 Feb 77

Dearest Elizabeth –

[...]

Nothing cld convey my profound and complete pleasure, dearest E, in your two-card message. [...] Then came, with some delay, yr letter of 16th, again giving me joy. I'm so glad it seems in important ways right to you – was dreading that it would not seem to Austs like the actual Oz. [...] Patrick wrote me v. kindly: I wonder if the Queen has ever read so many words at once? Also, won't she think Herodotus is a racehorse? Have so far heard from Eliz, dear Margaret, Patrick, and Mum. C'est tout in Aust. Sent 30 copies Austwards, so something will filter in eventually. [...] Imbecile reviews in general for Patrick's Fringe of Leaves. They cannot forgive him for having been good all the time while they slept, and for making a monkey of their parochial system. [...]

No, we had not known – but had conjectured – that Cynthia took her own life. It is all sad. [...]

Main thing I want to say is that Judah W is right – 'Write your book'. Yes. This goes for all of us. What of Margaret's also? One of the dividends of coming to Aust was meeting and reading M. To think that a year ago we were just girding ourselves to set out in face of horror letters from MM, and hardly knowing what splendour was in store – except that on the EH side we had a glimmering…

Love to you EH, from both your devoted Steegs – and especially grateful Shirley.

Mosman | 15 April, 1977

Dearest Shirley and Francis –

That was lovely – having your call the other Sunday. Since I confide in you, and send messages so regularly mind-to-mind, actually speaking is never a surprise, if you know what I mean.

Patrick is going off this week to look at some countryside he's writing about in the new novel. His play <u>Big Toys</u> is being produced in May/June. A film is being made of the short story <u>The Night the Prowler</u> and he has just been doing some work on that. He has been very active on the uranium front; was interviewed on radio and television when the moratorium campaign started, and has sent lots of us petitions to take around. At the time of the Queen's visit he travelled to Brisbane to speak there for the republican cause, and then spoke (marvellously) at the Town Hall meeting here in Sydney. We arrived at the Town Hall at 10 to 7 and left at 10 to 12. The streets were emptying by that time. A boy ran down the steps carrying a huge Eureka flag, jumped on his bike, and pedalled round into Park Street with the flag streaming out behind him. Patrick has been feeling disillusioned with some friends lately. There were some who rushed to accept invitations to the Queen's supper party on the Britannia. There were dear doctor friends who signed a public statement in favour of uranium mining. Others thought he might be interested in becoming Governor of South Australia (after he'd just spoken all over the place at republican rallies) – and so on. He still leads a prodigiously busy life, shopping for sick friends, seeing films, giving dinners – and so much more. The Chinese exhibition is in Sydney now. There are great queues. The critics seem bowled over.

[…]

Now we are round again to the accommodation thing. I didn't go on with the house painting or selling because till Christmas-time I was nervous (post-shingles) of the physical effort involved. You know, the house is full of objects and every one has to be moved or sold and so on. Now, Margaret is looking about for a flat to rent, but with our well-known housing crisis, and building crisis, and inflation crisis, flats are few and vastly expensive. So this all has to be worked out. My not very practical inclination is to catch a jumbo to India, China, the Canadian Rockies, Japan.

[...]

Francis, at least M found where copies of her books were – under the house. Now one has been posted off and she has sent a card to you.

Five of us went to the A.L.P. picnic that Sunday after you rang. It was held in the far-distant Western suburbs in a suburb whose name we didn't even know [...] In between times there have been little feasts with friends, great orgies of novel reading, some (literal) rose-gathering. Saw <u>Travesties</u>, the Tom Stoppard play.

Oh, Veronica Geng asked if I had an American agent. The people I used to know in London had some connection with Collins-Knowlton-Wing (can't even remember the spelling for sure). Then Cynthia introduced me to another agent in London – Richard Scott, but I don't know who he has in New York. In about 1959 when my mother started bringing me The New Yorker an agent sent them a story and they seemed to debate about it (I saw their letter) and asked for 'more of this writer's work' and then I let years go by. Presumably if the incredible happened and I wrote a story they liked, some agent would be willing to have me.

[...]

Greetings and much love and take care of yourselves – Elizabeth

New York | 22 April 77

Dearest Elizabeth –

[...]

I'll be relieved when Stanley Avenue's albatross is off yr necks. It must be pretty, but the burden is obviously continual, inexorable. I can feel those objects aiming themselves at your attention, those floors and walls and roof clamouring for yr attention as impeccably as if they were one's mother. Hope this next move is going to be a vast simplification.

[...]

Francis has been given a Guggenheim Fellowship to translate another volume of Flaubert letters – this a lot of work, and we can't quite see how to manage his work in libraries. He will go to Paris from Italy and bring back photostats – he already has masses. They are fascinating, terrific. Also ms. pages of Mme Bovary fascinating to see – incredibly overwritten with every change, seething with intense intention!

[...]

Was disheartened to read that those Aust writers are getting clique-ish like all the rest of the world. We felt, when in Aust, there was so much less of that than in England and America – here it is appalling, & a great deterrent to seeing literary folk in gaggles. Has to be said that 'literary' is often, here, NOT poets and novelists, but appalling critics, academic upstarts, analysers, interpreters, journalists, publishers. With these, obviously one would not be seen dead. But the writers themselves are often ingrown, patting each other on back; alas, there is something to be said against being with those comfortable people 'who all think the same way' – though I agree it's often a relief, especially during times of political stress. I do sympathise with writers who detach themselves from political and social causes in order to write their poems and novels: I find what I do in the public vein a hideous burden and bore most of the time, and would certainly have written more fiction without it. I suppose I'll always do some of it, but would like to give up most. [...]

Best love, and please be well, both of you – Shirley.

Capri | 22 June 77

Dearest Elizabeth –

Much, much to thank you for and discuss and say. [...]

Today came your pair of cards. We do not know whether MM is at Sydney, Hawaii, Los Angeles, New York, London, or Devon. And, after all that has passed, can hardly summon up a flicker of curiosity. I have no address for her (as she intends I should have to get in touch with you to find it out, thus revealing that I-do-not-even-know-where-my-own-mother-is). As I am in touch with you, would be glad to have this sometime. [...] Every letter from MM in four weeks has given a different & drastic programme, as you know. The latest, ten days ago, revealed the (insane) giving up of Sydney flat without having any other place to go, announced departure for Hawaii, and said with impossible archness that it was probably the best thing just to go on from there to England and Devon, perhaps eventually back to Australia, maybe America, etc. The efforts to get at us in the letter (all couched in loving terms) were so numerous as to become one single blow of steam-hammer, had we not long since been battered into a sheet of iron.

[...]

In spite of all this – which sometimes seeks its rightful pinprick size in face of world's realities – we've had beautiful times here [...]. Just back from a few days at, first, Naples – thrilling & filled with marvels & terrors as always; and on Procida, (perhaps you've been there?), the smaller, as yet unspoiled, island of the three – it lies between Ischia and the mainland (quite near to what the Procidani call 'il Continente' – Italy!) – but less visited even by mainlanders, partly because there is a gaol on the island, in the ancient fortress above the town. Elizabeth, what beauty – a riot of lemon-groves, vines, fields, flowers, wonderful rock formations, deep clear sea, a town or two in shabby bright colours honeycombed onto hillsides. Glorious day, with light breeze blowing from blue sea, a lovely purity to everything. Parts of Capri are still like this of course; but an entire island of it exhilarating and amazing. There were two little hotels – heavenly gardens; and next time we'll stay overnight perhaps. I was last there twenty years ago – it hasn't really changed. It is the island in Elsa Morante's fine novel, 'Arturo's Island'. People nice (so are the Caprese), & only ten thousand of them. Came back to Capri by way of Ischia – also not visited by us for some years. The port an appalling touristic ruin – there is nothing quite like that on Capri. The island beyond, marvellously beautiful & of course quite large – like a countryside rather than an island. Wonderful colours of everything, especially deep greens of land and sea. Came back on ancient ferry, rolling and tossing like mad for an hour and a half, with view of Capri rarely seen by us as we generally approach it from different direction. Feeling of antiquity and natural splendour, the light itself is sort of exaltation. Not least of this idyll was the reply received in Naples, when we inquired of a poorish person in the street whether one way or another was the more direct to a certain destination: 'È idem.'

So infinitely much more to say. We rejoice that Patrick is better.
And are sad about Sidney. It will be long before true equilibrium returns,
perhaps. Yet one feels it can and will, if only because of what is in his work.
(This presumptuous, and perhaps mistaken.) Graham Greene is here (are
seeing him this evening). He's so far in fairly good spirits (always on verge
of crisis of accidie, but his need to challenge every statement now almost
obsessive, which makes for some exhaustion and, also, for fewer statements.
It seems he likes to see us, as he always arranges to do so & we always give
him & Yvonne chances to be alone if they prefer; yet he has a need to give
me a sort of ritual slap every so often ('I didn't like the literary part of yr
Australia piece') in what seems mildly unnecessary way... He cannot bear to
be in receipt of any 'suggestion' that he should like or dislike; at once reacts
in predictably contrary manner. For instance, any book I'd recommended
or sent to him (now I never do it) unfavourably commented on – one feels,
mostly out of resistance to having a view 'imposed' on him, even in so
tangential a manner. (Obviously goes back to bedrock, all this.) [...] BEST
LOVE, dear Elizabeth, and our love to Margaret too. We hope that the
housing incubus is resolving itself a bit. We cherish you – Shirley.
PS: 23rd June – Just received 'departure' letter from MM, giving no
address henceforth for her.

Capri | 6 July 77

Dearest E – We may dread Aust stamps, but we glory when we discover
your hand, or type, on envelope. Thank you for all – we'd be in heart
of darkness otherwise. Latest development in saga of MM-v-the world
(doubtless superseded by the time this reaches you) is letter from Honolulu,
chaotic, about dress, V's pool, volcanic soil, red flowers, garden party, and –
casually – info that, although undecided, next address should probably
be c/o Bank of NSW, Sackville St, London. (A month ago, MM was
starving & could not afford an egg; now she is contemplating Magellan-like
expeditions...). [...]
    Could I ask, if you have any news of a definite move of MM – either
returned to Sydney or on to London – in next couple of weeks that you
cable us (Hotel Hassler, Rome until 16 July, then NYC)? Please forgive this
pestiferousness, but at the mo, I literally don't know if she's in Hawaii or

Piccadilly or Mogadiscio. How she loves this chaos and how hateful are both the chaos and the love of it. [...]

Today we saw V Nabokov had died – a weird & gifted chap, and unique. Sorry his eccentricities have disappeared from this drably uniform earth, as it sometimes seems nowadays. G Greene was quite often at his most agreeable this time here – he & Yvonne left yesterday. He is obsessed by The Hunt–the hunter & the quarry; sometimes on one side, sometimes the other. His life is haunted by cops and robbers & fascination with the same; with God as the ultimate detective & Bringer to Justice. Though he told me that his best, and frequent dream takes place in the peace of a beautiful second-hand book shop of the pre-war English kind...

Fond love from us both to you and Margaret – Shirley.

New York | 25 Aug 77

Dearest E – Kylie's news [cancer diagnosis] will have changed life so much for you in these weeks. As ever, one seeks for words to express the totality of it and doesn't find them. The shock is part of the tribute one pays to friends in these moments, but is terrible. Then, also, the inability to reach truly in imagination what it must be like to live with the consciousness of imminent death.

[...]

MM appears to have made the ultimate Catherine-wheel (sic) round the bend. What a peculiarly squalid and appalling bend she has managed to make it too. [...] I had sent MM a note, a brooch of no value but pretty, and got a book for her. These seemed to be safest means of maintaining contact while contact appeared vaguely poss. The book, however, was new (commercial-type) biography of Vivien Leigh, with whom MM has always identified herself, partic in role of Scarlett O'H. (Pity MM could not have led the South to victory, but there it is.) Looking into the book, I found that MM had weirdly been quite correct in identifying herself with VL, or more correct than she would know; because it is a tragic story of a schizo-paranoid, tremendous manic phases, bottomless depressions, hideous violent scenes, (to point of ripping off clothes, yelling, obscenities, etc. – this from someone reserved and fastidious the rest of the time). [...]

By the way, Sumner Locke Elliott has a good and lively new novel out this week here – he has sent Patrick a copy: 'Water Under the Bridge', said bridge being the Harbour Bridge and novel being set around era of Bridge's inauguration.

What about work? Between MM and interior of my head, I haven't done nearly as much as I'd hoped this August. But have got ahead and hoped to finish book by end of year. In late September, another chapter of it, in form of short story, is coming out in the New Yorker – if they stick to the schedule. And, if I may, I'll have a copy sent by air to you. (As the Japanese say of a present they are giving, 'Laugh at it and throw it away'...) [...]

Greetings go to Margaret as ever and always come with much affection and to Kylie, our admiration and helpless sympathy and solidarity. And to you, our thanks and best love – Shirley.

Postcard | 3/10/77

Your story arrived on Friday, dearest Shirl, and I send great THANKS and admiration. Everything is given with such lightness and subtlety! No words, no commas, no woods and no trees go unappreciated, and what we appreciate delights us. Really, you are GOOD. Margaret came in, all smiles: 'I've just read Shirley's story.' (And unlike Dr Jim Cairns and EH – frightful conjunction! – Margaret doesn't wear her heart on her sleeve.) Clearly, it made her happy, and she hadn't been especially happy moving house, having to think of furniture and objects. But what S wrote and how S wrote brought a whole lot of radiance to the scene as we discussed this remark and that remark and the total... More, more! And love and congratulations from

Elizabeth

P.S. Longish letter should be waiting for you, too. YM OK – no real change. Has TV back. Mrs Watt(s), of course, had NOT stolen it, merely stored – out of kindness. E

Postcard | 5.10.77

ANOTHER card from Elizabeth??! Just spoke to Christina (Stead) who is going to New York on Saturday for three months. If you'd like to see her she'd v. much like to see you. She is staying with friends: Jessie and Ettore Rella.

She has had an unsplendid time with half-brother Gilbert & wife in Hurstville, but got away often to congenial places & people in other cities & other parts of Sydney and is, herself, anyway splendid enough to make up for all circs. She has such a large, generous, stable nature. Judah Waten & Ron Geering, who knew her husband, say he was a 'lovely man'. She says he saved her life when they met. So – greetings, thoughts, best love, E
Saw Woody Allen's film Annie Hall. Loved it.

New York | 20 Nov 77

Dear Elizabeth –
    [...]
    What joy to hear you on the blower, dear Eliz. Despite the numerous bedevilments & sorrows of these past months, you sound very EH and – therefore – marvellers. Australia has been on our domestic scene – with Sumner winning the literary Melbourne Cup, Jim (as he kindly invited us to call him) McClelland making a splendid and much enjoyed appearance on our scene, & a good article in the Atlantic Monthly (otherwise usually boring magazine) on uranium, etc. If any press clips here on Sumner, I'll send them to you. If anything good there, could you send to me, and I'll pass to him? TA! It is terrible that Kylie's son tries it on again at this particular juncture. Terrible also, perhaps, that he did not long ago succeed... I wonder what state – & stage – Kylie is in?
    Good that Labour is ahead. (Even if Liberals return with reduced majority, it would be an improvement.) If Labour won, I wonder what practical course they would take after the jubilation was over – ie, on unemployment, inflation. I hope (don't have a fit), better than before. Here, Carter is useless. No surprise. As to those who would leave Aust – surely that is the intellectual's form of My Mum-ism? Point is never so much the wanting to leave, but the having somewhere better to go. People who left US in 1960 – to reside in Britain, Ireland (!), Italy (!!) etc. – stayed one

year, or two, or three; came back. Good reasons for leaving – Viet Nam, LBJ, Nixon, crime, violence; but you have to <u>love</u> the other place you go to. I could live in Italy, despite utter chaos; But F wouldn't want to be permanent expatriate. Then, I wouldn't stay in Italy if Fascism (or for that matter Communism) took over. There is always a fly in the Nirvana... All lucky to be able to travel sometimes, try other things... What do you think? I'm reading some good things – Do you like Arnold Bennett? I do. Love to Margaret, love to you – <u>Thank you</u>! – More soon – Shirley.

New York | 29 November 77

Dearest Elizabeth –

After posting that p.c. to you yesterday, we went to Lillian Hellman's for dinner for Christina Stead – and found (what you perhaps already know) no Christina, as she had had a fairly serious heart attack and was in St. Vincent's hospital. Lillian had talked to the Rellas but knew little more than that. Today I thought I would phone you after talking to Rellas and to Joan Daves (Christina's agent – NO great shakes – who inherited the practice of beloved Cyrilly Abels); but the news is both good and rather interim, and I thought not to alarm you but to wait a day or two and see what develops. Christina has responded very well to treatment apparently, and is to come home from hospital tomorrow if she continues as good as at present. That would mean only about a week in hospital, so it seems that it cannot be a drastic attack. Mrs. Rella says it was congestive heart failure (i.e., dropsical attack, with water in the lungs & difficulty of breathing); and I believe that is an affliction they can treat swiftly and well these days. She was stricken at 4:00 in the morning, and Mrs. R. got her to hospital in an ambulance. She is in a ward with eight beds; Joan Daves says she will not hear of moving to a private room (doubtless because of horrendous expense), and indeed is making notes on the other patients who, according to La Daves, seem very strange and evidently intent on providing Christina with material.

Mrs. Rella says the main worry other than the illness itself was the usual horrific NY hospital charge and the demand for large sum of money instantly from the hospital authorities. I said we would be glad to help if necessary, but she said she thought Joan D. was in the process of resolving – whether through publishers' advances on royalties or how else I don't know. We'll see what happens. There is apparently nothing else one can do at the moment. Christina wants v. much to return to Australia as promptly as poss. This seems foolhardy, though natural, because the exhaustion of the trip and the risk of making it alone in such a state might well do damage. She will be a short time at the Rellas when she leaves hospital, but Mrs. R. says she will then probably go elsewhere, to another friend.

Perhaps she will rest now and get better than before. Let us know if there is something <u>you</u> would like done here that we can undertake.

[...]

Love to you, dear Elizabeth, and to Margaret. Shall keep informed here – Shirley

New York | 22 Jan 78

Dearest Elizabeth –

How I hate to inflict the enclosed sinker on you; just to keep you up to date on the saga. I fear this has made more whopping holes in your working hours, and that I am adding to them. [...] As said, the situation seems in a new way to await some (indubitably ghastly) new event before change can be proposed or accepted. However, I wonder if Andrew knows of the falls. It was Andrew who, at Sydney in '76, urged us <u>not</u> to take on the idea of coming to Sydney for the possible installation in the non-home, and felt that he could handle such an eventuality professionally. [...]

Yes, of course, there are many consolations in living in the centres of the northern hemisphere. Yet there are consolations in Aust, also – as we greatly felt. All those places you mention (especially repulsive Madrid, where the Prado cannot after all house one indefinitely and where fascism exudes from every pore of the city) are in heart-rending convulsions. While still delightful to visit, Rome, London, etc., harbour their particular horrors, unsuffered yet by Australians; and wherever one <u>lives</u> becomes the point – one does not reside in a place because of the opportunities to get away from it. There is a lot of excitement to NY for people with means and good health and white skin and the luck not to have been the victim as yet of violent crime. There is also much that you above all people, living here rather than visiting, would soon find intolerable. That goes particularly for the 'literary' life, a phenomenon hard to convey in its full horror to anyone who has not experienced it. Italy to me is perhaps the saddest, though. Anyway, I do not say these things to be a killjoy, because joy there still is (as I believe there must be in a few pockets of Aust also); but because things are difficult everywhere and the 'consolations' are simply that – they console a while, and then you are back at realities of daily awareness. What we hope is that you will come abroad and be consoled.

[...]

Shall try Drabble Ice Age. Never liked others of hers. [...] Shall write soon to Patrick – have been thinking much of him. F was reading Margaret's novel again the other night and kept saying out loud, 'This is good'. New Yorker remarked to me the other day that the Australian they hope most to hear from is Eliz. Harrower. I've been corresponding a bit with Murray Bail about pictures. [...]

Love to you, dear Elizabeth.

<u>Write</u> <u>books</u> – love again from Shirl

Mosman | 16 February, 1978

Dearest Shirley and Francis –

Earlier, I hadn't seen that it would be helpful to describe YM's falls to you. Her face <u>was</u> badly bruised, and if Joan just happened on her, unprepared, she'd certainly have been shocked. The worst fall came when YM tripped over a manhole cover in the street, not properly fixed in place. The other fall was in her flat: she doesn't know how that happened. She has recovered from both and was lucky not to do any permanent damage. She is better about seeing the local GP now, and he seems to take an interest. Andrew rang the day before your letter came. I told him about V's letter. He said people often don't live very long when they go to those places. He said he didn't think Kit was ready for a place like that yet.

[...]

Recently, I've been reading the collected essays, journalism and letters of George Orwell. Last night I read: 'Now, it is clear that the decline of a language must ultimately have political and economic causes: it is not due simply to the bad influence of this or that individual writer. But an effect can become a cause... The great enemy of clear language is insincerity. When there is a gap between one's real and one's declared aims, one turns as it were instinctively to long words and exhausted idioms, like a cuttlefish squirting ink. In our age there is no such thing as "keeping out of politics". All issues are political issues, and politics itself is a mass of lies...' This is from an essay, Politics and the English Language...

I saw Christina twice. She was frail, but (as you know) has great natural dignity, fortitude, kindness. Her relatives are not young either, so her choice of accommodation was limited and the need urgent. She and David set off for Canberra to look at a room in Bruce Hall, A.N.U. Two trucks crashed into them just outside Sydney and David's car was written off. C and her sister-in-law then flew to inspect the place the following day. She had then to return here, gather possessions for one last time, and go back to Canberra. All this for a person so ill, so physically insecure! Ron Geering volunteered to drive her down, which relieved anxiety and made moving luggage simpler. Yesterday I had such a nice letter from her. She likes the Hall and has settled in – bedsitter, share balcony and bathroom with one or two others, and meals in a restaurant/cafeteria on the same floor. The warden is welcoming and considerate. I told you how much C appreciated your letters in New York, and your instant recognition of her voice on the telephone?

[...]

The editorials were all raging at Fraser about the Kerr UNESCO Paris appointment (with a huge G-G's pension, huge new salary, expense laid on, slaves laid on, marvellous apartment in new Australian Embassy building), when a bomb went off at the Hilton to frighten the regional Commonwealth P.M.s' conference, killing two garbos. All controversies temporarily shelved. Last Friday, Utah Development declared the highest profit ever made by any company in this country. Almost all of it went back to the U.S. Another item buried by the bomb. The Labor states have been in trouble trying to 'contain' A.S.I.O. (secret service).

[...]

Kylie had a good report from her doctor last week and was very much cheered. All seems to be calmer and quieter up in the mountains. Bim now has a permanent invalid pension. He's twenty-seven this year, incredibly. Poor boy.

I don't know Murray Bail. [...] He writes v. interestingly about pictures in the National Times. – Did I say before that there's a general feeling that Sidney has married again? Mary Boyd, Arthur Boyd's sister. She was married to another painter, John Something (name I know well, but forget), for years, but not happily. I think they're coming out in March.

Hope your snows and storms are over. What snow everywhere. Take care of yourselves. Best love –

Elizabeth

P.S. Ok! I'll write books!

New York | 25 March 78

Dearest Elizabeth –

This ultra-ratbag performance as correspondent is due to BOOK – of which today I typed the title page, and began the supposed finished copy. (This sounds better than is, I still have to do the last chapter, and the typing is to an extent a re-writing, as the ms. is a labyrinthine scribble. However – there is a tunnel, as they say, at the end of the light...) How can I thank you and bless you for your letters, your news, yourself? Well, one day I hope to try. [...] Murray Bail is here for ten days or so – he came to tea the other day, v. shy, v. real-seeming. Sumner Locke-E. is back from Sydney, only just, and we've spoken on the phone and will meet in a few days. He intensely regrets not seeing you (we had, sub rosa, hoped Patrick would arrange; but Sumner saw Patrick only once and thought him in v. low spirits). [...]

(Have been reading a pile of books on, and by Cavafy – a love of mine, if one can say that when one can only read translation. A pal of ours, Edmund Keeley, writes on and translates Cavafy, and I like also the Liddel book. He comes as close to anyone (Cav., I mean) to giving what Flaubert called the exact measure of thought in language – instead of what Flaubert described as the usual cracked kettle on which we tap crude tunes for bears to dance to, while pining to make music to melt the firmament...)

[...]

Our love and continuous telex to you and Margaret – happy Easter –

Shirley.

New York | 6 April 78

Dearest Elizabeth –

We've just received a 'letter' from MM, dated a month ago (we learned this week, only, from Sumner L-E that there had been postal strike), and find the terrible news of the death of Kylie's son. Her life is something only Thomas Hardy would have understood. Her great, countering piece of luck has been to have you as a friend. We imagine, or try to imagine, how you must be feeling, and this is to say that we think of you with much distress and with love. If there is any word that Kylie can bear to hear, then we would like to send our pain and sympathy to her. Please embrace Margaret for us, and know yourself much treasured by – Shirley.

Mosman | 16 April, 1978

Dearest Shirley and Francis –

Your feeling letter about Bim arrived yesterday. I did write a brief note to you at the time (although YM's was the one that got through), because I always count on your perfect understanding and moral support. Thank you as always for your loving words and thoughts.

It was all terrible. Bim had left home with money to make his way to Nepal. The next morning his mother was rung by detectives in Sydney; they had traced her through a medical card left in Bim's clothes. Everything else was taken – money, guitar, watch, sleeping bag. He never regained consciousness. The days all seemed to last a fortnight. The clock got stuck at a quarter past one. [...]

Kylie stayed with me for some days, then with her sister when Roddy came down. Then, since Roddy was failing, with stress and being out of his own environment, she took him back to Shipley, and that day Bim died. Next day, since Kylie was in the mountains, I had to go with the police to identify him. It was better that it wasn't his mother. [...]

Down here, when everything was happening, Kylie made it easier for everyone by accepting everything, not protecting herself. Doff and I kept some of the hundreds of calls off, of course. But Bim's life for years and years has been tragic and terrible. He used to be an affectionate, smiling boy. Kylie loved him greatly.

Kylie rang this morning. She had just taken her ninety-year-old father up there for a holiday. He's been proposing to me for twenty years, but now he suggests we should go and live in sin in Hong Kong! I gave her your messages and know she appreciated them.

There is more to say in a little while. [...] You can imagine that, while walking through the days with apparent calm, there's a sort of awful reaction that overtakes you when life supposedly settles down to normal again. Everything's a bit of an effort.

As ever, your words and friendship mean much. Best love – Elizabeth

New York | 18 April 78

Dearest Elizabeth –

I think so much of the nightmare of Kylie's son's death; and of you. So Kylie has been spared nothing. I wonder how her health is, and whether the prognosis remains as dire as originally. If so, then the timing of this ultimate blow is truly Hardy-ish.

[...]

Elizabeth, what a fascinating article on Patrick in the Nat. Times (and what ghastly clippings otherwise, about Bj-Petersen etc.). Reading it gave acute need to talk to you – there was so much in it of wisdom and fortitude. As I get (yes, truly, at last) into the last stage of my book I develop strong feelings abt the writer's craft, and the attitude of the world towards it (so well described by, among million others, Coleridge in the Bio. Litteraria, and by Auden in the first hundred pages or so of The Dyer's Hand). Even good friends are sometimes unable to resist hurting a writer, and of course it is the surest index of the unconscious wish to <u>hurt</u>, rather than just an accidental insensitivity. The envy is apparently intolerable. So much more so from thwarted creators – ie., critics. What is marvellous in Patrick on this score is that he has never done a single thing, in his writing or otherwise, to <u>oblige</u> these instincts in critics, or placate them; and yet he feels their evil (for it is a form of evil) acutely. [...]

I cringed to read that <u>Patrick</u> thinks he works 'so slowly'... Well, I hope never to be so long on a book again as this one. But I'm glad in a way I took the time on it... Bless You, dearest E. My love always to dear Margaret. Shall be in touch v. soon. Our thoughts and great love – Shirley.

New York | 6 May 78

Dearest, Elizabeth –

A note after talking with you. The voice was incredibly near. And dear. When you next think of fleeing the country, remember us and let's synchronise. We thought about your experience of these last months so much since getting your letter. As you say, you go on, but it is all different – or perhaps not 'all', but one is changed. It is not of course all change for the 'worse', but – change. Kylie's life is beyond fiction; perhaps by now, her feelings also. [...]

We are fine, but very fatigued. So much work – it's good to do it, though. I am very near the end of my book – it'll be close to 400 pages of typescript, I think. Want to keep it over this summer, then give it to publishers Sept-Oct-ish. It is to be called (this a secret – in case I discover another book has already had the title) 'The Transit of Venus'. At this moment it starts to seem like one whole, instead of many aberrant thoughts and feelings... Who knows what the world will make of it? – Truly, I don't much care. But want a few good readers to like it, and hope to like it a bit myself. (There will be so many ups and downs of feelings on part of author before ms. becomes book, of course...)

[...]

When book is finished, perhaps we will plan to get somehow to Aust again... Can hardly imagine life without book (this book, that is). Best love to you and Margaret, dear E – it was good to hear you – Shirley

Mosman | 10 May, 1978

Dearest Shirley and Francis –

The early news this morning was of Moro's death, Terrible. You'll have arrived in Rome presumably just as great demonstrations have been taking place. What happens now? Poor Italy.

[...]

Tell Sumner Locke-E I must be the only person in Oz who <u>doesn't</u> know him. Everyone knew him as a child, adolescent, worked with him before Fame, or met him (at the very least!) at the Adelaide Festival. Yes, like you, I had thought Patrick <u>might</u> arrange, but we had seen a fair bit of each other and he might have either wanted to see SLE alone, or felt others had a greater claim. He is such a generous and hospitable friend.

I was delighted when you said you'd been reading Cavafy and liked him so much. I love him, his tone, the way every word and thought seem to have been weighed on silver scales, yet so wondrously casual. The Rae Dalven translation, which I have, is troubling because of echoes of more congenial versions that get in the way. Wasn't there a new biography in recent times, and another translation of the collected poems? Must look them up.

Since the day I called on YM and found her in not very good form, other reports suggest that was a trough. These days, everyone finds her, by turns, not bad, good, not good. [...] Andrew spoke to me yesterday or the day before. He had gone to The Chimes, and caught YM just as she was going into town. The flat was clean and tidy, and YM well dressed and made up, with 'everything matching'. They discussed the future, and YM indicated that within a week she would decide on a telephone or a rose-covered cottage. She wasn't going to travel on one of those Greek ships. (Places were advertised on the Ellenis that day.) It's barely credible that she would have the strength to embark again...

No, I never think of any of the world's capitals as nirvana, or want to be part of any literary society anywhere. Even here I haven't much taste for it. It's a small literary world anywhere, I suppose, and (even here) nice people do each other over too much... Too much lively speculation, too much idle criticism, of acquaintances, strangers and friends really puts me off (puts me off myself as well as others, if I get drawn in). It takes a sort of cold childish energy (whatever I mean by that) and is v. jading. But I think in a friendly way of London (and other European places) where I was certainly not well off, but learning and producing work. No illusion about the glamour of foreign parts.

[...]

That is MARVELLOUS that you are getting into the last stage of the book. (I don't say this at this late stage in my letter because this is where such a statement belongs. On the contrary. But I do know what it means, and feel for you.) Practically nothing is more elating, more of a colossal relief. It calls for singing, dancing, noise, champagne. Fireworks! You were talking about the writer's craft, the attitude of the world towards it. All you say is true, except – alas! – when you say 'even good friends are unable to resist hurting a writer, and of course it is the surest index of the unconscious wish to <u>hurt</u>.' It's often all too conscious. A great friend set out to <u>stop</u> me writing and succeeded moderately well. (<u>Not</u> Margaret, of course.) The constant barrage of anti-novel comments, and barrage of phone calls during working hours, and more, were so terrible in their intention that I can scarcely believe it though I lived through it. People are peculiar. What would we write about if they (we) weren't? It's a pity to have to learn these things, and a greater pity if you learn them (as I did) so slowly. Patrick has been free (here) of critical attacks for a very long time. And he is so strong in so many ways. But he felt those early attacks very deeply.

[...]

David Malouf has gone to Italy. He and some other friends had lunch here. We were to have met in the last week, but I thought he was being optimistic about how much could be fitted in. I haven't got his address, but I think he'll be in touch. He's in or near Grosseto.

[...]

Take care. Best love,

Elizabeth

Capri | 26 May 78

Dearest Elizabeth –

This morning came yr lovely and so welcome – and so kind and good – letter. To get Mum over with (as if one could) right away – together with your letter came one from her, forwarded from NY. It merely said, 'I hate you and your sister'. Added to this cheer, a message outside on envelope, 'Leave me alone, both of you'.

[...]

As to Sumner – I will tell him. I was v. disappointed, so was he, that you didn't meet. He is a sweet person, funny and humane and talented.

Somehow he has kept his Aust. temperament and human honesty throughout his weirdo career in the US telly world. In confidence, he was sad about his evening with Patrick: Sumner is homosexual, and felt that a group of waspish Gays had been invited with poor Sumner in mind, when he would have preferred other people. Patrick was apparently in gloomy mood, and Sumner also felt the other guests (the Gays) were uncivil to Patrick, while PW returned acid remarks. Thus, not the setting for one's only reunion evening at the end of the earth... Sumner, great admirer and liker of Patrick, thus sad to leave Aust without seeing him in better context. We had such good times with PW – never forget the shrimp and artichoke in your Hunters Hill grove, dear E.

We arrived in Rome the day Moro's body was 'returned'. Eerie silence fell on the city – demonstrations subsided early, and a beautiful day was convulsed at evening by a thunderstorm (gods are angry). We notice that, at least for the present, there were fewer tourists – that is true here too, partly because of late spring and, until now, wet weather. The next day we went to the Farnesia – only three other visitors besides ourselves, glorious Roman morning of fresh green spring. [...] After this glorious morning among the Pagan gods, we strolled for ten minutes along Via Lungara, and sat down at deserted restaurant, Galeassi, in Piazza of Santa Maria in Trastevere to have pasta in the sun. It was as if peace, instead of barbarousness had descended. The It. govt is hopeless – de mortuis, etc, but when I see Moro – who had five futile terms as premier & closed his eyes to every corruption & idiocy of his party – now eulogised as a striver after sanity, my mind boggles. Poor devil, he was never anything but a no-hoper. These Dostoyevskyan factions of outlaw have profited greatly from the national sense that no govt will give the country honesty, justice or common sense. Of course, the fact is that the public have nothing like exhausted the peaceful means at their disposal to alter things – there is practically no community sense of bringing pressure to bear for decency, almost no idea of developing groups like the American Civil Liberties Union, etc. [...] The police in Italy are appalling – various separate factions, all in rivalry, and strong heritage from fascism. [...] The fact is that a prominent person is shot in the legs in the street in broad daylight in Italy now almost every day, and the assailants are never captured.

We're not exactly fans of the NY police, but it would not be possible, except in context of collusion with Mafia.

[...]

David Malouf kindly sent us his book – I think I mentioned it was very well reviewed in Sunday NYT Book Review (an appalling rag, usually) by a nice woman from The New Yorker, a poet Katha Pollitt? He gave us an address at Florence where he regularly collects mail, and we've written there.

Love to you, dearest. Please give our love to Margaret always. Shirley.

Mosman | 30 May, 1978

Dearest Shirley and Francis –

That is a <u>beautiful</u> title you've chosen for your book. It's an enchanting event, isn't it? – the Transit of Venus. Don't let anything keep you from it. How long – in words – is 400 pages? It's a big book – I know that much – and a prodigious amount of work when each word (and comma) has been weighed and considered and then, miraculously, I'm certain, been made to seem accidentally felicitous. It hardly needs saying that I'm so looking forward...

Don't be surprised to hear no word or sign of the Flaubert piece has been brought forth by YM. She had, however, assiduously saved for me a depressing article out of the Women's Weekly about shingles. I glanced at it and then ungratefully put it down, saying it looked too depressing. I received a Look that should be world famous. God! Anyway. [...]

Patrick's film The Night the Prowler opens the Sydney Film Festival on Friday night. He's been (naturally) interested and involved. He v. much likes films. I hope it's well received. Judah reviewed and sent me the Elizabeth Bowen biography. I really liked it. It was a pleasure to be in her company, reading it. And Judah, for all his life-long, far-left-leanings appreciated her, too. Did I say someone asked me if I'd think about going to a Sydney (Paddington) College of Advanced Education as writer in residence for nine weeks from beginning of September? Ken Levis asked me and I used to say no, regularly, when he asked me to even meet students in his house, so I thought it was time to agree to something. Also, it was just after I came back from the country after all the death and devastation of Bim's event, so it seemed a good idea.

[...]

Just had a call from Detective Finlay. He's arranged for us to meet tomorrow so that I can make a statement about Bim. Kylie rang this morning. She'll come down on 19 June, see the surgeon who operated on her on 20, then 21, 22, 23 will be the inquest and trial. Andrew spoke to me last night. I felt sorry for him. It's a terrible job. He holds the hands of people twice his age who are reliving German concentration camp experiences. Sometimes he must want to give it all away. He doesn't, however. Best love, Eliz.

ABC reading The Human Factor at 9 every morning. <u>Gripping</u>, with that special Greene tone. I listen.

Mosman | 11 July, 1978

Dearest Shirley and Francis,

Last night after being out with French friends who were turning into Australians (officially), I came home and switched on the radio to hear – Shirley, a talk recorded in NY. All you said was true and congenial, a total treat. You mentioned Auden's The Novelist, and I had his Collected Shorter Poems 1927–1957 by the bed. (A couple of nights earlier, thinking about The Chimeras, I wrote myself a note saying: The trouble with poetry is You only know what it's about After you know what it's about.) The next speaker was Antigone Kefala, a friend, a poet, whose first languages are Romanian and Greek, then French, then English, in which she works. Her talk followed yours as if to illustrate...

[...]

In June Kylie was here for a week at my place. It was very busy, visiting doctors, having people to dinner at first, then for three days we were at the Coroners' Court. These were the committal proceedings, and more stressful almost than what went before, and possibly more so than the actual trial. Yet to come. [...]

You asked what Patrick and Manoly thought about Cavafy, or work about him. Once, years ago, I spoke about his work with admiration – not a sudden thing, and not just following the reading of one poem – but they said they felt he was 'something for the English'. Whether that was a momentary or lasting view I don't know. [...] E

New York | 22 July 78

Dearest E –

As to 'only knowing what poetry is about after you know what it's about' – reading this in your letter just received, I went to look in Middlemarch remembering something of the same sentiment expressed by Ladislaw to Dorothea; And it goes like this:

'To be a poet is to have a soul so quick to discern that no shade of quality escapes it, and so quick to feel, that discernment is but a hand playing with finely ordered variety on the chords of emotion – a soul in which knowledge passes instantaneously into feeling, and feeling flashes back as a new organ of knowledge. One may have that condition by fits only.'

'But you leave out the poems,' said Dorothea. 'I think they are wanting to complete the poet.'

I thought that business about knowledge flashing into feeling and back again was rather like knowing what it's about etc.? Elizabeth, thank you for three marvellous letters, forgive delay (caused by either three million minor things or three larger ones). And – please – how is your health? [...]

We're thrilled for the Coll of Adv. Educ that they are getting a Go of you. Probably mates will think of you as 'employed' for that nine weeks, and you may in fact get more chance to work? I think, how good for the students to meet you and have different human levels to look to as well as different literary and articulate ones. [...] There will be some nice ones, no doubt. (Oh God Elizabeth don't take on the upset ones; steel your heart, please!)

[...] Left Italy beautiful, such a heatwave but of clear blazing sunshine. Such joy, everything one looked at seemed inspired. Publicly, things couldn't be worse in Italy. Privately, still much glory and much humanity. Even so, crescendi are being reached in various matters – the socio-economic-political area is like one of those stretches of boiling mud in NZ where boiling breaks through here and there all the time, though not simultaneously. Practical matters are endlessly difficult – strikes virtually continuous, some service is quite broken down, prices of essentials astronomically rising. The election of Pertini was moving – I wouldn't have believed any Italian appointment could move me now; his life is a long, calm, inflexible heroism. One dreads to see him dragged down, at the end of it, into the hopeless mire of present Italian politics of leadership – and it is doubtful he can do anything basic on the good side, the process is being all against any such development. Still, for what short time he is there, at least there should be integrity.

NY heat wave is thick and smoggy – as my allergist says, the pollution is so dense 'you could kick it'. I hope to finish my book towards the end of August. Then comes colossal job of typing it (I thought I typed it; then re-scribbled all over that clean copy). Anyway, it is near the end. As usual, the episodes I most dreaded getting to have turned out easier than expected, whereas the 'lesser' incidents are the devil. Our apt is a nice oasis – cool and light.

[...]

Love to you, Elizabeth – Shirley.

22 Nov 78 | New York

Dearest Elizabeth –

[...]

Sumner was here yesterday [...]. We're going to Patrick's film together (it's doing a one-night stand) in a week or two. I haven't written Patrick yet, though in my mind have often done so and will get to paper soon. Have had a spell of being able to get on with my ms., so have just stuck to it. Now at about p. 150 of typing finished opus – total will be over 400pp, I think. A great companion has been F's Flaubert letters – he is almost finished (500 pp.) his ms. The letters chronicling creation of Mme Bovary are marvellous – terrifying – exhilarating; just what novelists need to read. -[...]

You were utterly marvellous, as ever, to take MM for birthday lunch. I am sometimes desperate about her state. Just had a fairly ok note from her, and am about to write. [...] Yes, of course we remember Eliza's – it was lovely. Glad she wore the dress – (last dress was greeted with return letters saying 'One needs more than dresses'...) In the present letter she says she is sending us a Christmas cake, but not a good one. Goes on, 'That sounds like a threat – perhaps appropriate?'... Well.

Yes, of course we are like exiles; as you say. What has any self-respecting person ever been, of recent centuries in their country but in exile? What has old Shirl ever been, in all her life, in any country, but an exile? What is any writer worthy of his salt but an exile? Wait till you hear G Flaubert on this theme – complete with violent obscenities against the ultra contemptibility of French life... (I at once looked up an almost identical passage in Proust – Proust could not have seen that particular letter of Flaubert's – more decently expressed, but covering the same ground.) I fear I would remain in exile, if to a less degree, under even the benevolent stewardship of... well, the best politician one can think of. [...] The best thing is to do what only we can do, I think – write novels.

[...]

Eliz, it's good you've enjoyed A. Mackie – especially because I feel that means the students have had a splendid time with you. I can't help feeling it came at a propitious moment – if any interruption of real work can ever be propitious; the endless-seeming tragedy of Kylie's loss grinds into the souls, even of those who are not close to it (us, eg), and I wish you could be removed from the scene somehow, now that the event is past. I wish you didn't have to go to court again – a simple-minded thing to say; but the truth.

[...] Much, much love, dear E, and always our great affection to Margaret – Shirley.

Mosman | 9 January, 1979

Dearest Shirley and Francis,

It was terrific to hear you both, real voices, at Christmas.

M and I did visit YM on Christmas Day. In spite of having had a letter from me, she said she had thought we were coming on Boxing Day. However, we got over that, exchanged presents and had a drink and talked away...

Meant to ask, how have you got on with Patrick's film? What did you think? I haven't seen it yet. It will be shown here again in February. Many people have been bowled over by Woody Allen's Interiors, but I was bored, though I'd gone with high hopes and expectations. They all seemed one dimensional. It was like untransmuted experience. [...]

The court case. Kylie came down on December 9, a Saturday, and stayed till December 21, a Thursday. Every day we were in court from about 9.30 till 4 or 5. There were twenty-six witnesses, three QCs and three associates defending, and a Crown Prosecutor and associate. The defence selected a jury of people under thirty. Though I'd sat through it all for a week at the Coroner's Court, it was worse this time because Kylie was there, inside and hearing everything for the first time. The statements of the accused were read out and referred to again and again, so that details of the assault were constantly in the air. Bim's clothing, his watch, the broken flagon he was hit with, photographs of the scene, appeared over and over. At the end of the first week, one of the defence counsel thought to ask to see Kylie's first statement. In it, she had spoken about Bim's having experimented with drugs, and about his times in Gladesville and Parramatta Psychiatric Centres. This excited the counsel greatly, as though the law permitted an open season on psychiatric patients. The idea was to prove that Bim was a disturbed person who jumped out of the window for no good reason. [...] None of us could sleep at night, so we got tireder and tireder. And the old Central Criminal Court building has polished benches, bad acoustics, no air conditioning, no backs to the benches upstairs where you hear slightly better. So even physically it was demanding. [...]

At the end of that first week, at the week-end, which was the last before Christmas, we went out to the shops for food and things, and people were buying presents, and the tinsel everywhere was looking pretty sick in the hot sunshine, and we were really like visitors from another planet. All the week we'd been in the world of life and death, and truth and lies, and that real world made this seem so flimsy and nightmarish. Sometimes, in the court, while the judge read papers he'd called for, up to sixty people would sit in complete silence and stillness, for twenty minutes at a stretch. Outside, commerce and commotion; inside, the law turning over every grain of sand with wonderful patience.

[...]

Instantly, it was the date of Alexander Mackie parties, dinners with friends, belated shopping, lunches. This week, at last, there is almost an end to it. David Malouf is home from Italy next Sunday, and we'll do something about that, but it's been too much – the social life on top of Alexander Mackie, trial, Christmas... I did have lunch alone with Patrick and Manoly on the Saturday before 25th, and that was a rest-cure for me.

I say, friends, I had no idea that English and literature were in such frightful danger till I stayed at A. Mackie. If something was too difficult to be expressed in words (and, to the students, almost everything was) they could travel across the city to a building filled with radio, television, film equipment and fiddle around with technical things for a couple of hours, utter something spontaneous and fade out. It all counts towards a degree!! [...]

The wooden parts of this house are in process of being painted – burned off, sanded. Then we'll have to see what happens next. I'm very jaded (not glum, just tired of Sydney and Australia). I know work is the answer, but a change might be the answer – part of it, too. We'll see...

There was one film I enjoyed recently, a Greek production of Iphigenia. Wonderfully, the director hadn't felt it necessary to put them all in top hats, or to bring them into the twentieth century (since, of course, Euripides is in every century while there are people).

I do hope you made a cup of coffee, or a gin and tonic, before sitting down with this. As Christina sometimes says when she writes, 'This is all about me, but I'm really thinking of you.'

Greetings and best love –

Elizabeth

PS. There are cracks caused by subsidence at the front of the house (Stanley Avenue is on a sort of shelf on the hillside overlooking Balmoral); they look quite serious to me and have me hypnotized and paralysed. E

New York | 8 April 79

Dearest Elizabeth –

Some weeks, and many MM crises later, and so glad to have some news of you in the meantime. [...]

We saw that there was a march in Sydney just now about nuclear power, and wondered who of our dear mates was involved. Here we are, staring bemused at the skyline, waiting for a mushroom cloud. What madness. Last week, speaking with Lillian Hellman about civil suit brought against the Dept of Justice here, and against other organs of govt or big business, I mentioned that Whitlam had introduced measures whereby public money was made available to persons bringing civil suits against industrial violators. Lillian – who has a small foundation called, I think, the Committee for Public Justice, that does support actions of the kind – was v. interested and asked me to write out for her what I knew, as she wld like to try to introduce something of the kind here. I did write what I knew, but it was sketchy – and I wondered if you could, as ever, come to the rescue if it is <u>not</u> a fearful pest. For instance, where should Lillian (or I) write to Whitlam now to ask about this? [...]

Lillian H has been through a ghastly time with an eye operation, has lost most of her sight. A terrible drama with a lethal course of prescribed drugs followed the operation – she was rescued from this just in time, by new good doctor. She weighs, now, about 90 pounds – having put on about 12 pounds since the nadir. Incredibly courageous in all this, though always insanely continuing to chain-smoke – she has advanced emphysema, a disease she watched her lover, Dashiell Hammett, die of. She's maddening in many ways, but also good and fearless. The other day she and I went for a walk – she lives very near to us, and needs help to get exercise as she can't see anything but vague outlines. [...] She asked me if I had news of Christina Stead, and I said, only that she had been rather frail. Last night at dinner, also, Harry Ford of the publisher Athenaeum (a hard man to please) remarked out of the blue, 'What I'd give to find a book of Christina Stead's I hadn't read.'

[...]

<u>29 April</u>. Thousand interruptions later. My novel is now in copy-editing at Viking. [...] Viking so far very pleasant – no doubt I'll gnash my teeth over them one day. They have given me a handsome sum – first time I've been well paid for a book. Well, I try not to worry about their getting it all back – that is, presumably Their Problem. NY publishing is a fiendish affair, and one tries to find a human face in the conglomerate cloud and cleave unto it. In London next week, I'll do the English contract with Alan Maclean. Can't believe the stately pile of pages is actually completed. Wondering about getting galleys etc. back and forth through Italian mails (publication probably next March) this summer.

I never replied to your question about Patrick's film. Sumner went with us. I laughed like mad, and many things were good. Never saw a film like it. Very different from my idea of the story. However, some aspects repelled. Misogyny rampant. Why grotesque 'heroine', hideous, like male in drag? Then, some targets too easy – 'posh' house vandalised by girl, for instance; and its owners. Ending had not bothered me in story, but was pure treacle, I thought, in film. Strange that Patrick, who is acutely sympathetic to women in some of his writings, and has beautiful heroines, can also let rip in classic homosexual manner; pouring on a physically repulsive detail, savage jokes about menopause (as if this were a sin). On the other hand, his insight into the horror aspects of women – the Mrs Flacks – is true and exact. Francis also thought that P's film suffered from damp patches of amateurism also. I felt this less – I saw what he meant, but perhaps preferred occasional ineptitude to a professional gloss that varnishes the worst US products of film and telly, supposedly offsetting their total insincerity.

[...]

Wonderful here is an exhibition of Michelangelo drawings at the Morgan Library – a one-place, one-time loan from British Museum and other places. It is beyond adjectives – also an accompanying show of great drawings by approx. contemporaries – Parmigianino, Raphael, Perino del Vaga, and so on. Fearing not to see it before departure, I galloped down to the Morgan Lib., the morning after the opening – luckily found rather few people; by the time I left, there was a short line. The previous evening a friend took me to a beautiful evening of Guarneri Quartet – dramatic, splendid perf. of Brahms septet. These are the things this less and less lovely city still has to offer in abundance. Still, it is good to be leaving for the 'permanent exhibition'...

I too cannot abide Woody Allen, nor get the point. [...] The other evening we had dinner with Joseph Heller and his wife – They're coming to Capri for a month and wanted to ask various info. God knows what they'll do there – they are such NY types, and how can a man like that enjoy a place where no one knows or recognises him, or ever heard of him? People think they want tranquillity; but what they mostly want is for things to go wrong. I'll report. His new book is ghastly. It has some strong underlying satirical ideas. But the ideas are carried off on a crescendo of

NY crassness and false writing; and, if the reader doesn't remotely share the author's ambitions and values, there is no entering into the stream of the book. 'Catch 22' was a remarkable book, I think; but one scarcely recognises the authentic mind at work in that novel in these later efforts. One good book is something, though.

Murray Bail had a delightful story, very short, in a recent New Yorker: 'Healing'. 'They' have also taken a story by Michael Wilding. I lent my editor a couple of Barbara Pym's novels – most partic. 'Quartet In Autumn', which I think her best – and now they tell me they've taken a story from her; this is rather pleasant for the old girl, I imagine. I don't know her, but like these unauthorised risings of forgotten authors from their supposed ashes.

[...]

The New Yorker has taken a bit more of my book. One chapter – which can really stand alone, I think – is a childhood flashback to Australia, by far the most autobiographical part of the book. In fact, there is little autobiography otherwise in the novel (– and, if readers knew what portions are really invested with some of SH's characteristics, they might be taken aback). I find it is more and more attractive to me to make things up entirely, in the sense of events one can invent, or hold memories for unknown people. Am not expressing this well. Perhaps Proust has a lot to answer for, giving rein to the idea that our own impressions are enough. (All very well for him, he was a genius.) Anyway, now I'd like to do a fairly short book, fairly fast. So far – only have about three sentences...

Dearest E, forgive this long limbo; please show forgiveness by writing to your mates some keywords at least of yr news. We hope, some good things. [...]

Much love to you, and to Margaret. We always expect to hear, one day that E or M is embarking for... somewhere (and I don't mean in the MM sense.) It will be good to have a talk one of these days, on one continent or another, and we count on it – Shirley.

New York | 19 Aug 79

Dearest Elizabeth –

So many thanks for yr thoughtful and sustaining letters, answered many times in mind, but now on paper at last – and precipitately, because, when there is actually fairly good news about MM, one must quickly disseminate it before the reversal sets in. As F wrote from London, we left MM installed in the Onslow Court Hotel in Queens Gate [...]. The hotel, alerted by us, has taken a benign interest. The idea being that she should just sit quiet after the horrendous events of the previous weeks, the plan for suicide-at-Southampton, the Hate-S-&-F paroxysms; and let events suggest to her the next move.

[...]

The very fact of being unsettled keeps her sense of adventure up and her boredom a bit down. If we'd taken a flat for her on a four-year lease, she'd by now be suicidal. She has only one pal of her own – rather than a plenipotentiary of ours – who is an old dear, met on the ship, Mildred Tanner by name. When we first arrived in London & were getting hold of MM in Southampton, poor Milders, a raw recruit to the drama, greeted me with 'I very much doubt you'll find her alive by now.' MM, having declared adamant intention of doing away with self, to the point that poor Mildred rushed down to Southampton to dissuade her in the days previous to our arrival. MM's response, when I told her that Mildred had been v. worried, was 'Oh, Mildred likes to dramatise.' And then, 'I offered Mildred my best watch, but she refused to take it, although I saw she'd like to. When I offered her my second-best watch, she needed no pressing.'...

[...]

MM said aggrievedly that no one at Sydney had written her (!!). I repressed the logical response ('Why in hell shld they?') and said, 'Why don't you write them??' No answer. However, Alan tells me that yesterday at lunch MM related to him the whole story of how Elizabeth had taken her ('thinking I was a bit down') to 'a lunatic asylum', and done the wonderful service of introducing her to Andrew. She then added that I (SH) had suggested she ask Andrew if he could find her a place to go on return to Sydney; and that she would do this, by 'writing from one of the ports' when she was sailing back. Alan mildly proposed that right now might be the time to do this, & MM agreed to think it over. So I'll be sending word to Andrew in a day or two.

[...]

Saga this time must seem unending. Episodes of Greek dimensions have been omitted. Something incredible is the radiant appearance of MM, not a minute older; can't get over it.

Elizabeth, while these soap operas have been in full swing, you have been having real life. Blows heaped on Kylie appear endless; what huge fortitude she must have to survive all these calamities. [...]

Something GOOD is Margaret's precious freedom. Please tell her that not one day has passed since I escaped from UN bondage, that I haven't blessed my lot. A continuing, burgeoning satisfaction. Fine to hear that Patrick & Manoly are well – if Manoly goes to Greece in the New Year, we can't help hoping Patrick might go along and that our paths might coincide. Elizabeth, we've just read with the greatest admiration Patrick's new novel, which Viking sent me in proof. It is a tremendous feat, I think, we've both been engrossed by it, and in fact never expect now to be without it in our consciousness. Have you read it? We will be writing Patrick soon – have been getting our own respective proofs out of the house, and waiting for the next load. Viking so far are being ANGELIC to me. Hope it keeps up.

[...]

Please remember about The New Yorker. If you or Margaret – or any good chum – has something you feel like showing them, I'd be proud to be an intermediary. Not that you need one. I'm just trying to grab some of the glory. Much, much love, dear E – from Shirley.

Mosman | 18th September, 1979

Dearest Shirley and Francis –

[...]

A lot seems to have happened in the last few days. For one thing I met Murray Bail last night at a reception for the presentation of the Premier's Literary Awards – to David Malouf, Manning Clark and others... I liked him very much, though we met for a relatively short time. He's good company, interesting. I had been rung by the Premier's department with a request to ask Patrick if he would receive the award on David's behalf.*

So that all passed off agreeably, with numerous seldom-seen friends turning up – looking older! [...]

Yes, I've read Patrick's new book. A copy came from Cape a few weeks ago. Publication date here, and perhaps London, is 27 September. It's extraordinary, brilliant, a great feat. With a sort of stunning bleakness.

[...]

You must both feel light-headed & hearted with proofs finished. Terrific!

Much love,

Elizabeth

*P accepted because he likes David, & likes Manning Clark, who was there.

Mosman | 2nd October, 1979

Dearest Shirley and Francis –

A Herald acquaintance rang the other day to say she'd just read a marvellous story of yours, dear S, in a September New Yorker. She was thrilled about it. So I'm impatiently waiting for my copy to turn up. Sometimes NYs arrive in six weeks, but they can take three months. Helen told me how you'd described the trams in your story, and I instantly remembered those varnished slatted wooden seats, and the curved brass handrails on the outside carriages. It's a pity <u>everything</u> disappears and changes, though it might have been pretty stultifying in those times when objects and rituals seemed static forever.

[...]

Much love,

Elizabeth

Capri | 19 Oct 79

Dearest Elizabeth –

We are still here, as you see – glorious summer weather (interspersed by dramatic storms that arrive considerately at nightfall and disappear at dawn; these keep us clean and watered, while not interfering with swims, walks, breakfasts, lunches & dinners outdoors). Yesterday we were over at Naples, and went to a site near Pompeii to see a staggering (I mean figuratively) new excavation of a decorated Roman villa at Oplonti. May have been at one time a villa of Poppea – shades of Monteverdi – and certainly of imperial dimensions. Huge, with series of interior gardens, fountains, splendidly frescoed vast rooms. The site has been known of for about two hundred years, but only seriously excavated in the last ten years, & so far the recipient merely of 'serious' visitors – archaeologists etc. So one has the sense of seeing this extraordinary thing and its 'Pompeiian' paintings, almost as they are brought to light. Remarkable state of preservation of many of the paintings, some of them so closely resembling the Pompeiian scenes as to suggest they were executed by the same hand. This on the lowest slopes of the Vesuvius, in midst of an ancient & appallingly squalid town called Torre Annunziata. What a marvellous and beloved gulf this is, with its unceasing shocks, shockers, & revelations.

[...]

You will not be surprised to hear that MM is now in thorough dumps, England is an expensive wasteland, and the hotel staff are persecuting her. The room is dreary (that is true), & anything better that has been offered by the management too expensive to accept. Suicide is again raising its oft-lofted head. One groans. Our mates have been heroic, with outings and drives; but have also been abroad, absent, occupied with less deserving cases, etc; and the watch-snatching Mildred long since headed back to Adelaide. It is, as ever, pitiful and truly hopeless of lasting alleviation. Yes, the return to Sydney will be a corker. I suppose the next move will be back to the Onslow again.

[...]

Elizabeth, how nice of you, and of your Herald mate, to feel kindly to my story in The New Yorker. If I may, I'll have a copy sent to you by air now, from NY. It's an Aust chapter from my book – for the publication of the extract, I called it 'Something You'll Remember Always'. There will be one more (non-Aust) episode in the magazine before the thing is published in Feb in USA; probably a little later in Aust & UK. I'd forgotten dem brass hand rails – When you mentioned them, I could see the (quite elegant, I now realise) curve of 'em, and in fact feel them. It was not done for us gels to sit in the outside compartments, and any time we happened to do so, we felt devilish. Do you remember the slatted wooden floors, between whose ridges one's ticket or threepenny-bit used to lodge implacably? Think of the conductor swinging along, at risk of life, as the infernal machine plunged past another of its kind; and the souwester the poor man used to wear as he collected in the rain. As you say, keeping this the same didn't suit people either; but it was a relief to see, at Opplonti yesterday, the identical baskets, dishes, vases, etc. that are still used in the area (swiftly being replaced now by the plastic plethora).

[...]

Did I tell you that F and I are now rereading Don Juan (Byron's, ie) for about an hour each day, with breakfast. I read aloud, and he interjects with the copious notes – most of them necessary and fascinating – as required. For this purpose we have a splendid newish Don Juan put out by Penguin, vast paperback with infinite scholarly notes at the back. Only a few of the notes are of the American-academic-useless-pretentious variety; must have been culled from more than a century's attempts to annotate the work, and from Byron's own jottings concerning the content of the poem. Something staggering (staggers again!) is his erudition – he was thirty, & not only knew <u>everything</u> but could introduce knowledge like notes in music, the perfectly balanced, lightly touched addition to the entire harmony. This is Penguin's God's gift to the breakfast table.

F is well embarked on his second vol of Flaubert letters. We just had a copy of his introduction to the first vol, as published last week in the NY Times Book Review. Things do look splendid in public print. You will feel for the dreadful old monster GF, I think. Lillian Hellman has just gone home from hospital after another eye operation. She will retain enough reading-sight, they hope, to manage to read herself, with large lens. Otherwise, things have been pretty grim with her, but she is phenomenally tough and courageous.

[...]

Could I possibly ask you to send Manning Clark's review of PW's book to me in NY? – I'd love to see it. It will be nice to have a good mag or yarn about this opus. I've been writing letters to Patrick over and over in my mind, but nothing seems right.

[...]

High time we met. Please give our constant friendship to Margaret with much love – Shirley.

Mosman | 23 November, 1979

Dearest Shirley and Francis –

First of all, <u>thank you</u> for splendid, interesting story. Sydney and roundabout have been so lightly touched, as yet, by lit. that it's the story's special bonus for us here to have the place looked at and remembered by you. Dora, of course, is piercingly familiar. The prospect of YM confronting this story and the novel must be taking the edge off, but – I hope you won't let it.

[...]

Lately, not really for a change, I've been falling in love with novels all over again. I love them. You hear sociologists and specialists of different sorts, struggling to discover or make clear ideas set out wonderfully years ago (in different words, to find different audiences) by great, and less than great novelists. They don't know what they're missing. All of these beautiful, severe, true things, lying about waiting to be understood. There should be Billy Grahams for The Novel, on soap-boxes, on street corners. I suppose it would hardly do, but it does seem a pity.

With the Blunt affair in London, Burgess and Maclean are all over the papers again, on the news, on film. Patrick said he knew Blunt, or had met him, at Cambridge. Alan must feel it never ends.

[...]

M and I recently read Iris Murdoch's The Sea, the Sea. Years ago, everyone used to be grudging about IM's merits. I used to feel entertained, and thought her descriptive writing very good – landscapes, water, hair, dogs – but I forgot the people quickly. Now, perhaps still forgetting the people, I find these novels littered with treasures. That we grow in and out of novels according to what we are and where we are in our own lives is hardly a new thought, but so. M and I admired The Sea, the Sea (obsessions are interesting in books, if hideously boring to experience in life), and An Accidental Man. Kylie brought this last one to me, saying enthusiastically that she was <u>certainly</u> grudging about IM.

There was an excellent interview with Mary McCarthy in The Observer of Oct 14, and a good interview with Tom Stoppard somewhere else. Then Margaret Drabble was interviewed on the BBC. Women writers are rather too often dismissed – especially if they have university connections – as 'intellectuals' or 'blue-stockings'. Not allowed to think.

One of this week's near-disasters here was Rupert Murdoch's attempt to take over the Melbourne Herald and Weekly Times group. Governments had almost no power to intervene, but just after the Trade Practices Commission stirred, and after bonus issues by the HWT doubled the number of shares he'd have to acquire, Murdoch withdrew. He sold all his newly bought shares at $5.52 – an inflated price of his creation – an hour before it was known he'd given up, for the moment. He made a profit of 3.5 million. If he had gained control of the HWT, he would have controlled 75 per cent of all press, radio and TV outlets in Australia.

Your visit to the new excavations at Oplonti sounds thrilling. [...] Yesterday at an exhibition (very mixed) with Ferdi, looking at tiles in the pottery section, I remembered arriving in Las Palmas in 1972, seeing the mosaic footpaths, tiled roofs, thinking 'Europe!' and then, 'Home!' (Which Las Palmas can never have been to me.)

[...]

Dear Shirley, dear Francis, I hope (after allowances made for YM and the Ayatollah) you are both well, and in good spirits. I haven't heard from Andrew since that last interrupted call after he'd spoken to Mavis Lonsdale. He's a good person. When there's any word, I'll let you know.

With much love,
Elizabeth

New York | 16 Dec 1979

Dearest Elizabeth –

[...] Thank you so much for the clippings about Patrick's book, and about Randolph Stow – these came in marvellously handy, as Viking was anxious to have good reports of PW's novel for their sales conference, and as they have just taken a new book of RS's. So I passed them along. Viking so far have been very nice to me. The preliminary reviews of my books – in the trade and library publications – are good; so I just keep making the Neapolitan sign to ward off the Evil Eye.

With no change of subject, I note that MM is fast approaching Sydney. We've had nothing from the ship, other than a good cable, remorse (?) for a hideous letter sent to us after we left London. I forget if I told you that while we were in London she handed us, among some documents F was sorting out for her for the bank, a piece of paper with revilings of S and F on it. Unconscious strikes again. It is all pretty bad. How marvellous of you to get and send me the hotel brochure. It seems a very good 'solution' (?) for the short or long run – i.e., as long as it takes for MM to 'hate' it. She has a tremendous paranoia about people at hotel desks – how they have it in for her etc. Almost any form of 'authority' over her produces this – except, oddly, ships' captains and doctors of medicine (the latter are often suspect, but also have been revered). [...]

How good, what you say about novels. Yes, we love them too. I find it exhausting to think of the ground scraped over, as you say, by sociologists and psychologists, which has been covered beautifully and succinctly in art. The human race has no idea of transmitting knowledge of itself, really – except through art, which is usually ignored by those in 'power'. I loved what you said.

[...]

A dear friend of ours, Everett Fahy, the director of the (beautiful) Frick Museum here, is going with a friend to Aust at New Year for a holiday. [...] I introduced Murray Bail to Everett here – Everett asked him to lunch etc. (I'm really bouleversée when a thinking person like Murray is found to believe that 'painting' begins with Cézanne – i.e., that he really cannot see the great paintings, as many readers of current books cannot read Shakespeare or Milton or Pope, or the great poets... I think often – perhaps have already mentioned this to you – of what H. James wrote in connection with 'The Figure in the Carpet': that the very faculty of perception is being lost.)

I had given Everett Patrick's address, so that he might write & ask if it were possible to meet. Then it occurred to me that Everett might have written before I had, so the other evening I called Patrick. A thoroughly gloomy call. (Though indeed I perfectly understand that he is too busy for new people.) One wonders why on earth one did call. Patrick said he had just written me. This turned out to be a quite bitchy (or, more aptly, feline) letter: exactly the letter Douglas Cooper sends us when he feels <u>cafard</u>. It's as well one is surprised by nothing. I've answered it.

The Blunt affair. Oh Lord, so many friends of ours are involved in this (Everett, who knows Blunt well, has been hiding out from the press). Alan takes it with gigantic stoicism. The Blunt role is pretty dismal – or was, thirty years ago. The other interest, if it can be called so, is in the ferocity of savage self-righteousness it brings out in the 'civic-minded'. (Unbelievable, the letters to The (Lon) Times, the language, the revilings, the diatribes.) It gives a sense of what the atmosphere was during the Wilde case.

I should have said, re Blunt, that I do not mean to give my view as exonerating Blunt. One can sympathise with his desperate feelings of conscience, even admire them, as a young man of privileged class during the Depression; and he has behaved with dignity during this present frenzy. But, having signed oaths and accepted confidence and friendship from colleagues, to lead that life is pretty awful, I think – incredible after the Nazi-Soviet pact. Only, the other aspect – of bestial savaging and unearned moral supremacy – is just as repellent to me, and no one comments on it. (Blunt's (art) works are quite beautiful, I think – we had just read his Borromini when this broke; and had been commenting to each other on its rare passionate attachment to its subject, the joy and humility the writer takes towards the work, rather than the usual imposition of an 'authoritative' view. Well, those will last.)

The perverted delight in deceiving a society, while living within it in a privileged position (even accepting a knighthood etc.), is peculiarly intense in England. I suppose, the opp. side of the coin whose good aspect is the sense of privacy. Perhaps more complex than that. I've tried to explore this in my new novel – I hope without too heavy a hand.

Yes, I've been wanting to read IM's The Sea the Sea. She is so variable – sometimes really good, at other times almost ludicrously awful. I liked An Accid. Man. Mary McCarthy is a clever dame; she is a bit trapped in the parochial NY intellectual concept [...] We've just got the new Wm Golding in the house, 'Darkness Visible.' It is strange. But begins with a mighty first chapter. He's a real writer, a harder & harder thing to be. If you see The New Yorker for late Sept, early Oct, there is a fine short novel by William Maxwell, his best I think. It gets unbearable in the second part. He's been working on part of the same theme all his writing life, & now, in his seventies, hit it rightest.

As to hostages, Carter, barbaric world, demos at Mecca... As PW says, 'It's closing down on us.' We all feel like the last moments of Archimedes. The responsibility of this country (USA) is immense in this, not only for their mindless evil actions in Asia and elsewhere; but for having had the power to influence for the good, and thrown it away. The ghastly situation in Iran is the recoil, in part. If one tries to raise questions of experience, history, context, responsibility, here, one gets told 'We can't live with this albatross of guilt around our necks forever.' Privately and publicly, America does not want experience, does not want to reflect, or learn from itself. Or, on the other side, there is the cynical doom talk, pretty much self-indulgence. Of course we have friends who aren't like this. But in general the immaturity of America is a pretty aggressive element.

Eliz., I'd hoped to have an actual book to send you, via Everett. But shan't have copies until mid-Jan or so – when I'll shunt one off. It doesn't appear in Aust until about March, I think. Viking had sent PW a set of galleys without telling me – I wish this hadn't been done. Well, there is always something. Otherwise all goes well as yet with the opus. No, I don't much worry about MM – she can hardly excoriate me more than she does; and the character of Dora is only a tiny drawing on the MM material; with, in fact, none of MM's better qualities – which, let me quickly add before you are quite stunned, disappeared long before you knew her; or had only rare resurrections. As I wrote it, the character became someone else anyway. At first I thought that was because of different physical characteristics I'd given; but it was more than that.

[...]

Much love, dearest E., and a good Christmas – to you and to Margaret. Many many good things in 1980 – a good thing for all of us would be a piece of EH writing. Pl. forgive nagging. We hope somehow to meet in the coming year, and we keep this cheering idea in mind.

Shirley.

Mosman | 12 January, 1980

Dearest Shirley and Francis –

[...]

Your letter of December 16 was held up by Christmas holidays (and the effort of travelling across the harbour to Mosman from Redfern) till January 3. It arrived chewed round the edges by the Redfern machine when Everett Fahy, Channing Blake and the other friends were in the middle of lunch. Channing rang the day they arrived and we made a date for Jan. 3. I spoke to Patrick. He would love to come, I think, to be friendly to you, me and to your friends, but that was the day before Manoly set off for Greece, and he had to go to St Vincent's for treatment of some kind. I asked Salvatore Zofrea (painter), Margaret (so that she wouldn't miss anything enjoyable), and another friend who knows and loves NY and its pictures. I liked Everett and Channing so much. They're lovely guests. I quite wished I had kept them all to myself! The particular things about this place (Sydney and 5 Stanley Avenue) that make you feel you're on holiday are the weather and the view. It rained and was so misty and grey you couldn't see North Head. I showed them a print of Conrad Martens' version of the view, painted from a spot about thirty yards to the right of the terrace. [...] Gave them the crab, prawn, artichoke-heart casserole you had at my place (because that was a memorable night). Since that day others who obviously love the Frick have looked at me, so to speak, with reflected love at the thought of it. They say, 'It's so beautiful.' [...]

I was dismayed to hear about you and Patrick – your call, his reaction or mood, his letter. It's a pity, and unnecessary. A shame. He admires your novel, telling me and David Malouf that it's 'very impressive'. When we spoke – you and I – I knew nothing about your call or his letter... He is sociable and hospitable and has remarkable energy (or has had), but is sometimes oppressed by the overwhelming flow of things. If he does not say yes to all suggestions from the Aust. Council, universities and so on, he is thought to be churlish. So I think this too great pressure wears him down. That is not to say that I think you should receive a letter 'totally lacking goodwill'. Far from it. Although, like you, I feel that nothing is surprising, it is still rather like being shot at close range to be unexpectedly on the receiving end of 'no goodwill'. People do have moods, but things written down are peculiarly hurtful. As I am v. fond of you both, I feel fed up and sorry. The only hard words I've ever had from Patrick have come from his efforts to 'wake the spirit's sleep' and rescue me from some bad decision or bad situation. He thinks it a sort of crime not to work at what you can do, and what you might do better. Although I've done some suffering on these occasions, I've always known what it was about, that the intention was good, and often afterwards I wished I'd taken his advice.

There is much more to say but rather than wait another day to send this off, and I have to dash out, I'll break off here in mid-conversation reluctantly.

[...]

Much love to you both,

Elizabeth

PS. Delighted to hear such good book news. E

Mosman | 28 February, 1980

Dearest Shirley,

What can I say? What a piece of work! Your novel is an experience, a stunning, dense, complex work, one to be read over and over again if all its meaning is to be grasped. (I have read it twice already.) Warmest congratulations and great thanks for writing it and for the copy you sent me, so kindly inscribed.

Really splendid novels (and stories) always give the impression of speaking to large areas of consciousness that, as it were, hang about longing to be spoken to in the proper language. You've done me and all such waiters-about a great favour. I've written that to you before, and it was true before, too.

My God, what labour supporting that world in the air with your mind over such a period! Lucky thing, too! Because what a marvellous feeling to have brought it off. M and I discuss the people and the themes and single sentences. As you said of P's characters, they are part of our consciousness now.

I imagine you are likely to be besieged now and in the near future if publication date is mid-March. Do you mind, or do you enjoy interviews? No, you could hardly enjoy them. Presumably only rather bright people would be sent to talk to you. Protect yourself from all of that, and have (as I'm sure you will without exhortations from me) some beautiful rejoicings and celebrations with Francis and friends.

A dispatch containing other messages and views and things will be shot out of Sydney soon. Meantime, again, congratulations and best love –

Elizabeth

P.S. I took that mail over, of course, & had longish visit. M has seen YM a few times since then. E

New York | 9 March 1980

Dearest Elizabeth –

So many thanks for your lovely cable, and letters. As ever, the telex one most wants to send, and needs time and space for, remains in mind and heart while the inundation of bits of lesser paper takes over. My work-room is like a dump for scraps of papers from street-sweepers' carts – a reviews etc. pile, a UN etc. pile, an aborigines file, catalogues of paintings, supposedly relevant copies of magazines, a pile for a (fascinating) documentary film on the Hiss case, an Amnesty Internat. file, yellowing correspondence, a handful of pcs of a charming picture of Goethe at an Italian window, a typed out quotation from Montaigne, an illustration of a dress for which I want a new belt, a stack from the Academy of American Poets about three Aust poets arriving in April (Malouf, Murray, Buckley), and so on and on. Missing from any of these piles are the pages of my new novel that ought to supersede all the rest; and, which, like letters to you, get done in my head continually as in a resistance movement. [...]

Do you know Baudelaire's poem, 'J'ai plus de souvenirs que si j'avais mille ans'? well, my room is as he describes his soul.

[...]

We hope to go to Capri about 1 May, first stopping in England, during the first days of May, to see the Macleans and do a little for our books which both come out in British edition on – by coincidence – 27 March. Harvard Univ. Press have their own London branch, and are bringing out the Flaubert letters there; and Macmillan are doing my Transit. It is fun having our books out together, and so far they have had a good reception. Neither of us cares that much about reviews – no bravado in this; it is impossible to take the 'critical' scene here (or perhaps anywhere) seriously as a general phenomenon; but of course it's v. much nicer to get benign treatment and more readers, than the other way around; and I feel always anxious for the publisher's money. Several of Francis' reviewers tell the 'story' of the Flaubert letters as if they already had the info in their minds, scarcely stop to note that the letters had to be translated, annotated, etc; and then give their literary views on Flaubert. However, since they would not be reviewers if they really knew anything, and since it is all favourable, no complaints. My book is not officially out until this week, but already has had a lot of reviews and Viking are pleased.

Don Dunstan called several times – we are trying to get some publicity here for the rally on the 15th about aborigines being displaced in South Aust. It is difficult to get coverage for such things – not only because US press has little interest in Aust and south seas, but also because so many indigenous outrages here that their space for moral indignation is pretty much taken up (just as, alas, the space in their readers' minds is also used up).

[...]

I enclose a letter sent to Murray Bail, self-explanatory. Murray not only has no eye for painting; his eyes are closed. The visual arts in Aust are – what? – a busy desert. The publications of the Nat. Gallery (acquisitions etc.) are sent to us: and a conformist, uninspiring story it is. Like Murray, 'they' appear to have no knowledge, and an utter resistance to acquiring knowledge. Every contemporary formula and approved 'recognised' artist is trotted out, without reference to a greater standard, and without proper advice. They get some perfectly good things, of minor kind. They also get a lot of trash, and pay exorbitant sums for it. [...] It is the wretched paltriness of the attitude, and the sublime complacency of it, that annoys. And the ocker belligerence when challenged – or, not even challenged, but encouraged to move in a different direction or to share a greater pleasure. The <u>terror</u> of losing one's purity of ignorance. What I like in Murray must still be there, but this was a pretty contemptible letter I had from him, 'punishing' me for not accepting his parroted little views on art as gospel. [...] Murray gave me a run-down of an evening at Patrick's where, god help us, the conversation STILL seemed to turn on ridiculing Nancy Keesing's appearance. (How much mileage can be got out of that?) He made it clear that I was also the subject of malevolent jeers. Mrs. Jolley and Mrs. Flack are everywhere.

I feel that I – we – offered nothing but goodwill to these people, and got a tinge of evil in return. It is, furthermore, dispiriting to find a really great man like Patrick writing the letter of any spiteful old quean. I doubt the literary scales will fall from my eyes because he tells me that he didn't like some part of my novel when it was in the New Yorker, but did like it in the book; or didn't like my previous work much, but likes the present. These jabs are the classics of literary jokes here. His only criticism of 'substance' of my book (he also said some favourable things, I think) was that I needed more of the gutter. Yet – as I wrote him – I don't feel he 'lacks' something because he ignores the lower depths of working life, in offices and institutions, of hundreds of millions. His nature and perhaps also the comparative affluence of his early life have given him 'nostalgie de la boue'; but you need leisure and private means to pursue that taste, as he says he did in his youth; and those closer to la boue have no need of nostalgie. An author must choose. So: basta. What has attracted me – even, perhaps pleased me – is to look at, live, trace this strange caper of modern life lived in the constant presence and awareness of poverty and war; that is, what the undercurrent of my book strives to be – the endless 'music' of the two wars and the Depression that haunts a life-span like mine. Well, there is a lot else, I hope, besides...

[...]

Unpleasant episode. But how deeply Australian. Sometimes I have felt I couldn't continue living in the USA. But never, here, have I – for instance – heard the intelligentsia (sic), or, come to think of it, anyone else, jeer at the love for opera. In the end, Fraser may be the least of the destructive elements in Aust culture. There is also the inside job.

Part of the present hurly-burly that bothers me is the lack of time for reading. How one must fight to do the things that are the opposite of fighting. By the way, one of the reviewers of my book, today in the Washington Post, said the same things (less well perhaps) about novels that you wrote to us at New Year – how they 'say' what no other human expression can touch on or what 'analysis' misses. The other day the ABC asked me to give another of those little talks, and I gave one on the synthesising element in art – what makes the whole; what must disappear in 'critical' dissection. There is that in life too.

Oh, MM. MM. MM. We had a couple of better letters, then horrors. I have had gloomy times over some of this. [...] We've had true reason to delay sending her our books – other books sent to her were (apparently) stolen in the lobby, as they did not fit into her mail-box. But the moment is coming when they must go to her. I'll just send mine along and cover my ears.

It is remarkable how many people think they have met 'Dora', some quite unknown Dora, as far as I'm concerned. Dora is everywhere; like God.

Oh lord – Patrick wrote us of 'your charmed life with celebrities and the villa in Capri'. Remind you of anybody?

[...]

Much love, dearest E. From your curmudgeonly Shirley.

New York | 10 March 80

Dear Elizabeth –

[...] I am doing this instant word to say how greatly prized and loved your generous words are – they make me happy in a way no one else's could, and I am delighted my book gave you, of all readers, pleasure [...] Because, as Auden says in his delightful Letter to Lord Byron,

Art, if it doesn't start there, at least ends,

Whether aesthetics like the thought or not,

In an attempt to entertain our friends.

Meaning, as Proust (this time) put it, 'some friend of my thoughts.'

[...]

Forgive curmudgeonly content of previous letter re certain Aust vices. I really didn't see why Murray and Patrick should sit around saying poisonous things about me, nor why Murray should relay them. Mockery of absent friends is mortal sin. I too was raised to that indecency; and must wage war on it even now... at one time I would have been more affected by such things; now merely, and briefly, annoyed and disgusted. [...]

Dear and splendid Elizabeth, much love and more thanks than I can say – Shirley

Mosman | 16 July, 1980

Dearest Shirley and Francis –

[...]

Surely YM has sent the National Times piece? It came out during a journalists' strike in NSW, when managements were reporting news and other items direct from New York and elsewhere. I thought you'd possibly seen it in NY. Many friends rang to complain about the NT using a big photo of The Thorn Birds woman instead of one of Shirley, because of the headline (only Australian on NY bestseller list since C.

McCullough). [...] Transit had an excellent review in the SMH and came on sale the Monday afterwards. I saw the Observer review and the advertisement quoting reviews in The New Yorker. It's marvellous that your book has had such reception, been recognized so swiftly and, it seems, far and wide. You must both be happy, and rightly. The book has its own life now.

YM said in a note that it had been sold to Polygram Pictures. Heavens! This is big news, and I hope to hear more when your real telex comes. (I haven't mentioned this to anyone, not knowing what's what.)

Many Sydneysiders are now deep in Transit. (Have discovered I'm a mean lender, and have not persuaded myself to lend my copy. Won't.) One friend who gave up all else to read constantly, emerged saying, 'It's a whole world!' She was bowled over.

You say you've had good letters from YM, followed by distracted and ominous ones. (No, to my knowledge, she's not aware that you've been in Capri.) A few weeks ago Margaret called at The Chimes after not having seen YM for a while. She found her exceedingly distraught and angry. She had seen no-one for ages and had thrown her clock across the room. M said her best deed was simply to let YM talk. YM said she 'couldn't read' the book, and generally railed against her fate, her isolation. She seemed a bit better by the time M left. Shortly after that, the NY piece and the SMH review, and (I think) film news from you, she was elated. In other words, sometimes she's in total misery, and sometimes she isn't.

[...]

For two weeks I went to the Film Festival at the State, having been given a double subscription for Christmas by Patrick. Assorted friends came with me. Decades of human life, war and horror, and protest, rolled over us. The politicians and multi-national chiefs should have been forced to sit through it all. There were some splendid documentaries from the US (political – Vietnam protest, CIA, the Wobblies) and among the others I liked best a seductive, beautifully dream-like film from the USSR called The Mirror, by Tarkovsky. Patrick and Manoly had seats near mine, but did not go so often. Manoly's arthritis (in feet) troubles him a good deal.

[...]

Heard from Christina Stead last week. She is now living in Canberra again, at the A.N.U. in a small university room or flat. It's her birthday tomorrow, July 17. She'll be 77. [...]

Patrick, M and E reading Letters of Flannery O'Connor. And heard Borges on ABC radio couple of nights ago in long interview. Graham Greene, Updike, Robbe-Grillet spoke. The man talking to Borges patronized him. (This often happened to Flannery O'Connor, too. Well, not often, but did happen.)

[...] Greetings, best love –

Elizabeth

Mosman | 12 September, 1980

Dearest S and F,

When I said that, seeing YM in Bradley's Head [Hospital], I thought something like: how could you do this to yourself? Of course it wasn't old age, growing old, that I meant – more, how could you have wasted all that life along the way to this? There was so much intention in it.

[...]

Andrew said the Matron at Bradley's Head is in contact with several nursing homes, and if it should happen that YM must be moved, Andrew and Matron Patience would select what was best out of what's possible. It may never come to this. He was relieved to find that bed at Bradley's Head after three calls.

[...]

Margaret came with me to the flat that last time (in case I got depressed). Mrs Calvert, YM's solid-sterling elderly Scottish neighbour, saw us and came in briefly. I want to take/send her some flowers. She had some pretty dreadful times with YM, but was truly kind and compassionate (not her own pronouncement, but clearly so). The Grace Bros. men did all the packing expertly, and M and I went with them in the front of the taxi truck, because someone had to be present to pay and sign the goods out at the warehouse. Then I took the inventory and papers to Alan's office. Andrew and Mary came down from the Clinic and were there, too.

I couldn't find those crystal beads you mentioned, Shirley. They're quite possibly in one of the five thousand small packages. That flat was not the place to start undoing and spreading out and sorting.

Andrew suggested I should take photographs of you and V to the hospital, so I did, along with the nightdresses and other things. The hospital staff have asked me to get a couple of other things. So that'll happen.

Last week I took to the mountains to see the spring with a friend. And spring was beautifully present. This week-end I'm going away again. And last week-end I had lunch in a wonderful garden, with wisteria petals drifting down and freesias... An Aldous Huxley character said of freesias: they smell like angels. (Smell isn't a wonderful word. Perhaps I'm misquoting. But the sense is perfect.)

A good deal of the first week or ten days seemed to be spent in a state of aghastness. The facts, the small details, the sights and sounds, the waste, sadness, truth, inevitability. A great wearing mixture of feelings and reactions.

I've been wondering if you went to Paris or some other place. I hope it all worked out satisfactorily. Wonder who the scriptwriter is? It's another world, isn't it? The world of film-making.

Keep well. I'll ring if anything changes much...

With love,

Elizabeth

PS. Federal elections October 18. Announced last night.

PPS. Several quarterlies have recently published 'surveys' of my work. It makes me feel I must be going to die. Soon. When one dreadful interview appeared (with the interviewer ever so much brighter than the person interviewed), I really wanted to disappear to Tibet. Perhaps I told you David Malouf destroyed his first interview with this person and insisted on a complete second event. I thought the mortification of it wouldn't kill me, but I didn't like it. Maybe I've said this before. E

New York | 14 September 1980

Dearest Elizabeth –

A word of what will <u>not</u> be superseded by events when you receive it – to say that all you have done, including all the unknowable and unponderable goodness you've shown MM, is never out of my consciousness. There is no possible way to 'repay' those things, but perhaps one day we can give an idea of how much it has meant. That you and Margaret should have undertaken the monstrous task of closing up MM's flat has been a sort of last straw of ultimate largeness of heart. I don't wonder that it shattered you both. As you say, no matter how much horror one has allowed for in this case, there are always revelations – or, rather, another degree of revelation. A worst one hadn't wanted to know.

[...]

Her state, in England in Nov, was pretty close to unhinged a lot of the time – but truly far more so than before, and differently. It is amazing how much horror, and strenuous horror at that, this little being managed to generate. Knowing her makes for a weird inimitable bond – like having been together in a shipwreck.

With love always to you both – Shirley
PS our Italian landlord has suddenly died – another shock and portent...

Capri | 22 Oct 80

Dear E – As ever, the phone allows one to say much of what is already known and little of what one would like to reveal. To give here the main message of my call this morning, we would dearly love to see you; and to this selfish end urge you to think about some possible dates during 1981 when we would arrange for a trip for you – eg Sydney–NY–Sydney; or whatever other sequence you'd prefer. We will otherwise send you the ticket... (As long as it is understood that the ticket is ours, from us to you, and as long as we get to see you somewhere on the route, we don't mind how the details are worked out.) ... This idea is pure selfishness on our part...

[...]

Meanwhile – it is far from 'definite' as Hollywood's word went, that G Armstrong will do the film of my Transit of Venus (though not impossible). The writer of the screenplay seems more fixed – I won't comment on him at present. All should be 'clear' by beginning of the year but a lot of desultory contradictions seem to take place meantime... Having been assisted to get here, I've proceeded to make (my) most of it – we took the opportunity to go from Rome to Siena for some days, it was so lovely. Here, paradise. At Sorrento, a festival of Australian films, including The Night The Prowler...

[...]

Francis urges me to vote 'against Reagan' and cast my ballot for Carter – but I'm tired of that negative urgency, and will try to abstain (even if the spectre of Reagan does loom appallingly). How great and right on all these 'historic' matters does Tolstoy's view ever seem to me – I mean, his disquisitions on the multiplicity of factors conducing to the 'actions' known as history. Not because individuals cannot make single gestures that have effect, but because the gestures and effects can only come about in certain conditions. [...]

The disposal of MM's flat and effects is something you should never have had to do. I in fact had taken this up long before, as a possibility, and thought a different arrangement was agreed, not inflicting such a nightmare on a feeling friend. Had I thought it would devolve on you, then I would have come out. I don't know what to think about that question now – if it would serve any purpose, or spare some innocent victim – I should and would do it. If it would only or principally precipitate a scene of total horror, from which I shrink, then I'll try not to. Meantime, we must have a medical or analogous person at the Sydney end. That's what we'll have to dig out in our call to Andrew. [...] (I only wish you completely free of MM). Please – never mention your 'itemised account' again. When one thinks of what you have done, my lord – heavens.

[...]

With love – Shirley

Mosman | 10 December, 1980

Dearest Shirley and Francis,

Many thoughts sent, but not put to paper. Watching television film of Italy, I thought of you often and wondered about your friends and guessed how you must feel. The anguish and horror are beyond imagining even when they're there before your eyes. Your beloved Naples. Those suffering people. A very few have arrived here already, to join relatives who flew to the rescue. The Herald printed all details in Italian for some days. No light for the survivors anywhere. They can't even hope to be cared for, re-housed, knowing the fate of earlier earthquake victims. What might all this mean politically? There was something so pathetic about the news of aid arriving from all over Europe, the US and the USSR.

Your letter of November 10 and your cheque arrived, Francis. Thank you! Because I meant to write a longish, proper letter, I didn't acknowledge it immediately, which I should have done. Then, for the last ten days I was kept from my typewriter (some people will go to great lengths) by slipping in new slippery sandals and hitting my back hard at waist-level against a low brick wall. (Now I know why wrestlers aren't allowed to hammer each other over the kidneys!) So I've been lying low with hot-water-bottles and a great many books.

[...]

No-one would believe the complications and hysteria the move generated. Andrew said in wonder, 'We've "placed" three other people this week without any of this. They felt sad, and thought no-one loved them, but within hours they were drinking cups of tea and responding to someone friendly...' [...]

I hope you're both working and well and happy. Best love –
Elizabeth

New York | 1 Jan 81

Dearest Elizabeth –

Happy New Year. It's the early evening dark of New Year's Day, damp streets, snow expected. We hope for a good year for you and a year that will be good for us if we can see you here. Thank you so much for your letter. My mind has been a series of teleces in yr direction, and as usual, I've written innumerable letters to faceless persons, and almost never to the people I want to write to. [...] The writing of such letters has become an immense burden to me, and I fear this year the world will somehow have to do without me as a public-spirited missive-mailer. [...] But no one else will do these particular things. However, no one else will write my novel either. [...] We called MM Christmas Eve and she was v lucid, quite calm, quite <u>nice</u>, even moderately affectionate. She has terrific trouble hearing on the phone, but a hovering nurse came on from time to time and relayed our questions to her. Then we called Andrew; I said if MM was really getting into a thoughtful state, I would come out; as I feel I could be a brief comfort to her if she were (miraculously) transformed into a reasoning being, and got back any sincere feeling for me. He said it was very thin ice, and cracked at the least touch; besought me not to come under any such illusion. [...]

Elizabeth, how awful about your back injury. I could feel the horrid wallop as I read. I hope and suppose you've seen a doctor and that you really do feel better? Also hope that you've got to the typewriter with no further self-punishing episodes of that kind or any kind.

[...]

Murray wrote a pleasant letter, and I'll write him. Shall always keep a level voice, and level enthusiasms, now, however, so far as Murray's concerned. His letter – cordial to me – again brings in my mind the hostility felt and shown by so many many Australians – hostility of a peculiarly Aust type. He inveighs against Poms – 'What have they got to show in literature since 1950?' etc. etc. [...] Bruce Beresford gave interviews both in Times of London and here in which he talked like a Neanderthal man, playing to the hilt the sort of aggressive, jeering type, which gave rise to the anti-Aust attitudes of English people in the first place. Here, where there is no great engagement in or awareness of the particular situation, he turned up in the NY Times saying that making films 'gives me the chance to get back at the British, and the Americans too, for that matter' or words to that effect. Why can't his work speak for itself? Why can't the good things of the country be allowed to speak for themselves by now? (Rhetorical questions) Meantime, I've read Clive James' memoirs; which I was (again entre nous) asked to review, but won't. Groan-making – to me, because from your letter I think you've liked the book? But I felt it was one string of aggressive, untransposed, unexamined wisecracks and punch-lines attempting, again, to represent themselves as brutes and oafs and then to be enraged when the presentation is picked up as being significant. I felt if that James was sick into one more glove-compartment I would have to write to him on this theme. [...]

By contrast, I had a nice letter from a writer called Dal Stivens – perhaps I mentioned before that he thought I was a sort of talent-scout for the New Yorker in Australia; then we had a little correspondence, he sent some manuscripts for forwarding to the magazine, etc. He wrote me a pleasant and Australianly eccentric letter, and sent me some of his books. A lovely, unexpected phone call from David Rowbotham in Brisbane. I have many more Aust connections than I ever had – including a row of real charmers, girls who come to interview for Aust papers, and who are all interesting and nice, and sometimes beautiful. Each one has her story – and one sees how hard it is for such women to settle for Aust men with glove compartment tendencies. [...]

Meanwhile here we are Waiting for the Barbarians. We've already had so many threats from the Reagan administration that I feel it must be time for it to go out of office, not to come in.

Before the USA becomes entirely Reaganised, why don't you think about dates and about a reunion during the year? It would be cheerful just to start thinking and talking about it as a reality. Privately we are in v good form, it is the world that gets one down – I can't start to talk about south Italy, it is dreadful. I wanted to go over, but dissuaded by everyone both here and there. I had a tragic letter from a poor man to whom I regularly send a little money, at Naples, and to whom I've now sent a little more. He writes in the most dignified way about spending five nights in the open with his family, and with thousands of others in an open space where nothing could fall on them, and watching their teetering dwelling place. Other friends at Naples are all right, but stricken by events. Further South, of course, it is all the circles of hell. Even in Naples, almost every building is 'lesionata'. On Capri, no damage, 'only, fright'.

With the greatest good wishes to you and to Margaret, dear Elizabeth, and we'll talk soon. With love – Shirley.

New York | 11 May 81

Dearest Elizabeth – Forgive so long a silence – [...]

In April we were briefly at Charlottesville... What a beautiful place... Virginia – what extravagance of beauty: dogwood, coral and white; lilac, purple and white; wisteria; copper beeches, ash, maples; all this interspersed with white colonnaded 18th cent buildings – or extending off into green hills and blue mountains. At present (and indeed for a long time) I feel like Flaubert – that someone who brings politics into the house brings poison. How little is left of real civilised feelings. Flaubert says (after the war of 1870 really turned him into a melancholic completely) that he nearly wept when Victor Hugo, who had gone to see him, quoted lines of poetry to him by heart – the first breath of civilisation for a long time. (As I say this I'm plunged ever deeper into writing, writing, writing, on human rights cases...) [...]

My editor at Viking has given me a copy of P's memoir, or autobiography... Viking think v highly of it, are excited over it. I haven't written to P because – oh because – I don't believe he has any goodwill towards me. Perhaps you are the only woman he does have goodwill towards, and Margaret. Also, because anything I wrote him seemed to provoke a cheap shot of a joke or an easy sneer. A lot of sneering these days. He writes quite differently to Francis. Falling into the common error that F has a different viewpoint from mine; whereas F is far more taken aback by P's tone to me than I am and far more turned off. Well, heaven knows we haven't corresponded for so long it doesn't matter, though. Doesn't matter anyway.

[...]

A couple of weeks ago I read, in four days, two new novels I liked very much. One is The White Hotel, by an English poet & Russianist called Thomas; the early part of the book is too extended, I think (it is presented at first as a Freudian case history, and for me that goes on too long). But the rest of it & the cumulative effect are very moving and ingenious and beautiful. I imagine many people won't like it though. (It is having a surprising commercial success here for a good book, in part because of the closing section of the book and its mighty theme.) The other novel was Muriel Spark's new book, 'Loitering with Intent' – a good title for a book about a novelist picking up material, don't you think? It is her best for a dozen years, I think. What a clever little creature MS is, when she can cut away all the rubbish. Good initials, too, for a writer. (Her maiden name was Camberg; so despite the disaster of her early marriage she gained the Spark and the ms.)

[...]

With our love – Shirley

Mosman | 20 May, 1981

Dearest Shirley and Francis –

So good to have your letter yesterday and the earlier airletter when you returned from Italy.

[...]

You said that you felt as misanthropic as GF the night of writing. So did I the day the letter arrived. I'd just heard that another dinner party at Eliz. Riddell's – Patrick and Manoly, David Malouf, Murray Bail and his wife – had done me over (as the elegant saying goes): women novelists seem to have a thin time there. ER told the company she'd met me in the street and I'd announced I wasn't going to be a victim any more. The others all joined in laughing and went on from there destructively. I told Patrick that this conversational offering was a lie, and that ER didn't know me (we've never visited, and have met occasionally at gatherings). I was as likely to say I wasn't going to be Chinese any more. But I found this info very depressing. Was angry as well as sad. Patrick said I'd have to toughen up, but a world in which you could trust no-one seems not very desirable. If you're so tough that no-one can hurt you, you're dangerous. And you'd feel no affection for anyone. Having avoided all literary groups – where friends write reviews for each other, organize publicity and promotion – I imagined that I'd escape that sort of malice. Or, at least I hoped not to hear about it. I was extremely cast down for days. Massacres, where no-one stands up for you, are a bit grim. I think Patrick was taken aback that I minded so much. If he's ever said hard word to me, it's only ever been because he wanted me to be writing. But no, I'm not by any means his only woman friend. Some actresses are his good friends, and some women connected with film-making. Sumner sounds lovely. It cheers me up considerably to think that there are gentle persons incapable of hurting anyone still about. Though in fact that's what the friends I see regularly are like. Momentarily, however, I imagined the whole world like that dinner party.

(It has taken hundreds of years to write as much letter as this, friends. All because – frail, vain, childish – of that dinner party.)

[...]

Best love,
Elizabeth

Mosman | 5th July, 1981

Dearest Shirley and Francis –

[...] A few days ago, Murray Bail rang me. I told him I'd heard of
the dinner-party and wasn't pleased about it. He couldn't remember.
He mentioned the Flaubert letters, and I told him to read Cocteau.
That was about it.

Recently saw an excellent documentary at the Film Festival – The
Trials of Alger Hiss – made by John Lowenthal. Lowenthal arrived at
Mascot and drove straight to the State (terrifically refurbished and gilded),
and spoke to the audience before and after the film. Labor people like
High Court Judge Lionel Murphy and NSW Minister Paul Landa were
there with their wives, taking notice. Didn't you, dear S, mention someone
connected with this trial quite a long time ago?... The film was impartial,
with no narration, just statements, direct interviews, newsreel clips. This is
all still not settled?

[...]

At the moment boxes of books are arriving from the National Book
Council: with two others, have to choose best and second best book
published in Oz in last twelve months. As the 90 books include children's
books, biographies, anthropology, novels by liberated women, art books
and history, all other reading has had to stop for the time being. [...]
What of Mitterrand? What of the US and Britain objecting to his choice
of ministers? Wonderful! An Australian correspondent in Paris writing
for the Herald said the feeling in Paris was familiar to one who had lived
through the early Whitlam days. He said 'magic' (several times) and 'life
isn't dull, whatever else'.

[...]

Francis, thank you for ringing before you left NY. I felt better for some
kind words and comprehension. Perhaps I made heavy weather of that
occasion, but I was certainly laid low. I thought Patrick would be satisfied
to complain about me to myself. As for the book, I did know months ago
that there would be adverse comments. 'It's all in the book – how you raise
your throat to the knife.' This is something he says about women at various
times in the novels. Ah, well. Everything that could be thought or felt
about it, in all directions, has been thought and felt. I read Auden, Proust,
Cavafy; I read in The Observer, 'When you attempt to get back the good

things of one time while holding on like grim death to the good things of your own, you're up against Isaiah Berlin's implacable doctrine: "Not all good things are compatible."'; and on we go. Little tonics pick us up.

As you said in your last letter, Shirley, 'Things go on v. frighteningly here, and it is hard to be doing one's work for a future that may not exist.' That expressed very much my own feeling. Daily attention to the state of the world can be paralysing. When I swear to leave it to its own devices (!) some new outrage comes to light and vows evaporate: or it might be some new evidence of delight and interest in weapons, and unwillingness to meet and talk.

Nevertheless, I'm sure we all often laugh, and work must go on. Everyone seems to have rung in the midst of letter-writing today, so I'll stop rambling on, friends.

Best love to you both, dear friends –
Elizabeth

New York | 22 July 81

Dearest Elizabeth –
I'm sure I've told you one of my ten thousand favourite quotations from Byron – in a letter to John Murray, after Shelley's death: something absolutely frightful has happened (Leigh Hunt has got round to hearing what Byron has been saying abt him behind his back, and comes to Byron in tears, rage, etc), and Byron writes that at such times he misses Shelley acutely, because 'How we would have laughed, as we used to laugh sometimes at things that are grave in the suburbs'. So I thought, when I read your 'Nevertheless, I'm sure we all often laugh.' It is the only way.

[...]

Dinner at E Riddell's is, I hope, receding from your feelings and consciousness. It doesn't recede much from mine – how utterly right of you to take it up with PW. If he really tells himself that people don't get up from your dinner table unscathed, he has lost touch with reality completely. Perhaps has to disbelieve in any integrity in order to indulge the bad movie that he is running through his mind these days as Life. An appalling remark in his book is that, while those who have to do with him get a lot of bitchiness, he hopes they understand 'that the bitchiness is part

of the fun.' What a bully he has become. All this is awful. I don't want
to go on about the book; it is fundamentally off-key to me. However, the
lack of self-realisation is astonishing in someone who has written those
novels. Near the (ghastly) end of the book, he relates a story of having been
at dinner once, somewhere, seated next to Joan Sutherland. She said she
hadn't read anything of his; but had enjoyed The Thorn Birds. He says he
can't imagine why she was so rude. It doesn't occur to him that some friend
who thinks 'bitchiness is part of the fun' may have relayed to JS some
particle of the endless observations made by PW on her appearance. That
incident also seemed part of his apparent inability to bear with notable
achievement – it is grotesque to think he shld be jealous, of all people; yet
the book and his present antics make clear that a little court is necessary
to him – where he will be the indulged focus of attention, the centre.
This is all familiar stuff, and depressing. Also, from his memoirs, one
finally realises – at least I do – that he has no eye for painting; his interest
seems to be in the metier, the nature of the painter. It is painful to hear
him on certain works, but more painful to think that – with his means,
in the 1930s and even '40s – he could have loved and admired marvellous
pictures; and the NSW gallery would be something other than the tomb
of graffiti it is now.

[...]

When you wrote of the trials of Alger Hiss, I wished we had known
John Lowenthal was going to Aust. We met Lowenthal some years ago,
and he and I were in touch abt Americans at the UN who were fired in the
McCarthy years. Then he turned up in our lives with the preparations to
launch the film – we tried various ways to help publicise it. It was squashed
as much as possible here, but – against the NY Times' strong desires – the
film critic of the NYT Vincent Canby did several good pieces on it. It ran
v briefly, in several movie houses. F wrote to Vincent C to congratulate
him on his brave – for it is brave, in the context here – comments on
the importance of the film. Vincent replied that he was more than ever
glad to have a kind word, as he had got so much hate-mail from people
(who of course had not seen the film...) who denounced him as a commie
sympathiser. There is nothing that brings out primitive passions round
here so much as the mere mention of the name of Alger Hiss. We know
Alger a bit, see him at a friend's place. He is v dignified; his life has been

hell. One feels – I feel anyway – that something has not been told. It is obvious that the case was rigged. Yet this utter truth eludes.

[...]

Tunis – v little left of Carthage, that is of Punic Carthage. UNESCO (just wouldn't let it be!) have excavated some pitiful little boxes – or the floors, thereof – and are working them up to look like ruins. The floors are merely lumps of stone. We prowled among these on a day of mad heat. The Romans not only razed the city, but piled immense earthworks on top of it and then built their own town. So the excavation takes out the side of a small mountain. However, the port of Aeneas and Dido is very 'suggestivo', a small basin overgrown with reeds. The gulf of Tunis, ringed with low but dramatic mountains, v beautiful, turquoise water, unbelievably clear light. The city of Tunis, a mess of old remnants, elderly French remnants, and inundation of jerry-built modern housing (lowish skyscrapers). Where we were, it was heavenly – on the sea, the house on a small rise, marvellous gardens; and really charming white village, Sidi Bou Said. The most beautiful thing for me was the Musée Bardo – vast museum in an old palace; mainly Roman mosaics, in phenomenal state of preservation: many lovely, all fascinating. Whole vast pavements depicting way of life, seasons, agriculture, ports, etc. Some smaller, intensely refined – something of the quality of those at the upper town on Delos, if you know it? ...

[...]

Hope most of all you finished reading those ninety books. Such tasks seem impossible when one takes them on. When they materialise, I can hardly believe the horror of it. Elizabeth, I am hoping to go to Italy on the 8th. Francis remains until late Sept then joins me for all of Oct on Capri. Please begin to think about plans for coming to see us – what season, what continent. [...] Francis was so disgusted when he had the news of that party; he says the moment wld have been propitious to get you out of It All right then. By the way, we have both been very disappointed to think that Eliz. Riddell is an instigator of such evil feeling – we had liked her in our brief meetings, as Byron (also) says, 'The paper spares you.' With love, dear E, & much true friendship – Shirley.

Dearest and incomparable Elizabeth –

[...]

Thinking of Patrick and his awful memoirs (awful to me, anyway) I smiled as the foll. from Flaubert's letters came to mind: 'Almost all human beings are endowed with the gift of exasperating me, and I breathe freely only in the desert.' Indeed, perhaps that was truer of Patrick before he became public, social, and an extoller of 'bitchiness'. If one lives long enough, one sees that anything can come to pass. The English reviews – most of which I've seen – are pretty blah. No one as yet seems to have put their mind to the sources of such a book, such a temperament; and Peter Porter just wrote like a mechanical 'friend.' [...] I am writing a complaint to the Bulletin – thank you for telling me that they published the 'fact' that 'friends Randolph Stow and SH refused to review it'. A Melbourne paper also asked me to do it, and I cabled from Capri simply: 'Sorry cannot review PW thanks, regards'. 'Refusing' can mean that one is recently out of hospital, which I was, or has too much to do, or can't be bothered etc. The violation of professional trust strikes me above all as <u>amateur</u> (well, maybe not above <u>all</u>). Snake Gully ethics. [...]

'Gallipoli' was just abt unbearable. I thought Breaker Morant thoroughly dishonest (oh lord, Don's stricken look when I said that to him) – I defy anyone to tell me what the 'moral', the supposed principle, of that film was. Hated the ranting of the defence counsel, who seemed determined to break every one of Hamlet's rules for acting. Poor Don told me that 'the people on the set applauded' when this ranting was being filmed. Well, 'they' applauded Mussolini, they applauded Hitler; people applaud military parades. Applause isn't by definition critical or noble. The message to me seemed to be that Adolf Eichmann is all right as long as he wears a uniform. The theory that 'men will do anything in the context of war,' put forward as extenuation, did not extend apparently to the supposed villains of the piece. Also – rather distasteful to have blackened Kitchener with something he did not do. (Surely he did enough, in reality without film-makers having to invent something?) Well truly I thought it a film that played on the very emotions it professed to be against. ...

Have you seen anything in Aust about a young Italian woman's novel called 'Paese Fortunato' – ie 'The Lucky Country'? It won a prize in Italy,

and I am about to read it. Unusual case of an immigrant Italian brought
up in Aust, now returned to live in Italy; has written on her Aust life
and experience. Heavens knows what the book will be called if it appears
in Aust, as the Italian title is of course ironic – or at least knowing –
adaptation of the Aust one. Her name is Rosa Cappiello.

[...]

Much thanks, much love, dearest Elizabeth, Shirley.

New York | 21 Feb 82

Dearest Elizabeth –

I send this word to say that, for instance, June is good in Italy, and then
we are back in NYC in August. (F is only concerned that most pictures may
be out of the house in Aug, not here for your inspection; we sometimes
send them to the Metrop Museum summer loan show, particularly if we're
having a room painted or something of the kind.) [...]

In April I have to give my three lectures at Princeton – you'll think
I never do anything else but give lectures (and in fact we are both off to
Yale overnight this week); but I am at swansong stage – I take on to do
such things a year beforehand, then am amazed when. The Princeton
affair is 'serious' – I must do a lot of work to justify myself. But novelists
have no 'subject' – one has to think up things one never would've thought
of. I'm calling the 'theme', 'The Lonely Word,' from a Tennysonian context
I'll revert to. The first is 'Virgil and Montale'; which is rather pleasant to
do in a way; the second, 'The Defence of Candour' (exposure of language
pretensions, demonstrated through literature especially novels – eg Osric;
or Mr Vincy using the word 'demise' – well, I have to work all this into
something interesting (I hope); third, 'The Bright Reversion,' about
writers' views of posterity (Byron: 'He that reserves his laurels for posterity/
Who does not always claim the bright reversion'...), which I have a lot of
notes for but not much else... What a relief when these are done – for the
audience too, I fear. All I want to do is my novel.

[...]

I'm sending a separate envelope of other clippings – some about
the really staggering new 'primitive' wing at the Metrop. Museum. It is

exhaustingly presented, but full of fascinating things. You will see same. With love – Shirley.

It is thrilling to think you might come.

Mosman | 16 March, 1982

Dearest Shirley and Francis –

Where to start? That was a good talk, wasn't it? As ever, lovely to hear your voices. So much to say.

[...]

A real estate agent has brought a few people through the house, prospective tenants. Last year, I spoke to some agents. They were all interested in selling the place, but not in renting.

[...]

In between times, had lunch with some Bulgarian poets who came to the Adelaide Festival, dinner with Judah, lunch with Kylie for her 70th birthday, lunch with a Hungarian graphic artist, and so on. This is almost the first peaceful day for weeks. Heaven.

The Patrick/Sidney Nolan stir was all over the papers. While many people thought P would have done well to say nothing about Sidney and his marriages, no-one thought Sidney had done himself anything but harm by retaliating as he did. It was such an ugly painting, and not clever. Pretty alienating. In another area you thought I might have gone in for a little repartee, but I have no talent in that direction and have given up, anyway, having conversations with another person's neurosis/es. Freedom.

[...]

To be continued... Much love,

Elizabeth

Mosman | 24 March, 1982

Dearest Shirley and Francis –

I'd love to see you and certainly could do with a change out of Australia, but I don't think it can all happen by June. The boring house news in the other letter is part of it. Getting the right agent, tenant, new flat, could happen quickly, but that can't be counted on. If June, July, August were cool or cold I might close the door and go anyway, but summer as ever is something to endure. There's still not much airconditioning here in private houses and the humidity has laid us all out. Can't breathe. So, generally, I don't want to go away and come back to live in this house, and on the whole I'd rather not be hot. I took to London's grey skies and clouds and bare trees the way most people take to sun, sea and palms. Also, because of the distances, if I do trek out, I might stay away for a few months and do some work away, or at least I'd like to keep that option in mind. That's why I prefer to leave things in a tidy state here. Thank you both for these beauteous plans and suggestions. I <u>want</u> to see you and the islands and paintings, and I hope it might happen pretty soon.

I saw YM the other day briefly. Went once before lunch when she was up and dressed and eating in the room with others. In order not to distract her from the meal, I promised to return later. When I went back she was lying down and half-asleep. There is a real deterioration. Leaving, I spoke to the dreadful Dawn – poised, curious, smiling and throwing Christian names around as though no-one had a father. She said: 'As long as Shirley realizes what her mother's condition is.' I said that given YM's age and her admission to St Vincent's and the expectations then, I believed you did understand.

You spoke of meeting Margaret Fink and mentioned her comments about Christina. In recent times Christina has had a few minor heart attacks, and was at the Royal North Shore Hospital for eight days. She now moves between her half-brother at Lindfield and half-sister at Cremorne, taking an oxygen cylinder with her. She is very frail but in brilliant spirits, saying she feels about twenty-five inside. She was making notes for a book yesterday. She does love men very much, but she also has some good women friends. She doesn't like being claimed by feminists as a feminist, and as she is genuinely uninterested in fame and fortune she doesn't like anyone who cares much about them. She's a fine person. She loves to talk about words, language.

Went to the pics with Patrick and Manoly on Monday morning. We saw a documentary called <u>Home on the Range</u> about US bases in Australia. It was bad for the heart, nerves and blood pressure. The film maker sought funds from here and there and wrote to Patrick, among others, who sent a cheque by return (so Gil Scrine said in an interview). It was chilling. There is an anti-nuclear march on April 4 from the Quay to Hyde Park South. Patrick is taking part and then speaking. He had a happy time in Adelaide for two weeks, when his play <u>Signal Driver</u> was produced, but looked pretty tired on Monday. Manoly was walking with a stick. We had all been looking for candles, batteries and kerosene lamps because of proposed black-outs.

[...]

Friends, I hope you had happy times in March on your island and relaxed after finishing book and lectures. Lovely feeling! Take care. Much love,

Elizabeth

New York | 6 April 82

Dearest Elizabeth –

Just got yr letter, and thought I'd send a quick telex. Outside the windows, a blizzard; plus thunder and lightning. Branches that were showing green buds now burdened with snow, in our building's garden. Insane. A week ago, sitting out with straw hats at the gulf of Naples. Now, I didn't realise about you and heat. Then let us think of it for winter, here. Will you think abt something of the Dec-Jan kind for NYC? We did think you might be wanting to combine with longer absence abroad than just seeing us (that sounds like MM, but isn't!), and that's why we proposed June-ish in Italy, then some other time possibly here. But it can be the other way around, or any way you want it, of course.

[...]

Thank you dear Elizabeth for news of Christina (I sound like Dawn). She seemed v impressive & v nice when I met her chez vous. There is some movement on 'my' film – I'll know more in a month or so. Donald Keene's book is lovely isn't it? – He also brought me news that you have a paperback out, of The Watch Tower, and I've sent for some of it. [...]

I should have said a propos yr visit, that we UNDERSTAND about people needing time, silence, solitude. Not having to talk all the time, or do what others <u>think</u> they ought to enjoy... etc. But you know that – with love – Shirley

New York | [23] April 82 Shakespeare's birthday

Dearest Elizabeth –

A quick word to thank you, as ever, to send love and to wonder how you are and what is happening abt your house. [...]

Thank you for note, and enclosure about anti-nuclear march. Something is stirring at long last, even if it is only survival instinct. (Reason and humanity are apparently the last things we can depend on.) [...]

Yesterday I called The Mosman. Discovered that Valerie had been to see MM, but that MM did not know her... I spoke with Sister Hopkins... it is possible MM has had another mild stroke in all this. At present it seems a good idea for me to telephone on the weekend and get a little news that way: I gather that 'Dawn' is blessedly absent at that time.

[...]

When will we see you? We had such a nice message from Margaret – it would be good to see her too... These times require such seeings... On the Patrick-Nolan theme – they will end up by boring us all to death with their rancour. (Rancour is a boring property.) The picture (SN's) is absurd; but PW 'started it'. [...]

Love to you – Shirley

Mosman | 28 April, 1982

Dearest Shirley and Francis –

Today the third Jonathan Schell <u>Nuclear Arms</u> arrived. Last Saturday there was a big piece in the SMH, headed 'The machinery of the world's destruction is now complete', about the effect of the three articles 'on the news and opinion makers of America'. You do feel that only the dead or insane could fail to understand and respond to what Schell says. Patrick was bowled over by the Herald extracts and wants to distribute copies all over. Is it a book?...

[...]

Not finished but off to have hair fixed, so I'll post this on the way and finish later. Meantime, love to you both

Elizabeth

PS. In the SMH this morning a notice about a new exhibition of paintings by Sidney Nolan – twenty or forty at $2300 of Patrick and/or Manoly in deeply unflattering attitudes.

New York | 15 May 82

Dearest Elizabeth –

A quick telex to thank you for your lovely letter. [...]

I will send Jonathan your comments about the Aust reception of The Fate of the Earth if you don't mind. Alan Williams (my editor, & Patrick's, at Viking) – a lovely man – told me a couple of weeks ago that he had sent Patrick a copy of the book; then he had such an awful letter from him about something that he wondered if Patrick would pour scorn on Jonathan also (PW being no slouch at that NYr-baiting stuff). I now happily reassured him that Patrick was on the side of survival even if that had to be conveyed by the deputy editor of the NYr. [...]

My film is moving on a bit. Gillian Armstrong and Patricia have got together now with the Hollywood company. [...] A letter from Murray Bail (oh God, I haven't answered his last yet – I sent him a cable about his book; must write him tomorrow) tells us that David Malouf has been excommunicated by Patrick for standing up for God Save The Queen. Is this what people have to worry about out there? – the Lucky Country indeed. I fear I'd not get far with Patrick and his life sentences, sendings into exile, decrees from the throne etc. etc. It all seems to me to have got frightful, and of a pettiness... Sumner told me an exquisite – heart-rending – detail of his evening at Patrick's – the famous one. When he staggered down the garden path to the waiting taxi, consummately aware of what was happening as soon as he was out of earshot, Patrick's dogs shot past him, and one headed down for the gate. At this moment Patrick himself appeared on the verandah above, and called out, 'Come back!' Sumner then told me, 'And I like the idiot I have always been, thought that after all Patrick had felt remorse for the awful time he'd given me, and was calling a last message. And I turned and waved, and shouted, "Patrick, I will!" Whereupon Patrick yelled, "Not you! The dogs!"' ...

[...]

I keep writing (flowery cards) to MM – it wld be awful if she regained understanding & found she'd been treated as without consciousness; and we telephone the Mosman regularly. It is awful; and all part of the whole awfulness. Yes, I know that her appearance must be a shock, unbearable. Last Sunday 'they' said she was 'more herself'. One hardly knows what to wish for her. With love, dearest E – Shirley

Mosman | 19 May, 1982

Dearest Shirley and Francis –

Isn't airmail <u>slow</u>? Your letter of Shakespeare's birthday, posted on April 26, reached here on May 11. I know this is quite usual, but it's exasperating when you think how fast planes get to and fro. Thank you as ever for all good thoughts, words... I've spoken to Sister Hoskins, too, and she is very gentle and kind. As I said in that last letter, the very day I called in with your cards, YM had had what was described as 'a funny turn', and was unaware of anyone's presence. That was really the first time – through these many crises – that it's been impossible to exchange some words or signs of recognition. It's all beyond idle conversation, explanations or 'accountings'...

The British have never acted and sounded so much like caricatures of themselves. The language, the attitudes, the Union Jacks. They have all seen too many bad films about the Second World War. They must also be having a competition among themselves to see who can read communiques most slowly without losing the thread altogether. Then there is the cheerless rise in Mrs Thatcher's popularity, and the criticism of the BBC for being 'too even-handed'! Like you, I wouldn't want to be around during an Argentine invasion, but the islanders haven't got automatic right of entry into Britain as 'first-class' British citizens and the eventual handing-over was thought to be only a matter of time. It was also discouraging that everyone was surprised, apparently, when weapons and confrontations produced dead bodies. Imagination, where are you?

[...]

Trust you are both well, recovered from lectures and too much work, and trust, too, that we'll meet soon before we're all blown up by the world's patriots. (At Monash Univ., Christina used to be asked by students why she had become 'an expatriot'?!)

Greetings, dear friends, and love –

Elizabeth

Capri | 2 Oct 1982

Dearest Elizabeth –

A hasty telex, which I'm galloping down to town to despatch. About the time you get this, a (youngish, I think) American doctor, Jonathan LaPook, will be arriving at Sydney to work for a couple of months at Royal North Shore Hospital. He is bringing a book from Lillian Hellman for Christina Stead and does not know CS's address (which Lillian had mislaid) or how to get it to her. This morning here I received a letter from Lillian H asking for help in this. I telephoned Dr LaP in NY and found him extremely nice & v appreciative of any help. I suggested he call you. (I also suggested, since he knows not one single cat at Sydney, that he might like to get in touch with Andrew; he will be living at RNS.)

[...]

I had a long and good letter from Gillian A. Perhaps something will be salvaged. It is impenetrable to me; and of course worrying, somewhat, in case an icky film should result from all these wranglings. [...]

F's book comes out a couple of weeks from now. You should soon have a copy. So far, all early signals are v good... Francis tells me, 'You MUST tell Elizabeth how I admire The Long Prospect. Excellent. Admirable.' Most heartily and wholeheartedly agree. Congratulations, dear E, and much love from Shirley

PS 'They' – ABC – have been calling me here abt doing the Boyer lectures in 83. Not decided – it is the question of taking time from my novel. Got to stick at it – want to stick at it.

Mosman | 22 October, 1982

Dearest Shirley and Francis –

Thank you for wonderful New York letters, Capri letter and cable.
Possibly we'll have spoken before – and this was when the telephone
rang, Francis. High marks on the coincidence scale, surely? Lovely to hear
your voice, as ever. And, as I said, your prose and the prose of GF is doing
me a great deal of good. I'm trying to read slowly, to ration myself. It's a
beautiful book in all ways, and I do thank you for it.

That's interesting, that Valerie has written. Earlier, I think I said that
she did want to be reconciled with you. When I didn't respond to V's
taking for granted that I'd go through YM's things with her, she ceased to
be in touch. This doesn't matter at all because we basically have nothing
to say to each other. [...] No-one, as far as I know, goes to see YM. This is
not something she would be conscious of. Nurses seen every day might
spark a little recognition, but no-one else – unless there is a miracle. I
wouldn't call YM back to full consciousness if I could. It's scarcely to be
desired. Sister Hoskins gave me a list of things needed and I acquired from
DJs' ('acquired' sounds as if I'd gone in for shop-lifting!): 2 nightdresses
(cotton), 1 dressing gown (cotton), 2 pairs socks, 2 singlets, 1 pr slippers;
then, as instructed, I wrote 'Hazzard' on everything. They all – except
slippers – go into the washing-machines [...]

The call came from Dr Jonathan LaPook and Andrew and I surged
about being hospitable. Andrew has taken him out on the town a couple of
times, collecting and delivering, and is having a dinner for him tomorrow
night, to which I'm invited. I spoke to Christina and she took Jon (would
he spell it like that?) and me to lunch last Saturday. We met at her place and
transported ourselves around in taxis. (It's better to own a car when you're
Christina's friend, but, however.) She is frail. Anyway, we settled into a
place not far from Cremorne, where she is for the moment. She loved the
young New York doctor. She had a marvellous time. She blew me kisses
to thank me for my role in producing this congenial person. And so on.
He is 29 and way over six feet, and kind and sympathetic. He told her of
Lillian Hellman's admiration, and gave Christina an inscribed copy of
Pentimento. [...]

Australia has had its own amazing times, lately. Unemployed people
have taken to gathering outside the wildly conservative Melbourne Club

to confuse the members (easy tis). Sacked miners are staying down in the mines in Wollongong. Unemployed steelworkers and miners are planning a march to Canberra, and want to set up a tent city outside Parliament House. Every day factories close. Tradesmen imported from the UK less than a year ago with assurances of work and prosperity are laid off. Foreign students, migrants, are becoming less and less popular. Above all, what has happened here has been the Costigan Report. Frank Costigan, Q.C., once a Labor candidate in Victoria, was given the task of reporting, as Royal Commissioner, on the Painters' and Dockers' Union. This smallish union has so many murders to its credit, such a murky past, that investigation, all agreed, was overdue. However, no-one expected that Frank Costigan would be so thorough. He has uncovered an Australia-wide network of crime 'in high places' and tax avoidance schemes, involving the powerful, that have cost the country billions. Only relatively poor people are paying taxes in Australia. Since the relatively poor make up the majority, they're fed up and the government is wringing its hands and every day there are New Revelations. It's hard not to write about this in headlines. The government had brought down an election budget, giving things away without means tests, to buy votes. They had intended to have a federal election at the end of this year, before it was due. Then came the Report – or interim reports – and an election seemed less like a brilliant idea from the Liberals' point of view. With everything so dire, it doesn't look like an election Labor would want to win either.

[...]

As it's Friday arvo and must rush up to bank and P.O., think I'll post this first section of letter and send second half on Monday.

[...]

Much love to you both,
Elizabeth

Mosman | 22 October, 1982

Dearest Shirley and Francis –

Part II. Have returned from being 'up the street' and want to dash forward with more incoherent (only on and off, I hope) news on the southland.

A few weeks ago at the Premier's Literary Awards Dinner I had to collect Christina's gold medal and cheque. People clapped loudly, hearing her name, because she's known to relatively few. When I said my sentence and took the medal, it was the first time I had ever spoken from a platform. Christina told me ages ago that when she v. occasionally had to speak in public she felt like 'a very shallow person': perhaps I was a suitable substitute since I felt much the same. I like Neville Wran, though. He's a happy man, and has quantities of commonsense.

Women in the Arts have had a Week or a Fortnight of their own. They launched the Women's Who's Who in Australia and had a million exhibitions of pottery, other book launchings, strange plays showing liberation. I didn't go to the launching, and didn't speak on yet another platform and didn't even go to listen to others talking about writing. (Why 'even'?) You say you wonder if Australia can really come forward until numbers of women are released into public and active and creative life. I don't know. As you say, women are <u>not</u> all sweet reason and aesthetic power. I met Senator Susan Ryan at the Premier's dinner. She introduced herself, and said she'd met you. She seems an admirable person. Asked to name the novel she liked best a year or so ago, along with other people, she chose Böll's <u>The Clown</u>, a novel I admire, so I've liked her especially since then. There are some excellent women around. One who comes to mind is Philippa Smith, a lovely young woman who is chief of ACOSS – Aust. Council of Social Services. She is fearless and battles for the 'disadvantaged' – as poor people are called – without being strident. There are some women lawyers, women doctors, some known through newspapers and others accidentally encountered, who give hope. There are many more, like the dreaded Ita Buttrose, who have the opposite effect, but I think more idealistic and sane women of goodwill are on the loose here than ever before, and that's a good thing. They haven't been spoilt or spoilt themselves by browbeating and dominating men. There is a beauteous true equality here and there, and some of these wise people have children. Let's be hopeful!

This very day, Judah Waten sent me from Melbourne your TLS piece, dear S. My God! I feel like putting on a hat so that I can take it off to you. That is <u>real work</u>. It would inspire some teeth grinding in certain circles, presumably? You'll possibly have arrived home to – what sort of response from UN officials? I can't imagine. I was in mid-letter, typing Part I, when Judah's letter and clipping came, so I've only read it once. Tonight I'll read it with the concentration it merits and demands. I told Margaret on the phone about it: she has queued up. Congratulations. I'm relieved that it took you a long time!

[...]

Thank you for good words from Capri about 'The Long Prospect'. [...] It was published in London in 1958 when things Australian were (to the rest of the world) still lost in primaeval mists and slime. Patrick and Sidney Nolan had just begun, at that time, to clamber out of it, surprising people. But all along the way, over the years, single persons have come across it and been fond of it. Patrick and Christina, before they knew me, liked it. Max Harris 'discovered' it and wrote some reams. That's all long ago. What nicer thing could you possibly have said than that you wanted to know what happened to Emily, and wondered. Really, thank you.

25 October (Monday)

[...]

Patrick. He seems better now. They may do the other eye operation late this year or early next year. He's been working, working. Mostly, I suppose, I see the more homely non-famous person in Patrick. Years ago he made efforts to talk sense to me about myself, tried to rescue me from bad situations when no-one else did. He has a lot of credit in the bank with me, in spite of the ER dinner and his non-wonderful passing on of that, exchanges with you and so on. We talk often for longish times, and these conversations just don't consist of gossip or rage or tearing people down. Maybe, surely, with other people this happens, but it takes two to make a conversation. [...] I know Patrick and GD have been friends for a long time, but marriages fail and friendships do, too. Sometimes one person keeps the thing ticking over, when the other would let it go. I like ideal friendships that last forever, but commonsense and experience warn me that people change. To me, P is a bit like a relative with virtues and faults, but I try not to count on anything. If he had a coffee-shop, I'd enjoy his company. One last comment then silence: I don't think there's any truth at all in the 'ex-communication' of David Malouf. I recognize the justice of what you say, but affection's involved and I don't change easily.

[...]

Thank you again, dear friends, for GF, for letters and talks.
Much love,
Elizabeth

New York | 12–16 Jan 83

Dearest Elizabeth –

How splenders to have talked a couple of times in a couple of weeks.
[...]

Do you know – like – the work of Montale? Poems, and the essays
too? A difficult man and difficult work; but so much intelligence, such
strong ideas and feelings dispassionately presented. I've been trying a bit
to peddle a large vol of his essays just out here in translation. Some of them
excellent. Integrity. We were stunned that you'd already received Anita
Brookner's book, and read it. I'm glad you like it too. There were so many
good things in it. [...]

Christmas wishes from Patrick, 'in a sinking world.' [...]

Meantime, I get on with book. Too many other things, to hell with
them. [...] Another thing I have on hand is an article I accepted to do for
Napoli Nobilissima – did I tell you about this? 'NN' is a publication,
about a century old, of monographs on aspects of Naples, usually art
history, archaeology, history of the city, culture etc. but 'original research'.
These scholarly monographs are issued every so often, and bound every
few years into a new volume. [...] Dread starting it, because of complexity,
researches, time, time, time. Writing in Italian, more time. However, the
other evening, after a better day's work on my own ms. than for months, I
suddenly began this task and found myself whizzing on with it. What fun.
I suppose weeks will pass before I have such an experience again, but it was
a reminder that one must just seize the moment again and put pen to paper.
I'm unworthy to write for 'NN' but then so are others; and I at least would
<u>like</u> to be worthy, and know my unworthiness.
[...]

Let us hear about dates. Dates. Forgive ramblers. Haven't mentioned
the awful world. Too awful for mention. Flagrant. Blatant. But where are
'the public'? my experiences – strong ones – cause me never to rely on that
so-called public. Those who have rallied to any cause I have had the burden

of proclaiming have been almost nil: two cats, a stoat, a ferret, a weasel. The best company, no doubt.

Let's see you before more months go by.

Best & greatest love to you always – Shirley

New York | 21 Feb 1983

Dearest Elizabeth –

The pathos of MM is utterly appalling, the more for being an extension of so much else that is pitiful & wasteful & dire. The mad illogic of life, that she should go on like this. [...]

To complete the dire aspect – we read of these frightful fires in Aust. It recalls my childhood, when long drought produced conflagration across the land – the still, hot, portentous atmosphere, ash from the interior. All this compounded by Depression, the shadow of the Great War, the approaching 'next' war... It's a miracle we all can go on with things. I'm always marvelling at how much good and beauty has been produced by human beings, when one ponders the other side of fate, nature, wars, etc. Of course we are watching the March 5 election, & do not get our hopes up as faith in public common sense runs rather low in such affairs; however, surely we are due for a good surprise on the law of averages. [...]

With love – Shirley

Mosman | 24 February, 1983

Dearest Shirley and Francis –

[...]

Did I ever say that I visited YM on Christmas Day? I called in on the morning of 25th, taking small edible presents and stayed a little while. There was no recognition at all, and, really, it's virtually impossible for me to recognize Kit. Grim.

[...]

A Scotsman has been here painting the kitchen and putting new floor-covering down. The non-glamorous kitchen was a handicap when I asked agents to let the place last year. (I have <u>tried</u> to get away.) It still lacks items desired by tenants, but may pass. Whether to remove myself for one month, six or twelve is a choice I find difficult to think about. I should have extricated myself from this outpost at the end of 1975 when I had the energy and desire. A change is a necessity, however, and the possibilities are tossing about in my mind. Why did Europeans ever isolate themselves so from their own world? If only my Scottish forebears had gone to Canada, which is so much closer to Europe! Because maps of the world choose to put us at the bottom, you have the illusion of having to puff up hill getting away. (Put this rambling down to the humidity. We're all gasping like landed fish. Almost no-one has airconditioning.) I have your programme in front of me (understand your feeling in setting it out full well). Ideas surging while Mr Meek, my Scot, continues to improve the dwelling in minor ways.

[...]

Much love,
Elizabeth

Mosman | 15 March, 1983

Dearest Shirley and Francis –

[...]

Australia. What records have we not broken this year? The worst drought in history means the sun obscured by dust in Sydney; it means the State Rail Authority losing millions in freight and hundreds or thousands of jobs, and that in turn means trouble with railway unions. On television news you see staggeringly philosophical farmers shooting their sheep and cattle and walking off the farms. There isn't much water in the Snowy River Scheme so irrigation becomes a problem and today in Sydney we're asked to conserve electricity. While there are always bushfires, it's seldom that anyone is killed. Lately there have been some tragedies with volunteer fire-crews being wiped out. But seventy-one people being burned to death in fires of such ferocity and magnitude – that was something unheard of. It was difficult to understand that you were watching smoke from fires in Victoria and South Australia, but so it was. Great forests grown for logging, nearing the end of their fifty-year life, are now mile after mile of black sticks. The rivers were black with ash. When the BBC said the fires were burning on a front that stretched as from London to the middle of Europe, it gave a new and almost more awful perspective. The poor people. Again the herds and flocks were destroyed in vast numbers. Then there were sudden severe floods in South Australia. Dorothea Mackellar: My Country...

Sydney had its most humid summer and hottest March day in history. And so on... Driving to a pre-election fund-raising dinner in town, I heard on ABC radio that there had been one Labor Government in Australia in thirty-five years. Not news, but not bearable, either, when you think what that has meant to half the population. The suspense during the campaign was bad for everyone's health. As you might see in some of those clippings, Fraser thought he'd catch the ALP either with Hayden as Leader, or in mid-quarrel over the leadership. The timing was extraordinary. He was visiting the Governor-General while in Queensland Hayden was selflessly standing down and the ALP uniting behind Hawke. Fraser, judging others by himself, was so stunned by this vastly unselfish behaviour that he couldn't recover. He ranted away at an open-air meeting in Melbourne, telling people that their money would be safer under their beds than in the banks, if Labor came to power. Elderly people all over the country were frightened as intended, but lots more were sick of anger and suspicion as a daily diet. The Labor majority so far is twenty-five – the biggest since Federation. Hawke couldn't do anything wrong during the campaign. Only Tasmania voted solidly against Labor. This was because of the below-Franklin dam issue. Unemployment is severe there, and the people want the dam. Labor said they would preserve the river and stop the dam. (You may have heard from Max A. of the NO DAMS protest movement.) This won't be easy because it cuts across States' rights. They'll all go to the High Court, probably.

By Election Day the tension was terrific. Polls closed at eight, and the people in the Canberra tally-room started to tell us about trends half an hour later. Hours passed while our hearts and blood-pressure went up and down. The commentators tried to be impartial, but sometimes they had tears in their eyes, and sometimes we could hear great cheering as new figures went up somewhere out of sight behind their desks. At last, a simply wonderful little message started to run across the bottom of the screen: ALP WINS GOVERNMENT... ALP WINS GOVERNMENT... We waited and watched (ten of us at Hunter's Hill), afraid to believe it after all the suffering. We waited then for Hawke or Fraser to appear. Since that happy night, like a villain in a pantomime or an opera, Fraser has disappeared in a puff of smoke. There is a God. There is justice. Strangers talk to each other in the street. (Of course, it will never be 1975 again.)

That was lovely of you to ring me on Sunday. I'd have rung you, if not. There's a lot of radiance about... [...]

That's interesting and good that you'll be giving the Boyer lectures in 1984. Quite recently Patrick said something about this to me. So someone at the ABC or elsewhere has spoken. But yes, I'll certainly be there long before that. We're agreed.

[...]

Kylie was here last week-end before driving her aged Pa down to Patonga. She is now seventy-one, and her father is ninety-four. She will always be a Wild One of about twenty-three. Perhaps some resemblance to Lillian H.

Margaret seems to be fine. I always tell her news of you. We speak on the phone a lot, exchanging literary and political items. She's coming to dinner on Thursday with several others. Going to a reception to meet Melina Mercouri on Friday. It's Greece's national day. You don't meet or even want to meet people at these gatherings, but it might be interesting and I'll be with Antigone, who will know who all the Greeks are. It's at Neville Wran's office, so I'll know who the politicians are.

My feet (I feel) are going to walk into a travel place soon. I'll sit down and read your travel piece several times over later today.

My love to you both,

Elizabeth

P.S. Have taken a vow to think, speak & write henceforth only of Love, Literature, Human Nature & Travel, & Philosophy & History. E

Capri | 9 April 83

Dearest Elizabeth –

Just a note to say that we were sad today to see – in the Times (London) – the news of Christina's death. We at once thought of you. I know it wasn't entirely unexpected, but it can never come as a matter of course. A strong, purposeful life, pursued – I feel – over many difficulties.

Now, alas, no visit to New York. But her memories of that impossible place remained with her, and a wish to travel to it again.

Here – beautiful spring, rather cold.

[...]

We hope to find some word – and most particularly – of your plans – when we get back to NY in ten days' time. Meantime, dear E, our love to you and to Margaret, and our many thoughts and feelings about Christina's death. It's thanks to you that I ever met her – I'm v glad that I did.

With love – Shirley

Mosman | 12 April, 1983

Tiny note, dear friends, to accompany clippings.

Christina died on March 31, and there was a small private funeral on April 6: Easter intervened. Only seven of us were there. I've written to Jon LaPook and he and Lillian sent a cable from California. Christina was a great good friend. Her life was a triumph, though the last two years were not good. We understood each other.

[...]

Hope you had fine time in Italy, that you're both well and working well.

Our new government is good, intelligent, kind, calm, thoughtful, AMAZING.

Momentarily exhausted. Some sense later on. My last long letter would have been part of a mountain of post waiting for you on return.

Greetings, thoughts, love,

Elizabeth

New York | 15 May 83

Dearest Elizabeth –

So much to say. [...]

I do wish you would come before our walls are stripped & before a proposed 80 storey building gets built across the street and blocks our at present classic NY view. The city is beginning to be full of 80 and

100 storey buildings, cheek by jowl; has become a very jostled and jostling
place, intensified even over what it was: we find it different each time we
come back from Italy. Not for the better. It would be ungrateful to say
that all the validly extolled 'things to do' here, which indeed are manifold
& marvellous, add a bit to frenzy – if one is to survive in any lucid frame
of mind one just has to accept the fact that one will miss a lot of splendid
occasions, performances, events. Glad to say we did not however miss a
show at the Morgan Library of Holbein drawings from the royal collection:
one of the supreme exhibitions, for me. Not least for the mint condition
of these wonders. Also a show of English architectural drawings – we did
both these exhibitions on an afternoon last week, when NY was having a
rare clear, brilliant, beautiful spring day. The architectural drawings were
stunning, astonishing, lovely – beautiful pictures in themselves – from the
sixteenth to the twentieth century.

    [...]

    It is not impossible that Reagan – I dislike even writing his name –
will be re-elected: I have no confidence in the public in that respect (or
indeed in most other respects these days). It is a dreadful political situation
here, shameful & shameless; and the Reagan era is 'distinct,' if that's the
word, for introducing a new pr brand of flagrancy. They scarcely feel a need
to cover over or conceal their heedlessness and greed, their naked rip-off.

    [...]

    One of your clippings criticises 'Aust bashers abroad', saying in an
aside: 'They (foreigners) can hardly be blamed for cherishing the Awful
Aussie image'. [...] Please believe that this is not a simple matter. How ever
could someone like you, Eliz, not realise how Austs can seem compelled
to act out the very Aust caricature they claim to resent? [...] Why can't
such Austs simply disown the Barry Humphries type when it is brought
up to them? – but Patrick and others praise it, in fact, as a show of the real
nature of things. Why can't they get on with life & submerge all this? Well,
what sense to go on about it? I only feel this way because I mind for Aust's
sake & sense that it will get worse before it subsides or gets better, and that
hatred is needlessly being diffused...

    Perhaps I'll try – WITH INFINITE TACT – to say something about
this in my Boyer lectures. I fear no tact will be infinite enough, though.
But I won't go on to you about it again – only, we beg you, it is not just

'a few trendy yahoos' or that 'Nothing has really changed.' When you come away from Aust again, perhaps you will come to agree. It is outsiders who want Aust to mature and prosper who are concerned about this, not just wowsers.

Now – serious things. We have your promise that you are coming abroad before next year. So we want to know, only, <u>when</u>. I feel desperate in writing this to you, as if you will never come. It is so long that you've been promising, and so long since we saw each other. Nearly 8 years. The world isn't getting any better – things are being dismantled, things are being built, coastlines and countrysides encroached on. All this happens fast, and matters. We would like to talk to you about things we can't talk to anyone else about. Or think things one wouldn't think with anyone else. The other day I was wondering if I could send you a good new novel, there are several quite good ones around at present here, nearly all by women at the moment. Then I thought of the perfect one to send; and realised that it was yours. That is the sort of thing 'The Long Prospect' does for one. However, there's one form of long prospect we are rebelling against, and that is the delay in getting to see you. We are beginning to take this hard...

[...]

Meant to say, speaking of Lillian H, that she was here to dinner last night. Elizabeth, what spirit can still invest a shred of suffering humanity. Now entirely blind, a scrap, a bone; scarcely able to walk – comes with friends in taxi two blocks, met by wheel-chair, carried into our flat; carried to bathroom, food chopped for her at table, hand guided to glass, & to the fatal and inevitable cigarette. Why is she nevertheless so much more real and life like than many many others? [...]

She told me she feels terribly reduced in mind as well as body: 'I always had an idea of who I was. Now I lie awake in the night wondering who I am, what I seem to people now.' I told her that most people never even get round to wondering who they are. That produced her pleased and husky laugh – voice still deep in the frame of a little bird.

Eliz, I'll leave you (leave you in peace, as MM would have said)...

[...] I sense and see a new wave of nationalism – tribalism – almost everywhere. [...] The only haven from that still seems to be Naples. [...] What a good and true thing you say – that being born in Aust had the advantage of causing one to go out and cross the seas, look at things with particular eyes and high feeling.

Send us good news. Much love to Margaret, and always to you from us both – Shirley

Mosman | 31 May, 1983

Dearest Shirley and Francis –

So much to respond to, to thank you for, to tell... Thank you, first of all, for your letter about Christina – and the clippings. There was a gathering of C's friends (and some board members and administrators) at the Australia Council, and the archival film which was made two or three years ago was shown. She was sitting in the garden of Mary Lord's house in Melbourne, responding to questions and just telling how she felt about life and literature. No-one else appeared. It was strange to see this so soon after she'd died. On the one hand you thought: 'It's all right, after all. There she is, so like herself, and telling some of these people things they need to hear.' On the other hand you thought: 'This is the friend I've lost.' So spirits went up and down simultaneously. In recent months or years her life had ceased to be enjoyable; she was too ill. But her life was wonderfully fulfilled.

[...]

We have had very strenuous times here lately. When I last wrote or spoke we were all happy. Andrew wished (almost) that he needn't leave for his month's holiday, it was so interesting. That whole month was, too, pretty marvellous. People who had sadly closed down and disappeared in the seventies were meeting again. Hope lived again. The Economic Summit meeting called by Bob Hawke before Parliament opened, in Parliament House, was a sort of vision of how life <u>could</u> work if goodwill and intelligence were ever allowed to prevail. To see the country's leading industrialists, unionists and Labor ministers sitting together and listening with total silent attention to each other's papers for four/five days was a revelation. They all gave up some valued positions after hearing the other side. The proceedings were televised and no-one was grandstanding. Everyone unprecedentedly watched daytime television.

[...]

I had so many visitors and so many lunches, dinners and heaven knows what that I decided was either naturally exhausted or had become allergic to the telephone and social life. Have been lying low and just coping with ordinary things like natural gas being installed, and the roof leaking in a heavy storm and men coming to give quotes, and the telephone breaking down and four technicians coming to fix it. (It was lovely that it broke down.)

[...]

More today/tomorrow, but I want this to start travelling. Much love, Elizabeth

New York | 22 July 1983

Dearest Elizabeth –

[...]

Last Saturday afternoon in Naples, Francis was knocked down and dragged by a motorcycle carrying two youths who snatched and bore away something he was carrying. (This happens there often; we are usually careful not to carry anything – careless this time. It was at the end of the day, a day of walking in the city, when we turned to look for a taxi to go home.) Dreadful moments. He lay on the ground in pieces, covered with blood. I should quickly say, things have got better ever since. People were wonderful. Wonderful. Taken to emergency room of nearby hospital. Hospital disintegrating; doctors & staff magnificent. Staunching, scraping. X-rays. Broken shoulder, broken nose, broken teeth. Contusions. F wonderful, composed, even humorous. Transferred to new hospital after making police report. 'New' hospital, part of collapsed ancient convent, Hogarthian. Indescribable filth, squalor. Doctors & staff, magnif. Even the patients magnif. F in room with numerous beds; no linen on soiled mattress, stained pillow without cover. Chess game going on in corner, much crowding round to talk to F & me. Specialist in head injuries arrives – one a.m. – having driven from his seaside place. Takes great care, much attention. Says, nothing irreparable. [...] A Neapolitan driver, chum of years, comes out at dawn to get us to the hotel. Next day, drives us to Rome, after I make the 'denunciation' at the police station. [...] We marvel at the goodness of the world. Plane to NYC – first class provided to us free by Alitalia, who would not let me pay the extra. No one had so far let us pay anything, except the Rome hotel doctor who made up for the others. [...]

F says to tell you that he feels like MM on her arrival, ten years ago, on that doomed voyage to Southampton...

[...]

A loving embrace from us both – the only thing that F can do with ease, he says – Shirley.

Mosman | 26 July, 1983

Dearest Shirley and Francis –

I hope you arrived home safe and well on July 15. Thought of you on your birthday, Francis, and wished you were having happy times.

This note is just to explain the silence of your usually communicative friend. From some time in May I was unreasonably exhausted. Then there were pains in the head that would not disappear. About two weeks ago I visited a doctor. She said I had not had a cerebral haemorrhage, but with prolonged head pains you could not rule out brain tumours; we wouldn't start with a CAT scan, but I could take new pills for a week and my friends should be good to me. (This gave a definite impression that they might not have another chance.) Also blood pressure, which had always been normal to low was extremely high. I lay about in a sleepy way, and people were very good to me, as ordered, bringing food, flowers, books and pretty objects. The head pains have gone away, and more tests of a non-important kind have been done but not sorted out yet. I am still lying low, doing nothing much. This is the first approach to the typewriter for a very long time. Or so it seems. It's nice to feel not sick, though dimmish.

Hal Porter was knocked down on a pedestrian crossing on Sunday night and is unconscious. Did not mean to mention that but was just talking to Mary Lord, Christina's friend, who is also Hal's good friend.

[...]

Want to post this to show signs of life, and to thank you for your messages, and to send greetings and much love. (Be well.)

Elizabeth

New York | 21 Aug 83

Dearest Elizabeth –

So good to get your letter, and some news. We were about to telephone, and shall do so before long.

[...]

I've been reading on and off all summer poems of Camillo Sbarbaro – perhaps I mentioned this before – and wish I had a couple of other lives in which I could translate some of them; or attempt some unworthy renderings of these pure and beautiful and agonising works. He died about a dozen years ago. His poems are perfect truth, heartbreaking, so beautiful... He was 'by profession' an expert in lichens, something in harmony with his gift somehow.

Everett arranged, for one of his Frick concerts, a recital by an Aust pianist Kathryn Selby – a young protégé of Sutherland and Bonynge. Very good. [...]

More soon. Our love to Margaret, our thanks & greetings to all our well-wishers & friends. Our strong wishes & thoughts to you. <u>Be well</u>. With our love – Shirley

Mosman | 16 September, 1983

Dearest Shirley and Francis –

[...]

Since we spoke the world has shown signs of destroying itself again. The hypocrisy is hard to take. After attending one full-day and one evening meeting in April, when Dr Helen Caldicott and Dr Bill Caldicott spoke about war and peace, most of us felt as we did after reading The Fate of the Earth – not hopeful, but galvanized. Helen Caldicott (ex-Adelaide), had quite a longish interview with Reagan. She just shook her head telling about it...

[...]

Don't laugh. I became patriotic about the America's Cup and stayed awake (the night before last) <u>all night</u> listening to the wretched race.

[...]

Dear Friends, I hope you feel recovered and well and full of work and plans. Take care of yourselves. Much love,

Elizabeth

Mosman | 18 October, 1983

Dearest Shirley and Francis –

Many thanks for the beauteous stamps on your last Capri letter. They're so detailed, varied and interesting… (The 'C' of the Capri postmark looked like the tail of a monkey in a palm tree. Unlikely native.)

[…]

On an incredibly different note, I am bound to say that Australia smiled all over again when Australia II won the America's Cup. It was the first united smile since 11 November, 1975, and the papers said it was the happiest moment since the end of the war in 1945…

[…]

I had some underwear and nightdresses delivered by David Jones' to the Mosman. When I've spoken to Sisters Richards or Hoskins, I'll send the balance, if these things are all right. (I have the money you sent ages ago.)

[…]

Yes, please let me have a picture of F with the landlady's cat. Here in Mosman non-wonderful neighbours have a wonderful cat, Smoky, who sleeps on my front door-mat. Growing less playful with age is Smoky, but still has beautiful manners.

More soon. Much love,

Elizabeth

Capri | 23 Oct 83

Dearest Elizabeth –

[…]

We've had a beautiful time here. Weather, incredible. … made a v moving tour of the Naples hospitals where we'd been so kindly treated in July… It was so moving… reduced us to tears. We also had an extended visit to Caserta… Giardino inglese… a paradise. In Naples as ever, we've seen marvels, always new astonishments. Tomorrow we go there again, overnight, to dine with the mayor – this is not name-dropping, he is a v interesting man, a communist from Livorno, a Jew, interned in Tunisia by Mussolini (which doubtless saved his life; if he had been interned in Italy he would have been deported to Germany in '43, as perpetrator of the sin of Jewishness and anti-fascism), liberated there by – oddly enough – an English friend of ours. He has a fearful – and in many ways hopeless – task at Naples, compounded by the fact of his refusal to deal with the Camorra, who in turn strangle all his possibilities of action. [...]

At Naples, or at the rim of Naples, we have the drama of Pozzuoli at present; its poor, in all senses, inhabitants being evacuated as bradisismo takes the town up and down, and the Solfatara roars threateningly from practically beneath their feet. What will become of the innumerable antiquities – the entire town is an antiquity – no one has audibly mentioned.

[...] Yesterday half a million people marched for peace in Rome. Even the Mattino – the local paper, good on culture and pretty ignorant on all else – had to include in its headline a ref to 'manipulation'. If the march had been in favour of Reagan's diabolical missiles, rather than against them, this ref would not have been made. Apparently mankind cannot believe that some segment of the human race might genuinely and freely choose peace.

[...]

Did I tell you that F and I read Gibbon for about 45 minutes each morning with our brekkie here? This often happens (according to hour of rising, which dictates the ferocity of the morning sun) out on our terrace, in vast view of the sea and the Monte Solaro. We are nearly half-way through. We have identical copies (he has our old edition, which we bring vol by vol; I have a complete set of Everyman; in mine, the notes are sometimes truncated). I read aloud the text; F reads the notes (sometimes weasling out on the Latin). It is beyond praise; what genius, what intelligence, what superhuman application. The horrors, and the indefatigable repetition of same horrors, we read of teach us much about our own chances. Nothing all that good. Except that the good is manifest in the existence of such a work, and in the thousand thousand reminders Gibbon gives of human gestures and sensibilities & sufferings in their single forms underlying all the narrative. As my copy is a modern set, I am free to mark it up unashamedly; & freely do so. Yet we all need several lives. (But – how was it possible for one man – Gibbon – to achieve this in his sole allotted relatively brief existence? How annoying, such reminders of inspired diligence.)

Must either close, or go on forever – This with so much love – from us both – and most immediately from – Shirley

Mosman | 23 November, 1983

Dearest Shirley and Francis –

[...]

You asked about health. Had been urged to see another doctor and recently did. A case not of shutting the door after the horse has bolted, but after the horse has returned to stable and closed the door himself. If you see what I mean! Blood pressure back to normal, sun spots, blood tests, CAT scan (brain), and forget what else. As 'What Katy Did' used to write in her diary. Told Andrew that two or three things kill you and the others disappear with rest. 'Or death,' he adds. The CAT is tomorrow, I'm afraid the picture might carry a printed message: Elizabeth, you haven't put enough in or taken enough out, Your Brain.

[...]

Patrick flew to Greece on November 12 and came back November 20. This was at the invitation of the Greek government, to celebrate the overthrow of the colonels. It was strenuous for him but sounded like a highly stimulating adventure. He and Whitlam met at one of the many crowded receptions.

[...]

This jerky little note is more a telegram than a letter – just to say there is much to say and that you are thought about often. A real letter next time, and that will be soon. As always, much love to you both –

Elizabeth

PS. Don't like the idea of Christmas being almost here again.

Dearest Shirley and Francis –

As usual, I've <u>thought</u> many letters, but that's not the same as putting finger to typewriter. I trust you arrived home safely, in fine form.

[...]

It is now Easter. Last week-end was the time of anti-nuclear marches, here as elsewhere. Although the march is not so far in distance, it always takes hundreds of hours to get there, find friends, wait and wait, till these rather huge numbers sort themselves into groups. [...] It was Sydney's biggest gathering ever, they say. Helen Caldicott spoke. Patrick marched and stood for hours. (By accident, he and I met at the very beginning because we're always early, or at least punctual.) Last year I heard HC at Sydney University when there were about a hundred women and one man in the audience at a day-long gathering. This time she spoke to 120,000 or more.

[...]

Hal Porter (Watcher on the Cast Iron Balcony) still lies unconscious in Melbourne months after having been knocked down on a pedestrian crossing at Ballarat. The doctors and relatives should let him go.

Geoffrey Blainey stirred everyone up by saying what many think – that there is something unbalanced about the immigration programme. People from the UK and Europe have trouble getting in to Australia. The feeling in the country is changing rapidly. They say (Bill Hayden, for one) that it's inevitable that Australia will be 'Asianized'. Powerful people on multicultural boards attack Sydney University when it tries to set reasonably high standards in English language courses. And so on. Ambitious people do attach themselves to 'liberal' causes, and hammer certain topics almost to death.

Andrew is working in administration at Rozelle, implementing the Richmond report – the gradual closing of psychiatric hospitals and sifting and moving of patients to more appropriate, small places. It will take years.

[...]

Margaret told me she has just re-read <u>People in Glass Houses</u>; she shook her head with admiration. And I've just read Geoffrey Scott's The Portrait of Zelide, and loved it. So much intricate analysis so well expressed.

[...]

Thank you for telling me, suggesting, that I might stay in your apartment in NY. Like all unvisited cities, New York still seems mythical to me. Is it really real? If only New York, Paris and London lived just over the equator, more or less where Tokyo is. I'll visit it, anyway...

[...]

Having the August arrival date makes the Sydney visit (unlike New York) real. That's really terrific. I look forward to seeing you so much. There's always so much to say. Then, if there are some people you'd like me to ask over, do say. I hope my visiting cat, Smoky, calls in from next door. Smoky is beautiful and has perfect manners (more than I can say for his owners). Closer to the time you'll have more idea of a timetable, I suppose. You'll have a strenuous but, I think, enjoyable time. What larks!

[...] Take care of yourselves. So look forward to seeing Both.
Best love, dear friends,

Elizabeth

Mosman | 13 May, 1984

Dearest S and F –

[...]

Yesterday had a good visit from Rosemary Dobson and Alec Bolton. Alec is taking a series of photographs of writers for the National Library. We all met last at Christina's 80th birthday party.

Immigration and race have taken over the newspapers and interviews and conversations. Geoffrey Blainey's more complex thoughts have been grabbed, simplified and turned into weapons by the stray maniac. Hawke has spoken very well on the subject.

[...]

The Observer last week went on about plastic surgery in the US. It does make one feel it mightn't be safe to appear there. My face seems to have decided to follow the path of Auden's. I don't think this can be attributed to some inherent literary inclination of the flesh; it has more to do with the wondrous skin specialists of the late forties and early 50s who irradiated me with so much X-ray treatment for adolescent spots that it's a marvel I haven't been carried off yet. One of a legion of medical guinea pigs.

Sister said today that YM was better and actually up a little bit and walking, with help. She had just spoken to you when I rang. It's Mothers' Day, so the hospital was busy. It's another beautiful autumn day... Can't remember if I told you about Anzac Day. At nine o'clock hundreds of taxis came down Martin Place, each carrying an old soldier. On and on, lines of taxis and old soldiers. Then, from nowhere, riding straight out of a dream, came the Australian First Light Horse from Gallipoli, about twenty frail horsemen wearing the slouch hats and feathers, and old khaki felt uniforms of the First World War. A staggering sight. Everything else was an anticlimax. Though it's a curious and sad truth that Australian men of the old familiar kind never appear to such advantage as at the Anzac Day march. It was a brilliant day like this one.

[...]

Much love to you both,

Elizabeth

New York | 17 May 84

Dearest Elizabeth –

Tomorrow we fly away, and I'm surrounded by bits of scribbled paper, plastic folders, god knows what. Impossible that it will get done – easier to send the papers on a trip than to cope with them, so for once I write a letter I want to write instead of all the others. Yesterday the first two Boyer lectures went off – they have nearly killed me... I leave here 1 Aug, get to LA, change to QANTAS, fly into the night; stop at Tahiti – without sighting the transit of Venus – in the dark; then should arrive 3 Aug at about 8am (supposedly). Can we see each other that evening, or perhaps earlier? On Monday I start with the ABC; but of course they won't take up all my evenings, or even perhaps all my days. I do hope so much to see you and Margaret, and almost don't believe it can happen. [...]

Subject of lectures – well in a way, Australia. Changes there; and, more to the point, things that don't seem to change. I'll be safely departed when these are broadcast.

[...]

What larks, what larks. We'll have 'em.

[...]

Thank you, Margaret, for liking my People in Glass Houses. I once re-read it (almost never re-read own books); and laughed myself. Far too lenient, though.

Best love to you dearest Elizabeth – Shirley

Postcard, Capri | 17 June 84

Dearest Elizabeth –

[...] I am toiling and slaving with the concluding parts of the Boyer orations. [...] Good to think that soon we can really say things; also, can make plans for your flight. Here, perfect hot summer day today – Spring of weird storms in Italy; we've been spared a lot in this region. I made first – last I should think – talk in Italian to group interested in salvaging monuments at Naples. Was particularly asked, as foreigners' words count somewhat in embarrassing officialdom; but never so nervous... Lovely, kind audience; I had made notes but deplore speeches that are just read off, so it ended up conversational. Beautiful room – ballroom of Villa Pignatelli on the Riviera di Chiaia. Next day we lunched at a house of splendour – truly – on the Posillipo, 'Villa Emma' (name only of Hamilton's Posillipo house; this is a nearby house that assumed the same title later on) whose owners hope to found an endowment for restoring some Neapolitan monuments... More to say – thank you for butterfly stamps always – Love to you – S

Mosman | 29 June, 1984

Dearest Shirley and Francis –

[...] I can't believe you'll be here in August. Yes, as soon as you feel half-awake, able to meet, I'll be there. Whatever you like. We could set a time or – what you choose. I'll flit over soon or late.

[...]

Australia... Long to know what you've said in those no doubt exhausting-to-write lectures. Fashion has a stultifying effect on thought in this country. A few 'in' topics are regularly thrashed to death. Academics talk all the time about aborigines at the moment. Not the best academics:

they're the ones who've retired and gone home to write their books. I can think of some.

Items: Marg. was present at Geoffrey Blainey's last Sydney meeting; it took place just across the street from her flat. The National Front and the Trotskyites were there in noisy numbers. A horrible night had by many.

Patrick and I received calls from the Soviet Embassy in Canberra inviting us to Moscow – not fares, but all else.

The crumbling marriage of friends – hearing too much about it – caused my blood-pressure to fly very high then crash with the help of medication. Stress. Doctors.

[...]

I thought at first that you would want to go alone to the Mosman, but on second thoughts I'd to some extent urge you to meet me there (unless someone else) and afterwards have lunch, coffee, something.

[...]

Saw a marvellous <u>Macbeth</u>, and read Painter's biography of Proust (a bit late in the day), and am reading <u>Dr Faustus</u>. Friends come from Melbourne, Canberra and England. No wonder a Dutch sociologist announced to us the other night that Australians are the happiest people in the world!! Think of that.

I wish you were coming over, too, Francis. Best love, dear friends,
Elizabeth

P.S. Seem to have said everything.

Mosman | 22 August, 1984

Dearest Shirley and Francis –

Exactly twenty-four hours ago we were in the Captain's Lounge (or whatever it was called) at the airport. It was a beautiful, lovely visit. What larks! And much better even than the very great larks were the conversations – really times of happiness. Francis, you should have been here. You were missed. And people asked about you all the time.

Another heavenly day today... Yesterday, I flitted back to town with a friendly Maori taxi-driver, a philosopher, and felt not – as in the best school compositions – 'tired but happy', but rather, and more confusingly, 'sad but happy'. Well, you know what I mean. The dead marines left over from the party were carried up to the Stanley Avenue footpath for the quarterly Mosman Council clearance (and today carried back down because they don't take bottles!). Andrew rang: 'What's this about thinking you'll get lost?' and promised psychotherapy. Richard Hall rang and was very disappointed to know you had gone home. Richard the Cool said twice that the 11th was 'a magic night'. He admires your work very much, and he's going to write to you about the UN/TLS piece I sent him. Also, that night, he spoke to Whitlam about UNESCO at length. [...]

Next day. And another perfect spring-like day. The birds are wonderfully noisy, almost too talkative, making Smoky look persecuted. It's possible that they're nesting under the eaves somewhere.

Enough rambling, dear friends.

Thank you again for the lovely glasses and treats galore: I still feel so touched and pleased about the dedication that I can almost not think of anything to say. Happy times.

Something more coherent later. Best love, dear S and F –

Elizabeth

Mosman | 12 September, 1984

Dearest Shirley and Francis –

When you put your 'all' into writing a letter, Francis, it would take someone much less susceptible to the word than I am to resist. And not only the word, but the spirit of the word. You said things that seemed true. Yes, Shirley and I did have happy times in Sydney and asked always why you were not there.

[...]

I don't think the US Consulate will give visa without a ticket. They're a bit severe and want arrival and departure dates and deep knowledge of one's worldly wealth. So far there is a tiny collection of goods – the 1972 Edinburgh suitcase, a Mastercard, a handkerchief with 'E' on it, and a passport. The accountant, Bill Reid, was rung as a reference for Visa and Amex cards. He told me to work out my budget carefully and not to stay away very long, because he and I know that it's by staying in Sydney and putting first things first (seeing friends and fixing the roof) that the budget has just broken even. Earlier on, before I moved into this house, before I sold the flats, before I went to the aid of a friend, if I had been more interested in my own affairs and applied more intelligence, I could have arranged for more prosperity. I might have gone away then and stayed for a while, but people had nervous breakdowns and died, and it didn't happen. Then a while ago there was talk of a film of The Long Prospect, but that fell through. At various times a holiday has seemed possible, but hasn't worked out. If I sold the house, too. But the bad experience of selling the flats at the wrong time has made me nervous of that. Almost all of the time I feel lucky and enjoy my life, apart from guilt about writing. Sometimes not having the freedom to go to Melbourne (Judah has asked me for years) and Canberra or Ayers Rock or the Barrier Reef is trying for about half an hour (perhaps more the idea, even, of not having the option), but then happiness, even-mindedness returns and remains. High spirits.

Forgive this interminable ramble. So. What I thought was, if this all comes to pass, I'd stay away for about six weeks. After Italy, a week in Paris or London or flitting in a circle round the US, then perhaps a week in New York? Several of the people I really cared about in London, England, have died. I'm very fond of Steph and Alec, but they'll be here. Or perhaps that week could be a circle round Scotland. I love Auntie Minnie but she is now very old and that's sad. Her daughter, Anne, M's and Steph's sister, is good, but a bit stern and conservative with me (and them). Perhaps new ground, certainly new ground, carries no memories. In Perth, in Scotland, that first time, the bells of the little church were playing Ye Banks and Braes...

[...]

No, if I have a chance to see Francis, Shirley and some of the beautiful world, I'll think I'm very lucky. Ferdi has assured me no-one gets permanently lost at a great airport, and wishes we could meet in Europe to go about for a while. Ambitious man! All of this rambling is to say that you can see it's sane, wise and dignified not to destroy all the future budgets to be worked out at 5 Stanley Ave by staying away for an extended period. If Francis tells me seriously to work, then I'll come home and work and then very likely be more prosperous and return.

[...] A couple of weeks ago when I mentioned going to the airport to say goodbye, Patrick was totally silent. When he heard, a bit further on, that we'd spoken on the Saturday morning of your return, another silence. What is this? Are people not to have friends? There was an outburst because I chose to go to the Premier's Literary Dinner and enjoyed being at the table with Graham Freudenberg, J.D. Pringle and his wife, and Evan Williams (Wran's cultural chief), and Les Murray.

[…]

Blue, blue days, and grey Smoky cat asleep on the prickly front door mat. Thank you for everything. Best love,

Elizabeth

Long Meadows, Brookledge Lane, Adlington, Cheshire, England SK10 4JU | 21 November, 1984

Dearest Shirley and Francis –

Where am I? And how do I thank you for Rome, Naples, Capri, Naples, Paris and London? I think you know that I did love those places, see wondrous things, have happy times, and that I did notice and appreciate the thousand thoughtful small (as well as large) deeds that occurred for my benefit, comfort and enjoyment. Thank you both many times over. With silver stars round the edge.

[…]

Tomorrow I go by train to Edinburgh. Anne (sister of Margaret and Stephanie) has booked me in at a small hotel near their house. The house has quite a bit of space, but only two bedrooms, and I'm not going to disrupt their sitting-room in view of Auntie Minnie's excellent but considerable age. Steph tells me they go out to lunch twice a week (at ninety-two/three!). A.M. is always ready for an outing, and used to read very solid works till her eyes deteriorated a year or so ago. Shame.

When I left here, after eight and a bit years, the newspapers were what I missed most, and it's always a pleasure to see them again. I tend to be attached to the Guardian because we agree with each other. Perhaps a weekly airmail Guardian at home would be the thing. The countryside is autumnal, wintry, ravishing. The villages dream away and smoke comes from the chimneys and you are relieved not to be part of them, they seem so enclosed. A hunt clattered down the village street outside my window. We've seen two things on television: The Dismissal (Whitlam-Kerr,

1975), and a long BBC interview with Francis Bacon to celebrate his 75th birthday. It might be less difficult to see his paintings now. It was a very good interview with an inconspicuous but concentrating questioner who knew what to ask, and how to let a silence run on. The Dismissal, which I'd seen before (in four parts), was bad for my health.

So to Paris. It's marvellous and beautiful, of course, and didn't seem to be crowded at all. And was notably orderly after Naples, as you had said it might seem. Freda Whitlam (E.G.'s only sister) was very welcoming and kind. On Sunday we went out in the morning, suddenly we had to get a taxi home and (as I sd on the phone) I was in bed for two days. Not my idea of how to make a grand entrance or good impression, but no choice. It was rather awful. Margaret and Gough arrived home from Spain on Sunday night. Saw little of him, and we can never think of anything to say, but that doesn't especially matter. Margaret and Freda were so lovely to me, so kind. They were like old friends. Of course there were great thanks to you from him for your letter and that beauteous book. He and Margaret are so good together. We did some considerable sightings and outings before I left. But since I'd felt so rotten and couldn't be certain when I felt a bit better that I was going to stay better, it seemed a wise idea (if collapsing permanently and finally) to be near Steph and Anne.

[...]

This is all old news because I told you most of it on the phone on Monday. Patrick and Manoly made their NZ visit and he spoke about peace and war and had to go to St Vincent's immediately on return. He may have to wear a brace forever (which seems a long time). A vertebra in his back cracked or broke, or else is it porosis (I think a crumbling of the bones). Much pain, and he's been there in hospital for quite some time now.

Numerous letters and phone calls from a variety of friends have disturbed the peace of Adlington. Several have told me about the Boyer Lectures. All say interesting and pleasing things. I'm sure, dear S, you've had masses of letters already, and more will no doubt follow the completion of the series. (Someone's volunteered to acquire some cassettes and the book for me.)

[...]

Now, the thing is – dates, New York, your Christmas trip to Italy, the convenience and lack of convenience to have your wandering mate to think of. I know the only cloud was my feeling that I wanted to go sooner and yours that I should stay longer. It isn't a question of 'can't wait to get back to the Heads' at all. You know I've had terrific times and wouldn't have been dragged away, and I expect to have some more terrific times, and see more, and meet more friends again and new people. The best result of all this is to be shaken out of ruts at home, galvanized there and – it goes without saying – to have spent time with you both, and had those many experiences of a rare kind. The limit of what can be accepted has been exceeded. My God! The beloved Hassler to start somewhere... When I sell the house and do some work, I can return to NY for a visit under my own steam. As it is, I have a ticket to leave NY on Dec. 16, so I may flash through when you have already gone or are on the verge of going back to Italy. Quite apart from my limits, although they are highly relevant, I have the workaday responsibilities of my own life that we all have to take notice of for ourselves or else suffer the consequences. I feel you hope something wonderful and lucky will happen to me if I wander about enough. What is all this but something wonderful and lucky? But I'm not going to wake up having written a good book unless I work, or wake up speaking a foreign language unless I work. – I am sitting in silence in Auntie Minnie's kitchen thinking more than I am writing. Left Cheshire yesterday (Thursday) and came by train to Edinburgh. A.M. is still lovely and so kind and smiling and has all her wits together. Anne says she repeats the same thing over and over, but she hasn't done that with me. I stayed (am staying) at a little bed and breakfast place nearby, owned by a dear little Scottish body, Mrs Drummond. So <u>pleasant</u>. I could not refuse the cooked Scottish breakfast, part of the deal, so warmly produced this morning. My poor conquered Scots. Coming up in the train, I remembered finding a book of Scottish ballads in Whins House in Alloa in 1951, and picking them out on the piano, and singing them all through the house – My Heart's in the Highlands, Scots Wha Hae, All the Blue Bonnets are over the Border. Stirring stuff. [...] It's lovely that you would like lucky things to happen for me. I'd like that for people I care about, too. Again, more thoughts that I'm writing down, and long silences, no doubt, for Auntie Minnie, who hopes I'll stop tapping and come and talk. After lunch, a bit of exploration alone in Edinburgh.

I am causing too much of delay to the workings of the household and not being sociable enough, so perhaps I'll have to flit off and ring up or send a cable or something to sort out the dates.

There is much that I want to say, but dishes are being produced and time is passing.

[...]

Don't know your dates of exit and entry, and wretched Christmas is on the way.

Take care of yourselves, dear friends. You were so good to me. What times, what larks! Great thanks again. Best love,

Elizabeth

Postcard, Sydney | 10/11-12-84

You said not to write a letter (although that would seem a natural thing to do) so – a pc.

Arrived Thursday and still have not surfaced much yet.

I've cared about you both a great deal for years and refuse to be not cared for back because all of a sudden I got worn down and ran out of energy. This doesn't surprise anyone who knows me here.

So. I came back from London, but I'm a constant friend. Believe me. The disappointment of missing you and New York and everything there is all mine. But it's obvious from the way the organism feels now that that just wasn't a possibility.

Take care of yourselves. Thank you again for beautiful times.

Love, Elizabeth

New York | 22 Dec 84

Dearest Elizabeth –

[...] This being hastily written in Christmas intensity – soon, a real letter. No – please – I did not 'say not to write a letter'; merely that you needn't tackle a long letter on exhausted return. Nor, as said on phone, do you have to 'refuse not to be cared about' – there is no question of that. Well, you know these things, one really should not have to write them. Many pleasant things since return, but not enough work. On New Year's

Eve Francis to Paris for a week – cannot bring himself to miss Watteau exhibition and also vast Diderot show, about to close, on which he may write something. I can't let myself be tempted to go, must seize chance to be desk-bound in January. Today is our anniversary – twenty-one years, seems like five minutes – we were married on a day of snow; today, however, warm & beautiful reprieve from winter of which we've had mysteriously many such, only sparsely mixed with ice-age moments, so far. Along the streets where we live, fir trees banked up in thousands to be sold for Christmas – in the mild air, smell of pine. (Some of these quite big, Douglas spruce I suppose...) Last night, Royal Shakespeare 'Much Ado', which we approached with caution, but delighted in... The year concludes with Donald at Tokyo, Everett at Palermo, Elizabeth at Sydney, Francis at Paris, Shirley in NY.

Love to you and many many good things in 1985. As Gauguin's favourite salutation (apparently) goes: 'We pinch your claws...' S.

PART THREE

1985–2008

Signs of hope came with the fall of the Berlin Wall in 1989, the seeming end of the Cold War, and the 1994 election of Nelson Mandela as President of South Africa. But Harrower noted with concern the 'breaking-up in Europe into smaller and smaller groups'; at home she was appalled at John Howard's Coalition government, elected in 1996. In the US George Bush Sr, Bill Clinton and George W. Bush each brought problems to the presidency. The Gulf War presaged the attacks of September 11, 2001, which passes almost without comment in the letters, and the Iraq War. Prime Minister Silvio Berlusconi heightened Hazzard's constant worry about Italy's corrupt and unstable politics. After the death of Kit Hazzard in 1985, friends and loved ones fell rapidly: Kylie Tennant (1988), Patrick White (1990), Graham Greene (1991), Francis Steegmuller (1994), William Maxwell (2000), Manoly Lascaris (2003).

New York | 3 Jan 85

Dear Elizabeth –

Happy new year, and many many thanks for envelope with your goodies. I just came in with groceries on a raw day and found with great pleasure the lovely paper-weights — <u>air</u> mail — of Ellen and Lord B. And card of the same Westall portrait – which B liked – engravings from it supplied the ardent requests of his public, and private, for a likeness; B referring suppliants to 'Mr Westall of Charlotte Street' in their 'entusymusy' as he wld have called it. 'A restless and impatient subject... a <u>hurried</u> sitter', he styled himself. And thank you for the 1882 piece by John Weightman on J. Hope Mason's DIDEROT, which F will be most grateful for. He is busy at Paris, as I in New York. A statement of Doctorow's read the other day – that 'only the person who goes to his manuscript first thing every morning, and stays there can call himself a writer' pierced my heart and, more important, my mind, and I do my best to reclaim the designation, in that respect at least.

[...]

Just before leaving Capri, ran into David Malouf in the 'street' with a young friend, I think Australian. We chatted a moment, I had to run and he was only there overnight; the first dark day. Here we have occasional cold like yesterday, and capricious snowfalls; but amazing warmth maintains... Last week, being driven from a library meeting by a friend, I sat waiting in the car outside a row of old houses, whose front drapery of bare creepers and wistaria vines looked almost late summery in the dim light – thanks to atmosphere of open windows, people strolling without coats, me leaning on sill of open car window. Fine sensation of beating the rap. At Princeton where we spent three December days, forsythia was trying to bloom. Am on a committee there to hear grievances; which for commendable reasons, seldom needs to meet, most grievances being of a nature dealable with internally.

[...] Muriel S telephoned – she has been suffering from multiple fractures resulting from slipping while making her bed: 'I've lived all my life with danger, and never come to harm. This is what happens when you go domestic.'

Back to the Doctorow regime. With Byron airily holding down my pages, something must come right. Be well, best love to you, & best thanks from Shirley

Mosman | 19 February, 1985

Dearest Shirley –

In the middle of the morning, this morning, I remembered I'd dreamed about you last night. Whatever it was, it was something pleasant – as though you'd made a flying visit and had champagne at the kitchen table.

[...]

A few days ago the ABC (Peter Morton) sent me a complimentary set of Boyer cassettes. Before this, ever since I came home, I'd heard comments from acquaintances, friends and friends of acquaintances. They seemed to cover all conceivable reactions. I felt that I'd almost certainly agree with your general propositions, though I might quibble round the edges here and there. And that is how it's turned out to be. Someone pressed to borrow the cassettes, which I'd heard just once, and as it was a person who is constantly giving me chamber music on cassette, I couldn't refuse – though inclined to. The book will be published at the end of this month, they say, so I'll soon be able to read them. There's no substitute for print. Your voice sounded clear and pleasant to listen to. I can imagine that sustaining an even and unstrained tone would not be easy. Quite a few people who were away during the broadcasts are waiting to read the lectures, and looking forward to their appearance in print.

[...]

In the Botanic Gardens on Saturday it was rather like heaven – very warm, ideal breezes, scented air, many flowers, dense shadows under trees. Blessings on the one who set aside the land. You had said that the British came with all the forms and institutions – and with the idea, clearly, that such oases could and should exist.

[...]

Keep well and keep working, dear S and F. Best love,
Elizabeth

New York | 3 March 85

Dear Elizabeth –

Our many thanks for letter, whose tattered enclosures cause imagining of fire and flood – or, worse, of apocalyptic mergings of bad luck & averages ominously near.

[...]

Lange was here: brave. Also here was Mrs Thatcher, who denounced him. Hawke was here – apologising for the 'radical wing' of his party. Reagan is here, and so is his electorate. Some good writing appears; beautiful music pours. John Pope-Hennessy's Caravaggio exhibition opens at Metrop Museum: resplendent. (None of the Caravaggios we saw together in Rome and Naples is included; many others are. Much as we deplore the sending, we enjoy the result. Critics write as if no one had ever cared for Caravaggio before. This exhibition goes to Naples shortly, then disperses back to its mostly Italian origins.) What else? – Buildings go up, up, up. Time flashes by.

[...]

Nothing more ever heard from Whitlam by us. The papers here report Fraser among other predictable and awful nominees for the new head of UNESCO. Perfect. The UN as repository for the nationally unwanted has some interesting aspects. [...] Thinking, and not indulgently, of such matters the other day, I came upon a piece of writing by Dal Stivens – so good, so true and unflinching that I took up pen to write him. And it seemed to me that at your door on that immortal night the person who mattered most was in fact the artist, not the power-person. Dal was not merely in the way of Whitlam. And looking back it somehow seems right that Dal was unprepossessing and immortally shuffling there; like civilisation itself as a 'battered bag' in Muir's poem 'The Combat'. Much has changed since an emperor could pick up the dropped brush of a painter and humbly say it was an honour.

Valerie. Valerie. Nothing more since a note at Christmas. All rendingly unchanged at The Mosman [...] Yes, paradise in those Botanical Gardens: I never forget my morning there. One should have such mornings frequently. Westall's Byron continues to glow. I'd recent occasion to think of Westall's briefly 'Australian' brother William, brave young painter who sailed with Flinders to sketch the new continent. [...]

We hope Patrick continues better. Shall perhaps write him. Be well, dear E. Always much love from Shirley

Mosman | 12 April, 1985

Dearest Shirley and Francis –

[...]

The film of Christina Stead's <u>For Love Alone</u> is going ahead in Sydney. There were photographs in the local paper of actors in Mosman at one of the old wharfs. I think of Christina often, and miss her.

Yes, Dal Stivens is all the good things you say. He's fairly frail these days and has to lie low quite often. But he rises up again. We've had some fine conversations and I have clear and detailed memories of meetings over the years. Christina first introduced us.

Saw <u>A Passage to India</u> at Easter. Went quite reluctantly, but liked it very much.

[...]

Not many books have arrived yet for the Age Book of the Year award. That isn't settled till November. Premier's Department in NSW asked me to join their judging panel, too, but decided against it. I'd like to be in that group, but they've asked before when the National Book Council has asked first.

[...]

In between visits from friends there are acres of silence, sky, clouds, golden moon on water. Smoky the cat deserted me for a while but is actually rattling his bell as I type, and was asleep on the doormat this morning.

I hope you had happy times in Italy, and that Galiani still makes his presence felt. How lovely Lily and Annette and their mother were. So many people have asked: 'Who is that?' 'That is Shirley's friend, Lily, from Naples, and her admired dog, Archibald.' [...]

Trust you are both in the best of forms. Trust work goes well. Greetings and best love,

Elizabeth

A BORDO DI UN JET ALITALIA / ON BOARD AN ALITALIA JET –
or about to be | 21 May 85

Dearest Elizabeth –

[...] I wish I had time and state of being to write a real letter. Am flying
in a few hours in the air; and already flying on the ground with thousand
thoughts and necessary deeds; and flying also in my attempts to sort out
details in my mind. But soon I'll send real words.

You were so good – immeasurably good – to her. What was bearable
in her latter life was in great part thanks to you.

F joins me on 12 June. He is finishing some work here; and I'll be
finishing a section of work there. His 'essay' on his Neapolitan mugging [...]
will be in The New Yorker later this year.

I'll be calling Andrew. I know you will have told Yolanda, who
was lovely to my mother. Many people did show her understanding and
kindness – if only it got through to her. Well, it's over now –

With love from us both – Shirley

Francis has been wonderful, undertaking so many of the tasks – calls,
letters. We feel rather unrealising as yet. It was expected for such a long
while, in this last twilit time.

Capri | 26 July 85

Dear Elizabeth –

A year ago I was getting ready to fly to Australia. Now getting ready
to fly to NY. That year seems to have dissolved, in spite of many many
moments and events consciously grasped. F went back from Rome, where
I accompanied him, last week. I stayed to finish a section of work, not
yet finished but under some measure of control. Great heat has kept me
indoors away from temptations to walk to mountain-tops or seabeds. I've
also had so many letters about MM, from more continents than the atlas
appears to hold. People often understood – even when they couldn't take
any more – that something original had been wasted there. The waste –
which she in later years doggedly cultivated, alas – was one of the saddest
features in a general sadness. What you describe, of good conversations
& some fun, was hardly ever present for me after childhood, although
we did have sporadic good times, and, in the 1960s when I had prospered

enough to be able to help her, some sustained periods when it seemed something could be changed for the better – two months in NY in 1962, and then several NY trips after F and I had married. Then it all went down, down. [...]

Thank you for going to the service, for receiving all those calls, for everything. Valerie wrote me about the funeral – I should say, the 'non-service' in what are for her subdued tones, though with her usual bitter-archness, perhaps some pointlessness; no sign of philosophical trends, however. Her children all live far from her and apparently are not closely in touch... [...] What would be the point of our getting together in any sustained way, I wonder – we have nothing to say to one another and no common interest. A pity, but a fairly usual pity in families – or at least not a rarity.

Andrew was a prince... we hope we can do something for him one day and that we'll meet around the world. Yolanda, Joan, Daphne, and a cast of hundreds showed kindness beyond imagining. You and Margaret were not only beyond imagining but beyond expression. As I say, the people who were pitched into the saga cover many continents. Again, the sad thing is that she couldn't believe in it, somehow.

[...]

Be well – and we'd like to hear how health is. My best greetings always to the nice people of the great evening. And love to you – from Shirley

Mosman | 29 December, 1985

Dearest Shirley and Francis –

Thank you for the beautiful stamps (which I'm looking at now) on the Silence envelope from Capri. I can never bring myself to pass those Italian stamps on to deserving stamp-saving children. The painting itself keeps drawing my eyes back. It has the look of an icon, almost.

[...] The Age awards were handed over at lunch at the Regent. The winners were Peter Carey (fiction) and Hugh Lunn (non-fiction) and were both good writers and unaffected youngish men.

[...]

Have just read Saul Bellow's <u>Him With His Foot In His Mouth</u> with, as ever, admiration. Have also read some of Martin Amis's novels. Brilliant and hair-raising stuff. Have so far not got on well with the Booker prize-winner, <u>The Bone People</u>. Sometimes judges can't or don't like to choose between several already admired writers, so strike out in search of the unusual, not to mention sometimes the incoherent. However. Pleased to see in some oldish copies of the NY Review that Julian Barnes' <u>Flaubert's Parrot</u> was receiving such praise. One day some time ago now read Gail Godwin's <u>Dream Children</u> and liked that collection v. much though then felt disappointed by a big novel that followed. It seemed just sociological. Then there was a long and v. favourable review of a novel by your friend, Paula Fox. It sounded complex and not at all sociological. But the award books took time and not all, by any means, were worth it.

[...]

We had one day of 39 degree heat on one of those 'last shopping days' before Christmas. But apart from raining at night and watering the garden, which is nothing to complain about, it's been breezy and blue by day, and glamorous and balmy at night. Friends had lunches at various sites round the harbour, under trees.

[...]

Greetings and love to you both –

Elizabeth

New York | 18 Feb 86

Dearest Elizabeth –

11:00 pm, and we are both at our typewriters, determined – after a day of continual interruptions – that we'll do some of the things we set out wanting to do this morning. (In truth, Francis is often at his typewriter at this hour, especially when he has done library work in the day and wants to attach it to his narrative. His Galiani ms. is going at a great pace and he has found all kinds of interesting docs and sources.) Yesterday evening the Keeleys were here. [...] Mike has just brought out a volume of translations of Yannis Ritsos, the best, perhaps, of contemporary Greek poets; reading these poems, I marvelled that anyone had the courage to attempt them – they are so arcane, and often surreal in effects. The other extreme of difficulty in translating poetry seems to be limpidity – for several years I've been trying to translate an Italian poet, dead now for almost twenty years, whose quality is a pain-filled simplicity. Over and over, these piercing lines translate into banalities in English – I have three or four short poems to show for intermittent slavery over as many years. No one has translated him into English, and I am beginning to see why.

[...]

We are so much at Naples, and increasingly so with F's work in libraries recently, that we now have taken a little place there. How we're going to divide our time among the three places that don't belong to us we don't really know. But our Naples place fell into our laps, as like a dream, and we could not have repudiated it. It is very beautiful, on the sea, not far from where I lived thirty years ago. It belongs to friends, who have a house nearby and own quite a lot of land. So it is protected, in all senses. As we could not possibly give up Capri, we just signed on for this one too. Who knows where all this is leading? – perhaps to bankruptcy, but with pleasures on the way.

[...]

Today I wrote to Julian Barnes to tell him – confidential for a few weeks yet – that he has won the EM Forster Award (a trip to the USA, and some money: Forster left his royalties from certain books to Christopher Isherwood; and Isherwood turned them over to the American Academy & Institute of Arts & Letters to set up an award for a British writer, fairly young, to visit this country.) I am the leader of the selection group at present. We had several good possibilities – Richard Holmes, Andrew Harvey, and two or three novelists. A youngish poet called John Ash (not Ashbery). But everyone liked the idea of Barnes. The series of deaths of poets over Christmas was strange and touching – Larkin, Grigson, Graves, Isherwood. Isherwood was not a poet, really, but must be considered one by osmosis. Larkin was sometimes inspired; unbearable. At the time of his death we read some poems of Larkin aloud – but it was often intolerable. What simple-seeming, even laconic, penetration to the bone. Graves was one of the last real ones. And he lived – the opposite of Larkin – twenty times to most people's single effort. I liked much of what he wrote, and the full life in his work. [...]

Pat Lovell is often on the phone, expects to be in Europe again in coming weeks. Her proposal for a film of my E of the H has advanced a fair bit. These things are beyond me. She is a very pleasant woman, & has life and purpose. The money they offer me seems, however, inconceivably little. Who knows if the thing will ever be made, but have not signed for it yet.

[...]

Now it's tomorrow – this seems to be continually the case. I'll run out with this – running also seems to be the case. Grateful that the whirl is of good things, but sorry, it has to be a whirl. We find ourselves reading at 1:00 am, in order to be able to read in peace at all. Time to fly away. Friendliest greetings, please, to all our and my Sydney friends; love, please, to Margaret – and our love to you – Shirley.

Mosman | 30 April, 1986

Dearest Shirley and Francis –

Since your letter arrived and the card with clippings just before you left NY, I've thought of you so often. Thank you very much for all. When the news of the Libya bombing was broadcast, I wanted to ring you, but the time was wrong for Capri and you might anyway have been in Naples. To this point, we've all survived and most of the world, but wish Reagan had more imagination or that the rest of us had less.

[...]

Where else to start? Why not with the many star-filled nights looking for and looking at Halley's comet? The first sight of it was heart-stopping (not, of course, because it was spectacular). Three or four in the morning, making coffee, fixing binoculars and finding the sky at that hour wonderful with or without comets, studied the Herald's star-map, lifted the glasses at random and found it – an apparition, Hamlet's father's ghost, wanderer. Other nights, found it again at different times with its 'veil' or 'tail' more or less obscured. Friends who live in other parts of town came to dinner and star-gazed. Luckily it was never cloudy on those nights.

Have been reading Auden's biography, Dr Faustus (noticed passing reference to the Abbé Galiani), Kenneth Cook's life, Anne Tyler's novels, Patrick's new book, Charles Ritchie's diaries Siren Days (a vivid, zestful, delightful book: he and Elizabeth Bowen deserved each other). Reading Waterland, novel by English Graham Swift.

Had lunch with Freda Whitlam one day, and dinner with Yolanda and (unexpectedly) Valerie. Asked Valerie what she'd change in her life if she had it to do again. Nothing, said Valerie, except the TB. Perhaps she meant it. (No utterance ever from V about you or YM). Have no plans to repeat meeting.

[...]

Patrick's had his new book appear. There was a premiere of the opera, Voss, at the Adelaide Festival. It opens here in June. Some of his poems were set to music by Moya Henderson and sung by a visiting English soprano. He has just completed another work.

The Golden Summers exhibition was a huge and somewhat unexpected success at the Art Gallery of NSW. Presumably Edmund Capon would have been pleased. Australian paintings of early days were brought together for the first time. Extracts from the painters' letters were displayed beside the works mentioned. They added to the pleasure.

[...]

The Adelaide Festival came and went. Antigone was one of the invited. The overseas and local writers were settled in a charming out-of-town hotel to get to know each other for two or three days before the official opening. Antigone seemed to get on best with Robbe-Grillet. They liked each other.

[...]

Greetings and best love,
Elizabeth

Naples | 12 Oct 86

Dearest Elizabeth –

We are fine, and I've been wanting and intending to write you for many weeks, only impeded by daily and hourly demands. Most of all, in the past months, by the fitting up of our Naples place, which has involved a thousand items, interventions, crises, interruptions. However, all this is at last receding, & the beauty of this place begins to seem 'ours.' Tonight, the moon on the sea, the shapes of the mountains and islands, the complete silence except for the lapping of the shore. Yesterday we could hardly bear to leave Capri, however, a dream of beauty at this season. There, too, we've had household matters bedevilling us – a burst tank in the flat above us devastated our little living-room a month ago; and nothing can be done until the walls dry out. Even so, we have been loving our times there and must find out how to juggle all these places – none of which is in fact ours by ownership.

And tomorrow to Rome, to see a painting we've applied for permission to visit; to see a few friends, and to see the translator of F's Neapolitan 'incident', who has sent her typescript – pleasing and good in spirit, and in general, but with perhaps a hundred errors, some of them essential ones. The Italian version should appear around the end of the year, in the 'good' literary magazine called 'Nuovi argomenti'. [...] Last week we hired a little boat and went along our Posillipo coast. Such sights, such light, such antiquity, such colours.

The only things completed in the past three or four months have been an article on the Vesuvius, long promised to the NYT; and a long piece on Waldheim, which the TLS now tells me they want longer still. That will have to wait.

[...]

How infinitely interesting to me the city is, like another consciousness. Strange place.

Francis sends his love. So do I. More before long. Forgive silence. With love – Shirley.

Mosman | 7 January, 1987

Dearest Shirley and Francis,

I was so glad to find your beautiful card and Christmas note in the letter-box yesterday.

[...]

Just recently three women have started to write biographies of Christina Stead, and two or three more are writing critical works about her books. Two of the women have visited, and the third rang this afternoon and comes next week. Luckily, I liked and admired Christina, and knew her quite well, so it's almost a pleasure to be cross-examined. This first young woman, Chris Williams, [...] said that in some old printed interview, Christina had said that writing a book, a novel, was like being in love. Something along those lines. I said, 'Yes, that's true.'

[...]

Saw Patrick and Manoly on Christmas Day. They're not in very good form, but Manoly's garden looked beautiful and they were very welcoming. Patrick is still working, naturally. He was invited to Moscow not long ago, but had no remote chance of going anywhere much.

Think in my last letter, of months ago, I remembered saying something adverse about novels turned into films. Just after that I saw <u>A Room with a View</u>, which everyone (just about) enjoyed, including me; and then with Patrick I saw Christina's <u>For Love Alone</u>. It had had terrible reviews and was destined, as they say, for a very short run. Feeling that everything that made the novel memorable, original, prickly, unique, could never be seen by the eye, I had no thought of seeing it. Went because Patrick asked, and we both enjoyed it so much. It was quite sad to realize so many missed it because of the reviews. Early scenes photographed around Watson's Bay were ravishing.

[...]

Next day.

Very humid. Clouds of steam (it must be) low over the harbour. Up Awaba Street for a back X-ray at 10.00, having done something strange to back carrying two bottles of wine <u>down</u> Awaba Street. Probably needs the sort of treatment Henderson the Rain King received. (Applied feet.)

Best love,

Elizabeth

Mosman | 12 February, 1987

Dearest Shirley and Francis –

I've been writing this letter in my mind for some time, but this seems to be the day to get it on paper. (Trust you are still in NY and still grappled to desks?)

First of all, what do you think of showing letters to biographers? This is about Christina Stead. Three biographers have visited me. Two, at least, seem to be writing about CS for the right reasons – that is, they care about the books and they have allied themselves mightily to the task. I like these young women very much. They've had access to some letters now held by the National Library in Canberra, and the family members kept letters from 1928 on. (Only one person has been shown letters at this point.) Ron Geering is C's literary executor and he seems to be opposed to showing letters. When I look at those I've kept, they sometimes seem, appear, very personal, vulnerable and recent, and I wonder why any stranger should see them. C did speak about living people – people still living, relatives and others – very frankly. But even if she complained about friends and others, she could always see that they had a point of view and was extraordinarily impartial and un-angry. Should the biographers closest in time to the subject see all the letters? When I look back at the letters, I sometimes hear her say, 'Dear girl, what does it matter?' and at other times I feel a need to protect them, her and private life from view. Please tell me what you both think.

[...]

I hope you're both very well and working well. Take care of yourselves. Best love,

Elizabeth

PS. Andrew arrived in Manila just as the shooting started. He's sent a postcard since then. Was on the point of seeing Cory Aquino and was thrilled about it.

Mosman | 24 March, 1987

Dearest Shirley and Francis –

Thank you both very much for your good February letter. I was really grateful to know in a general way how you feel about showing letters, Francis. While I know that, in the long run, you should suit yourself in this matter, I couldn't decide – after quite a lot of thought – what <u>did</u> suit. Someone had said that if you showed letters to one you must obviously show them to all. I couldn't see the logic, and was relieved that you mentioned this very point. All is sorted out in my mind now (on this front at least!). Thank you again. Recently, Ron Geering gave me a copy of Christina's novel, <u>I'm Dying Laughing</u>, just published by Virago. The manic protagonist, Emily, is a person you would go a long way to avoid. C had kept this novel by her unpublished, but gave Ron permission to go ahead if he chose. It's uneven, but has brilliant things in it.

[...]

Whole areas of Doris Lessing's work – outer space, the future – were unreadable to me, but novels before and after that phase I could read, and this last one (about London terrorists) I tht very good. The worst ones became very fashionable – perhaps with feminists?

Have just read Marguerite Duras' The Lover. I liked it. I like her. This reminded me of Tarkovsky's beautiful film The Mirror. A deep dream that you breathe in.

[...] Trust you're very well, working well, enjoying the world.
Best love, Elizabeth

Mosman | 17 January, 1988

Dearest Shirley and Francis –

Thank you for the marvellous letter, dear S, and a card that produces laughter at every reading. [...]

After fairly prolonged heat and humidity, lovely, heavy rain last night which continues. The only sad thing about that is that it meant cancelling the opera in the park at Parramatta. Last Saturday sixty thousand or so saw Traviata in the Domain; this was the Aust. Opera's second performance that had to be cancelled last night. We have about two hundred Tall Ships or First Fleets converging on Sydney for Australia Day, January 26. Kylie used to say, 'Never give a present that eats.' Other nations have given us sailing ships, and while they may not eat, they will have to be maintained and used in some way after the famous birthday. However, though I'd felt there was a definite surplus of ships, the sight of one, alone, against a wooded hillside in Hobart was strikingly beautiful and exactly like an engraving or water-colour of the period. Far and away the worst aspect of 1988 and the celebrations is the irrational and sentimental attitude taken towards aborigines and the founding of the colony by self-righteous (but irrational) white Australians who always like to be 'agin the government'. No one really plans to give his own house to an aborigine, or to sail back to Europe, but they rage and rage about something that happened in 1788. They want to do good, and be good, but this is surely not the way to go about it. Some, like Manning Clark, speak so much of 'blood staining the wattle' that it's difficult not to feel they'd find it interesting.

[...]

They tell me Balmain has stopped making Ivoire. Is that not a great pity?

For some weeks or months I've been visiting Kylie in hospitals scattered all over Sydney. She has weeks or days to live. Like everyone else, she has her faults – and more than some; but this does not seem the best moment in the world to tell her about them, as her daughter has chosen to. She has always been physically brave. Why heroin should be denied to people at this time, I can't imagine. (Your mother used to rage about drugs and addicts and people like herself who really needed something.)

Had dinner with Patrick and Manoly the other night at a friend's house. They brought me a pot plant of rocca which, I think, is that interesting, slightly bitter plant they put in salads in Italy. Is that what it's called? Must make a space for it in the garden. Evidently its seeds scatter and it 'takes over'. Hope it does. It was good to see P and M. Some TV man is interviewing Patrick on Wednesday so that he can say something adverse about Australia and the Bicentennial year.

[...]

Sydney does at last look much better. The holes in the ground have been filled in, and all around The Rocks, the Quay, the Opera House and Macquarie Street the plans are completed. The only thing I can say to console anyone about the Monorail is that it is not like the Pyramids and can't possibly last as long. [...] I haven't set eyes on Darling Harbour yet. It was a derelict part of the city. No-one ever went there. There was no access to the harbour-side as there is now. It is so fashionable to oppose everything the government does here, that even sensible people sometimes condemn automatically without looking or thinking. Unthinking cynicism is as boring as unthinking enthusiasm, I suppose. Anyway, I believe that some good things will come out of the effort, money, work put in to celebrate this year. People complained ceaselessly while the Opera House was being built, and now it's the soul of the city, and everyone goes there. Parks, colleges, theatres have come into existence in the west of Sydney, where most of us never go. Still it isn't the wilderness that it once was, where everyone was at a disadvantage.

You mentioned the Renoir film, The River, which I saw, too, and of the homesickness for the orient that it gave you. You were in Hong Kong at that probably turbulent time after the war. Is that right? Where so many vivid and brilliant people congregated, or were assembled by fate. Did you read Ballard's Empire of the Sun? Many thought that should have won the Booker instead of Anita Brookner's novel. Then there is Marguerite Duras' <u>The Lover</u>... Years ago when I lived in Hunter's Hill, I had a letter from poor, beautiful Bim, Kylie's son, from India. He described all that he could see from his hotel window, the doorway. It was such a brilliant, complex picture of everything in life happening simultaneously that I've always remembered it. Afterwards, I looked out at Hunter's Hill: it was like a terrifying, super-real, empty painting of suburbia, no sign of life... I wonder how old you were in Hong Kong, and how long you stayed. Fate was surely friendly to take you there at a young age?

[...]

As ever, I send much love to you both –

Elizabeth

Mosman | 15 February, 1988

Dearest Francis –

You wrote on Australia Day and that was an extraordinary day – in Sydney especially. Although I could see the Tall Ships (as they're called) from the sitting-room, it was my good fortune to be with friends who live in a big unit at Kirribilli, on the eighth floor. This is close to the Harbour Bridge, opposite the Opera House, with the harbour and foreshores laid out below. We were all there from about ten in the morning, till eleven at night, with a walk over the Bridge in the middle of the day – the day human beings overcame the motor car. We all felt glad to be alive and exactly where we were. Wonder, admire: that's what we did.

[...]

Affectionate greetings and thoughts are sent to you by Margaret, Andrew, the Geerings, Patrick and others, and others, and especially from me with much love,

Elizabeth

Postcard, Mosman | 25 February, 1988

Wish I could give you five minutes at the Zoo, standing watching the platypus I saw last week-end, dear Shirley and Francis. It was such an active, joyful, well-made little creature. Patrick sd he used to see them in and around rivers when he was a jackaroo. The Zoo is much improved these days and provides what the platypus must assume to be a very real river and river bank.

[...]

Reading Leon Edel's Henry James. Liked this sentence: 'Turgenev himself gave proof of his own psychological sagacity by telling H that he found it difficult to judge someone else's critical appraisal: that he felt the praise too great or the blame too weak, and this not through "diffidence or modesty", but perhaps this was "one of the many disguises which self-love enjoys."' How well Turgenev emerges from this whole account. No wonder HJ loved him.

Hope you are feeling much improved, well, and thinking of Flaubert/ Sand.

Much love,
Elizabeth

New York | 11 March 1988

Dearest Elizabeth –

This afternoon in The Times, which reaches NY a day late, I found the enclosed obituary on Kylie Tennant. I knew from you that she was near the end, I know too that this will have been an important farewell for you. How much your love and friendship and understanding sustained her in all these later years I can only imagine. I remember her name from the time when I first knew my own. [...] We both remember so well meeting her in 1976 at your party – we went into the bedroom, and spoke with Christina and with Kylie. Had it not been for you I'd not have met either of them. And was always sorry that Christina's trip to New York foundered before we could spend any time together. At an earlier age one imagines there will be other opportunities. Later on you realise it may not happen, and that there are important encounters you'll miss.

[...]

Then, of course, the Bicentennial – and now the little picture with X marking the Kirribilli spot. It brings intensely the Coronation night of over fifty years, yes, ago – I remember so well going out from Balmoral on the yacht of friends of my parents, from the jetty at the Balmoral baths, in the dark. What adventure. Valerie and I allowed up nearly all night. There was also the daughter, V's age, of our friends, Janet, after whom the beautiful boat (nearly seventy feet) was named. I do know that we lay off Kirribilli while terrific fireworks went up, including a double portrait of king and queen (I hope they didn't do Hawke and Mrs. H). Oh, it was wonderful. For us (I was six, I suppose – 1937) there was only a dry ginger ale to drink, good but tingly. I recall what I wore...

As to aborigines – surely there is something between giving up one's house to an aboriginal or 'sailing back' to Europe [...] and reverting to indifference or, wildly worse, the sort of thought and talk about native peoples that blighted the world of my childhood? (and that MM was forcefully maintaining at the close of her conscious life). Is the trouble in part at least that almost no Australian knows an aborigine? Some have not even met one. That is the case here with the American Indians. Whereas 'blacks' and whites, while still in heaps of trouble, work together, deal together, are intimate with one another in some measure; often intermarry, and more often live together. For all the ghastly things still attending the black–white circumstances of this country, when I look back to the time of my arrival here I see an immeasurable improvement; not only in the possibilities for at least some millions of blacks, but in the education of white people, a great many of whom simply had to become accessible to the existence of a difference. It's hard to see how the aborigines of Australia can ever have a valid context for authentic life again – it has been demolished. But surely there can be many alleviations, less attitudinising about them on the one hand and more receptivity on the other? I wd say, more simple humanity; but that simplicity is the hardest thing to find.

[...]

Serious matters: I didn't know that Ivoire had been abolished. This is awful. Thank heavens, I have a good supply – F brought me a big packet of it in various splashy bottles from Paris to Naples last year, but I'll nose around and see if there's any left in the shops. That dandelion-looking salad plant from Italy is variously known as rughetto, rúgola, radichiella, and even arrúgola. Rughetto that I pick on Capri is my favourite, quite sharp when you bite into it, distinctive. Also, the greengrocers sell it in Italy in great quantities, already washed and plucked from the coarse stems. One re-washes it, but easily. It does grow like a fire.

I forgot to say that on Bicentennial day there was a huge party given by the consulate here, to which we are not stalwart enough to go. However, we were asked to a 'small lunch' at the consul's flat (extremely luxurious, on the east River, near the UN). F too ill to go but I went thinking there wd perhaps be Aust writers, musicians who live in or were visiting NY... However, a call from Sumner alerted me to the fact that he had not been invited (not to anything, in fact). The consul and his wife (just gone back to Aust) are very simple, friendly, always extremely pleasant with us; but somewhat aghast-making to arrive and find myself the only woman (apart from C's wife) in a lunch of twenty Aust-US big businessmen, one of whom was Rupert Murdoch. I spoke to Murdoch for a few minutes, he was the least boorish of a strikingly simian assemblage. But I really didn't want to find myself in that company. A beautiful day, very cold. The toasts, by Murdoch (US citizen!) and the consul were in the one case utterly mechanical and in the other well meaning.

That part of NY, where I used to live, is still the most charming, I think – many parts of Manhattan are more handsome with streets of old houses well kept up, etc. (those are still in profusion in the 'Village', the section of NY where the rock is too soft to sustain the weight of monster buildings; many scattered still throughout the town). But I loved being beside the river and in a sort of enclave of quiet. However, all is being torn up now wherever possible, to make 60 and 80 storey buildings, and the city changes every day. I do think one must speak out against this most deadly aspect of the money game, the destruction of space. I don't see why, when there's a derelict Darling Harbour, it can't be recreated with pleasant structures and open spaces rather than made the immediate victim of a new kind of dereliction. [...]

Lots of pleasant things here, mostly with friends. Last evening to Khovanshchina at the opera – stupendous. We seldom go now to the opera as, to the vulgarity of the opera house there is added, often, a costly cheapness of production; and the performance seldom moves us as once it fairly frequently did. But Khovanshchina was v. impressive – such music, such singing, such solemnity and force. And beautiful sets, I thought. I've been sunk in two Waldheim pieces – one, the lesser, a review for the NY Times of a (wretchedly written but informative) book on the Waldheim case. This will be out in a couple of weeks, I'll press one on you.

The other is a longer, far more complex affair. When this broke on me, I was working so well on my book, and can't wait to return to it. But this time shd close down my UN business forever.

How are you, dear E? Well, we always hope. And Margaret? – we wish her a happy birthday in retrospect and in prospect. I have no time to be anything but well. We are lucky. Many good things happen, we like our work, we like our friends. We leave for Italy on 27 March. [...]

Our love to you – Shirley.

I re-read Voss and The Tree of Man this winter. How marvellous these books are. They go on existing in spite of much that went off the rails thereafter. Splendid, really.

Mosman | 16 May, 1988

Dearest Shirley and Francis –

So many good things to thank you for, all so welcome and read to pieces. Most recently I had your note and the very grim Waldheim piece. Mysterious, his wish to rise and rise in the world, to become prominent and known, in view of his life. Then, not satisfied with the UN, the need to become President of Austria. Now and again in these months I've seen Waldheim being interviewed on television, defending himself, and seen his wife standing by – no sign of his 'winsome manner' on these occasions. I told Patrick about 'Chaos was his opportunity' and he was interested though he couldn't remember writing it.

[...]

Thank you for writing about Kylie's death and for the obituary from The Times. She had been in and out of hospitals from last October, sometimes darting back to the mountains to die up there. [...] Because she had been famous here for so long, from a time when there were few famous people about, the curious gathered round. [...] Although I sometimes had to force myself to trek over to Chatswood to visit, I was almost always glad I'd gone because it did make a difference to her. She knew great quantities of poetry by heart, and I heard her say for the last time familiar lines she'd quoted hundreds of times over the years.

[...]

Glad that was a false alarm about the disappearance of Ivoire. The local importers gave up or lost the contract, then months passed before the new people shipped some in. Having heard from you that this life-enhancing fragrance still exists, asked again and was embraced by the ladies of French perfumery for Ivoire had returned that day. Serious matters, as you say. Thank you, too, for the various names of rughetto. These good leaves bite back and make salad-eating interesting. My plant from Manoly grows and grows.

[...]

Saw a very fine film version of the Thomas Hardy short story, On the Western Circuit. Chilling, so well done. Also saw excellent and heart-rending short films about Oscar Wilde and Callas. You seem to enjoy opera less than before, and I feel like that about the theatre. This is a sorrow, because it once meant a great deal.

What are you both reading? After the Henry James biography, I seem to have settled down with literary essays. You must have been occupied with the Waldheim pieces for weeks and months. I hope you now have a chance to get back to the novel. Politics. I regret having taken so much interest, wasted so much time.

Patrick is often frail these days. Their little dog, Nellie, was run over in front of Manoly a couple of weeks ago, and they'd had her for twelve years. A friend miraculously persuaded them to acquire a new Jack Russell terrier, Millie, four months old. So that will keep them busy and cheer them up.

[...]

And I must speed up Awaba Street – always a thought. I hope you're both restored and working well after the change in Italy. With love,

Elizabeth

Capri | 5 July 88

Dearest Elizabeth –

[...] Two days ago was Francis' birthday, which always brings him many Neapolitan and Capresi greetings, some nice prezzies, a good dinner, etc. As often in the past, we dined à quatre with Graham Greene and his Yvonne – Graham in exceptionally genial form, invited again to Siberia by

Gorbachev, planning visits to Latin American strongholds, etc. Graham is 84, F is 82. They seem to be doing more than almost anyone else I know. Although, on the forthcoming trip to Russia, I don't know that Graham will want to go over quite so many tractor-factories and farm cooperatives as on his recent last trip. What interesting things are happening there. As the Western world belligerently turns to the right, to Thatcherism, etc, the Soviets at last seemed to clank their ghastly chains and take responsibility for their existence. Strange to think that Gorbachev could retain what so far seems an almost visionary sense of transformation while presumably going along with decades of repression. A man so much part of the power machine almost never conserves the ability to break out of it, don't you think? – which is one reason we have such a wretched bunch of 'candidates' around the world. The reporting in such Italian press as La Repubblica, a daily paper of considerable quality, is ample and straightforward on the Russian events. Whereas the NY Times (at least until our departure at end of March) seemed heartbroken at the idea that something might conceivably improve in Russia; and even their full and interesting reports of certain events were accompanied by editorials or signed articles urging us, virtually, to take no notice, not to be taken in, and to go on growling in our supposed corners.

[...]

Our Naples place is beautiful, we've made it very comfortable. At this moment it's very hot, being exposed all day to the sun on the sea side; always cooling as soon as the sun goes away and delightful at evening when we sit out to dinner. However, Capri is divine at present; and the crowds are all at the sea, where we seldom go at this season. Here one is always speaking about the light being 'just like that of the Neapolitan gouaches', but so it is; and yesterday was supreme in that respect, the whole gulf radiant. In the evening, F and I walked to the Arco Naturale, where we could see the entire great bay of Solarno spread out, and, through binoculars, even the hilltop town above the temples of Paestum (I don't mean the temples are visible; impossible). There were about a dozen people in trattoria, while hundreds or thousands are huddled elsewhere on the island. It was cool, beautiful. Awoke at midnight to tremendous red-white-and-blue fireworks exploding from the annual party given on the Fourth of July, by a grateful local jeweller, to all Americans in the best hotels.

(They have often asked us, but Uncle Sam is not really a close relative of ours.) The fireworks were lovely, made me think of Empire night. How I remember the smell of sparklers. A couple of weeks ago, the Queen Mother 'steamed' across the Bay of Naples in the yacht Britannia, flying – on three masts – the white ensign, the royal standard, and (I think) the standard of the Cinque Ports. A sight. The Britannia is a very nice shape, built when boats looked like boats instead of outsize armoured tanks. She (QM) had been to Paestum by sea – oh, what a treat. She came to 'tea' (champagne and mozzarella di bufala) at our landlords', and – for God sake, don't tell Patrick – was in fact very nice. I gave her a copy of 'Rammage in South Italy' – another Scot who went to Paestum by sea, although seducing girls all the way. How MM wd have loved it. (Not the Rammage part, the queen part.) [...]

The foll day we went to a neighbour's, again for champers and mozzarella (he has his own buffaloes north of Naples), not far from where we are at Naples, and also on the sea. They live on the edge of the vast remains of the villa of Pollio – of Vedius Pollione, that is, who left his property to the Emperor Augustus: the place that was called 'Pausylipon', and gave this luxurious name to the headland of Posillipo. Beside our friends' garden, a 'small' private theatre, perhaps seating 200 or 300 people, is being exposed. We walked down the tiers. Beyond it, as the 'scenery', so to speak, for the Roman stage, there is a brief descent of shrubs and pines, all wild, and the sea. The whole place, called the Valley of Gaiola, is extremely ancient, beautiful, mysterious – very close to the city and yet untouched by the modern world except for the everlasting motor-car, snorting around the winding, walled country road that leads down to the place.

[...]

Poor Manoly, to have seen their Nellie killed. Poor Nellie. They're brave and 'right' to install Millie. It's hard to start up again with a new little creature, but they bring powers of their own. Did I tell you that one of the homeless cats I feed in Capri has only one eye? I called him Nelson. The remaining eye is most compelling, as was no doubt the case with his great namesake. He is otherwise very pretty, a golden tiger. Then there is Miscia, who wants to have her kittens among F's sweaters. That quotation from Patrick, adapted, is from The Tree of Man. When Stan comes back from the Great War, his contemporaries all have their 'yarns' to tell, but he falls silent about it: 'Chaos was not his opportunity.' What a splendid thing to write. A good moment, when that came into PW's head. We wonder what he is writing now.

[...]

Thank you for all your news, and thoughts and affection, heartily returned. And with best love always from Francis and Shirley.

Capri | 2 Oct 88

Dearest Elizabeth –

We only received this week your letter, forwarded from New York just after our departure, telling us of your broken wing. What a shock, and what a ghastly nuisance for you. [...]

So many things going on. The last two days at Naples have been stupendous. 'Our' foundation for restoration unveiled their greatest work, a splendid overhauling of a sculptured triumphal arch, of Renaissance sculptures, at the Castel Nuovo in the middle of the city (You might remember, a great castle of huge round towers overlooking the port?). The towers are of dark grey stone; the arch was originally of blond stone, had become as grey as the towers; now is blond again with its decay arrested. A floodlit opening, beginning at 10 pm.

[...]

Elizabeth, I liked so much 'The Cost Of Things', in the short stories anthology edited by Murray. From what vintage is this? It made me think of a story – by Chekhov, or Tolstoy, about a young man sent to a provincial town who marries the daughter of the town's leading citizen, can't believe his luck, a nice little house, wife, children soon, furniture, money saved up. One day realises, this is all there will ever be. Wants to die. Not really 'like', but that emanation of nullity got up as achievement. I must look for the Russian tale. In the anthol., I liked best 'The Cost Of Things', and 'The Persimmon Tree'.

We've been working, working. I left NY exhausted – from long hours of work and from an incubus of extraordinary heat (which did in fact break in the latter part of August, but left us all in constant terror of its murderous return). [...]

Shall hope to speak in a few days. Take care of yourself, dear Elizabeth
– With love always from us both – Shirley.

Mosman | 10 October, 1988

Dearest Shirley and Francis,

Here, for some cosmic reasons, numerous friends young and old
seem to have been laid low by dire life-and-death events. I trust that this
is a purely local phenomenon and that you are both very well, happy and
working. Lately, here, it's been quite startling and sad. On a better note,
though, Patrick, who was very ill for weeks at St Vincent's Hospital, is at
home and has an intelligent, interesting nurse. He's very, very thin and I've
looked up diets to see what he should eat to gain weight. When he started
to rail about something on my last visit to the hospital, I said accusingly,
'You're <u>better</u>,' but in truth he's alarmingly frail.

[...]

We are in the midst of spring, but the temperature rose to a stunning
thirty-eight degrees last Tuesday. Now it's idyllic again – radiant, cool,
sunny, scented. One day last week as I walked along this street, the morning
was so inspiriting, so beautiful, with this same combination of flower-
scented air, warmth, coolness, light, that I was enraptured. Quite what the
difference is between one beautiful morning and another, that would lend
one some extra, poetic, almost heavenly dimension – God alone knows.
It was like paradise.

The right hand, having been fallen on 8 ½ weeks ago, is almost normal
to look at, but only feels happy when unused. A second X-ray showed the
bone hadn't yet mended. But it will soon be well.

[...]

Read Muriel Spark's new novel. It is quiet and hasn't the fire and
originality of her early books, but the London of the fifties is very
familiar and interesting to me, and – best of all – she has generously
inserted throughout the novel very, very wise advice about life. There is
commonsense; there is practicality. By falling down mine-shafts et cetera,
I've learned most of these things for myself, but younger people might be
saved some troubles and bad decisions if they heeded Muriel S.

[...]

Smoky put a dead rat on the lawn at the front door the other day, and David, who cuts the grass, took it away. Now Smoky has brought me this lovely present once again. Too kind!

Be in excellent form, dear friends. I'm sure you are. But <u>be</u>.

Best love, Elizabeth

Mosman | 5 November, 1988

Dearest Shirley and Francis,

[...]

Thank you for what you say about 'The Cost of Things'. When Murray said he liked it, I was quite surprised. It's chilling to see a captive in such a partnership – the demonstrated power of one, and the trudging through life, staying alive for no reason, of the other. Even in these days it's not uncommon.

Tonight I and much of Sydney will witness yet another spectacle. This one is a birthday present from Japan and is likely to be extremely dazzling and loud. Scotland has given us a lot of stones and they're being cemented into a cairn at this moment by a Highlander, Duncan Mathieson, who travelled out for this purpose. There's a stone from every parish in Scotland and the cairn will be in Rawson Park, Mosman, on a headland – more or less.

[...]

What else? People here as elsewhere can't believe the way the US election seems to be going.

Patrick is still at home, with a daily nurse, and can't put weight on, but has many visitors and is reading Pushkin.

There is more to say but mundane tasks clamour for a bit of attention.

Happy days, dear friends.

With love,

Elizabeth

Naples | 14 May 89

Dearest Elizabeth –

This is the feast day of Capri's patron, San Costanzo, whose silver image (a life-sized bust, wearing bishop's mitre) is at this moment being carried through the streets to the sound of a small brass band, followed by maidens who have exchanged their usual blue jeans for white smocks and who carry open baskets of bright petals (geranium petals, mostly) to strew about in the wake of the Saint. We are in fact at Naples, but have seen the procession many times and marvel at its survival [...]. From the beginning of February on, I haven't lifted my head from words, work, whether in regard to what has become a shortish book on the Waldheim case, as it 'touches' the United Nations, or my 'own' work, which I now must press on with and conclude. The Waldheim opus, an intense labour, will bring me a tirade of abuse, but it has been worth doing. Wanted to get it done with, and also – as it, or most of it, will appear first in The New Yorker – there was a kind of pressure to conclude it, so that it could go to press if they suddenly chose to run it. [...]

Here, with work and events and waiting tasks, [...] it seems that one has not drawn breath. Only today we sat out on our terrace, looked at Capri as it was blessed by San Costanzo, and re-entered a more rational state of mind. Francis is galloping towards the stable with Galiani, Diderot, Mme Depinay, who have now become a great tribe and a large ms. Meantime, his colleague on the George Sand–Flaubert letters seems at last to be coming through with her side of the work, so there will soon be a date for publication. All these words, words, rushing towards the printers.

What of Elizabeth? What doing, saying, reading, writing? What about your arm? If beginning truly to return to normality, such a relief, almost a luxury. Thankfulness becomes philosophy – 'it' can be relegated to experience. [...] Why isn't one thankful all the time when one is not afflicted by such aggravations? – I am, often, conscious of the luck and grateful; but it wd be demeaning to make a full time occupation of such appreciation, it's better as an undercurrent – a George Herbert sense of quiet wonder. [...] What news, too, of Margaret?

When I was reading – but one scarcely 'reads' such things – a tonne of dreary official writings for my Waldheim work, I was thinking in something of this way of the time when I would be restored to real books and could read for delight. Return to books celebrated by reading three favourite Dickens, some good new – new to me – Italian writing, 'A Passage to India', two early Iris Murdoch, many poems English and Italian; and our reading aloud Herodotus each morning for forty mins or so. The translation, Penguin, by Aubrey de Sélincourt (with introduction, eccentric and beguiling, by A. Burn) is delightful. The translator has much lively freshness, and is not too grand to put things plainly. Today, describing the capture of Babylon by Cyrus, he tells us that city was so large that the inhabitants at the centre did not know that the besiegers had penetrated the town and went on, at a local feast, 'drinking and dancing until they found out the hard way'.

Having had no winter, Italians have had a tantalising spring of glorious near summer-days, abruptly eclipsed by damp chill. Today, warm, humid, misty, greyish bay, with regatta of colourful spinnakers passing with a rushing sea-sound by our walls. Some churning from an occasional hydrofoil. Flowers everywhere, and yesterday I bought what seems to be a thousand sweet peas from a barrel in Naples. In Rome with Everett, this past week, we saw such beautiful things. After Everett had flown off to the conf. tables of the Metrop Museum, (where he has just opened a huge Goya exhibition), F and I sauntered, in a way we hadn't done for months. In NY, now, we never seem to have time to <u>flâner</u>. The whole world has lost the gift – the taste – for sauntering. Dear Elizabeth, please excuse silence, send news. Our love to you – Shirley

PS: In Florence I met for the first time Peter Porter. What an extraordinary, nice and knowing man.

PPS: We both wonder what Patrick's state is. I would call Manoly, but it seems – what? – pointedly unusual.

Mosman | 17 June, 1989

Dearest Shirley and Francis –

Have we been going through the threatened change of climate? After living in a radiant universe more or less forever, we've been all but drowned in Sydney for months, with record-breaking rains that now seem as eternal as our previous state. This is mid-June. There has been one fine week-end this year. I like rain and get tired of paradise from time to time, but even so...

[...]

During all these wet weeks more people have come to talk about Christina, Judah, Kylie and Patrick. I haven't minded yet, but could get bored if this keeps up. It's ideal weather for reading and writing. No-one European should ever leave Europe. After his Chekhov and Pushkin, read two of Troyat's novels – The Children, which I admired very much, and The Web, which was not of the same order – thought up and fitted together like a lesser Mauriac. I've read more of Julian Barnes, Ian McEwan, Rachel Ingalls, Martin Amis, the John Cheever biography (somehow not satisfying, although illuminating in unexpected ways). I've read good pieces about/by Bellow, Genet, Duras, Milan Kundera. An excellent (not new) Cocteau documentary film was shown; and a cassette of the music from Fellini films definitely brightened a dark day. Biographies have been unsatisfactory because the subjects are seldom as gifted and never as humanly wonderful as Chekhov. This wasn't news, but kept striking afresh.

[...]

You ask about Patrick. While other people of 77 are hearty and well, flitting to all parts of the globe, Patrick and Manoly are both frail. Patrick has a nurse with him four days a week. He rings on Sundays, and on a good day we talk for about an hour. [...] He wants to be around to see how his biography is received.

[...]

Yesterday someone came from Sydney University to ask me about my own books. Then just this afternoon a marvellous box of flowers arrived as thanks. I'm delighted, but never surprised when good news arrives at the door.

[...]

Keep well, keep working and sauntering.

Love from Elizabeth

New York | 3 September 1989

Dearest Elizabeth –

[...]

I'm at my desk, surrounded by a million New Yorker galleys, a million Waldheim documents & scraps of scribbled paper with supposedly vital information on them. In a week, the issue of the magazine 'closes', then it will be on the stands on 20 Sept, the day the General Assembly opens. [...] The weather is either torrential rain, or – as for the past ten days – divine. Unprecedented clear, fine days for August, and cool nights. Astonishing. I wish I could go out and enjoy this light, but Waldheim has his fangs into me. The long weekend – Labour Day holiday – means that, in all the residential skyscrapers surrounding us, scarcely a window is lit at evening: all out of town. However, the streets are busy with young people; and with tourists, European, Latin American, and from the rest of the USA. At this moment, we have a spate of illness among our dear friends – hospitals, operations, strokes, AIDS, therapy... Among these, I'm so sorry to say, is dear Sumner Locke Elliott, who was operated on last week for intestinal cancer (he is not generally telling this news). When he recovers from the operation, will have to have treatment. What a shame – a good and lovely man. The kind and admirable man he lives with (in a building very near us, where they have a flat with lots of room) tells me today that Sumner will soon be home, and we'll be able to visit him. We always laugh so much together; and shall do so again.

Francis is working incredible hours – yesterday until 1am. He loves it. I too, but things will subside for me soon, at least in that sense. Then, must finish my novel. (The book of my Waldheim writings now has a draft jacket – very nice, and definitely not with a picture of Waldheim.) Love to you, Dear Elizabeth; and our love also to Margaret, with great commiseration for that terrifying episode of 'rustiness', which we hope she is now putting behind her. If you can send us a word about Andrew, we'll be more than grateful – Shirley.

4.11.89

Dearest S & F,

It's 10.00 at night and I'm alone in a 4-bed ward of the Royal North Shore Hospital. Big black windows off to my right with some scattered lights of St Leonards, or North Sydney, Crows Nest. In the last few weeks I've been rushed in twice – the first time following blood tests & X-rays – for blood infusions, then for tests as an outpatient & a second immediate admission. Came in last Friday at 2.00 & didn't see the surgeon till 2.00 today, Tuesday. A tumour. Operation Friday. People have said some cheerless things, but friends have been wonderful. [...] I certainly haven't been lonely, so much loving support – I don't look forward to the next days, especially since the last medical man came in this evening to give me his thoughts. He took a somewhat dismal view of my future – perhaps he was truthful, perhaps he emphasised the bad news cruelly. Anyway Marg. Brink turned up as he left, having listened behind the drawn curtains. She was crying, but I think I had better not cry or it will be too hard on everyone – including myself. Later the dear Madigans turned up. I'll have to think of Col surviving in the shark-filled ocean for days & days when his ship was sunk during the war. With the best friends there's been a lot of laughter. Why not? I can't quite believe this is all happening. I've never been in a hospital before – except as a visitor, & always thought my weakness would be – like my mother & father – the heart. Not to be.

If you'd been in NY I'd have rung, but this has been v. sudden & no access to phones coping with OS calls here anyway. Too much happens in wards & there have been so many visitors I haven't wanted to read. Margaret (Dick) brought in the metaphysicals – for me to read Marvell's Garden yesterday. Like some solitude & have seldom had less. Tonight I'm alone for the first time for ages. I enjoy reflecting, thinking. It always feels interesting inside my head. This may be an illusion, but I like it.

When the registrar spoke to me tonight, such a handsome young man with an angular pale face, I felt my head slowly freeze. However it's all right now. Just shock. I'm not very interested in medical matters or interiors of bodies. I'd hate to have been a doctor or nurse or anything like that.

There seems no space there, no need there, for intuition or poetry or – they just carry us about, like carriages. Our consciousness has to be able to get about the world. My taxi is in need of repair.

Best love,

Elizabeth

P.S. In the light of history, eternity & all the rest, we've all been lucky.

E

Mosman | 24 February, 1990

Dearest Shirley and Francis:

[...]

Since we spoke I think I've seen the surgeon, Dr Fielding. He didn't organize any more blood tests. They happen on 2 May, but as I feel so fine I trust they won't produce anything interesting. The warnings and comments of the younger doctors have begun to fade away, or have entirely faded, but they could scarcely have been more threatening. Dr Fielding said it's the fault of medical education that they ever approach patients in this way. [...]

So much for all that... There are grey skies, huge storms and humidity. It will probably change on 1 March. So often on the 1st of the month the season decides to change completely. I love that first morning when I go into the courtyard early to pick up the Herald before breakfast and the air and the light say <u>Autumn</u>. Saw <u>Crimes and Misdemeanours</u> the other night and enjoyed it: it was like a novel – than which there can be no higher praise (unless it's Fellini and then it's ineffable). The Adelaide Festival starts soon. I was invited to Writers' Week, but didn't want to go. Everyone in the world has been to see <u>Tristan</u> at the Opera House and all are enraptured. [...]

With many South African friends I waited up to watch Nelson Mandela walk out of prison and into the arms of his supporters. Bitter but not surprising that Mrs Thatcher so rapidly lifted sanctions, renewed investment in S.A. However, she's a minority of one, and events will move without her help... I wonder what people say where you are about a united Germany? There are world-wide doubts and fears, and now the Poles want the Russians to stay until they can agree about borders! When will that ever be, with populations so extremely scrambled? Enough of rhetorical questions and deep thoughts. What I like to think about is the Abbé, and Francis at his desk from early till early. Happiness. Look forward to seeing and reading the Waldheim book soon. It will be released here, too? Keep well.

Much love
Elizabeth

Dearest Shirley and Francis –

I was so pleased to find <u>Countenance of Truth</u> in my letterbox. Thank you very much. It's a tremendous piece of work and no doubt had a tremendous reception. [...]

Over here, the great rains have gone, and there are crystal days and huge, glamorous moons by night. Winter is lovely. The Italian class is highly enjoyable. Of course, two hours a week won't take you far, but daily application yields not startling but noticeable results.

Events around the world have one moving from hope to concern as the globe spins. On the one hand, the founding thinkers of The Shining Path and the Khmer Rouge and on the other, Vaclev Havel, Dubcek, Mandela and heroic, largely unknown people in Colombia (editors, judges), in most troubled areas. But this breaking-up in Europe into smaller and smaller groups, quarrelling about ancient borders and producing more dead bodies is not cheering. For a change, I like to think about the Hubble telescope out there looking at the universe. And the photographs the other day of the earth from another Voyager.

I told Patrick of your reading <u>The Aunt's Story</u> again and perhaps ringing at some time. He was interested, though saying little, doubted that you had the number, but I reminded him he'd given it to you in 1976. A bit later I went over on his birthday taking some edible presents, hoping to help reverse the weight loss. So happy to see him, but sad that he should be so frail. Still, he's absolutely his familiar self and a loved friend.

[...]

Hair. Told Dr Fielding about the great fall-out. He assured me it won't <u>all</u> fall out. I'd wanted to hear it would return thick, long, glossy, dark chestnut... The fall has stopped, but it's not my hair. I wonder what you should eat to help? (I know you know what I mean by all this.)

[...]

Thank you both for your enlivening and affectionate calls. When there is so much going on, everything takes thought and effort. I'm aware of that. I'm always trying to catch up with wants and oughts.

[...]

Best love,

Elizabeth

Mosman | 10 October 1990

Dearest Shirley and Francis –

It's now almost ten days since Patrick died. Difficult thought. On Sunday, a week after his death, I went to see Manoly again. He was alone. We went through the house, looking at books and pictures, and it seemed so empty and quiet. We seemed to be looking for Patrick.

There have been some very fine readings on radio and television, arranged by his theatre friends. On one, while Kerry Walker and John Gaden read, there were many close-up photographs showing the young, middle-aged and finally the very frail Patrick of recent times. It was affecting.

Of course he was infuriating and hurtful and said many non-wonderful things about everyone, but equally, he was extremely lovable, kind and funny. He tried to rescue me from myself when no-one else did. In the days when I had a strange obligation to save people's lives, he said, 'You're an artist, and you're acting like a social worker!' Another time, he said, 'I get depressed when I think you're not writing.' Not many people deeply mind whether other people write.

[...]

David Marr, his biographer, said Patrick was brought up like a prince. He was always very rich, and might have been a playboy all his life. Fortunately, he was driven to write, and to return to Australia, where his work and his presence changed forever the awareness and appreciation of the arts. No-one can do again what he did. His biography depressed him, although his desire to read it probably kept him alive.

These days I have to think about boring things like getting plumbers to find broken water pipes under the courtyard, but in no time my head is full of Patrick again. I am also clearing out ancient furniture and sorting out cupboards with the intention – real estate crashes or no – of selling the house when possible. And this room where I'm typing is hideous with papers overflowing from filing cabinets. So those not destroyed will go to a library soon. When there is only one of you all these things seem tedious, not to say mountainous, but must be done.

Italian starts again tomorrow. Just four more classes this year, which is a pity.

You'll be arriving home with work completed, proofs on the way, good events all over the place. Take care of yourselves. Thank you again for your call from the phone box. That was nice.

Best love, Elizabeth

New York | 11 Feb 91

Dearest Elizabeth –

Since we came back from Venice – and found your passion-flower message – I've been trying to establish a serene time to write you a serene letter. Now I snatch an interim mo to send an interim word [...] and send you the originals of the Sbarbaro poems I've so far published. His work is difficult to approach because the tone is low key and deceptively simple; and in English could easily become banal. He was a friend and mentor of Eugenio Montale. They knew one another from youth. He had a very solitary inner life, without human intimacy, until in his forties he fell in love (with a woman, married & with children; I knew her, she was wise and beautiful), and found his love returned. He never married. He was a scientist, an expert in lichens. I think his poems sometimes have a lichen-like quality.

We hope for news, and very good news, of your health. Francis is fine, working long long hours – useless to try to deter him, and anyway he loves it. Venice was more than miraculous – one of the most beautiful things we ever did was to take that trip. We came back just as this terrible, mindless war broke out – a war 'authorised' by the United Nations, which is supposedly dedicated to prevention of conflict... Events in Lithuania, too, are deeply discouraging. (Lithuania, Somalia, The Gulf War itself undiscussed now at the UN). Well, we try to think as little as possible about these matters, otherwise one would never do any work and one might go mad.

I'm reading David Malouf's 'Great World' – a big enterprise done with much heart and mind, one feels – and much else – a beautiful Italian novel, le Strade di polvere by Rosetta Loy (soon to appear in English). Tonight, very cold after many mild days. Strange atmosphere, strange world. With love always from us both – Shirley.

Mosman | 8 April, 1991

Dearest Shirley & Francis

[...]

Graham Greene. A great figure in the world, a great life & an immense contribution to the lives of so many. And to you, of course, a good friend. [...]

I had a good report – blood count did – from Dr. Farhenblum. He decided against the cardiogram & chest X-ray, thank goodness, since I see the surgeon early May. He gave a talk about cholesterol & asked if I ate ice cream which I don't even like. Don't see how a spartan diet can be much more spartan. Life & death & ice cream. Dear, oh dear!

Surely a relief to you to be out of NY & away from the US version of the aftermath of the Gulf War. Even for a genetic optimist it's hard not to have some deep unfavourable thoughts about human nature & the future of the species. [...]

Beautiful autumn is here, but gardens are DRY & having trouble keeping plants alive. I do some selective watering.

[...]

Much love,

Elizabeth

Postcard, New York | 25 July 91

Dearest Elizabeth –

An interim and most apologetic word, because I've begun but
not completed the letter I spoke of on the phone. I am staggering under
(1) a chapter of my own work, which is in fact my joy but needs silence &
seclusion, and which I'm determined to finish next week; (2) F's completed
ms. – nearly 1000 typed pages – of the Flaubert–Sand correspondence,
with his narrative, notes, introd, etc; (3) desk-load of papers, any one of
which causes me to gasp if I turn it up, since these are all tasks long long
overdue. As MM said, when Francis, after weeks of telephoning, writing,
filling out forms, got hold of the last of her eight missing pieces of luggage:
'Just what I always say: if you leave things alone, they work themselves out.'

Among the above tasks are certain of the many books from
publishers – the ones to which one feels some sort of obligation. One of
these is the biography of Patrick, to be published by Knopf, by David Marr;
of which I've read about a third. If it can be said of a life that produced
those best and great books – it's a tragic tale, I think.

Letter follows. We're pretty heat-struck here, and thrilling
thunderstorms rarely seem (as EM Forster noted) to clear the air.
With love as ever to you both – Shirley.

New York | 3 Sept 91

Dearest Elizabeth –

When I sent a card a month ago, the seas were closing over us. [...]
Against all the odds, I've completed a long chapter of novel. I'm now at my
desk, it is 1am, tomorrow we leave for Italy, and the small hours of the night
are the only times I have for silence and 'leisure'. One hopes someday to
recover a sense of time rather than an unremitting anxiety about it. Thank
you for letter, for news, for interview – oh my – with Manoly. Thank you
for all. So much has happened, hasn't it? – not only to all of us, but to the
world. One morning a couple of weeks ago, we awoke to torrential rain
and the high wind of a nearby hurricane, and the news that Gorbachev
had been arrested and that the populace was rising – at last, that erstwhile
passive populace. Well, another roll of huge events passed over us, as in the
autumn of 1989: and again, something favourable. It is obvious that ghastly

difficulties lie ahead. But there have always been ghastly difficulties; the difference now is that there are positive elements as well. And God save us from these 'experts' who foresee nothing, and then 'explain' after the event.

As I wrote you, I've been reading the Marr Life of Patrick. It's an awful story, really, and in some ways impenetrable. Marr has done a lot of work, assiduous, and has had the difficult task of providing the quarry from which future opinions will be drawn. Sherry is now well embarked on another colossal volume of his (good, so far) life of Graham Greene. We had a remarkable letter from Yvonne – Graham's companion – about his death. [...] Many thoughts abt PW and his life. We are told that he read the ms. of this book 'often through tears', and one would like to know the source of such tears. Remorse – by the time one's got through with the story – seems unlikely. In any case, it wd be appalling to read the story of one's own life like that, I shd think. To remorse, you say you never cared for it. That is very strange to me. I suppose psychiatry has made us (or tried to make us) suspect remorse as being invariably a manifestation of 'guilt'. What abt sense of responsibility, which is the rightful source of 'guilt' or remorse? One can't wallow in regrets, one doesn't have time for one thing; but the adult ability to question oneself, to try to find out what sort of character one truly has, to feel more than a passing pang for wrongs one has done to others – that seems to me a form of grace, the central civilising factor, perhaps. How difficult and beautiful to be able to say, as one is older, 'I'm sorry', 'I was wrong.' [...] (Rather than be Valerie, who declares she 'wouldn't do anything different.')

[...]

I don't enjoy remorse, but I need it. Otherwise, it wd be in my case a disinclination to <u>consider</u>, of which no doubt there's plenty in any case.

[...]

Much more to say, always. But brain is failing. Our weeks here have included many nice things, it's only the lack of hours and days. After many soggily hot stretches, the temperature abruptly fell last Saturday evening – 40 degrees F. We were sitting in friends' garden in Brooklyn, to the scent of night-flowering stock, when a real wind swept over us. Since then, clear light, lovely sky, autumnal cooling. I'm glad to be returning, in Italy, to extended summer, which is not the uncomfortable variety, but something mellow without the autumnal sadness that, here, comes so early.

[...] Please remember us with all affection to Andrew and to Margaret, whose health we hope is good these days. Francis sends his love, and so do I – Shirley

Mosman | 26 July, 1992

Dearest Shirley and Francis –

How are you both? Even a short letter or a postcard, please. I miss hearing from you.

Over here, as in many other places, it's impossible to escape from the economic depression for very long: the newspapers, radio and television, people in shops and at bus stops, talk about little else. Many of the golden lads and lasses who thronged the restaurants in the eighties are in prison, bankrupt or overseas avoiding arrest. The city had its 150th birthday last week, and the bands of foreign ships marched through the streets and flags waved and it was rather pathetic. Luxury hotels built to accommodate tourists offer bargain rates to locals in desperation. Unemployment is higher than in the US or the UK, though it's a far cry from the Depression, and from Sarajevo, or Lima, or an endless list of tragic cities and countries. People – except the young who've dropped out – do seem to realize that. Opposing sides from what was Yugoslavia parade with banners, as do the Macedonians and Greeks and so many other groups now living here, but there's no violence except for the occasional scuffle round a soccer-field. This is the time when some 'leaders' in Sydney choose to bid for the Olympic Games for (I think) the year 2000, spending millions and courting, like the other contending cities, what seems to be a very corrupt little group with the power to signal yes or no. The pleasant, handsome lawyer leading Sydney's bid also says 'mischievious' constantly in interviews and English is his native language.

Italy. The deaths of Falcone and Borsellino and their bodyguards are so tragic. The Mafia seems to be everywhere and all-powerful. But what heroes these men were to stand up against that force, as were many others in the past. In the Italian class some say they would take risks for their families, but marvel that anyone would risk himself for the general good. And I marvel at that point of view.

Ron Geering edited the <u>Selected Letters of Christina Stead</u>, 1928 to 1983, in two volumes, and that ends his arduous task as literary executor. He saw into print the big collections of short stories, <u>Ocean of Story</u>, and the novel, <u>I'm Dying Laughing</u>, but this work was the most strenuous and time-consuming. Reading the letters confirmed my feeling that she was, as Henderson the Rain King might have said, 'a great human being'. I agreed to write a short piece about the letters and enjoyed the thinking while making heavy weather of it.

[...]

What else of deep significance? The outside of my house has been painted and that's a relief to the eye. Some relief inside would have been welcome, but impossible. A wattle tree that I planted – it seems, six months ago – when it was eighteen inches high, is suddenly 25/30 feet and golden all over, so beautiful, so surprising. The japonica is in blossom, too, and Adamo, from Trieste, comes occasionally to help in the garden and, unlike former helpers, knows a weed from a plant.

[...]

America. Who will become President in November? Should Mario Cuomo have entered the field? Will Bush have a war or find some lost prisoners in an effort to win? Clinton and Gore would surely be a great improvement? Though you wish they would not choose to call on JFK for support. Why not FDR? (There are splendid documentaries around about FDR. He wears well.)

If you've read so far, you'll realize I have a lot to say to you. I wish you'd send a letter back saying something to me. Sometimes I've wondered about Lily, in Naples, how she is, what happened about Enzo, and her sister. Lovely women.

Have you read anything new that's very good?

Lots of wishes for work and health. (Madame d'Épinay smiles at me as I walk up and down the hall.)

Much love,

Elizabeth

Naples | 20 Sept 92

Dearest Elizabeth –

More, and more intense, mortification than usual for not having responded at once and with gratitude to your so welcome letter of late July. To begin at the end, I shd start by saying that all is more or less alright with us now, and – as you see – we've been able to come to Italy as usual for the autumn. However, just when yr letter arrived in NY, we were peering reluctantly into that abyss described by Homer as 'horrible to mortals and to the immortal gods alike'. Francis had an awful fall, down the escalator at Bloomingdale's one evening. Miraculously, nothing broke, but just about everything else happened; and the following weeks were rough indeed – as well as being crammed with bone scans, CAT scans, X rays, orthopaedist, neurologist, dermatologist, (for awful wounds on legs, cut by emerging risers of escalator)... Now at Naples, we're in more cheerful state, partly because of a course of therapy for muscular weakness, is already producing results – stronger legs, better walking, etc. AND the therapist comes to us here, rather than inflicting a waste of hours and days with arriving at and waiting in offices and hospitals.

[...]

Oh yes, what a 'mischievious' – as that lawyer would say – world. How much time, in our time, has been wasted, how much mindless enmity nurtured, what stupid obsessions – of football or Disneyism – have prevailed at the expense of common sense or tolerance. What trivial (in both the Italian and the English senses) uses have been made of our years of prosperity, and of what folly that prosperity was in large part composed – armaments, speculation, mad consumerism... Not only was there the erosion of the Cold War, there was the tearing apart, the sacrifice, of helpless smaller lands, and the stimulating of useless minor conflicts into huge conflagrations, so that the Big Powers could wreak their will while not going directly at each other's throats and risking annihilation. [...]

Here, it seems incredible that we are, with a little exaggeration, almost within sound of the guns of 'Yugoslavia', and Italy, by and large is still enjoying its beautiful late summer, the bays full of boats going to the islands and to Amalfi, there are fireworks for football, and for the liquefaction of the blood of San Gennaro. There is also the collapsing

Italy, the Italy of self-inflicted wounds that has no reason not to be strong and prospering in this otherwise insecure moment; but seems intent on doing itself in. The Mafia in Sicily (and all over the Earth), the Camorra at Naples, the 'Ndrangheta in Calabria, these are like some force, ferocious yet highly organised and efficient on their own terms, never ceasing to consolidate power. Useless to ask, as outsiders do, why the authorities don't 'act'; in many cases, the 'authorities' are the same people, the mafia, etc. have high positions in the national government (the head of one of the leading Camorra families of Naples, Gava, was until recently minister of the interior in the government of Italy); evidence is destroyed, nothing comes of commissions of inquiry... Now indeed there is movement, and a new generation not raised to accept civility as the only means of a quiet life, and not all that interested in a quiet life either. But the power, the fear, the lack of belief in improvement comes from so far back, and the rapacity too, that it is hard to discuss merely in the context of what is happening today, even if the elements of world-wide drug traffic and arms peddling create a new dimension.

What is said in yr Italian class, that people wd take risks for their own families and own interests, but not for the general good, is alas a wide truth; and as a platitude is often declared by outsiders to be the root of the Italian 'problem'. Like most platitudes, it has some reality. However, Italy is still, to a large extent, many nations, with distinct histories and characteristics; there is still a strong contrast between north and south, between educated and uneducated people, (although the word 'educato' in Italian does not mean 'istruito' as it does with us, having gone to school, having read, thought, etc; it means, a marvellous thing, 'good-mannered', well-bred in the profound and not the social sense. A king could be 'mal educato', and so could a univ. professor; while a poor, retarded young man who carries heavy loads on Capri for a living, was described to me recently as 'sempre molto educato' – always so polite). And the history of the unification of those regions is a stupendous story of idealism, endurance and sacrifice – and terrible martyrdom – for the common good. The country largely did accept, and in some degree worship, Mussolini and the rise of fascism; but the segment that held out against that, not only the socialists and communists (many of whom gave their lives, many more, who went through terrible years in prison) but also 'intellectuals' and those eternal free spirits who cannot be designated, were heroes for the common good. So the truth is, as usual, very complicated and cannot be simplified into cynicism or universal self-seeking. It's true, at Naples there is inextinguishable scepticism about efforts for the common good. Yet even here there are changes – such as our own landlady and her foundation for restoration – there are younger people not tied to the attitudes of the past; and there is some well-founded apprehension about the approaching crisis, illustrated all over Eastern Europe and pointing very much this way.

This seems to suggest that I have some ideas to offer, or think I have. No I don't. One never gives up on individuals, but I do at times give up on the human race. [...] 'The war' – ie, 'our' war – begins to seem historic indeed to me now, and the states of mind of 'our' countries engaged in it sad and touching as far as they represent individuals. People had more sense of absurdity then, and it helped them bear the unbearable. (I remember Sumner describing himself in his awful AIF uniform – diminutive Sumner, carpet-like khaki hanging formlessly on him, and, in the rain, a wet emu feather drooping and dripping over the brim of his digger's hat.)

Since I began this letter, I've had to put it aside not only a thousand times for arrivals, deliveries, phone calls, but also to make my trip overnight to Capri, where the days were, as here, an outpouring of golden splendour, such light... Yesterday evening, F met me at the boat, and we went to dinner at Lily's – I was so pleased to see her. We had dinner on her terrace, Enzo was there, looking much older and being fairly mellow; terrace, where I first dined thirty-six years ago... After so many fine days, it seemed scandalous to find ourselves coming home, by taxi, in a sudden downpour, which today turned into a dramatic storm – much needed rain, and we do expect to revert to warm days for some weeks to come. But, well, well, summer is ending.

[...]

Please forgive delays, and don't forget the love and friendship of your Francis and Shirley.

Dearest Shirley and Francis –

I was so glad to have your letter, and then appalled to hear of the accident. Particularly, I was averse to that rare man to whom I had expressed undying love at the time of our last phone call (about the Abbé Galiani) getting damaged in any way. Francis, when I call you up in my mind, you are always smiling, and make me think of sunshine. [...] In every possible way, it's cheering to think of you concentrating on Proust's letters for the TLS.

Shirley, thank you for the beautiful stamps and for answering my need for a conversation about the state of the world. Had not expected that it would look better from where you are, and of course it doesn't. Everywhere you look there is calamity. Even skimming the paper or inadvertently hearing the 'news', one is assaulted by disasters and, at best, other startling signs of the times like Disneyland in France (!), and the Royal Family in Britain, and the US elections, and so on. [...]

I was extremely interested in everything you had to say about Italy. [...] Clearly, Italy still throws up such people – men and women – in heartening numbers, considering what they have to stand against, deal with. Until recently, Italy seemed to be flourishing remarkably, and managing the huge number of migrants – legal and illegal – with humanity, but even since you wrote there have been those other currency crises, cut-backs, strikes. SBS, the (dreaded word) multicultural television station, has had some very good documentary films about some of these matters, and shows the news in Italian on Sundays. (News-readers speak at the speed of light.) After the chilling, but brilliant, La Piovra, there is a terrible soap-opera which I sometimes watch for the sake of listening to the language, and this week there are two films. The Guardian Weekly is useful and even the SMH carries pieces from the European papers. Seeing Roberto weekly gives a strong feeling of being in touch with the place and the history. [...]

This morning (it's now another day) they were reporting on the third and last debate between the presidential candidates in the US. It will be a relief to so many when this is in the past. All the rhetoric appeals to patriotism while, so to speak, Rome burns.

Adamo came early to fix the overgrown garden, but a peculiar hurricane/ice-age descended with branches flying about dangerously so he had to go home. Pity. He's a gentle man who came from Trieste long ago.

What else? A stroll through the Botanic Gardens while the azaleas were out and the white wisteria, wonderfully glamorous, scented air. Saw the Imperial China exhibition at the Gallery and imagined Ed Capon camping out amongst these treasures while they're around. Bring back Confucius!

Visited Manoly and heard how he rolled, slipped, down the steep garden right to the violet-bed without hurting himself, because he remembered his training with the parachute regiment in the Middle East. He had also been to see, and had loved, <u>Strictly Ballroom</u>, an Australian film which is a tonic sent to the rest of the world.

Dear S and F, may there be great good recoveries, work that satisfies and happy times.

Best love from
Elizabeth

Mosman | 2 October, 1994

Dearest Shirley and Francis –

Where to begin? Because I think of you often I have the impression that I've already told everything that merits telling, and asked all the questions that no-one is answering...

In late May/early June I heard from Sybille Smith that you'd met in the Post Office at Capri, and that you were going back to New York within a few days. Now, in a letter from Jinx that took two weeks to travel from Boston to Sydney, I hear that you've just gone back to Naples. It makes the world seem smaller and friends closer when news flies in from unexpected quarters. Also, most important, it's pleasing to feel that all is well, and that the seasons bring the seasonal changes.

This seems to be the season, too, of news, books, speeches, prizes, reviews, interviews and literary lunches with writers from every country. It's big business and alien – you'd imagine – to many writers, but it's clearly congenial or recognized as a necessity by many others. Sybille edited an English translation of the poems of the Greek Archbishop Stylianos, Primate of the Greek Orthodox Church in Australia. Les Murray gave the launching speech and David Malouf was there. Les had had a piece published a day or so before about the 'multicultural mafia' of the Australia Council, mourning somewhat old Anglo-Celtic Australia, but he paid tribute to the Archbishop's work. The Archbishop, however was doing his own mourning – 'Do I laugh in English? Do I cry in English?' – and said he'd never read anything written by Les. He gave the impression to some that he had no particular interest in ever reading anything in English. The handsome and brilliant young professor of Greek who had translated the poems was enraged (I heard later) by various matters linguistic and multicultural, and all in all it was a vivid occasion. It was good to see David looking relaxed and informal. There are many – no doubt desirable – demands on his life these days.

On Friday, I went with Vivian to my second literary occasion of the year when David gave the speech that launched the Patrick White letters at the Art Gallery. Both Davids – Malouf and Marr – spoke extremely well. For David Marr this is the end of a decade of work on the biography and letters. He was speeding about, punctilious, pale and – he said – hyperventilating with anxiety. Film-makers, politicians, composers, actors, poets, critics, Australia Council people and so on were all there. Manoly carried on with his routine at home, but David Marr asked if he would give an interview on television – his first ever – and he agreed, wanting to help David and the book. The medium has no dangers for someone so dignified, self-possessed, truthful and fair. It was heart-warming to see him.

[...]

Assassinations, unemployment, droughts and bushfires notwithstanding, I've never known a time when so many different people have recognized that we've been living through a period in this country that will be remembered very favourably. Something good under the surface of things has been going on. Nothing lasts forever, but it is interesting to have been here and to have been aware of it. (Olympic hysteria as 2000 draws closer could ruin everything.)

Saw an exhibition of artefacts from Pompeii at the Museum the other day, and enjoyed it so much. There was even a garden, with lemon trees and twittering (invisible) birds. The responsibility of packing and dispatching such fragile objects must age those involved. Yet it's invaluable that galleries and owners round the world take the risk and share the treasures.

Roberto, who teaches Italian, now teaches the opera singers, too. Understandably they have, as he says, special powers and can mimic his words and accent perfectly. They are lucky to have him, and he adores them. We surprised him with champagne and cake at 9.30 on the morning of his 40th birthday.

[...]

I have now told you a thousand things you didn't need to know, twittering on like those invisible birds in the garden in Pompeii, and possibly omitted the one essential point. Please tell me some things I'd like to know – such as how you both are, and what's happening, and what you think of what's happening. Practically anything, I'd like to hear. I'll send clippings with this or separately.

Great good wishes and love,

Elizabeth

Mosman | 15 November, 1994

Dearest Shirley,

It was good to hear your voice and exchange a few words last Thursday night. I had written to Capri but know how long letters take to arrive.

Shock freezes poor human heads and makes it impossible to accomplish much and give an impression of some reassuring kind to everyone around. But it's another world, even to the light in the sky. But what Bill Maxwell said was true – ever-present in the heart.

I think of you going in to the apartment in New York, everything double-edged and unbelievable – Francis's presence and absence. The extreme busyness will be a blessing even if it doesn't seem so. I'm sure friends will be wonderful though nothing anyone says or does is what you want. How can it be?

[...]

The Australian published The Times obituary and Michael Costigan sent it to me. So well-said – true and deeply felt.

Francis's presence will be wherever you are, always.

Loving thoughts,

Elizabeth

New York | 16 January 95

Dearest Elizabeth –

I'm sending these enclosures to you, dismayed at not yet having written a letter. My days are consumed by (apart from the wonderful kindness, and tactfulness, of friends) lawyers, tax people, bank colloquies, insurance re-arrangements, reappraisals of possessions, dentist (broke a front tooth)... and all manner of such time-devouring, nullifying, necessary tasks. I said as much to our lawyer, who told me that 'this is a very simple will'. Also, much paperwork and correspondence. However, in recent days some hours of my own work, real work; which is the thing that helps me.

Otherwise – one gets deeper into loss, incredulously.

Forgive lamentations.

Many pleasant appointments to do beautiful things – dinners, music, paintings. And I've begun again to have guests at home to dinner – which at first I had some trepidation about, that there being no Francis wd be intolerable to me. But no, it is a little as if he is present because of the continuity – i.e., that all who come loved him and think of him. What lovely friends we have, extraordinary. Lucky. It's also been spring weather, in the 60s, for some days, no one knows why. This in its way is lucky too. Hard, though, to believe in 1995. I note that young-ish (or formerly young people) have stopped saying 'I'm a child of the 20th century'. Soon, in fact, that won't do them any good at all. What a century – well, we know that successive centurions have always said that. But ours really did throw it away.

I'm reading wonderful books. That, and my own pages, are the episodes that do their best for me. All the familiarity of 'home' is both a comfort and a wound. And I long to be free of the 'tasks' – which will soon slacken off, I trust. Thank you for messages, thoughts, words, teleces, clippings, news. All precious to me. I had such a kind letter from Margaret, and shall write as soon as I can. I love to answer these letters, it's only the other papers – the paper impediments – that weigh on me. (But I am falling again into complaint – we'll talk soon...)

Be well, be cool – with love – Shirley

Mosman | 20 August, 1995

Dearest Shirley,

I often wonder how you are, and where you are, and wish that I would hear. I haven't needed anniversaries either, like Francis's birthday, to think about you both. Far from it. Things read, things seen and thought. If we were nearby it would be such a pleasure and a consolation to talk sometimes.

At the beginning of May I had a horrible accident, my own fault. The courtyard was like a giant banana-skin with algae and moss. I went down like a bullet, shattered knee, called for help and was rescued by three neighbours – one a surgeon. Shock, ambulance, operation, Royal North Shore Hospital for ten days, leg in brace for six weeks and then physiotherapy three times a week to bend knee again. Eighty minutes of knee exercises daily. Three and a half months later, I'm still incarcerated at home. Not such a hardship. Friends have been heroic, bringing food, shopping, flowers, books, driving me to physiotherapy, providing company. Hills and steps have still to be conquered – soonish, I do hope. Shock has its own laws, I learned, and takes its own time.

[...]

Manoly rings fairly regularly in the evening. He talks of Cairo and Alexandria as they were in his youth, of Islam and the Turks and Bosnia. Younger friends who live nearby see him quite often, and his little dog, Millie, is very dear and important to him. I look forward to seeing him again.

Margaret is all right except that her eyesight has deteriorated so that she must read with the help of strong magnifying glasses. For someone to whom reading has always been of primary importance, this is a blow, though she says nothing by way of complaint and continues with Italian conversation classes. It still cheers the young ones that she can untangle grammatical puzzles better than any of them. Speaking and quickly understanding are more difficult for her.

[...]

The last of the ceremonies commemorating the end of the Second World War happened just a few days ago. So many across the globe looking back to that particular time, so many tears... The news of current wars leaves everyone speechless.

I hope you will send a postcard at least. I would really like to know how you are and not be so out of touch.

Best love,

Elizabeth

New York | 6 Sept 95

Dearest Elizabeth –

What a forbearing friend. I was so pleased to see your 'typewriting', and need not say that I've been sending teleces for months. But – overwhelmed. Now I learn, so long after the event, that you had that brutal accident. How mindless such things appear, one keeps re-running them through one's mind, to do them differently in retrospect. One careless moment, and then months of hellish inconvenience. Almost the worst thing, beyond the accident itself, seems to me the eighty mins of knee exercises. The boredom of exercises. And then, Mosman is peculiarly unfair to those who have difficulty with slopes and steps and stairs. I well remember trailing home from Queenwood, when we lived in Stanton Road, in the fearful heat. The walk uphill ended in what seemed like a million steps. Capri is also fiendish to people with leg or foot trouble, especially our part of it where there are (mercifully, however) no cars. Nowadays, little electric carts take the heavy merchandise, and the infirm or injured. I remember when everything was by manual labour and physical struggle. Glad to think that something mechanical, at least one thing, has been useful. [...] I'm so extremely sorry not to have been in touch and not to have known, not to have sent solidarity.

[...]

I am about to leave for Italy, on the 10th. [...] Hard thing will be to close, forever, our little Capri place. [...] We lived in such close quarters there, and for so many years, that every little thing I look at has been charged with its memories and associations. Sometimes it seems that the whole world is like that, for me. Soon it will be a year since Francis died. It has gone by in a kind of delirium, so that I hardly know whether it has been slow or swift. In such circumstances people say – I used to say it myself to the bereaved – something about time, that it helps, or heals or will pass, etc. Not knowing what else to say – since what else is there? But when it happens one realises that all that is meaningless. One does not want to be 'healed' –

by which is meant, that closeness will diminish, memory become somewhat dimmed, a measure of forgetfulness set in. Francis is still more real to me than any living person, and I don't see why that should alter. He <u>has</u> been more to me than any living person. Well – enough of this, it's self evident...

[...] With love – with apologies – with dismay for accident – with gratitude for forbearance – Shirley.

Mosman | 4 October, 1995

Dearest Shirley,

I was so pleased to find that large packet in the letterbox, with your writing on it. Sadness that we were so out of touch had been creeping up on me, and I had determined to set up a clamour if I didn't hear soon. I did and do understand that it's not only having time, it's feeling able at so many levels to assemble thoughts for letters, but I was concerned, and very much wanted to know how you were, what you were doing. So thank you indeed for the so-welcome letter, the wonderful photographs of and words about dear Francis. I settled down in my semi-incarceration with everything you'd sent, very much comforted with so much to absorb and appreciate.

You won't believe this. Your package arrived 18 September, Monday. On Saturday 16, Margaret was coming over by bus for her weekly visit. It was raining and I wondered if it was a good idea for her to trail over. Half an hour after she was due to arrive, I had a call from Sydney Hospital: M had been admitted by ambulance, having had an accident at Wynyard Bus Station where roadworks were going on. They kept her there for a week, in a good deal of pain, with three broken ribs and danger of pneumonia and concussion. Ferdi brought her here at the end of the week, and that was almost two weeks ago. M said it was ludicrous that she should fall after my spectacular and long-lasting effort, and Eleanor said it was 'unseemly competition'. She has just been sitting in the front room, reading, doing Herald crosswords, recovering well. I've just cooked a little more. She's anxious to get back to her little flat.

[...]

Not long ago I saw a documentary series about the life of F.D.R, and I remembered Francis talking about those times and wished I could tell him what I'd seen and ask questions. Earlier this year there was a French film that I liked so much, and I wondered what he'd have thought – Colonel Chabert. I encouraged Margaret when her eyes became worrying by telling her that Francis had had trouble with eyes, but hadn't allowed it to deter him. Recently, across a room, I heard his name when a retired biologist acquaintance was telling someone else about Cocteau, what a great biographer Francis was. He's often in my thoughts. I appreciated the obituaries and photographs so much.

[...]

You wondered what I'd been reading, or if I'd been working. For the first long time I felt mute, unable to take in or give out, amiably passive – stunned, I suppose. People came with shopping and stayed for tea, coffee, conversation. It was all a dream. Tomorrow must learn to catch a bus again with walking-stick.

Before interruptions interrupt, I'll say goodbye for the moment, dear Shirley. I'd missed you. It's so good to have heard, and had a conversation. Take care of yourself.

Best love,
Elizabeth

Mosman | 9 October, 1996

Dearest Shirley,

I imagine you are in Capri and perhaps established in your new apartment. I wonder where it is and what you see from the windows or balcony. Nowhere is very far from anywhere else on that magical island. I hope it feels good to be settled there, with no feeling of its being provisional, dependent on your landlady's family's needs, and with books and familiar possessions round about. Do you see the sea? Did I dream it, or did you tell me that there are songs about that so-beautiful merging of fishing-boat lights and stars?

[...]

From being an exceptionally surprising and enjoyable country to live in for thirteen years, Australia has now turned into something quite other following the March election. All the tattered Thatcher ideas, all the worst of the American religious right, have taken over. It was such a defeat for Labor. There were so many good people on the front bench, and so many lost in the 'massacre', as the journalists said. No-one could really account for the size of the defeat. The journalists, viewing everything with terminal cynicism, were tired of writing about the same people year after year, and did their best to pull the government down. Young people hadn't been here long enough to know what beneficial changes had been brought about in so many areas. Now, with the Liberals in power and the Olympic Games on the way, it's hard not to see this as a very Dark Age that's fallen upon us. It crosses my mind to flee to the north of Scotland, a not entirely rational thought.

[...]

Martin Amis's <u>The Information</u> has many dire things to say about writing and novelists, as well as some very funny and true things as when an interviewer asks: 'What's your novel trying to say?' 'It's not trying to say anything. It's saying it.' 'But <u>what</u> is it saying?' 'It's saying itself. For a hundred and fifty thousand words. I couldn't put it any other way.' 'Richard Tull? Thank you very much.'

[...]

Andrew retires on 2 January next year and can't wait, though he will be only 53/54. Margaret is pretty well, enjoys the lovely spring weather, enjoys reading, Italian grammar, crosswords, and Manoly is fine, too, though both are frail. Ferdi is still a great friend to me.

[...]

These 'telegrams' seem like the wrapping of a package that contains the message, and I suppose the message is simply that I wonder how you are, think about you both and send love.

Elizabeth

Mosman | 20 June, 1997

Dearest Shirley,

You'll be coming to a very grumbly, discontented place in August – mean-spirited, grey. It has so changed since the arrival of the Liberals. Before that no-one wanted to be anywhere else, and now it's exactly the opposite. (Of course, I don't know any Liberals, but can't imagine that even they think all this is an improvement.)

Meantime, fortunately there is another world.

I had meant to say would you like a breakfast, brunch, lunch, dinner or gathering here when you're in Sydney? A smallish party/gathering? You will be swamped with invitations, I know, and I certainly don't want to add to inundations, but if you would like anything of this kind – something totally quiet and different, walks along the esplanade and whatever, please say.

[...]

Let me know if there's anything I can do.

With love,

Elizabeth

Mosman | 16 July, 1997

Dearest Shirley,

I thought of you and Francis on his birthday – like many other friends, I'm sure.

Thank you so much for your letter – and beautiful butterfly stamps. I begin to believe you're really coming over and that's lovely. I smiled at the news that you'd been dreaming of Superba Parade and Mandalong Road! In those eight or nine London years I used to have real nightmares where I found myself back in Australia. I'd wonder desperately how this terrible thing had come about. Such a relief to wake up. I hope the Balmoral streets weren't quite as horrific as the thought of Sydney was to me.

[...]

Yes, I'd so much like to be at the dinner to hear your talk. Thank you so much for including me... As you'll know, the Institute has a tiny staff and organizes many events during the year, but the Larry Adler dinner is the highlight unquestionably, and possibly attracts what Labor Prime Ministers call 'the big end of town' – corporate people, lawyers, bankers, economists, money-market people, senior people from the press, radio and television. The other night when Gough Whitlam gave a talk for them at the Wentworth about his new book <u>Abiding Interests</u>, three-quarters of the audience were young men in suits. (Gough was eighty-one last Friday, 11th, and has never stopped travelling, working, speaking.)

[...]

You'll notice we suffer from an excess of 'icons' in Sydney; there are also too many people 'living life to the fullest' and walking out of somewhere or other 'with my head held high'. There's 'culture' on every street corner. And the Olympics, and fireworks, and festivals. Some of it well-meant.

On a better note, saw the dress-rehearsal of a beautiful production of Madame Butterfly at the Opera House, and the Morandi exhibition at the Gallery, and read Tabucchi: Declares Pereira and so on...

With love – we'll talk soon

Elizabeth

Mosman | 17 September, 1997

Dearest Shirley,

With so many here in a frail state I'm not surprised that you wondered if something had happened when I rang. No, I was sad to see you go and had wanted to write before you left NY, but 'details, details', as you said in your last letter, got in the way. Constantly, friends go away for four or eight weeks, but then they return. Everyone is irreplaceable. Some more than others, of course.

Your visit was lovely, and Sydney shone. Thank you for all the so enjoyable involvement, but especially some chances to talk together. I have promised many, many copies of the unedited version of your speech when the Sydney Papers publish it towards the end of the year. I'll have photocopies made.

[...]

Margaret is reading Zélide, as she read your introduction, with real appreciation. A feat to describe someone's life and character, disposition, so persuasively, in a style not mannered at all, but full of air, light and magnanimity. This is how Francis writes about his people, don't you think? They remain so vividly in the mind.

[...]

What of the amazing, sad phenomenon of Princess Diana's death? Archaic ritual, alarming future.

It's so good to have seen you, dearest S. Wishes for work, health and happy times.

With love,

Elizabeth

Balmoral | 2 November, 1997

Dearest Shirley,

[...]

Was Italy lovely? Fewer details to distract you and more time to think, work, be with friends, I trust. It's been beautiful here, too – sunrises, more birdsong than ever, white wisteria, ideal breezes. Love this time of year.

[...]

Visited Manoly one day, feeling that I should have gone sooner, and for the first time it was something of an effort. The dear man has deteriorated and actually fell over in front of me. Luckily, Alida, the housekeeper, sorted out this fallen body as though it were a problem in geometry. He was all right, but I was unnerved.

[...]

Did you know Nugget Coombs, Dr H.C. Coombs? He died last week and has received great tributes from all sides. Born in 1906. Many regarded him as the most outstanding Australian of the century. It's sad when people disappear. He used to come and see me, and take me to lunch down at Balmoral.

The young Greek heroes who risked so much to take down the swastikas from the Parthenon while the Germans were in Athens, were Manolis Glezos and Lakis Santos. They were wonderful. I'm sure you don't need to know this but such bravery has to be remembered.

Ferdi is coming over soon and we're going to see a film, have a Thai dinner and a glass of wine. That will be nice.

I'll hope for a postcard. Be well. You must be receiving good thoughts from around the globe.

Love and wishes, Elizabeth

Mosman | 5 July, 1998

Dearest Shirley,

I think you might be back in New York... The clippings sent recently will be already out of date. Caught up in the turmoil of the region and the global economic revolution, the country is like an upturned beehive. There's confusion and anger everywhere, and in addition, at a different level, every street and building in the city is being dug up or pulled down to make way for the dreaded Olympics. Not a happy country. And perhaps for the first time for many decades the general feeling is of deep insecurity. Every country would have something to say on this front.

[...]

Two or three months ago we drove to Canberra for a day or two to see the landscapes exhibition at the National Gallery, and there was the Paul Mellon exhibition from the US in the Gallery here. So little and impermanent, but better than nothing. Friends visiting the US for the first time marvel at the museums of NY, Washington, Chicago, all the great cities – and at the Getty. The isolation of this continent seems more apparent than ever, with the collapse of the A$ not helping. It's like a very sick patient.

I wonder what you're reading. I wonder what you think about the way things are going in Italy. What you're thinking... Send postcard at least, closely written!

[...]

I'm being collected soon to walk down at Balmoral. Keep well. Be in touch.

Much love,

Elizabeth

New York | 10 Sept 98

Dearest Elizabeth – forgive, please, a piece of typing paper, which seems to be the only sheet that ever comes to my hand these days. Forgive such silence. And thank you so much for your forgiving letter, and for the clippings that preceded and accompanied. Thank you most of all for remembering Francis' birthday, and keeping the memory of how he was. It is terrible without him always.

I have virtually finished my GG memoir, and I gave 90% of it to my agent last Monday (she likes it). Never turned in a book incomplete before, but I am going to Italy tomorrow, and could not surrender the last pages without working them over. Although I couldn't work on my novel in these recent weeks while I was preparing the ms. for the last time, I have done quite a bit more of it during the year; and shall hope to finish that, too, in 1999. This millennium; it always seemed far off, and now its head and shoulders are discernible in the fog. You will have seen the melancholy news here – I could murder Clinton for being hopelessly irresponsible, with so many of us depending on him. He walked into this mess, with his terrible taste in girls and his compulsion to sleaze. On the other hand, the hypocrisy of his accusers is unspeakable; and when he had to go on the telly and 'apologise' and 'confess', I felt as if he were being gleefully put in the stocks by persons with faces out of Hieronymus Bosch. All this while the world swirls around in a morass of incoherence. I haven't been taking a newspaper while I was trying to finish my GG book, which spares me a good bit, but it's impossible, I find, not to be aware of the squalor, it has a quality of seepage. [...]

I wonder how Manoly is going on. I think of him quite often, and Patrick, and their house, their dogs, garden, books... (re-reading those words, I see I've made it seem like a kindly, roses-round-the-door household...). I'm glad that Andrew's only 55, that seems a pleasant age, and how right that he retired, or semi-retired, and can work as he pleases and not tax his heart. Please give them great greetings from me, if I may send them. I'm staggered to think that I had all those lovely days at Sydney a year ago. I might have come back last week, it is all fresh and insufficiently absorbed.

[...]

I'm reading lots of things – although I could scarcely manage to read while finishing GG (did I say that the book is called GREENE ON CAPRI?). And just finishing Murray Bail's Eucalyptus book, which I'm liking very much. It will be published here in November, I think?

All this about me – I'm sorry. I was glad to have the news of Margaret, whose Scots resistance evidently keeps her on track. But, oh, what a disaster when one's eyes begin to give out – yet she seems to be bearing even that and persisting. Please, always, my love to her. I'll try to be a better correspondent, I'm so bedevilled by papers I don't want to see, and to which I have to respond (or the skies will fall, apparently), that it uses up precious time for writing to precious friends.

With love, as ever – Shirley.
On 20 October – the day I return here from Rome – it will be four years since Francis died.

Mosman | 3 November, 1998

Dearest Shirley,

I was <u>so</u> pleased to have your letter. It made the day happy for me. Thank you for writing in the midst of everything, and for your good call from NY recently.

This is the most tedious day in Australia – Melbourne Cup Day – with deserted streets and the occasional sight of overdressed women rushing to lunch. In America it is the moment for important elections, I think. On the Jim Lehrer News Hour I have seen numerous candidates and supporters telling their stories. They show the Republican advertisements stressing Bill Clinton's well-known failings. These must have been nightmare months for all his supporters and friends – not to mention, as you said, his wife and daughter. With the world burning around us, I often wondered, as I watched Kenneth Starr's dimples and smiles, what someone from Mars or Outer Space generally would think of this concentration on happenings in a broom-closet at the White House. The hypocrisy of the accusers, as you say, has been quite mind-turning. The mind reels again, of course, at the thought of his recklessness and irresponsibility in view of what he knows about his own capacity to do some good and useful things. Lewis Lapham wrote about meeting him at some White House gathering earlier this year and was amusing about the degree to which he was charmed; but in the most recent issue of Harper's he's been very severe and unforgiving. But let us hope the Republicans don't sweep away all reform and commonsense.

Yes, we did have our election here on 3 October, more or less. There was no likelihood that Labor could win after the huge defeat and loss of seats last time. Even so, because of the projected GST (Goods and Services Tax) and its unpopularity, Labor did actually win more 'raw' votes, across the country, but lost in marginal seats. So we have three years of Liberals smiling smugly, hectoring and lying. Labor has many faults, but the good hearts and best minds are on that side.

[...]

You mentioned The Reader, and Murray's novel, and I'll watch out for both of them. I've read Ian McEwan's <u>Enduring Love</u>, Camus <u>The First Man</u>, Javier Marias <u>A Heart So White</u>, Jay McInerney <u>The Last of the</u>

<u>Savages</u>, Tabucchi <u>Piazza D'Italia</u> over a period. That's what I can remember. The Guardian Weekly is always full of reviews of books I'd like to read – as well as enlightening/depressing news about the state of the world.

[...]

How can it be more than a year since your visit? Mysterious. Have happy times in Italy, and keep well. I think of you and Francis often.

With love, as ever,

Elizabeth

Mosman | 25 April, 1999

Dearest Shirley,

I was so pleased to have your letter and news and clippings. Thank you for all of them. Yes, Don's death. There were documentaries about his life and works from the seventies. Everyone looked so young, with hair, with deeds ahead of them. I remember going to a concert at the Town Hall with Patrick. At the very last moment Don [Dunstan] and entourage swept in, noticed by all, white suits, coats flapping. He did a great deal to improve the lives of so many people. Was clearly loved.

[...]

Like you I've been struggling with boxes of books, in my case because I've sold the house. This is my news. It happened very quickly, but not agreeably, since it involved real estate agents. [...] I'm glad to go, although I haven't found anywhere to live yet, but it's been wonderful to see so many sunrises, moonrises, rainbows, cloudscapes, birds. Because I must start somewhere, I started with books, though this was a bit half-hearted, not to say dusty.

[...]

In Mosman fairly rickety red-brick flats cost about half of the house price. If I wanted to live in Melbourne, Adelaide or Hobart (heaven forbid!) I could buy a tiny stone mansion. However, I have no such ambition and will probably settle for something at the top of the hill (important), with enough space to have friends to dinner. Probably something like the Hunter's Hill flat of long ago. There are hordes of young people looking for 'investment flats' every week-end, and most are auctioned, which is a bit unnerving. The whole city is being 'developed' in an uncontrolled manner at a phenomenal rate. In addition to the development, the poor city was hit by a phenomenal hail storm about ten days ago. Authorities were slow to recognize the scale of the disaster. After the Darwin cyclone and Newcastle earthquake it was the worst natural disaster to hit the country. Now they've called in the army to help. Even here it seemed that bricks were being thrown on the roof and at the windows, a bit like the end of the world, but mild compared with events in the southern and eastern suburbs.

[...]

Many major distractions of a tediously practical nature, but at night I'll read poetry, some Italian, and some ancient history to calm down and restore balance.

Keep well, work well and enjoy time with friends. I think of you and Francis often, with love

Elizabeth

21/26 Cranbrook Avenue, Cremorne, NSW 2090 | 12 December, 1999

Dearest Shirley,

Thank you for marvellous letters. I loved hearing all this, a tonic.

This year has been torrid – not so much because of selling, searching, buying, auctioning furniture and odds and ends, giving away, hunting for quite ordinary things, receiving oceans of help and advice from friends, but health has loomed. Margaret was in hospital four times, twice for extensive tests, then an operation. Her tiny flat chose this moment to collapse – well, the bathroom ceiling, more or less literally. I saw numerous doctors on my own account, having inherited faulty wiring here and there. There is no-one else to manage things for Margaret – no relatives, and contemporaries frail or departed. It was all too much.

Improvement all round. I've never regretted moving, and like the flat. The red-brick building has eight storeys, was built in about 1970, and is geographically wonderfully convenient – to the city, transport, friends, cafes and so on. I'm on the fifth floor, two balconies (small) and a view. Camphor laurels grow up to eye level so I can see the birds nearby. (One of the bedrooms has desk, books and filing-cabinets – so it isn't a bedroom.) The pictures aren't on the walls yet, and there's no coffee-table or dining-table and chairs, but it will happen when handymen and supplies can be assembled.

[...]

Take care of yourself. Have happy times with friends, and send a message when you can. Much love,

Elizabeth

New York | 29 March 2000

Dearest Elizabeth –

[...]

I have the feeling that your health has been erratic? Could you tell me how you feel? Also, I think of Margaret in her ordeal. Always, to her, my love and remembrance. Are you well settled into your new place? My region here, of 10021, is a forest of skyscrapers these days, new ones being added continually in what seemed to be minimal spaces – not quite like the Lord's Prayer on the head of a pin. The terrific granite base of Manhattan so far sustains it all. My rent will go into the same stratosphere 18 months from now, when I pass over some regulatory threshold. At present, the garden of this building – garden where I just now have no time to sit – is wonderfully coming into bloom: flowering trees, and pansies, narcissus, crocus etc. How we treasure these little signals in our private park, where the surroundings are now extensively denuded of nature – except for a wonderful variety of white flowering pear tree that lines the streets, a discovery by the Parks Commission as they are resistant to bugs, pollution etc.

I've been to Washington, to Princeton, and, a few days ago to the (magnif.) art gallery at Philadelphia, to an enormous and beautiful exhibition on eighteenth century Rome... This morning I read of Anthony Powell's death – writer whom one followed closely, admired, respected, and, in a long way, enjoyed. Sometimes, in a short way, greatly relished – an occasional offhand brilliance one could not have elsewhere. He – with private cause – intensely disliked GG (they knew each other from Oxford days), and wrote scathingly about the Greene oeuvre. Powell was 94, one of the last of that wave of masters of our language: no tricks needed, they brought singularity, quality, their respective gleams of genius.

With loving thanks, with love – Shirley

Cremorne | 23 July, 2000

Dearest Shirley,

[...]

The Olympic Games will open here in seven or eight weeks. The citizens have been advised by some authorities to stay home, stay away from public transport, streets, their cars, taxis, footpaths; others have said we must all go into the streets and smile at the strangers in our midst and give advice when it's needed. Many friends are flying out, others are holing up, and others will venture out of mouseholes to see what the fuss is about. There are exhibitions – Dead Sea Scrolls, Greek marbles – and many good things happening, great concerts... Many people have slaved, I'm sure, to bring fine things to the city, to produce something more than the vast athletic event. Sydney is being pored over as never before. Robert Hughes has produced or presents a six-part programme called <u>Beyond the Fatal Shore</u>.

[...]

I'm enclosing one or two things though I'm sure that, like me, you dread the arrival of more papers to look at and dispose of. (That's not true for all items, of course.) Anyway, a photograph of the view from my place. In the distance the Opera House looking tiny, and close-up a tennis court...

[...]

With love and wishes,
Elizabeth

New York | 6 September 2000

Dearest Elizabeth –

Receiving your lovely letter, a month ago, and the note with thoughtful clipping about the death of William Maxwell, I stood in the kitchen – where all too much of my life seems concentrated in NYC – and sent mental faxes and reverberations, and thought I'd go at once and answer it.

[...]

Thank you too, for the photographs. Now I can picture you in context. The light was a Mosman light. The tennis court and some houses and gardens were familiar Mosman-Neutral Bay-Cremorne.

New 'developments' fell into place in my mind along with the truncated
Harbour Bridge – so few moments, now, to approach and cross it – and the
telescoping of distance between Balmoral and the ferry... What used to be
an expedition.

Now, 10 Sept

Various Australians have been to see me in these weeks, including an
'oral history' interviewer from the National Library: a very refined and
quiet spirit, a musician and musicologist called James Murdoch, about
seventy yrs old, who lives in Bali. I too have an island, where I'll be a few
days from now, leaving for Rome tomorrow. On the 29th Sept I am getting
the honorary citizenship of Capri – a fun thing, touching. Italian friends
initiated this without telling me, and to my astonishment the thing went
through. There will be a ceremony, the mayor speaks, I give a brief speech,
etc. I'll report.

[...]

As to hubbub, the world is increasingly a place that needs, wants, and
creates hubbub. You'll be in gridlock Olympics. Here for a week we've just
had the UN 'summit' of world leaders, the centre of the city paralysed, the
airports under siege. [...] In Rome, meanwhile, 'youth rallies' with a million
present. A few of us still want some measure of solitude, silence, reflection,
and what Samuel Beckett called 'staring into my old friend, empty space';
but these are elements that most people now fear, and young people in
cities have been conditioned to continual noise, interruption, telephone,
telly, films exploding with bullets. I try not to be a curmudgeon out loud,
but inwardly often feel like one. This city has given me much, and I cannot
imagine having my headquarters anywhere else: also, my friends are, with
infinite variety, people with affinities, talents, tender manners, liveliness.
We are all struck by the acceleration of city life, however, which happens as
soon as I set foot in NY on return from Italy. This winter, I must somehow
have many more days entirely to myself, going out only at evening into
company. Mornings without phone calls (and the era of the three-minute
phone call, so that my poor word-box doesn't diminish). Reading when I
choose, rather than late at night when I find myself still awake at 2:00 a.m.
with book... Have you read a wonderfully (I think)-written novel by an
Irish writer, John Banville? – 'The Untouchable'. A treatment of the
Anth. Blunt case, Blunt is the narrator. What matters is the extraordinary

intelligence and beauty of the writing, the level of thought, penetration of character.

[...]

Now I go to pack, to deal with an acre of papers. We'll be in touch. Be well, be joyful. We have to have good times on behalf, too, of our friends who aren't here to enjoy them? Please remember me always to Margaret, whose ordeal and whose courage – and whose spirit – I think of so often. I wish I could think that I might do as well. Could you some time give me a list of all Margaret's fiction, if that's not an imposition? With year of publication and publisher if possible.

With love – Shirley

Cremorne | 31 October, 2000

Dearest Shirley,

Thank you for the lovely September letter, for the clippings, the conversation. Immediately I sent so many thoughts in response by mental fax and e-mail – that I now feel you must know everything I'm about to write. But perhaps not.

You told me about The Untouchable, so I bought two copies for birthdays and subsequently read a marvellous reference to it in a review of John Banville's next book (Guardian). Then another friend, at lunch, asked out of the blue if I'd read it and said how much she was enjoying it. Now I look forward to it myself, drawn magnetically by your singling out 'penetration of character'... That was precisely what made your GG book so marvellous. [...]

The very last of all the Olympic events happened yesterday. It was a parade for the athletes in the Paralympics. I don't want to hear 'fantastic' or 'awesome' again ever. On the other hand, for years, months and weeks we were bored and intimidated by the gloom and cynicism of all radio, television and newspaper reports of what would happen when it all started. These were often the same people who jumped for joy when the city 'won' the games. Many friends flew off to America, Japan, Canada, France. Those of us who were left in the about-to-be-destroyed city said that we'd just buy enough food to survive the siege and stay in. Sydney was unveiled, looking wonderful. Overnight a sort of celestial radiance descended on the mood, organization, public transport, population and weather of the whole city. We were all, mysteriously, like people who drank champagne night and day with no ill-effects and all the joy. Something happened to us. If it sounds difficult to believe I can only say that most of the friends left in the city, like me, know nothing about sport and care less, so it had nothing to do with sport. They're all people who live at the Opera House, to whom all the arts are their reason for living. Nevertheless, this happiness happened. Crime disappeared. People were wonderfully friendly, kind and helpful to each other. It was a huge organizational task, so many aspects to be thought of, and there were geniuses at work who had thought of everything. Those who escaped have now come back to the realization that they missed something rare.

Outside my window there is a huge camphor laurel tree. Currawongs have built a nest, sat on the eggs patiently in all weather, and now have – as far as I can see – two eternally demanding young ones waiting for food. They're so close to me, swaying about in the wind, so high up. Every time I go to the kitchen sink I look to see what they're doing. And visitors follow, equally charmed by this domestic scene.

[...]

You say you try not to be a curmudgeon out loud, but inwardly often feel like one. That is a familiar feeling. I often have to reason with myself about human imperfections, and try to remember that standards have been falling since the beginnings of recorded history. But still, it's impossible to avoid deep thoughts about the springs of behaviour.

[...]

I'm being urged to go away somewhere, and might yet fly off if they bring the rest of the world a bit closer. Today I don't think I have the energy, but maybe tomorrow. Meantime Andrew and Clem come over on Sunday with some congenial others. To this point I haven't tried to fit too many people in at one time, since crowd scenes are – too crowded. Be well, dear S, and have happy times. Good working days.

With love
Elizabeth

Naples | 8 May 2001

Dearest Elizabeth – I moaned when I read your letter, received here just now. What life de-railing, mindless things are these accidents: one wants to run the whole scene through the camera again and not allow 'them' to throw their spanners in the works (Mixed metaphors, but much felt). By now, I trust, you are regaining your rightful dexterity every day – la mano lesta, la mano prensile. The necessary therapy – but what a pest exercises are, so boring and repetitive. Thank you very much for writing, especially when writing must be a burden. Yes, I did call you. I was in rather a grim patch of lung trouble – how unfair, like your accident, my lung trouble, when I've never smoked. [...] Not grave, but a month of low strength and low spirits this past winter, when I need high energy to get my book done. Winter, long and dark grey. Well, now I'm here in the beautiful spring; and fresh air is helping lungs. [...] Here in Italy, elections are giving us all the creeps – next weekend, 13th, Berlusconi may get elected, a really frightening possibility, the more so because it will be a present to him from the Left, whose diverse factions are mired in petty differences and, having had a mandate for several years, could not get into action on the simplest possibilities...

Arriving here at Naples, again immediate visitors, all nice but I need a duplicate day, another 24 hours, to have inner life, working hours, no doorbells or telephone calls. [...] Among other nice things in these crowded days, I was asked to a performance of Don Carlo at the San Carlo, it was wonderful. I don't think Verdi ever was in Spain, although he travelled much and went to Russia; but that long and deep opera is suffused with sombre Spanish character at every level. Otherwise, much reading of engrossing novels. I remember you once said, What would we do without novels? The thought is in itself terrifying. I re-read a lot, especially when I had my debilitating lung trouble I clung to novels I knew would be guaranteed bliss, laughing and crying over Dickens as if I'd never heard of Mr. Dick or Steerforth in my life before...

Something unnerving is change of established things in one's life: friends give up houses one has loved for thirty years, that enshrined one's own memories let alone theirs; couples whose stability one has relied on get divorced after twenty-year marriages; most inconsiderate of all, great friends die. Don't you find this disappearance of beauty and affinity intolerable? – yet nothing to do but tolerate it. [...]

I wonder how you like your new surroundings? – rooms, streets, neighbours? How Margaret goes along, how Andrew is. How, as wrist returns to normal, you spend your days. Whether Sydney is still recognisable; and whether I'll see it again. Here, a sunny spring afternoon, the sea moving against the embankment of the house, SH preparing for departure in an hour for Capri, for a week. With love, dear Elizabeth – Shirley

Cremorne | 14 June, 2001

Dearest Shirley,

I posted a letter to Capri and came home to find yours in the letter-box. Beautiful stamps, words of sympathy for the wretched wrist, all appreciated. [...]

The wrist and physiotherapy have dominated my life since 27 February, because it didn't set well. [...] Apart from that, lots of outings with friends. [...]

I understand very well what you mean about the unnerving nature of change in the established things in one's life. Nothing to do but tolerate it and be aware that this is the new pattern... Not easy. The great friends with love and understanding, shared intuitions, flowing to and fro... Everyone is irreplaceable.

You wonder if you will see Sydney again. I wonder if I'll collect myself together enough to fly (so far) to far-flung places.

Meantime, Max and I have copies of the Inferno – Italian/English and seventeen cassettes in which a scholar reads in both languages then analyses not quite line by line. It must have been a labour of love.

I so much hope that sunshine, some time to work and be alone when you choose, friends, too, have helped to restore physical health, energy, spirits. Be in touch when you feel like it. A card.

With my love, dear Shirley
Elizabeth

New York | 26 October 2001

Dearest Elizabeth –

An early return to NYC, precipitated (literally) by a stupid fall on my Naples tiles (my foot had gone to sleep, I got up and tried to walk on it, and broke 'the fifth metatarsal'); final result, after seven weeks in plaster nearly to the knee, I'll be liberated on 12 Nov... You know what a pest such an incautious two seconds can inflict. Was treated in exemplary fashion at Francis' old hospital, Loreto Mare at Naples – free hospital in the dock area, excellent and lively. Came back at insistence of an orthopaedist friend here, but so far only needed to change the plaster (fibreglass) cast and wait and wait. Everyone marvellously kind, including all the help I had for the flight back from Rome. (Flying over was a great relief, <u>on 15 Sept</u> by the Alitalia Rome flight on the first day that the airports here reopened.) I was 'glad' to have been here for the appalling event; but Italy was a reprieve. One has long felt that reprieve is all that one can expect, at best, from this world. Of course, the city, (NYC) remains obsessed, and that state of emergency is kept boiling, unpardonably, by 'the media'.

[...]

In Italy and here I've seen such good friends, done beautiful things – even when all involved hobbling on F's stick. Now I can walk about the neighbourhood, in slow motion, and get small things done. Today I get back to my own work, interrupted by this homing journey. I was able to get on with my ms. quite a bit in Naples. Could not go to Capri after my fall. Felt like flying back right now to 'complete' my Italian autumn. Fair, fair, Là bas. Weather ripe, clear, warm, splendid, there and here. Last Saturday, 20 October, was the seventh anniversary of Francis' death.

[...]

Everett will 'take' me through two magnificent small exhibitions at the Metro Museum next week – one of them drawn in part from F's 'Flaubert in Egypt'.

All through the city, trees are as on this card – with love – Shirley.

Cremorne | 9 December, 2001

Dearest Shirley,

Thanks so much for your card from NY, now quite some weeks ago.

[...]

Here, it's been an extraordinary and almost too-great effort to organize Margaret's move to the James Milson Retirement Village. Because she is so frail physically and almost blind she could only do so much for herself. The little flat had deteriorated and tiny things had collected over the years. The home help didn't clean very well. [...] The good thing is that she is very glad to be there, relieved [...].

What is the world doing with itself? While acknowledging the wonders of humans at their best and over the ages, you feel, on bad-news days, that something is peculiarly wrong at the moment. The birds in my camphor laurel continued their nest-building, and went through the whole cycle till the young ones had learned to fly off. Right outside the kitchen window it was a deeply reassuring and pleasing sight.

The elections. Everyone was wondering where to go, what country. Meantime, of course, we all fitted in some beautiful things, true small things that really matter.

With love,

Elizabeth

PS. I remembered the anniversary of Francis's death. I often think of him.

Cremorne | 23 June, 2003

Dearest Shirley,

I've thought of you often, wondering if you're still in New York, wondering about the progress of the book through the publishing events – like proof-reading, wondering how you are in general.

Here, it seems to me, the best hearts are depressed. [...] Locally, the populace supports wars, cheers troops, is easily frightened by the PM's tales of bogey men, foreigners. They've learned the lessons of propaganda very well, and they still work. The cartoonists battle on quite brilliantly, but most journalists are comfortable, don't stir themselves. Once upon a time people like Patrick and Manning Clark spoke out, but there's almost no-one who does that now.

Anyway, we're in the midst of radiant, supposedly wintry days. Just so beautiful. The opera season has started again – always looked forward to, and there are concerts in Angel Place and the Opera House. There was a Bonnard exhibition in Canberra that we all enjoyed, although some people said some important pictures were missing. That must almost always be true, but I thought – let's concentrate on what is here.

I saw a film set in Finland and in my present mood, of wanting to live permanently anywhere but here, it seemed a place sufficiently far away. Or there would always be Indonesia, Vietnam, India – somewhere with an impenetrable language where you wouldn't understand the lies. The Finnish film was very, very dry and dead-pan; no-one smiled, they just looked at each other and moved rather stiffly. It was a change.

People are still reading, though mostly in groups and clubs, strangely enough. Yesterday, Sybille and I were having coffee and an adult man was sitting in the sun nearby reading Harry Potter.

[...]

Andrew has a 60th birthday in July and friends are arranging celebratory lunches and dinners for him. He's taking some of us out for the official occasion. He and Clem have a holiday house in the Philippines and they'll go there for a holiday soon. Bombs and rebels in the areas don't trouble him. Quite right.

[...]

Be in touch sometime, with a p.c. even.

With love,

Elizabeth

Cremorne | 8 October 2003

Dearest Shirley,

Your book arrived and everything was laid aside till I had read it. Thank you for sending me a copy, above all for writing it.

You know what you have achieved, what the achievement has cost and the so much more it has given you. I have a consciousness of the weight of each word, really wondrous detail, existing within and making up the great picture. That is art, of course, and the artist's work, to know the whole while bringing thought to the finest point. Like a great work of architecture, or music.

You've created a marvellous panorama of a time and place, with all the subtle colours and hugely varied characters of an ancient Japanese screen suddenly come to life. The immediacy of it all is something to treasure, giving rise sometimes to smiles, and sometimes – like the young man in the book whose photograph on a book jacket showed thoughts too deep for tears – to deep reflection indeed.

In your characters and in that view both intimate and vast of what is in life, and what matters, and what human beings do during their brief stay, there is so much poetry.

And now that I have read it, I must read it.

Congratulations, dearest S. I wish Francis had been here to share this time with you, but unquestionably he knew this would happen and knew what you would continue to achieve. I always thought how lucky people were to have him as their biographer. He had a magnanimous soul, and didn't judge. He was always so proud of you.

More congratulations and thanks,

With love, Elizabeth

New York | 19 October 2003

Dearest Elizabeth –

How to express the profound pleasure your letter gives me? – all your letters (so shamefully belatedly answered – I hope now to reform that, when time is restored to me); but this wonderful one in its deep feeling and generosity. Thank you for such words, for having read in this unique state of receptivity and understanding. I am practically unhinged by all that's happening to me. As I hadn't had a 'prominent' book out in so long, I hadn't realised the changes in 'marketing'. All must now 'happen' quickly, intense publicity, many appearances and appointments to 'establish' a claim before the next inundation of books sweeps mine away... [...] It is having a miraculous time, and the 'sales' are almost embarrassing. Sensitive and fine reviews (except for a first one, weirdly equivocal, by that very John Banville whose novels I so admire – I have never met him – however, this has now evaporated in the inundation...). Telly programme (interview) that sells many copies was wonderfully interrupted by a bulletin that I'd just been nominated for the Nat. Book Award (to be judged a month or so from now). A surprise for me, fortuitous enough to make me suspect the hand of Francis... (I won't get the award – one of the nominees, we are four in the fiction category, is a black novelist who has written about a weird aspect of enslavement; sounds good, and almost certainly the winner.) However, I now must be present in NY when announcement is made, delaying a trip to London for publication there. Virago is bringing me across the Atlantic... Meanwhile, Elizabeth: Toronto, Chicago, Washington, Yale... and innumerable events in NYC. Can you believe any of this? It is so unlike my writing, and my temperament.

I'm already exhausted. But of course much of this is not only favourable for me, creating readers, but it is interspersed with pleasant encounters and with the great kindnesses of my friends. I want so much to begin a new novel; impossible. After November, when I'm back from London and everyone has forgotten me in favour of the cataract of Christmas books, and I've slept for a week, some ideas may filter back to my brain, soul, spirit, or at least through the soles of my feet...

Forgive all this. I should only have said that there are precious events such as your letter; and a private letter from a director (woman) at Gallimard who will publish, now, three of my novels in French translation – a great pleasure to me. Francis' 'Cocteau' has just gone back into a fresh French edition thirty-odd years after its first French publication. How I miss him acutely in all this. Tomorrow, 20 October, is the ninth anniversary of his death. What fun we'd have had with all these jinks high and low.

[...]

Always, my love to Margaret, my love to Andrew. I hope Andrew wasn't in the Philippines for the visit of 'our' inexpressible president. It's better not to begin on that theme, one will go mad. Cruel, wicked, imbecile fully. [...] Donald Keene, returning from Japan sometime ago, said: 'I can't believe this is my country.'

You had an idea of writing – perhaps? – a story. Of returning to the page. Many many people will rejoice if that happens. I've been very happy in this restoration to fiction – very hard, but so pleasurable. I only want to continue.

Thank you, Elizabeth, also for such good clippings and enclosures, which keep me in touch with Australia in their way.

With best friendship, with love – Shirley.

Cremorne | 25/11/03

Dearest Shirley,

The days of cables are long past or I'd have sent one immediately on reading the news of the National Book Award. It's wonderful news. I'm so happy for you, as all your friends must be. Other friends here send many messages, warm congratulations, realizing something of what's achieved.

[...]

I'm sending news and words about dear Manoly's death. Desmond Digby rang to tell me. So much remembering. I wonder where you will soon be – London for Virago, or Italy or NY for Christmas.

Take care of yourself. Love & wishes, Eliz.

Cremorne | 17 May, 2004

Dearest Shirley,

It was so good to hear your voice, have a conversation – and about such great and cheering events. But I was so bedazzled by your timetable that I've no idea where you might be at this moment. It does sound as though a great many wonderful and heartening things have been happening in your life. I marvel at your stamina and envy it, though I know good things bring their own energy somehow.

It will be a pleasure for me too, if the Miles Franklin happens. We'll wait and see, although they're fairly certain to let you know well beforehand. The news about the short list appeared the morning after we spoke and I'm enclosing the clipping. And the Orange Prize is a very important and highly regarded prize. I only know Margaret Atwood's name among those writers and don't get on very well with her work though obviously many people do.

[...]

Apart from the state of the world, which is unspeakable, everything is pleasant and interesting now that autumn has arrived. My only writing lately, unfortunately, has been letters to friends after the death of some loved person. Then we've all come together in beautiful places with very good and diverse memories and that's been important. I've seen some operas (had never seen The Cunning Little Vixen before & it was directed by someone very – well, an artist), been to some concerts and exhibitions.

Now that autumn's here I've been walking a lot in the Botanic Gardens and across the Domain, and at certain times of day the light makes the scene so significant and joyful.

In Andrew's kitchen tiny parrots come in the window and walk up his arm to his shoulder, or take seeds from his fingers.

Margaret does well, maintaining her interest in words and the world and observing, even without seeing much at all, the people around her. She says very Patrick-like and Margaret-like things sometimes and is ready to laugh, be amused. These are good things when you're eighty-eight.

Warm wishes, love,

Elizabeth

Cremorne | 20 June, 2004

Dearest Shirley,

So much to say. I'd really like to talk to you, but must make do with what email people call snail mail.

[...]

Today I watched the 'Sunday' programme with your Jana Wendt interview and felt very sad that it was so long since we'd seen each other. It's not surprising that after so many years you should seem very familiar to me, but it was affecting to see you and hear you again.

Jana had rung before the [Miles Franklin] dinner in need of photographs. I took the few I had to the dinner and a charming young man from Channel 9 copied them on the spot; some were used today. You'll know – and will perhaps even have seen the programme somehow – that David Malouf and David Marr spoke, both eloquently, and that there were newsreel flashes of the times and places in your book. In an earlier conversation Jana asked me, as a few other people have, about Aldred Leith. You were patient, but the idea held by many intelligent readers that a novel is simply an elaborate autobiography has always made me marvel. Silently, for the most part. You had told me of this time in your life long ago. [...]

In 1957 the Miles Franklin prize began – afternoon drinks and quite a small prize, but prestige. In those pre-Labor days the arts received almost no support. When we were all cast down by Gough's dismissal, our will to live (politically) was restored when Neville Wran became NSW Premier – dashing, likeable, effective. It was at an early Premier's Literary dinner – grand event at the Opera House – that I accepted Christina's special award (from him). By this time the prizes covered non-fiction, poetry, ethnic writing (?) and many other categories. The prizes were quite substantial. Now other states have Premier's awards and the novel prize is called the Christina Stead Award. There are now many prizes where none existed, so things have improved greatly for writers and artists of all kinds. The fiftieth anniversary of Miles Franklin's death was the occasion for the splendid dinner and promotion and greatly increased prize money. This went along with an exhibition of her papers and times at the State Library.

Since Valerie and Kathie weren't at the dinner, the young Penguin/ Viking people in Melbourne suggested I should take two friends along and 'just enjoy yourself', which duly happened. The young woman promoting the event did well to capture Cate Blanchett, a real actress, rather than a film star and celebrity. She is here to play Hedda Gabler at the Wharf Theatre, lives a private life out of the limelight with a nice playwright husband and two very young children, catches buses, would not be robbed in the street. She spoke quite briefly, was unaffected, beautiful. There were quite a few speeches – not long, and the librarian had probably the best night of his life. Your interview showed on the big screen as soon as the announcement was made. It was good to see you and to hear what you said. Everyone applauded and seemed very pleased.

[...]

With love,

Elizabeth

New York | 4 August 04

Dearest Elizabeth –

How to thank you for marvellously extracting and sending these clippings; and most of all for your letter and notes? [...]

I am in NYC until late September, after which I snatch the month of October in Italy. On the dreaded 2nd November, the election will hold us all in thrall: important for the world, not only for this increasingly weird and divided land. Last Sunday, Everett and I went to see Fahrenheit 911, the filmed exposure of Bush. One is always hesitant about such a gleeful hate-fest. But it is important, if imperfect, and moving. Certain astonishing moments the audience grimly laughed, and at the end applauded at length. Soon we will have the Republican Convention here in NYC – another demonstration of self-destruction by the Republican Party, having grotesquely chosen the city that most hates them.

I arrived, very tired from a thousand 'events' (all lovely, but unremitting over months), in Rome at the end of May, dumped my bags, and almost at once went to London at publisher's request. Had the only days of good weather London has enjoyed this summer. Managed to see some of many friends. While there, learned of Miles F. Award – delighted and grateful. But impossible to go to Australia to receive prize – apart from commitments, I think the double journey might by then have killed me. Returned to Rome, collected luggage, crawled as if on all fours to Naples and Capri. Then re-entered into myself. I've begun a new novel, but get so little time to work on it. [...]

'My' Chinese publishers ask me to Peking. Meanwhile, the Hong Kong Literary Festival (early March 2005) invites me to H.K. (last seen at end of 1948) and Shanghai. This, theoretically to be followed in June by Sydney high-jinks. In principle, all marvellous and interesting. But when would I ever write again? [...]

Forgive details. Just talking out loud. What I really might do is go to an island (Torcello) on the Venetian Lagoon, to spend Christmas and New Year in absolute peace. Always a difficult time, now, for me if I remain in NYC over those holidays.

[...]

In England, I was 'taken' to Hay-on-Wye as part of the Orange Prize 'events' – fine bookish little town in magnificent forested Welsh countryside. My friend Christopher Cooper – survivor of my Hong Kong office days of miraculous memory – lives fairly nearby, drove over to hear morning's 'event'. Then he drove me around the surrounding hills. The vastness – impossible to think of such ancient hills and woods as 'cramped little Britain'. Very different in form and feeling from Scotland, and without that deeply affecting sadness of the Scots beauty. Lucky to have had these adventures, which are not yet absorbed, really. Good people everywhere.

Again, forgive rambling. Late at night – my only time, now, for communing in silence with kindred spirits. 'Col favore delle tenebre,' as Italians say.

With a close embrace, with love – Shirley
I would never have seen these clippings but for your kindness in sending them... S.

Cremorne | 4 October, 2004

Dearest Shirley,

You will be in Italy now, I think, but back in NYC for your November election. Our election takes place next Saturday, and the almost certain return of the Howard government is depressing absolutely everyone I know. Only Blair is suffering in the polls, and Bush and Howard flourish. To our stupefaction. Not that the British population is so moral or intellectual or thoughtful. I remember how they cheered Mrs Thatcher over the Falklands War and sang Land of Hope and Glory.

[...]

You were saying that you might go to Torcello on the Venetian Lagoon for Christmas and New Year. I always imagine disappearing to a non-Christian country for that whole period, but this year I must have – on December 1 and 15 – cataract operations. While this is now a commonplace operation/procedure on eyes, it doesn't feel so ordinary when the eyes are your very own.

I haven't been reading so much because of the misty eyes. The problem I suppose is brought on by sunshine and age and I'm not sure what. With any luck this will all improve soon. It's just sustained and concentrated reading that becomes a trial.

Stay well. Take care of yourself. I like to think of you walking with a friend and saying aloud great speeches from Shakespeare. I couldn't do it, but have been known to reel with appreciation. Words transport.

Much love,

Elizabeth

Cremorne | 27 October, 2004

Dearest Shirley,

This letter will be in mid-air, probably, on what you call 'the dreaded 2nd November'. So important for the world, this election. It seems almost impossible that Kerry might win when you think of the powers ranged against him and the Democrats. There have been so many documentaries – revealing, but not cheering. You saw Fahrenheit 9/11, as I did, and the other Michael Moore before that, then Outfoxed about Murdoch's world-wide influence over 4½ billion people. In the Gobi Desert outside a yurt sits a satellite receiving Fox News. If that's what you could call it.

Ancient clippings about the election here would await you on your return from Italy. We are stunned, in recovery, imagining what we would do and where go if we were all younger and fitter. Between imagining a younger self divided between Scotland, Finland and Italy, I exchange political news with friends and then think of December 1 and 15 with some apprehension, since these are the dates of the cataract operations/procedures.

[...]

Here, numerous breakfasts, lunches and dinners with friends – some for profound political conversations, some because there's always much coming and going to the world. Saw Der Rosenkavalier recently – and reeled out, overcome by the music, the wonderful voices. After an opera I usually ring Desmond Digby, Patrick's great friend – painter, opera designer – to hear his opinion of the production, the singers.

You wrote in your last so-welcome letter about the happiness of driving with your friend from Hong Kong in the beautiful Welsh countryside. Extraordinary how different Wales and Scotland are from England; you know you are in 'foreign' countries when you cross the borders. There's a sort of ancient familiarity that's very affecting. Never feel like that here. If you're European, you can see too many eucalypts.

Let us pray for the Democrats and John Kerry. Please stay very well.

Many wishes, best love,

Elizabeth

Capri | 3 June 2005

I am looking, dearest Elizabeth, at the 'programme' sent by my 'handlers' for my Australia trip – I arrive Sydney late on 14 June, staying at the Intercontinental in Macquarie Street until I 'depart' midday on Sunday 26th. [...] I hope we can meet as soon as possible – a prompt lunch or even cup of tea in immediate days? – and perhaps, again according to your own plans, dinner on the Friday 17th or even the 18th, which seem unencumbered in this list? I'll call you on arrival, unless the plane gets in very late. [...]

Looking out a favourite book for my Sydney flight, I took down Iris M's 'The Sea, The Sea,' to re-read in mid-air. What an idiot I am – of course I looked into it and was hooked all over again. For me, the best of her novels, along with 'Bruno's Dream' and 'A Word Child'. I remember – early 1960s when her first books appeared, one after another, so intelligent and alive and individual. It was also the time when Muriel Spark's work was at its inventive best and she and I saw each other in NY continually. Her NYC, and New Yorker, connection culminated in 'The Girls of Slender Means' – lovely book, as I think, in which I have a walk-on role... Different world. Added to which, Muriel introduced FS and SH, another culmination.

This week, Italian translation (good) of my Great Fire appears here. Einaudi are doing nice things for it, but have made what I consider a vulgar jacket (despite the fact that I have a contractual right to an opinion; the draft was sent to me when already gone to press). Surprising, for they are a fine pub. house and I like my vis-à-vis there, himself a novelist.

Ghastly vibes from Valerie. What bitterness. Otherwise, I look so greatly forward to reunions, and only hope to be recognisable.

With eagerness, with love –

Shirley.

Cremorne | 13 June, 2005

Dearest Shirley,

Too much to say – except that I look forward so much to seeing you. The sooner the better. If we can speak when you arrive, we can arrange times, places.

You suggested prompt lunch or even cup of tea, and perhaps dinner on Friday 17th or the 18th. I'd like any or all of these.

You say you hope to be recognizable, and I look much more worn than I feel, but we'll know each other.

With love,

Elizabeth

[Undated Christmas card, 2008]

Dearest S,

This card – a light in the darkness.

It was good to hear your voice when you left a message some weeks/months ago. Then weeks ago, I rang when it was too late for me and too early for you. You seemed to say, or I seem to remember your saying that you'd been in bed since January because of trouble with your left leg. But perhaps I was dazed – or am now because of lack of sleep! Then I told you Margaret would be 93 in January, and you spoke a little of getting on with your work.

Not sure where you will be for Christmas. You're often in Italy, I know. I hope to stagger through the day and survive.

I think of you and Francis, of YM (somewhat differently), the prodigious letters / thoughts exchanged, the girl in your story who often comes to mind, hoping to see things less clearly.

With love

E

Acknowledgements

A book is always the product of many different kinds of labour and generosity.

The editors would like to thank our families, friends and colleagues who have enthused about and assisted with this project.

Susan Wyndham would like to thank the friends of Elizabeth Harrower whom she interviewed.

Brigitta Olubas's work on this book has been supported by an Australian Research Council Discovery Project grant (DP230101797) and by a period of sabbatical leave granted by the Faculty of Art & Design, University of New South Wales, Sydney.

The editors would also like formally to thank the following:

The Estate of Elizabeth Harrower, for permission to publish her letters.

The Estate of Shirley Hazzard, for permission to publish her letters.

Librarians at the following libraries for their important work in processing and making available Hazzard's and Harrower's letters: National Library of Australia, Canberra; Rare Book and Manuscript Library, Columbia University Libraries, New York; State Library of New South Wales, Sydney.

Elspeth Menzies, Executive Publisher, and Kathy Bail, CEO at NewSouth, for their excitement about publishing the Hazzard–Harrower correspondence; Sophia Oravecz, Joumana Awad, Briony Neilson, Debra Billson, Josephine Pajor-Markus, Rosina Di Marzo, Caitlin Lawless and everyone who helped produce a beautiful book and send it out to the world.

Sources

In our Introduction and Notes, we have provided full citations of published sources in a source's first note; subsequent references have a short-form citation. The notes provide a full bibliography of published and unpublished sources used in the book.

Shirley Hazzard and Elizabeth Harrower's correspondence is held by several archives:
Shirley Hazzard's letters to Elizabeth Harrower in Papers of Elizabeth Harrower (1937–2005), National Library of Australia, Canberra.
Elizabeth Harrower's letters to Shirley Hazzard in Shirley Hazzard Correspondence and other papers 1966–ca.2005, State Library of New South Wales MLMSS 10249.
Additional correspondence from Elizabeth Harrower to Shirley Hazzard in Shirley Hazzard Papers 1920s–2016, Rare Book and Manuscript Library, Columbia University Libraries, New York.

Notes

Introduction

p. 2   '*It seems odd*': SH to EH, Jan 5 1973, Papers of Elizabeth Harrower (1937–2005), National Library of Australia.

p. 3   '*one of the most beautiful*': Paul Horgan, cover endorsement, Shirley Hazzard, *The Evening of the Holiday*, Knopf, New York, 1966.

p. 4   '*almost miraculous ability*': Charles Poore, 'Books of the Times: Intermezzo', *New York Times*, Jan 15, 1966, p. 25.

p. 4   '*angry and in tears*': John Leonard, 'Books of the Times: *The Transit of Venus*', *New York Times*, Feb 26, 1980, p. 45.

p. 4   '*in a sort of enchanted jeopardy*': John Malcolm Brinnin to SH, Sept 10, 1980, Series II, Box 13 Folder 37, Shirley Hazzard Papers, 1920s–2016, University Archives, Rare Book and Manuscript Library, Columbia University Libraries.

p. 5   '*because I don't like Newcastle*': Harrower, Elizabeth, 1928–2020 & De Berg, Hazel, 1913–1984. 1967, *Elizabeth Harrower interviewed by Hazel de Berg for the Hazel de Berg collection [sound recording]*.

p. 5   '*I must have cast off mine*': EH to Margaret Dick, May 31, 1972, Papers of Elizabeth Harrower (1937–2005), National Library of Australia.

p. 5   *often drunk and abusive*: NRS-13495-16-342-1891/1942 Divorce papers Helen Hughes – Robert Hughes [Incorporates 127/1940] Contents Date Range 09-10-1940 to 15-11-1943, State Records NSW.

p. 6   '*never saw any happy marriages*': quoted in Susan Wyndham, 'Elizabeth Harrower doesn't want spoilers to her own novel', *Sydney Morning Herald*, May 3, 2014.

p. 6   *around the age of eight*: Susan Wyndham interview with Andrew Robertson, Aug 24, 2023.

p. 6   '*an unloved, unwanted*': Elizabeth McMahon, 'Moments of Being in the Fiction of Elizabeth Harrower', in E McMahon & B Olubas (eds), *Elizabeth Harrower: Critical Essays*, Sydney University Press, Sydney, p. 136.

p. 6   '*The emotional truth*': 'An interview with Elizabeth Harrower', Jim Davidson, *Meanjin*, May 5, 1980 <https://meanjin.com.au/blog/an-interview-with-elizabeth-harrower/>.

p. 7   '*little despot*': Fiona McGregor, 'Introduction: Aces from Hell' in Elizabeth Harrower, *The Long Prospect*, Text Publishing, Melbourne, 2012, p. vii.

p. 7   '*more than anything*': Elizabeth Harrower, *The Long Prospect*, Text Publishing, Melbourne, 2012, p. 110.

p. 8   '*insight into evil*': John Colmer, 'Feminine Achievements', *Australian Book Review*, September 1966, pp. 218–19.

p. 8   '*simultaneously illuminating*': Colmer, 1966.

p. 8   '*square stone house*': Elizabeth Harrower, *In Certain Circles*, Text Publishing, Melbourne, 2014, p. 6.

p. 9   '*The subtlety and even brilliance*': CH Derrick, Reader Report, March 19, 1971. Papers of Elizabeth Harrower (1937–2005), National Library of Australia.

p. 9   *'an accurate though morose'*: CH Derrick, Reader Report, Jan 20, 1963, The Macmillan Archive, Macmillan Publishers International Ltd.

p. 9   *'I suppose I have been very good'*: Wyndham, 2014.

p. 9   *'Were alarmed to hear'*: Patrick White to EH, Aug 20, 1971, Papers of Elizabeth Harrower (1937–2005), National Library of Australia.

p. 9   *'gradually became involved'*: EH to SH, March 24, 1971, Shirley Hazzard Correspondence and other papers 1966–ca.2005, State Library of New South Wales, MLMSS 10249.

p. 9   *'absolutely frozen'*: Wyndham, 2014.

p. 9   *'living a novel'*: quoted by EH, EH to SH, July 25, 1973, Shirley Hazzard Correspondence and other papers 1966–ca.2005, State Library of New South Wales, MLMSS 10249.

p. 9   *'Elizabeth keeps her principles'*: Patrick White to SH, June 22, 1980, in *Patrick White Letters*, (ed) David Marr, Random House, Sydney, 1994, p. 533.

p. 10   *'I wouldn't mind the stress'*: EH to Margaret Dick, July 24, 1972, Papers of Elizabeth Harrower (1937–2005), National Library of Australia.

p. 11   *Harrower was prickly*: Shirley Hazzard Diary/Notebook, Dec 1, 1984. Series VIII, Box 36, Folder 4, Shirley Hazzard Papers, 1920s–2016, University Archives, Rare Book and Manuscript Library, Columbia University Libraries.

p. 11   *'There you go again'*: Shirley Hazzard Diary/Notebook Nov 4, 1984. Series VIII, Box 36, Folder 4, Shirley Hazzard Papers, 1920s–2016, University Archives, Rare Book and Manuscript Library, Columbia University Libraries.

p. 11   *'To Francis'*: Shirley Hazzard Diary/Notebook, Dec 1, 1984. Series VIII, Box 36, Folder 4, Shirley Hazzard Papers, 1920s–2016, University Archives, Rare Book and Manuscript Library, Columbia University Libraries.

p. 11   *'far more complicated'*: SH to Donald Keene, Dec 18, 1984. Series II, Box 10, Shirley Hazzard Papers, 1920s–2016, University Archives, Rare Book and Manuscript Library, Columbia University Libraries.

p. 12   *Hazzard's 'tone'*: Interview with Susan Wyndham, April 26, 2017.

p. 12   *'Why aren't there lots of Francises'*: EH to Margaret Dick, March 18, 1972, Papers of Elizabeth Harrower (1937–2005), National Library of Australia.

p. 13   *'makes the next one possible'*: SH to Murray Bail, March 13, 1983, Papers of Murray Bail (1950–2001) [manuscript], National Library of Australia.

p. 13   *wrote an introduction*: Cynthia Nixon, *Outback and Beyond*, Angus & Robertson, Sydney, 1994.

p. 14   *'beautiful little nightmares'*: David Barrett, 'Nightmares in dream homes,' *Australian*, Nov 3, 2013, p. 23.

p. 14   'In Certain Circles *is subtle'*: Jessica Au, '*In Certain Circles* by Elizabeth Harrower – book review,' *The Guardian*, April 28, 2014 <http://www.theguardian.com/books/australia-culture-blog/2014/apr/28/in-certain-circles-elizabeth-harrower-book-review>.

p. 14   *'witty, desolate'*: James Wood, 'Rediscovering Elizabeth Harrower', *The New Yorker*, Oct 13, 2014.

Part One: 1966–1975

p. 23   *My organization book*: *People in Glass Houses*, Macmillan, London, 1967.

p. 23   *Like Herzog*: Harrower often refers to *Herzog*, 1964 novel by Saul Bellow, partly written in letters, many of them mentally composed but unsent.

p. 24   *I am beginning*: *The Bay of Noon*, Macmillan, London, 1970.

p. 25   *delightful adaptation from Luigi Barzini*: *The Italians*, bestselling 1964 book written in English.

p. 25   *'Christening Party'*: Francis Steegmuller, *The Christening Party*, Farrar, Straus & Cudahy, New York, 1960.

p. 25 *Apollinaire*: Francis Steegmuller, *Apollinaire: Poet Among the Painters*, Farrar, Straus, New York, 1963.

p. 31 *Dr. Andrew Robertson*: Robertson was not a doctor, as Harrower learnt, but a psychiatric nurse and counsellor at Erskine Street Clinic, Sydney.

p. 32 *the original long-winded lady*: Maeve Brennan wrote for *The New Yorker* 'Talk of the Town' column under the pen name 'The long-winded lady'.

p. 39 *agley*: Scottish adverb meaning askew, awry.

p. 44 *M. Hulot's Holiday*: 1953 French comedy film directed by Jacques Tati.

p. 45 *Hal P.*: Australian author Hal Porter.

p. 45 *Boulestin's*: legendary French restaurant in London, opened 1927.

p. 56 *Artur Lundkvist*: Swedish writer, member of the Swedish Academy committee that awarded the Nobel Prize for Literature to Patrick White in 1973.

p. 60 *1973*: Harrower mistakenly wrote 1972.

p. 62 *The book*: *Defeat of an Ideal: A Study of the Self-destruction of the United Nations*, Little, Brown, 1973.

p. 69 *Bill Cantwell*: Mrs Ida 'Bill' Cantwell, a Sydney arts patron.

p. 77 *GG*: English writer Graham Greene, subject of Hazzard's 2000 memoir *Greene on Capri*.

p. 77 *The Anguses*: Max and Thedda Angus. Max Angus was a notable Tasmanian landscape artist, and Kit became friendly with the couple during a brief stay in Hobart in 1969.

p. 78 *H of Commons day*: Hazzard was invited to address the British Parliamentary Group for World Government.

p. 83 *sonsie*: Scottish adjective meaning lucky, attractive, jolly.

p. 88 *Isadora*: Steegmuller edited a book of the correspondence of the American-born dancer and choreographer and her lover Edward Gordon Craig, English theatre actor and director, son of actress Ellen Terry.

p. 94 *I'm being given a grant*: In August 1973 the Literature Board of the Australia Council for the Arts granted Harrower a two-year Fellowship valued at $6000 a year.

p. 102 *P. White is giving away his prize*: Patrick White used his Nobel Prize money to establish the annual Patrick White Award, for an Australian writer of achievement who had not received adequate recognition. Harrower won the award in 1996.

p. 107 *North South West*: David Foster, *North South West: Three Novellas*, Macmillan, Melbourne, 1973.

p. 108 *Alger Hiss*: Hiss was a US government official accused by the HUAC in 1948 of having spied for the USSR in the 1930s. He was indicted for perjury in 1950.

p. 109 *crocodiles waiting at Edgecliff*: Hazzard's sister, Valerie Barnes, was living at Edgecliff, in Sydney's eastern suburbs.

p. 111 *one of his most recent novels*: *Edens Lost*, 1969.

p. 118 *his new short story collection*: *The Cockatoos: Shorter Novels and Stories*, Jonathan Cape, London, 1974.

p. 120 *cockle-warming brochure*: *Recent Fiction*, Oxford University Press, Melbourne, 1974.

p. 123 *John Colmer*: Professor of English, University of Adelaide 1964–78.

p. 123 *Gordimer novel got good prize*: *The Conservationist* was joint winner of the 1974 Booker Prize.

p. 124 *'Darwin's been wiped out'*: Tropical Cyclone Tracy devastated Darwin on December 24–26, 1974.

p. 135 *the Oast*: Macmillan publisher Alan Maclean's home in Dorset.

p. 135 *The exhibition*: Modern Masters: Manet to Matisse at Art Gallery of NSW, April–May, 1975.

p. 152 *Blue Poles*: painting by American Jackson Pollock, bought by the National Gallery of Australia in 1973 for A$1.3 million with approval of PM Whitlam.

Part Two: 1976–1984

p. 158 *what a splendid story*: Harrower's 'The Retrospective Grandmother', published in the Melbourne *Herald* in 1976.

p. 159 *Dunstan*: Don Dunstan, Labor Premier of South Australia 1967–68 and 1970–79.

p. 162 *Prince Andrew*: Andrew Robertson.

p. 176 *The Chinese exhibition*: 'The Chinese Exhibition: a selection of recent archeological finds of The People's Republic of China' at Art Gallery of NSW.

p. 179 *departure for Hawaii*: Shirley's sister Valerie was now living in Honolulu.

p. 183 *Sumner winning the literary Melbourne Cup*: Sumner Locke Elliott received the 1977 Patrick White Award, always announced on the Friday after the Melbourne Cup horse race to turn public attention to literature.

p. 187 *A.N.U.*: The Australian National University.

p. 188 *John Something*: artist John Perceval.

p. 190 *Bj-Petersen*: Joh Bjelke-Petersen, arch-conservative Queensland Country Party Leader and Premier 1968–87.

p. 195 *David Malouf kindly sent us his book*: *An Imaginary Life*, Chatto and Windus, London, 1978.

p. 195 *Elizabeth Bowen biography*: Victoria Glendinning, *Elizabeth Bowen: A Biography*, Weidenfeld & Nicholson, London, 1977.

p. 198 *Eliza's*: restaurant in Double Bay, Sydney.

p. 203 *His new book is ghastly*: *Good as Gold*, Simon & Schuster, New York, 1979.

p. 206 *Patrick's new novel*: *The Twyborn Affair*, Viking, New York, 1979.

p. 210 *Dora*: Hazzard described the darkly comic character as 'a very mild dose of my mother'. 'Shirley Hazzard: The Art of Fiction No. 185', *Paris Review* 173, Spring 2005, p. 166.

p. 211 *a new book of RS's*: Randolph Stow, *The Girl Green as Elderflower*, Viking, New York, 1980.

p. 229 *P's memoir*: *Flaws in the Glass: A Self-Portrait*, Viking, New York, 1981.

p. 230 *dinner party at Eliz. Riddell's*: Elizabeth Riddell, poet, journalist, critic.

p. 237 *The Patrick/Sidney Nolan stir*: In his memoir White attacked Nolan for remarrying soon after Cynthia's death. The public feud continued with Nolan's crude portraits of White and Lascaris in 1982.

p. 239 *Donald Keene's book*: Keene was professor of Japanese literature at Columbia University and a good friend of Hazzard's. She put him in touch with Harrower during his 1981 lecture tour of Australia, and they continued to exchange letters for some years.

p. 239 *you have a paperback out*: Angus & Robertson reissued *The Watch Tower* in 1977, and *The Long Prospect* and *The Catherine Wheel* in 1979.

p. 240 *The Mosman*: The Mosman Nursing Home.

p. 241 *My film is moving on a bit*: Proposed films of *The Transit of Venus* and *The Evening of the Holiday*, with Patricia Lovell as producer, did not eventuate.

p. 241 *Sumner told me*: There are several different versions of the story and of the evening in question in circulation. Shaun Bell provides a neat summary in his essay '"The Writers' Picnic": Genealogy and Homographesis in the Fiction of Sumner Locke Elliott', JASAL 27.2, 2017, np. <https://openjournals.library.sydney.edu.au/JASAL/article/view/11852>

p. 242 *The British*: a reference to the 1982 Falklands War between Argentina and the United Kingdom.

p. 247 *Patrick and GD*: Geoffrey Dutton.

p. 266 *group interested in salvaging monuments*: Hazzard's landlords Maurizio and Mirella Barracco established Fondazione Napoli Novantanove (Naples 99), which began the slow process of opening historic buildings and sites to the public, to alert them to the wealth of art in their city.

p. 268 *Richard Hall*: journalist, writer, political adviser, private press secretary to Gough Whitlam as Leader of the Australian Labor Party, 1969–72; Harrower sometimes attended his well-known Friday lunches.

Part Three: 1985–2008

p. 283 *I wish I had time*: Kit Hazzard died in the Mosman Nursing Home in May 1985. Harrower and Valerie Barnes were the only mourners at her funeral.

p. 284 *The Age awards*: Harrower was on the judging panel that chose the winners, *Illywhacker* by Peter Carey and *Vietnam: A Reporter's War* by Hugh Lunn.

p. 287 *Patrick's new book*: *Memoirs of Many in One*, Viking, New York, 1986.

p. 292 *this last one*: *The Good Terrorist*, Jonathan Cape, London, 1985.

p. 292 *Ivoire*: Ivoire de Balmain, perfume launched by fashion designer Pierre Balmain in 1979.

p. 294 *Anita Brookner's novel*: *Hotel du Lac*, Jonathan Cape, London, 1984.

p. 303 *Muriel Spark's new novel*: *A Far Cry from Kensington*, Constable, London, 1988.

p. 305 *The Waldheim opus*: *Countenance of Truth: The United Nations and the Waldheim Case*, Viking, New York, 1990.

p. 309 *the dear Madigans*: Col Madigan, architect of the National Gallery of Australia, Canberra, and his wife Ruby.

p. 310 *Crimes and Misdemeanors*: 1989 film directed by Woody Allen

p. 312 *His biography depressed him*: White read the final manuscript of *Patrick White: A Life* by David Marr, Random House Australia, Melbourne, 1991, which was published three months after his death.

p. 324 *Vivian*: Australian poet Vivian Smith, married to Sybille Smith; the couple were good friends of Harrower's.

p. 325 *It was good to hear your voice*: Francis Steegmuller died aged 88 in Naples on October 20, 1994.

p. 332 *the Institute*: The Sydney Institute, current affairs forum run by Gerard and Anne Henderson.

p. 346 *Meantime, Max and I*: Max Henningham, a friend who took Italian classes with Harrower.

p. 347 *the appalling event*: September 11, 2001, terrorist attacks by al-Qaeda on the United States, including the World Trade Center in New York.

p. 349 *Your book arrived*: *The Great Fire*, Farrar, Straus & Giroux (US), Virago (UK), Hachette (Australia).

p. 351 *nominated for the Nat. Book Award*: *The Great Fire* won the 2003 (US) National Book Award for Fiction.

p. 352 *if the Miles Franklin happens*: *The Great Fire* won the 2004 Miles Franklin Literary Award. Hazzard was unable to attend the Award dinner but travelled to Sydney the following year to receive it.

p. 354 *Aldred Leith*: character in *The Great Fire*, based partly on Hazzard's early love affair with Alec Vedeniapine.

p. 359 Undated Christmas card (2008): Harrower's last Christmas card reproduces a Japanese colour woodblock print, Woman Admiring Plum Blossoms at Night, by Suzuki Harunobu, 1725–70, from the Metropolitan Museum of Art in New York. It shows a woman in a kimono holding up a lantern to the tree.

INDEX

Hazzard's mother and 26, 36, 53, 82, 221, 224, 284

health 327, 329, 330, 331, 336, 339, 340, 353

reviews by 41–42, 55

travel 138, 141

writing 7, 84, 86

Digby, Desmond 357

Dobson, Rosemary 264

Doctorow, E.L. 279

Down in the City 6

review 14

Dr Faustus 267, 287

Drabble, Margaret 186, 210

The Ice Age 186

Duncan, Isadora 51, 88

Dunstan, Don 159, 161, 218, 338

Duras, Marguerite 142, 292, 294

The Lover 293, 294

Dutton, Geoffrey 89, 91, 106, 143–44, 146, 247

Edel, Leon 295

Henry James biography 295, 299

Eliot, George 146

Adam Bede 146

Daniel Deronda 146

Felix Holt 146

Middlemarch 146, 197

Eliza's 198

Elliott, Sumner Locke 109, 111, 124, 125, 130, 162, 182, 183, 188, 192, 193–94, 198, 241, 297, 308

Careful, He Might Hear You 111

Edens Lost 111

The Man Who Got Away 174

Rusty Bugles 111

Water Under the Bridge 182

EM Forster Award 286

Encyclopaedia Britannica Awards Committee 27

Ehrlichman, John 87, 105, 108

The Evening of the Holiday 3–4, 8

proposed film 286

reviews 3–4

Fahrenheit 911 355, 357

Fahy, Everett 212, 214–15, 259, 274, 306, 347, 355

Falklands War 242, 356

Farhenblum, Dr 314

Fielding, Dr 310, 311

Financial Review 172

Fink, Margaret 238

Fitzgerald, R.D. 107

Fitzgerald, Robert 132

The Iliad translation 132

Flaubert, Gustave 8, 188, 199, 229

Rae Dalven translation 192

Ford, Gerald 145, 170

Ford, Harry 202

Forster, E.M. 41–42

Maurice 41–42

A Passage to India 306

Foster, David 107

North South West: Three Novellas 107

Fox, Paula 285

Franklin River dam 251

Fraser, Malcolm 143, 147, 152, 155, 158, 159, 169, 187, 251–52

Fraser Government 164, 168

Freudenberg, Graham 270

'The Fun of the Fair' 6

Gaden, John 312

Gallipoli 235

Geering, Dorothy 173

Geering, Ron 120–21, 157, 173, 183, 187, 290–91, 318

Recent Fiction 120, 157

Selected Letters of Christina Stead 318

Geng, Veronica 177

Gibbon, Edward 261–62

Gittings, Robert 127

Gladesville Mental Hospital 106

Glendinning, Victoria 195

Elizabeth Bowen: A Biography 195

Glezos, Manolis 334

Godwin, Gail 285

Dream Children 285

Golding, William 213

Darkness Visible 213

Gorbachev, Mikhail 300, 315

Gordimer, Nadine 84, 85, 122, 123, 124–25, 126, 131, 132

The Conservationist 122, 123, 124–25, 132

Gore, Al 318

Graves, Robert 286

The Great Fire 4, 14, 349–51, 352, 357